NEW ILLUSTRATED

WORLD HISTORY

This is a Starfire Book
First published in 2001

02 04 05 03

1 3 5 7 9 10 8 6 4 2

Starfire is part of
The Foundry Creative Media Company Limited
Crabtree Hall, Crabtree Lane, Fulham, London, SW6 6TY

Visit the Foundry website: www.foundry.co.uk

ISBN 1 903817 20 X

A copy of the CIP data for this book is available from the British Library

Printed in China

SPECIAL THANKS TO EVERYONE INVOLVED WITH THIS PROJECT:
Anna Amari, Frances Banfield, Lucy Bradbury, Roger Buckley, Helen Courtney, Claire Dashwood,
Giskin Day, Karen Fitzpatrick, Vicky Garrard, Phil Hempell, George Keyes, Lesley Malkin,
Geoffrey Meadon, Sonya Newland, Colin Rudderham, Mel Shaw, Andrea Simmonds,
Graham Stride, Helen Tovey, Helen Wall, Sharon Weiss, Nick Wells.

NEW ILLUSTRATED

WORLD
HISTORY

Guy de la Bédoyère, Alan Brown, Gerard Cheshire, Ingrid Cranfield,
Judith Hodge, Michael Kerrigan, Jon Sutherland

GENERAL EDITOR: PATRICK O'BRIEN

STAR
FIRE

CONTENTS

THEMES

Each A–Z entry is tagged by themes which can be followed as threads throughout the book

 Art & Culture   Industry   Religion   Science & Technology   War

 Exploration & Empire   Politics   Royalty   Society

INTRODUCTION

AS THE GLOBAL integration of nations and communities accelerates, the demand for concise information about the history of our interdependent world from schools and universities, and for an educated public at large, becomes clear and urgent.

Several developments promote a need for histories of the world. Firstly the sheer number of publications and the volume of data about the past stimulates demands for compressed, attractively presented but reliable sources of information about a universal past. Secondly, the branching out of history's traditional concerns (namely with states, warfare and diplomacy) in order to take into account a plurality of contemporary interests, such as ecology, evolutionary biology, ethnology, botany, the health and wealth of populations, human rights, gender, family systems, private life, fashion, popular music, to name but a few, points the study of history towards comparisons across cultures and national histories. Thirdly, in an age of travel and electronic communication, the young quickly acquire portfolios of knowledge and develop curiosities about other places, peoples and cultures. These new generations are less easily persuaded to feed on diets of national, let alone regional and parochial histories, than previous ones. Thus, schools and universities need to provide spatially unfettered, ready access to the kind of historical understanding that will satisfy the capacious interests of this generation. To nourish the cosmopolitan sensibility required for the next millennium, history needs to be widened and repositioned to bring it into fruitful exchange with geography, geology, evolutionary biology and the social sciences. Barriers between archaeology, ancient, classical, medieval, early modern, contemporary and other 'packages' of traditional, but now anachronistic, histories must be dismantled.

As new technologies enable our world to 'shrink', for problem after problem and subject after subject, national frameworks for political action and academic enquiry are recognized as unsatisfactory. People require historical perspectives on the ubiquitous technological, political and economic forces that are now clearly transcending and transforming traditional frameworks for human behaviour and reshaping personal identities around the world.

Thus this excellent work of reference to world history is not only propitious, but it has been well-designed, structured and written by a team of experts in order to help teachers of history in high schools and universities communicate a truly global historical perspective to their pupils and to students in general. Histories of the world cannot be taught or read without a clear comprehension of the chronologies and spatial parameters within which political, economic, social and cultural activities of different empires, states and peoples have evolved over very long timespans. This book is an ideal text for the easy acquisition of basic facts upon which an understanding of world history can be built and studied. It encapsulates hard knowledge and reunifies history with geography, providing a perspective which goes back to classical civilizations in order to help its readers appreciate the significance of people, places and locations for seminal events in world history.

Works of reference must be accurate, accessible and display the unfurling chronology of world history in words, illustrations, maps and captions that are memorable. The team of historians, illustrators, cartographers and editors who collaborated in the production of this book set out to produce a popular work of reference that could be adopted for undergraduate and high school courses in world history.

World History is a concise, fully-illustrated, up-to-date, single volume reference book for readers aged 16 and above. It features: over 700 clearly written entries, compiled and authenticated by professional historians and more than 300 coloured illustrations, covering millennia of history, from Ancient Egypt to the present day.

The entries provide readers with authoritative, yet accessible, information on every period in history. Due weight has been given to all regions of the world – Europe, the Americas, China, India, Russia, the Middle East, South-East Asia and Asia. Entries have been organized alphabetically to enable fast fact-finding, while cross-references give directions to associated entries and illustrations. References to people, dates and events from Ancient Egypt to the present day cover every inhabited continent on the planet and have been organized into nine major themes: Art & Culture, Exploration & Empire, Industry, Politics, Religion, Royalty, Science & Technology, Society and War.

Although books on world history must accord prominence to such traditional, historical topics as the rise and decline of empires, states and civilizations, a serious effort has been made to include the communal concerns of mankind, including religion, economic welfare, trade, technology, health, the status of women, human rights, etc.

World History offers chronologies, perspectives and geographical parameters which aim to subdue the excesses of nationalism, ethnicity, chauvinism and condescension. The length and breadth of this world history, covering, as it does, all continents with a chronology which goes back hundreds of years, works to separate the provincial from the universal, the episodic from the recurrent. It will elaborate upon the decline as well as the rise of societies, nations, cultures and civilizations. This volume contributes towards rapidly growing aspirations for an education in universal history and will also contribute towards the nurturing of a cosmopolitan sensibility for the 21st century.

PATRICK K. O'BRIEN FBA
Centennial Professor of Economic History, London School of Economics,
Convenor of the Programme in Global History at the Institute of Historical Research,
University of London

ABORIGINALS

The most famous Aboriginals are the Australian Aborigines who had settled there and in Tasmania when the Europeans reached there in the eighteenth century. It is believed that the Aboriginals made their way to Australia via a land shelf connecting it to New Guinea and that 500 tribes originally settled there, amounting to a population of some 300,000. It is estimated that 230,000 still exist in Australia alone. Factors such as changes in culture and marriage between different tribes and different cultures have affected the way the Aboriginals live, as well as their physical appearance.

ABRAHAM (b. c.1900 BC)

Abraham was born in Mesopotamia around 1900 BC. The Old Testament tells how God appeared to him and offered him and his people the Promised Land in Canaan. The Bible also tells of how Abraham was instructed by God to sacrifice his son Isaac, which the prophet was about to do when angels intervened and saved him.

))))▶ *Islam, Judaism*

ACROPOLIS

Rocky outcrop overlooking Athens, Greece. A natural stronghold housing the citadel of Athens' first aristocratic rulers, the Acropolis might have been rendered redundant by the advent of democracy had the statesman Pericles not seen the opportunities it afforded both to promote the state's prestige and create employment. It was on this site that, from 449 BC

onwards, an ambitious programme of public works was undertaken. The great temple to Athene, now known as the Parthenon, is merely the most celebrated of the monuments built at that time, a lasting symbol of the enterprise and achievement of the Ancient Greeks.

))))▶ *Ancient Greece, Classical Period*

ACT OF UNION (1707)

Formal union of the governments of England and Scotland. Although the Stuart monarchs had jointly ruled both countries since 1603, this treaty created the United Kingdom of Great Britain. The Scottish parliament was dissolved and would not sit again until 1999, but Scotland kept its legal system. The main purpose of the Act, however, was to stifle Jacobite hopes of a Stuart restoration to the throne: under its terms the throne passed to the German House of Hanover on Queen Anne's death. There was also economic union with free trade on both sides of the border.

))))▶ *Stuart Dynasty*

ACTIUM, BATTLE OF (31 BC)

Navan confrontation at Akri in western Greece. The members of the second triumvirate of Ancient Rome were Mark Antony, Lepidus and Octavian. Having sought out and killed those who had murdered Julius Caesar, they began quarrelling among themselves. Mark Antony and Cleopatra were eventually defeated by Octavian in the Battle of Actium. Octavian became Emperor Augustus, while Antony and Cleopatra fled to Egypt and ended their lives.

))))▶ *Ancient Rome, Mark Antony, Cleopatra*

AFGHAN WARS (1839–42, 1878–80, 1919)

Three wars between Afghanistan and Great Britain caused by the threat of increasing Russian influence in British India. In the early nineteenth century Britain had a garrison of soldiers at Afghanistan's capital, Kabul. At that time Russia was nurturing ambitions of

LEFT: Australian Aboriginals: anthropologists believe these indigenous tribes did not migrate but settled in a particular place.
FAR RIGHT: The Battle of Agincourt demonstrated the superiority of English longbowmen over French knights.

expansion and its influence was being felt in Afghanistan. India was an important part of the British Empire and the British began to perceive the Russians as a threat so they instigated a war with the Russians. This First Afghan War lasted 1839–42. Britain fared badly, however, losing the entire garrison at Kabul.

For 36 years tension remained between Britain and Russia until Britain decided to enter Afghanistan once more. Under General Roberts (1832–1914) British troops began their push in 1878. The Second Afghan War lasted until 1880 and saw Britain recapturing Kabul, relieving the Kandahar, the Afghan leader.

Another 39 years of tension passed before Russia and Britain once again did battle over Afghanistan in 1919. Before the year was out, though, Britain had won the Third Afghan War, partly assisted by the appearance of the first aeroplane ever seen in the skies over Kabul. Afghanistan regained its full independence as a result.

))➤ *British Empire*

AGE OF REASON (1794)

Influential book by republican philosopher Thomas Paine (1737–1809). The latter half of the eighteenth century was the era of Revolution – in France and America. Paine, an Anglo-American philosopher, experienced these events first-hand. Paine had emigrated to Philadelphia in 1774. Two years later he wrote *Common Sense*, in which he asserted that the American colonies gained no advantage from their association with Great Britain. It also criticized the monarchy. American independence was declared six months after the book was published. Paine wrote several pamphlets between 1776 and 1783 inspiring the Revolutionaries. He returned to England in 1787 and wrote *The Rights of Man*, which put forward the idea of a republican government. Paine fled to France in 1792 and there found Louis XVI about to be executed. Paradoxically Paine supported exile rather than execution and as a result was imprisoned. It was while incarcerated that he began writing his book *The Age of Reason* in which he outlined his objections to religion. Friends and foe alike denounced him as an atheist and he returned to America in 1802, dying there seven years later.

))➤ *American Revolution, Enlightenment, French Revolution, Louis XVI of France*

AGINCOURT, BATTLE OF (1415)

Battle fought during the Hundred Years' War. In the 78th year of the longest-running campaign in history a battle was fought at Agincourt, northern France. On 25 October 1415 English troops under the command of Henry V managed to defeat a considerably larger French army, thereby conquering Normandy. The French had a divided command and this proved their downfall. Some 6,000 French died as Henry took the initiative with only a quarter of the manpower. English losses were minimal.

))➤ *Henry V of England, Hundred Years' War*

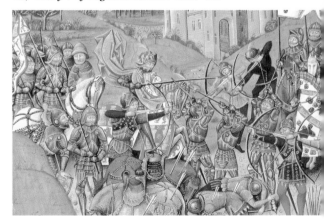

AGRARIAN REVOLUTION (18TH CENTURY)

Term applied to the changes in agricultural practice that began in the late eighteenth century. In Britain almost all traces of the ancient 'open-field' system of arable farming vanished. Wealthier landowners gained title to huge enclosed tracts of land. Farmers now began experimenting with livestock breeding. Extra fodder could be grown to feed animals year-round. Similarly, crop rotation meant all fields could be used fully each year. Improvements in crop production derived from inventions such as new types of agricultural machinery. Mechanization reduced the need for human labour, causing unemployment, hardship, the eviction of peasant farmers, riots and revolts and even mass emigration. However, wherever the agrarian revolution impacted, people on the land were able to produce more food for the growing urban population, partly thanks to artificial fertilizers and the cultivation of high-yielding, reliable crops. The term Green Revolution is sometimes applied to the movement to increase yields and diversify crops in developing countries.

))▶ *Industrial Revolution*

AIDS (1981)

Acquired Immunodeficiency Syndrome. There are several forms of the AIDS virus that can be passed from one person to another and attack the body's immune system by destroying white blood cells. The virus can be spread through unprotected sexual intercourse, transfusion of contaminated blood or sharing of contaminated intravenous needles. The first outbreak in the West occurred in the US in 1981, but the virus is believed to have originated in Africa.

AIX-LA-CHAPELLE, TREATY OF (1748)

Treaty that ended the War of the Austrian Succession. Between 1740 and 1748 war had raged in Europe initiated by the succession of Maria Theresa to the throne of Austria, following the death of her father, the Holy Roman Emperor Charles VI. The war was won by Austria and her allies and was concluded by a general peace agreed at Aix-la-Chapelle.

))▶ *War of the Austrian Succession, Holy Roman Empire*

AKHBAR, EMPEROR (1542–1605)

Most powerful ruler of the Mogul Empire. Jalal Ed-Din Muhammad Akhbar (meaning 'the Great'), a Muslim, was descended from Genghis Khan. He succeeded in 1556 when India was ravaged by civil war. In 1560, when he was 18, he embarked on a 40-year war at the end of which he controlled all India. He saw that Muslim–Hindu rivalry spelled disaster so he married a Hindu princess and tried to create a new religion combining the best of all faiths. He ruled India by dividing it into 18 provinces, each administered by an aristocrat. Akhbar reformed the law and taxation, and encouraged art.

))▶ *Genghis Khan, Mogul Empire, Emperor Babar*

AKHENATON (1379–1362 BC)

Pharaoh of Ancient Egypt. Akhenaton was responsible for widespread changes in pharonic rule in Ancient Egypt. He came to the throne as Amenhotep IV, but changed the focus of worship at his court from Amun to Aten and moved the capital from Thebes to a new city which he named Akhenaten.

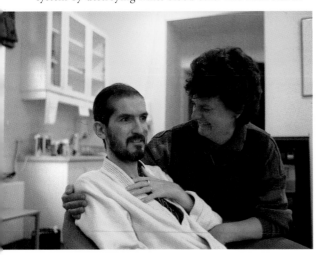

LEFT: An AIDS patient at the Lighthouse Hospital in London. The number of people with the disease is on the rise worldwide despite millions that are continuously invested in research.
RIGHT: American astronaut Edwin 'Buzz' Aldrin, one of a select group of men to have walked on the Moon.

His preoccupation with religion meant that little attention was paid to the empire and its enemies, and many previous conquests were lost. Akhenaten's son Tutankhamen reverted back to the original form of worship early in his reign.

))))➤ *Ancient Egypt, Nefertiti*

ALAMO, THE (1836)

Siege during the Texan War of Independence. In San Antonio, Texas, there was a Franciscan mission fortress called the Alamo. It housed a garrison of some 180 Texan soldiers. Outnumbered 20:1 the garrison held out under siege for 11 days but all were lost by 6 March. Among those killed were Davy Crockett (1783–1836) and Jim Bowie (1796–1836).

))))➤ *Texan War of Independence*

ALBUQUERQUE, ALFONSO DE (1453–1515)

Portuguese navigator, statesman and founder of the Portuguese empire in the Orient. He made his first trip to the East in 1503, travelling with a Portuguese fleet around the Cape of Good Hope to India. King Emanuel of Portugal later appointed him viceroy of all Portuguese possessions in Asia and in that office he captured Goa, Malabar, Ceylon (now Sri Lanka) and other territories in South Asia.

ALCUIN (AD 735–804)

English scholar and theologian. Educated at York, Alcuin later taught there before travelling a great deal throughout Europe. The Emperor Charlemagne

appointed him to preside over his Palace School at Aachen (AD 782). Alcuin was critical of the forced conversion of the Saxons and the brutality they suffered. It was pointless, he said, to baptise those who had no understanding of the faith – an astonishing criticism of Charlemagne that the Emperor allowed. Alcuin went on to become Abbot of Tours.

))))➤ *Charlemagne*

ALDRIN, EDWIN 'BUZZ' (b. 1930)

American astronaut. Aldrin fought in the Korean War before entering the astronaut training programme. In 1966, as co-pilot of Gemini 12, Aldrin achieved a record five-hour space walk. In 1969, during the Apollo 11 lunar mission, he became the second man to set foot on the Moon.

))))➤ *Neil Armstrong, Space Race*

ALEXANDER THE GREAT (356–323 BC)

Macedonian ruler and conqueror. Son of Philip II of Macedon, Alexander was 19 when he succeeded. By his death 12 years later he had conquered a vast empire stretching from Greece to India, including Egypt, founding cities, of which Alexandria is the most famous. A brilliant general, but a drunkard, he also believed he was a god. His greatest rival was the Persian Empire ruled by Darius, defeating it finally in 331 BC at Gaugamela (in Iraq). In 327 BC Alexander invaded India but his troops were exhausted. In 323 BC he died at Babylon. His empire was immediately divided among his generals.

))))➤ *Persian Wars*

ABOVE: Alexander the Great of Macedonia inherited a Greek empire which he expanded to the edges of the Indian subcontinent. Dying childless, his kingdom was eventually divided among his most trusted generals.

ALFRED THE GREAT (AD 849–99)

Anglo-Saxon King of Wessex (England south of the Thames). Alfred was threatened by the Danes who controlled much of England. They demanded money to buy them off. Alfred paid, but the Danish ruler Guthrum

soon returned for more. Alfred had prepared his armies, and defeated Guthrum at Edington in AD 878. The Danes left and Guthrum was converted to Christianity. In AD 892, the Danes returned again but Alfred had organized a cycle of military training for everyone, and had built a fleet. By AD 896 the Danes were forced out. Alfred reformed laws to protect poor people, encouraged education and founded monasteries.

))) *Anglo-Saxons, Vikings*

ALI, MOHAMMED (b. 1942)

First man to win three heavyweight-boxing titles. Born Cassius Marcellus Clay in Louisville, he started boxing in 1954, winning amateur championships including the Olympic Games. He defeated Sonny Liston (February 1964), Ernie Terrell (February 1967), lost to Joe Frazier (March 1971), defeated Frazier (January 1974), defeated George Foreman (October 1974), lost to Leon Spinks (February 1978), defeated Spinks (September 1978). Ali remains the best-known boxer of all time.

))) *Olympic Games*

ALSACE-LORRAINE

Region of north-east France, bounded by Belgium, Luxembourg, and Germany. Its geography (and valuable mineral deposits) have made the area a political football. In the sixteenth century, Alsace and Lorraine were part of the Holy Roman Empire. The Peace of Westphalia (1648) gave control to France, but much of the area was annexed to Germany following the Franco-Prussian War (1870–71). After World War I Alsace-Lorraine was returned to France – it was again annexed (1940–45) to Germany during World War II. The German dialect 'Alsatian' remains the region's *lingua franca*, although both French and German are taught in schools.

))) *Franco-Prussian War, World War II*

AMERICAN CIVIL WAR (1861–65)

War between the northern (Union) and southern (Confederate) states in America. The reasons for the Civil War were primarily ideological. The populations of the northern states had a more progressive approach to their politics. They proclaimed the emancipation of slaves in 1863, but this issue became overshadowed by a determination to maintain the Federal Union of the States; the people of the southern states were claiming the right to secede from the Union in order that they be able to satisfy their instincts for political conservatism. This included the continuation of slavery, which was a far more significant element of society in the south – and the foundation of wealth for many white families. In reality many northern and southern families were divided on the political issues. This meant that relatives ended up fighting on opposite sides, making the war a bitter struggle.

The war began on 14 April 1861 when President Abraham Lincoln proclaimed a blockade of southern ports in reaction to Confederate rebels taking the Federal-run Fort Sumter in South Carolina. In July the Battle of Bull Run was fought. This first major engagement was won by the Confederate side.

ABOVE LEFT: Alfred the Great, one of the great Wessex kings, drove out the invading Danes and introduced new legislation from which the poor and the uneducated could benefit.
LEFT: Mohammed Ali, the world-famous boxer, a legend in his own time.

In April 1862, at the Battle of Shiloh, General Grant won a victory for the Union and the Confederates began conscripting men. The next three years saw counter-attack followed by counter-attack, including the decisive Union victory over General Lee at the Battle of Gettysburg in July 1863. Eventually, though, the end of the war was hastened by a further Union victory at the Battle of Petersburg in March 1865. Hostilities stopped in May.

))))▶ *Confederacy, Battle of Gettysburg, Abraham Lincoln, Slavery*

AMERICAN REVOLUTION (1775–83)

Also known as the American War of Independence, the conflict began when British North American colonists revolted against the policies of the British government.

In 1773 an event known as the Boston Tea Party occurred in Boston Harbour. It was a demonstration of the antagonism felt by colonists toward the British parliament for having attempted to introduce a tax on tea. The purpose of the tax was to raise funds to pay for a standing army in North America to fend off threats to the British colonies. The policy backfired, though, serving only to fuel anti-British feelings in the colonies,

which were beginning to nurture ideas of independence.

Hostilities between the British and the colonists began on 19 April 1775 when the Massachusetts militia, led by rebel leaders John Hancock and Samuel Adams, attacked British troops in Boston as they attempted to seize military stores. The Battle of Bunker Hill on 17 June, the first proper battle, was a victory for the British, but George Washington was soon to become commander-in-chief to the colonies.

A series of battles over the next three years saw the frontline move back and forth, but Washington proved to be a tenacious foe to the British. Following the winter of 1777–78, when Washington reached a low ebb having been deserted by many homesick troops, the French entered the war on his side. The British then had a run of success but the introduction of conscription alienated potential support from loyalist factions. The British general Charles Cornwallis surrendered his army in 1781, leading to peace negotiations. Eventually, at the Treaty of Paris (3 September 1783) American independence from Britain was recognized.

))))▶ *Boston Tea Party, Battle of Bunker Hill, George Washington*

AMIN, IDI (b. c. 1925)

Ugandan dictator (1971–79). Army chief Amin overthrew the government of Milton Obote in 1971. His brutal regime plunged the country into chaos. The economy broke down following the expulsion of 60,000 'non-citizen' Asians, and tribal persecution resulted in the murder of 300,000 Ugandans. In July 1976 he was involved in the Palestinian hijacking of a French airliner to Entebbe. Amin was finally driven into exile in 1979 by Tanzanian troops and now lives in Saudi Arabia.

AMUNDSEN, ROALD (1872–1928)

Norwegian polar explorer. In 1903–05 Amundsen achieved the first voyage through the North-West Passage in a single vessel, the sloop *Gjøa*, having spent two winters on King William Island calculating the exact position of the North Magnetic Pole. In 1910 he set sail for Antarctica. On 14 December 1911 he and four companions, using dog-sledges, became the first men to reach the South Pole, a month ahead of Captain Robert Scott.

))))▶ *Captain Robert Scott*

ANCIENT EGYPT

The civilization of Ancient Egypt began about 3100 BC and flourished for over 2,000 years. It was one of the earliest and greatest civilizations, remarkable for its richness and sophistication and its lasting achievements.

In 3100 BC the kingdoms of Lower Egypt, on the Nile delta, and Upper Egypt south of the delta were unified by the legendary king Menes, who ruled from Memphis. The first major phase of the civilization was the Old Kingdom established in 2686 BC. During this period the great pyramids at Giza were built and hieroglyphics, or picture writing, developed. This script covers clay tablets, manuscripts and the walls of buildings, describing every aspect of life in Ancient Egypt. In the Middle Kingdom (1991–1786 BC) Nubia was conquered and became part of the Egyptian kingdom. Trade links with Asia were established and the kingdom prospered. The Egyptian Empire reached its largest extent and Egyptian civilization its greatest heights during the

ABOVE: The funerary mask of Tutankhamen, part of a vast treasure unearthed inside the Valley of the Kings.

New Kingdom (1554–1196 BC), when the capital was also moved to Thebes. After the eleventh century BC Egypt was often divided and sometimes subjugated to Assyria and Persia and ultimately to Alexander the Great. The empire survived until Cleopatra's death in 30 BC.

To Ancient Egypt is owed not only the construction of the pyramids and other monuments such as the rock temple at Abu Simbel (built by Rameses II in the thirteenth century BC), but also the invention of irrigation, early discoveries in astronomy, mathematics and medicine and the legacy of a rich pantheon of deities and totemic animals. The arid climate has preserved a wealth of treasures and other objects. The most famous find was that of the tomb of Tutankhamon (r. 1358–53 BC), the young pharaoh who succeeded Akhenaten and reversed his monotheistic policy.

))))▶ *Akhenaton, Alexander the Great, Cleopatra, Great Pyramid of Giza, Rameses II, Tutankhamen*

ANCIENT GREECE

The civilization of Ancient Greece lasted from *c.* 800 to 300 BC. More than any other civilization except that of the Jews, it bequeathed ideas about politics, society, philosophy and culture to modern Western civilization. The first Greek civilization, the Mycenaean (*c.* 1600–1200 BC), probably spread by the marriage of Greek-speaking invaders with indigenous inhabitants. At the two great centres of this era, Knossos on Crete and Mycenae on the mainland, royal dynasties developed palace societies in which writing evolved and art (notably frescoes) and architecture flourished.

Between the fourteenth and twelfth centuries BC, Greece and Crete were invaded by the Achaeans and the Dorians, who founded Sparta. Between 1100 and 800 BC the great city-states arose. The mountainous terrain of Greece prevented the cities from attaining any national unity and compelled them to take to the sea. Thus from 750 to 550 BC the Greeks became great traders and founded colonies around the coasts of the Mediterranean and the Black Sea. These wealthy ports became the main centres of Greek culture, where philosophy, science and lyric poetry originated.

In the fifth century BC the focus of the Greek world shifted to Athens and here tragedy, comedy, sculpture and

ANCIENT ROME

The centre of the Roman Empire, which became the greatest of the ancient world and for its duration was the predominant world culture. According to tradition, Rome was founded in 753 BC on seven hills and ruled in succession by seven kings. A republic was established in 510 BC, governed by two consuls (chief magistrates), elected by a popular assembly, and by the Senate, a council of elders. One of Rome's arch opponents was the North African port of Carthage, with which Rome fought between 264 and 146 BC. In the first Punic War with Carthage the Roman navy was founded. Roman conquests became provinces ruled by Roman governors.

Civil wars, unrest and revolution marked the transition of Rome from a republic to an empire. Julius Caesar took over Rome as its dictator. Assassinated in 44 BC, he was succeeded by a triumvirate of rulers. Under Augustus, the first Roman emperor, Rome began to prosper again. At its greatest expansion, in AD 117, the Empire stretched from Scotland to Egypt and Spain to Mesopotamia, and had a population of over a million. The last emperor was deposed in AD 476, completing the fall of Rome.

The Romans were essentially pragmatic, militaristic people, remembered especially for the efficiency and discipline of their army. They imitated the best of Greek culture, including its coinage, units of measure and fine arts. Roman law was codified in the sixth century. Roman roads were unmatched in the ancient world and Roman city planners and engineers excelled in the building of houses, temples, monuments, aqueducts and dams. The Colosseum and the Forum are testimony to their architectural skill. Roman religion, like the Greek, was pantheistic. Latin, the language of the Romans, was the medium for a multitude of brilliant and enduring literary works.

))》 *Augustus Caesar, Julius Caesar, Punic Wars*

architecture reached their glorious height. Ultimately Athens was surpassed by Alexandria and then by Rome. Homer, Hesiod and the lyric poet Pindar were the three greatest names of Ancient Greek literature. Socrates, Plato and Aristotle laid the foundations of moral philosophy. The city-states, *poleis*, which included both rural and urban areas, passed from monarchy to the rule of landowners or merchants and then to democratic communities of citizens. For the first time in known history ideas of freedom and autonomy emerged and the art of politics was practised. Greek religion included many gods, who were honoured with animal sacrifices, gifts and offerings.

))》 *Aristotle, Trojan War*

ABOVE: A high-relief stone carving of life in Ancient Greece shows the wealth and sophistication enjoyed by this advanced civilization.
RIGHT: In its heyday, the Roman Empire was a nexus for world culture and commerce. The discovery of Roman coins is a testament to the wide-ranging trade network established by the Romans.

ANGLO-DUTCH WARS
(1652–54, 1665–67, 1672–74)

Three wars between England and Holland in the seventeenth century. This was a period of intense rivalry between Britain and Holland – both nations had vested interests in newly discovered parts of the world where they had established colonies and set up trade links. With vast profits to be had from these colonies it was only a matter of time before both countries went to war.

In 1600 Elizabeth I of England had chartered the British East India Company. The Dutch East India Company was established in 1602. Both countries used their companies for founding new colonies in the East and West Indies and by 1652 rivalries had initiated the First Anglo-Dutch War, which lasted until 1654 and culminated in English control of the seas. Tensions remained through the 'Golden Age' and war broke out again in 1665 in which the Stadtholderless Republic regained control. The Dutch became preoccupied by war with France in 1672 and the Third Anglo-Dutch War contributed to the Netherlands' eventual fall from power.

)))➤ *British East India Company, Dutch East India Company*

ANGLO-SAXONS (AD 597–1066)

Germanic rulers of England. The Roman army left Britain (AD 410) and to help the Picts, Scots and Vikings defend themselves against raiding parties, mercenary Angles and Saxons were employed from Northern Germany. They brought their families and were paid in land. They colonized the Celt's kingdoms; by AD 850 Mercia, Northumbria and Wessex were Anglo-Saxon. The Vikings invaded (AD 865) and overran Mercia and Northumbria.

BELOW: After the Romans' departure from England, the Anglo-Saxons were employed as mercenaries by local tribes to defend themselves against invaders.

Alfred the Great, King of Wessex, counter-attacked (AD 878) and drove the Vikings to the sea. By AD 955 Edred, Alfred's grandson, ruled a united England. During Ethelred the Unready's rule, the Vikings returned and on his death (1016), the Viking Canute ruled England. When he died Edward the Confessor became king, dying in 1066 without a male heir. Harold, the Earl of East Anglia, claimed the throne but his reign was abruptly brought to an end by the Norman invasion, culminating in William I's coronation (Christmas Day 1066), ending Anglo-Saxon rule of England.

)))➤ *Alfred the Great, Canute, William I of England*

ANSCHLUSS (1938)

Meaning 'union', Hitler's invasion of Austria in 1938. Adolf Hitler led the Nazi Party from 1921. He was Austrian by birth and harboured an ambition to annex Austria with Germany as part of his plan for expanding the Third Reich's territory. He invaded Austria and achieved a peaceful union on 12 March 1938.

)))➤ *Adolf Hitler, Nazi Party*

ANTONY, MARK (c. 82–30 BC)

Roman politician and Cleopatra's lover. In 44 BC Marcus Antony was consul with Julius Caesar when Caesar was murdered. Antony joined a triumvirate with Lepidus and Octavian (the future emperor Augustus), fighting a civil war with Caesar's killers, who were defeated at Philippi in 42 BC. Soon after this Antony met Cleopatra, whose gifts made his loyalty to Rome suspect. In 32 BC a civil war broke out between Antony and Octavian, who defeated him at Actium in 31 BC. The following year, Antony and Cleopatra committed suicide in Egypt.

)))➤ *Battle of Actium, Augustus Caesar, Triumvirate*

ANTIOCH, SIEGE OF (1098)

Siege during the First Crusade. The ancient capital of the Greek kingdom of Syria – Antioch – stood where the modern Turkish town Antakya now stands. Antioch became an early centre of Christianity under Roman rule, but was taken by the Arabs in AD 637 after the fall of the Roman empire. In 1098 Antioch was reached by the First Crusade which set off from Western Europe in 1096. The Muslims surrendered to the crusaders after a siege lasting five months.

)))➤ *Crusades*

APARTHEID (1948–94)

South Africa's racial segregation and separate development policies. Before the National Party came to power (1948), racial segregation had been sanctioned by law. The Land Acts (1950, 1954 and 1955) set aside over 80 per cent of land for exclusive use by the white minority. Non-whites carried documents authorizing their presence in restricted areas and further laws established separate education, banned non-white unions, access to government and use of public facilities. The Bantu Self Government Act (1959) created 10 black African homelands and the Bantu Homeland Citizenship Act (1970) made all black South Africans homelands residents, thus excluding them from South African society. Without participation in politics, strikes, demonstrations, protests, assassinations and sabotage became widespread. Condemnation of apartheid led to South Africa's withdrawal from the Commonwealth in 1961 and economic sanctions in 1985. President F. W. de Klerk repealed the apartheid legislation throughout the 1990s and a new constitution was established in 1993. The first all-race elections were held in 1994.

)))➤ *Nelson Mandela*

AQUINAS, ST THOMAS (1224–74)

Born in Italy, Thomas became one of the great thinkers of the Christian Church. A Dominican philosopher and theologian he systematized the Christian revelation along the lines of Aristotelian thought. He produced five arguments for the existence of God – all suspect – but God creating out of nothing is central to his theology. He influenced the development of the Church, particularly Catholicism but Protestants have also used his methodological insights. His best-known work is *Summa contra Gentiles* (1261–64).

ARAB LEAGUE (1945)

Organization of Arab countries, formed in 1945 to coordinate political and economic interests. Its 21 members include nearly all of the Arab states and the Palestine Liberation Organization, and its headquarters are in Cairo. In 1948 league members attacked the newly formed Jewish state of Israel. Egypt was suspended (1979–89) following its peace agreement with Israel, and the headquarters were moved to Tunis. The Iraqi invasion of Kuwait in 1990 and subsequent involvement of Western countries (invited by Saudi Arabia) caused a deep rift between members.

)))➤ *Gulf War*

LEFT: Elizabeth Taylor (Cleopatra) and Richard Burton (Mark Antony) convincingly brought the two ill-fated lovers back to life on the silver screen.

ARAB-ISRAELI WAR (1956–57)

In 1948, following the horrors of the Holocaust during World War II, world leaders made a goodwill gesture to the Jewish survivors by establishing a homeland for them in Israel. Many Palestinian Arabs were forced to become refugees in the Gaza Strip and West Bank areas as a result, causing much resentment and unrest. The Israelis soon nurtured ambitions to take more land. They did so in 1956 by invading Gaza and Sinai. The war that ensued was ended by Israeli withdrawal in 1957 due to Egyptian resistance. In 1967 the Six-Day War saw Israel defeat Egypt and Syria. Much of the land seized has subsequently been returned.

))⯈ *Six-Day War, World War II*

BELOW: Yasser Arafat, Palestinian figurehead and leader of the Palestinian Liberation Organization (PLO).

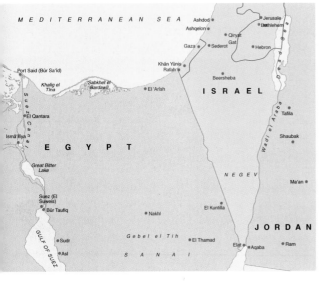

ARAFAT, YASSER (b. 1929)

Palestinian leader. Chairman of the Palestinian Liberation Organization (PLO) since 1969. Arafat, who always appears in public wearing the symbolic kaffiyeh, presided over the PLO's move from terrorism to diplomacy in the late 1980s. The 1993 Oslo Peace Accord with Israel led to limited Palestinian self-rule in Jericho and the Gaza Strip in 1994, for

ABOVE: The Arab-Israeli conflict remains unresolved to this day with deep tensions colouring relations between Israelis, who were given a part of Palestine as their homeland, and Palestinian Arabs, who had that land taken away from them.

which Arafat, Shimon Peres and Yitzhak Rabin received the 1994 Nobel Peace Prize. Agreements since then have led to a slow expansion of self-rule in the West Bank and Arafat was elected President of the Palestinian-controlled territory in 1996.

ARCHIMEDES (c. 287–212 BC)

Ancient Greek scientist. Ancient Greece was where science and civilization merged. One of the greatest scientific or natural philosophers from that world was Archimedes. He is described as mathematician and engineer, because he used mathematical principles in explaining how things worked and in designing things *to* work. Archimedes' principles of fluid displacement is probably his best-documented achievement. It demonstrates that the water displaced by a vessel weighs the same as the vessel.

))⯈ *Ancient Greece*

ARISTOTLE (384–322 BC)

Ancient Greek philosopher. Long before scientists began to properly understand chemistry and the elements, Aristotle came up with his own theory to explain the way things are made. For Aristotle there were just four 'elements': Earth, Air, Fire and Water. He believed that all earthly matter comprised these elements in different proportions. He claimed that a fifth element called aether made the celestial bodies seen in the sky. Interestingly, Aristotle was the first to consider the Earth to be spherical, although he did mistakenly think it was the centre of the Universe as well.

))▶ *Ancient Greece, Plato*

ARMSTRONG, NEIL (b. 1930)

American astronaut. A former fighter pilot in the Korean War in 1962, Armstrong became the first civilian to enter the astronaut training programme. In 1966 he was command pilot of the Gemini 8 mission, which achieved the first physical joining of two orbiting spacecraft. In July 1969 Armstrong, as commander of the Apollo 11 lunar mission, became the first person to set foot on the Moon. His companions were Edwin 'Buzz' Aldrin and Michael Collins.

))▶ *Edwin 'Buzz' Aldrin, Space Race*

ARNHEM, BATTLE OF (1944)

Allied aerial attack during World War II. The Allied landings of World War II began on 6 June 1944. By September Allied forces had reached the River Rhine. On 17 September the allies launched an airborne operation designed to secure a number of bridgeheads over the Rhine, intending to capture the key area of the Ruhr – the industrial heartland of the German military. The Battle of Arnhem, part of the campaign known as Operation Market Garden, lasted for nine days and resulted in 7,600 Allied casualties. It was judged only partially successful.

))▶ *World War II*

ÁRPÁD (AD 840–97)

Chief Magyar and national hero of the Hungarians. Árpád led the Magyars from Asia to the Avars-occupied region of what is now Hungary in

AD 890 and founded the Árpád dynasty and line of Hungarian kings. The Holy Roman Emperor Otto I defeated the Árpád dynasty at Lechfeld in AD 955.

))▶ *Magyars*

ARRAS, BATTLE OF (1917)

British attack on German forces during World War I. The Siegfried line was a defensive line marked out by the Germans in 1917; it was a sub-division of the Hindenburg Line at the Western Front. In support of a French offensive, British troops launched an attack on the German frontline during April and May 1917. The Siegfried line was partially breached during the operation, but casualties were extremely high. About 84,000 Britons and 75,000 Germans were killed or wounded.

))▶ *World War I*

ABOVE: The great Greek philosopher Aristotle.

ART DECO (1920s)

Style of design dating from the 1920s and 30s. Its name deriving from the 1925 Paris Exposition Internationale des Arts Décoratifs et Industriels Modernes, Art Deco can be seen as having taken up where Art Nouveau left off in the attempt to produce a style of design and interior decoration for the machine age. Where the Arts and Crafts Movement had arguably attempted to put back the clock to pre-industrial times and Art Nouveau had used industrial processes to represent patterns and images drawn from the natural world, Art Deco made a virtue of streamlined shapes, geometric lines and uncompromising angularity. These values are as evident in the jewellery and glassware of Renée Lalique (1860–1945) as they are in Donald Deskey's design for the interior of New York's Radio City music hall (1932) and in the ship's-bridge bay windows of so many English suburban villas of the period. To begin with, a fashion of the rich, employing luxurious materials like lacquer and jade, Art Deco's industrial inspiration meant that it adapted well to mass-production in much cheaper materials to meet the more austere requirements of the 1930s' Great Depression.

))) *Art Nouveau, Arts and Crafts Movement*

ART NOUVEAU (c. 1890–1920)

Decorative style, popular in the late nineteenth and early twentieth centuries. A reaction at once to the perceived soullessness of machine-production and to the stolid, superannuated romanticism of so much late-nineteenth-century art and design, Art Nouveau sought to bring energy and fun back into the field of ornamentation. Named after the Parisian gallery, L'Art Nouveau, whose owner Siegfried Bing did much to champion its principles, the new approach was characterized by the bold asymmetries and swirling lines of what were often highly stylized plant-forms. Though first coming to prominence in France, Art Nouveau was recognizably rooted in the English Arts and Crafts Movement, whose anti-industrial values and whose affection for nature it obviously shared. The illustrations of the English artist Aubrey Beardsley

(1872–98), the glass and mosaics of Louis Comfort Tiffany (1848–1933) in New York, the interior designs of Charles Rennie Mackintosh (1868–1928) in Scotland and the extravagant constructions of Antoni Gaudí (1852–1926) in Spain: all clearly show the influence of this vital and varied school.

))) *Art Deco, Arts and Crafts Movement*

ARTS AND CRAFTS MOVEMENT (19TH CENTURY)

Aesthetic and political movement of the late nineteenth century. Inspired by the writings of the critic John Ruskin (1819–1900), and his condemnation of a system of industrial production which he believed debased both the skills of craftsmen and the tastes of consumers, a growing number of artists and critics called for a return to medieval standards. The spirit of collective creativity which Ruskin believed had gone into the construction of the great Gothic cathedrals of the Middle Ages had been made possible by the dignity accorded in those times to the craftsmen and their guilds. An abstract theory to begin with, Ruskin's ideas were soon being realized by the poet and artist William Morris (1834–96), producing hand-made furniture, wallpaper, cloth and books for popular consumption. Not until 1888 did the movement finally crystallize into a formally established Arts and Crafts Exhibition Society: by that time its influence had spread to the continent, where it prompted the rise of Art Nouveau.

))) *Art Nouveau*

ARTHUR, KING (AD 5TH OR 6TH CENTURIES)

Mythical British king enshrined in legends surrounding the sword Excalibur, the castle of Camelot, the Knights of the Round Table, and the search for the Holy Grail, elaborated in more recent times to associate him with Tintagel (Cornwall) and Glastonbury (Somerset). Geoffrey of Monmouth, and other twelfth-century writers, developed the myths. Arthur may have

LEFT: This vase by Émile Gallé (1846–1904) is an example of work produced by the arts and crafts movement known as Art Nouveau, which sought to bring spontaneity back into artistic expression.

RIGHT: *During the Battle of the Atlantic, cargo ships transporting vital wartime goods to British armies became prime targets for maritime attacks by German bomber planes and submarines.*
BOTTOM RIGHT: *The Acropolis in Athens, Greece.*

had a loose basis in historical fact as a fifth- or sixth-century descendant of the Romano-British, leading resistance against the Saxon invasions.

))))> *Anglo-Saxons*

ASOKA (269–232 BC)

 King of India. Asoka ruled India for 40 years. At the beginning of his reign he embarked on a military campaign of empire expansion, but he is reputed to have been so shocked at the horror and bloodshed that he turned to Buddhism – then just a small religious sect – and adopted it as the state religion. He is responsible for the spread of Buddhism to Sri Lanka and central Asia.

))))> *Buddhism*

ASSYRIANS (c. 900 BC)

Civilization of the Ancient Near East. The Assyrians replaced the Babylonians in the area of Ancient Mesopotamia (present-day Iraq). They were a warlike people and the first to form a military state, which assisted in the successful conquest of other civilizations and the expansion of their empire. The Assyrians are also noted for their love of learning; they took care to preserve the libraries of the states they conquered. The most famous of these is that of King Ashurbanipal, discovered at the Assyrian capital Nineveh.

))))> *Babylonians, Hittites, Sumerians*

ATHENS

Capital of ancient and modern Greece. The city is dominated by the Acropolis hill, on which stands the Parthenon, temple of Athena, erected in the fifth century BC. Athens became the capital of a united Attica before 700 BC. Under Pericles it was the first city of Greece in power and culture. After its defeat by Sparta in the Peloponnesian War the city began to decline, although it flourished as a philosophical centre until AD 529.

))))> *Ancient Greece, Peloponnesian War*

ATLANTIC, BATTLE OF THE (1939–45)

Naval campaign during World War II. Essential to the success of any campaign in wartime is the regular supply of fuel, equipment and goods to a fighting force. For this reason battles raged in the Atlantic Ocean throughout World War II. Cargo ships needed to sail between Britain and the USA to keep Allied forces in

supplies, so they became prime targets for German warships and submarines. The battle began on the very first night of the war in September 1939 when a German U-boat torpedoed the British ocean liner *Athenia*.

))))> *World War II*

ATOMIC BOMB (1945)

Weapon with a huge explosive force released through splitting nuclear atom. Further destruction is caused by radioactive fallout. The first secret test took place in the desert in New Mexico on 16 July 1945. Two atomic bombs, thousands of times more powerful than any previous weapons, were then dropped on the Japanese cities of Hiroshima and Nagasaki by American aircraft in the final stages of World War II. Bombs were later developed by a number of countries, including the USSR, France and China, which led to a build-up of nuclear weapons. Others, including Iraq and Pakistan, are thought to be able to manufacture them.

))))> *Hiroshima, World War II*

ATTILA THE HUN (c. AD 406–453)

King of the Huns from AD 434. During the closing period of Roman rule in Europe the Romans became increasingly troubled by tribes from the north. Attila the Hun became king when he murdered his own brother. He attacked the eastern Roman Empire (AD 441–443), to increase his tribute payments. He did so again between AD 447–449. Then, in 450 AD, Attila turned his attentions to the western Roman Empire. He entered Italy but was persuaded to withdraw in AD 452 by Pope Leo I (c. 390–461 AD).

AUGUSTINE OF HIPPO, ST (AD 354–430)

A native of North Africa, Augustine was a professor of rhetoric until his conversion at the age of 32 in AD 387. Ordained in AD 391, by AD 394 he was Bishop of Hippo in North Africa. He became one of the most influential thinkers in Christianity, using his considerable intellect to defend the Christian faith and refute heresy. He argued that all humans are born into an inherited state of sin, the penalty for which is death. This was caused by the disobedience of Adam (*Genesis* 3). His *Confessions* (basically autobiographical, *c.* AD 400) and *City of God* (AD 413–26) are classics of their kind. His feast day is 28 August.

))) *Christianity*

AURANGZEB, EMPEROR (1618–1707)

Most powerful Mogul Emperor. In 1658 Aurangzeb organized a palace revolution, becoming Mogul Emperor of northern India. A Muslim fanatic, his despotic rule provoked opposition. He continued the work of his father, Shah Jahan, fighting to extend the Empire into southern India, reaching Bijapur and Golconda, but overstretched Mogul resources.

))) *Mogul Empire, Shah Jahan*

AUSTERLITZ, BATTLE OF (1805)

Battle during the Napoleonic Wars. Napoleon Bonaparte proclaimed himself Emperor Napoleon I in 1804. A year later, at the height of his powers Napoleon scored one of the greatest victories of his campaign of expansion at a small town in the former Austria, known as Austerlitz. The Battle of Austerlitz saw

the French army defeat a coalition force of Russian and Austrian troops. The outcome was that the Russians retreated to their own lands and the Austrians signed the Treaty of Pressburg.

))) *Napoleon Bonaparte, Napoleonic Wars*

AUSTRIAN SUCCESSION, WAR OF (1740–48)

War between European states over the right to succession of the Holy Roman Empire. When the Holy Roman Emperor Charles VI died in 1740 his daughter Maria Theresa assumed succession to the throne of Austria. This was supported by England and Holland, but disputed by Prussia, France and Spain. The result was the War of the Austrian Succession, principally between Austria and Prussia, and thus sometimes described as the Austro-Prussian War.

The first act of aggression came from Frederick the Great of Prussia who seized an area of Austria called Silesia. The Battle of Dettingen (1743) saw an army comprising Britons, Austrians and Hanoverians, under King George II, victorious over the French. The Battle of Fontenoy (1745) saw an Anglo-Austrian army beaten.

The war was not solely confined to land: action was also seen at sea. Eventually British naval superiority began to tell, particularly around America and India. Eventually, after eight years of fighting, the war came to an end. The Treaty of Aix-la-Chapelle (1748) was the official end to hostilities. Maria Theresa's husband subsequently became the new emperor of Austria until 1765.

))➤ *Treaty of Aix-la-Chapelle, Holy Roman Empire*

AVERROËS (1126–98)

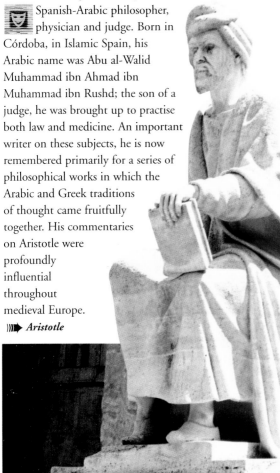

Spanish-Arabic philosopher, physician and judge. Born in Córdoba, in Islamic Spain, his Arabic name was Abu al-Walid Muhammad ibn Ahmad ibn Muhammad ibn Rushd; the son of a judge, he was brought up to practise both law and medicine. An important writer on these subjects, he is now remembered primarily for a series of philosophical works in which the Arabic and Greek traditions of thought came fruitfully together. His commentaries on Aristotle were profoundly influential throughout medieval Europe.

))➤ *Aristotle*

ABOVE: The Spanish-Arab philosopher Averroës was reknowned for his commentaries on Aristotle's works.
RIGHT: This striking Aztec skull artefact bears witness to the ferocity of these warrior Mexican-Indian people.

AVICENNA (IBN-SINA) (AD 980–1037)

Persian-born philosopher. Central Asia was at the forefront of Islamic civilization from the ninth to fourteenth centuries; Avicenna was born into that milieu: often regarded as the greatest philosopher to write in Arabic he was a scholar, physician and scientist. His major work, *Kitab al-Shifa* ('Book of Healing'), is an encyclopaedia of eleventh-century Greek and Islamic thought. He was not a great original thinker but synthesized the ideas of his predecessors. He was an influence on Thomas Aquinas. Avicenna also published *Kitab al-Najat* ('Book of Salvation').

))➤ *Thomas Aquinas*

AZTECS (1325–1521)

Mexican Indian Empire. Originally hunters and gatherers in Northern Mexico, the Aztecs established their city Tenochtitlán in 1325. Through the cultivation of all land, including swamps, within 100 years they had become dominant in the area. By 1519 with an empire covering over 200 sq km (125 sq miles) and a population of six million the Aztec empire had absorbed about 500 smaller states. War was a part of Aztec culture and human sacrifice played a role in their rituals and ceremonies. When the Great Pyramid Temple in Tenochtitlán was dedicated, 20,000 human beings captured in battle had their hearts removed. The Aztecs were occasional cannibals, believing that by eating the flesh of victims they could absorb their virtues. The Aztecs worshipped an elaborate collection of deities, including Quetzacoatl. In 1519 with the Aztec Empire still developing, Spanish explorers arrived in the area. Montezuma II, the ninth Aztec Emperor, had been on the throne for 17 years. He was captured by Hernán Cortés and, whether by design or accident, died whilst being held. Cuitláhauac and Cuauhtémoc, Montezuma's successors, waged an unsuccessful war against the Spanish but when Tenochtitlán was captured and sacked by the Spanish in 1521, the Aztec Empire collapsed.

))➤ *Hernán Cortés, Montezuma, Tenochtitlán*

BABAR, EMPEROR (1483–1530)

First Mogul Emperor. Descended from Genghis Khan, Babar (also spelled Babur, and meaning 'tiger') became ruler of Turkestan from 1495 but by 1501 he had lost Turkestan and Samarkand to the Uzbeks. However, Babar retained enough support to enter Afghanistan and seize Kabul in 1504. In 1512 he finally abandoned attempts to regain Samarkand. Seeing potential in the political dissent on the subcontinent he made several raids, climaxing in 1526 with the defeat of the Afghan emperor of Delhi, and in 1527 the Rajputs. Although further wars followed, by 1530 Babur could bequeath the core of the later Mogul Empire to his descendants, who were left with the task of organizing its control and government.

))➡ *Akhbar, Mogul Empire*

BABBAGE, CHARLES (1791–1871)

British mathematician. Charles Babbage is considered the father of the computer. He was interested in developing mechanical calculating machines that could automatically solve complex mathematical problems. Two of his brain children were the 'difference engine' and 'analytical engine': theoretical computing machines that were eventually built after his death.

BABYLONIANS (c. 1792 BC)

Peoples of the Ancient Near East. The Babylonian Empire became significant in Mesopotamia *c.* 1792 BC under Hammurabi. Babylon is renowned for its decadence, but also its advanced technology. Most famously Nebuchadnezzar II captured Jerusalem in 586 BC and exiled the Jews to Babylon for 70 years to help on the Babylonians' hydraulically irrigated Hanging Gardens. Astronomical and mathematical developments included the establishment of an hour of 60 minutes and 360 degrees in a circle. In 539 BC Babylon itself fell to Cyrus the Great. From then on the civilization was in decline, but from the palace at Mari, which had 12-m (40-ft) thick walls, clay tablets survive with extensive information.

))➡ *Assyrians, Cyrus the Great, Sumerians*

BACH, JOHANN SEBASTIAN (1685–1750)

German composer. Orphaned at the age of 10, Bach was brought up by his elder brother, a church organist in Ohrdruf: it was he who taught the boy his keyboard skills. Though respected for his work in composition – and, by 1723, court composer to the Elector of Saxony in Leipzig – Bach's fame in his own lifetime rested mainly in his dazzling flair as a performer, especially on the organ. Subsequent ages would recognize the revolutionary innovativeness of such keyboard compositions as the *Goldberg Variations* and the *Art of Fugue* as well as the enormous emotional power of choral masterpieces like the *St Matthew Passion* and *Mass in B Minor*.

LEFT: Babar, the first Mogul emperor and a direct descendant of Genghis Khan.
ABOVE: The German composer Johann Sebastian Bach.

BACON, FRANCIS (1561–1626)

English statesman and thinker. A successful courtier under James I, Bacon became Solicitor General in 1607 and by 1621 had risen to the rank of Viscount St Albans. He has, however, been known to later ages primarily for his writings. In his *Essays* (1597–1625) and above all in his great longer work *The Advancement of Learning* (1605), Bacon underlined the need for knowledge to be based not on traditional wisdom but on active experiment and observation. Dying of a chill caught after stuffing a chicken carcass with snow to test the effects on decomposition, he became not only a pioneer of modern scientific method but also its first martyr.

BADEN-POWELL, ROBERT (1857–1941)

Founder of the Scouting movement. After serving the British Army with quiet distinction in India and Afghanistan, Baden-Powell became a public figure in the Boer War of 1899–1900 when he won fame as hero of the Siege of Mafeking. In 1908 his book, *Scouting for Boys,* became the basis of a worldwide movement of Boy Scouts. With his help, his sister Agnes founded the Girl Guides two years later, while a movement for younger boys, the Wolf Cubs, followed in 1916.

))♦ *Boer War*

BAGHDAD

Capital of Iraq. Baghdad was founded in AD 762 on the western bank of the Tigris and became a great commercial and intellectual centre under the

Abbasid caliph Harun ar-Rashid, whose reign is celebrated in the *Arabian Nights* story collection. In 1258 Baghdad was overrun by Hulagu, grandson of Genghis Khan, who destroyed the irrigation system, converting the fertile

ABOVE: The colourful, tiled dome of an Islamic mosque in the ancient city of Baghdad.

fields into a barren waste. Another Mongol, Tamerlaine, sacked the city in 1401. Baghdad fell under Persian control in 1508, then that of the Ottoman Turks in 1534. The Persians recaptured the city in 1623 and held it until its reannexation by Turkey in 1638.

))♦ *Genghis Khan, Tamerlaine*

BAHA'I (1844)

On 2 May 1844 the Baha'i Faith began. The Bab (1819–50) (meaning 'gate' or 'door') was born in Persia and was a descendant of the Prophet Mohammad. He proclaimed himself the Messenger of God and was executed as a result in 1850, on a charge of heresy against Islam. Three other figures were central to the development of Baha'i: Baha'ullah (1817–92), often considered the founder of Baha'i), Abdu'l-Baha (1844–1921) and Shoghi Effendi (1897–1957). The guiding body of Baha'i is the Universal House of Justice based in Haifa, Israel. Baha'is believe in One God; the common foundation of all faiths; the oneness of humankind; the harmony of science and religion; universal peace; elimination of prejudice; and the equality of the sexes. They are regarded as heretics by Islam and subject to persecution.

))♦ *Islam, Prophet Mohammad*

BAIRD, JOHN LOGIE (1888–1946)

Scottish inventor. The television started life as the brainchild of John Logie Baird. The first working prototype was demonstrated in 1926. It was primitive, but showed that the idea worked. Eventually the familiar television, using a cathode-ray tube, became the preferred format. The design has gone on to be used for computer monitors. By 1928 Baird had also perfected the workings of colour television.

BALACLAVA, BATTLE OF (1854)

During the Crimean War there was a Russian advance on British positions at Balaclava, 10 km south-east of Sevastopol in the Ukraine. The Battle of Balaclava took place on 25 October 1854. British cavalry unit the Light Brigade made a foolish charge at Russian artillery, suffering heavy losses.

))♦ *Charge of the Light Brigade, Crimean War*

BALBOA, VASCO NÚÑEZ DE (1475–1519)

Spanish explorer. Balboa joined an expedition that established a settlement at Darien (now Panama), the first European settlement on the American mainland. In 1513 he led an exploratory expedition of 190 Spaniards and 1,000 Native American guides to the shores of the Pacific. They were the first Europeans to reach that ocean from the east. Balboa claimed both sea and all the land within it as the property of the Spanish king.

)))➤ *Conquistadors*

BALFOUR DECLARATION (1917)

Statement from British statesman Arthur Balfour supporting the creation of Israel. As foreign secretary (1916–19), Balfour wrote a letter to Baron Rothschild that contained the so-called Balfour Declaration: a promise of British support for 'the establishment in Palestine of a national home for the Jewish people'. The declaration was endorsed by the Allied powers and included in the British mandate over Palestine, approved by the League of Nations in 1922.

)))➤ *Arab-Israeli War, League of Nations*

BANDUNG CONFERENCE (1955)

Meeting of 29 different countries (18–24 April 1955). Sponsored by Indonesia, Burma, Sri Lanka, India and Pakistan, the conference took place to discuss a number of worldwide issues and the 'declaration on the promotion of world peace and co-operation' was adopted. Further conferences arranged in 1961, 1964 and 1965 never took place.

TOP: The Portuguese explorer Vasco Núñez de Balboa.
RIGHT: The medieval Arab pirate Khair-ed-din, also known as Barbarossa because of his trademark fiery red beard.

BARBAROSSA, KHAIR-ED-DIN (c. 1483–1546)

Arabian pirate. In the late medieval period the Barbary Coast – the Mediterranean coast of Africa from Morocco to Egypt – was home to Arab populations who saw Christians as their enemies. Two notorious pirates who emanated from there were Horuk and his brother Khair-ed-din, otherwise known as Barbarossa, 'Red Beard'. They both had great success attacking Christian vessels in the eastern Mediterranean sea, looting them of their valuable cargoes and killing their crews. Horuk was eventually run down and killed by the Spaniards in 1518. Barbarossa and his band of cut-throats took Tunis in 1534 and he eventually died in Constantinople (Istanbul).

)))➤ *Barbary Corsairs*

BARBARY CORSAIRS (16TH CENTURY)

Pirates from the Barbary Coast. With very active trade routes established across the Mediterranean sea there was a rise in piracy in the area. Often these were Arabs attacking Christian vessels. The term 'Corsairs' comes from the Latin for 'raid' or 'plunder'.

))) **Kair-ed-Din Barbarossa**

BARBIZON SCHOOL (1840s)

Group of French painters. Taking their name from the village near Fontainebleau, France, which their leader Théodore Rousseau (1812–67) made his head-quarters in the 1840s, the Barbizon School represented a radical new departure in European landscape-painting. Reacting against the academic, classically inspired work until then conventional in nineteenth-century France, Rousseau moved landscape from the background into the artistic foreground as a worthwhile subject in itself, to be captured not in the studio but directly in *plein air*. Breaking with recent French tradition, he turned instead to the work of English landscape-painters such as John Constable (1776–1837). Rousseau's following at Barbizon included Charles-François Daubigny (1789–1843) and Constant Troyon (1810–65); Jean-Baptiste-Camille Corot (1796–1875) and Jean-François Millet (1814–75) maintained a greater degree of independence.

))) **Impressionism**

BARNARD, CHRISTIAAN (b. 1922)

South African surgeon. On 3 December 1967, the pioneer of cardiac medicine Christiaan Barnard performed the first human heart transplant on a 54-year-old patient. The operation took place at the Groote Schuur Hospital, South Africa, and the patient lived for a groundbreaking 18 days.

BELOW: This baroque candlestick belonged to a florid form of neo-classicism first used in late fifteenth-century Europe and later adopted in Britain.

BAROQUE (17TH CENTURY)

Style of art and architecture. Conventionally associated with the Counter-Reformation of the seventeenth century, when the Catholic Church attempted to win back the spiritual initiative from the Protestant rebels, baroque art sets out to overwhelm the viewer by its sheer emotional intensity and technical skill. The work of Gianlorenzo Bernini (1598–1680),

and especially his *Ecstasy of St Theresa* (1645–52), represents baroque art at its most extravagantly theatrical. Challenging the pointed austerity of protestant architecture and its stern disapproval of religious images, Catholic churches sprouted stucco flourishes, gilded statues and marble colonnades, while in elaborate ceiling-paintings saints soared heavenwards in triumphant *trompe l'oeil*. Such exuberance is, however, only half the story: the riotous excess of baroque art in its detail always found resolution in the classical balance of the work as a whole. The baroque found more sombre expression too in the play of light and dark in works like Rembrandt's *Night Watch* (1642) or Velázquez's *Water-carrier of Seville* (*c*. 1619). The human depths dramatized in these paintings suggest the inadequacy of any simplistic yoking together of the baroque spirit with Catholic spirituality. Though undoubtedly produced in an age of Counter-Reformation, baroque art belonged too to a time of scientific advance, and of increasing psychological awareness.

))) **Counter-Reformation, Rococo**

BASTILLE, STORMING OF (1789)

The Bastille, a fortress and prison in Paris was built by Charles V (1370) and was used to detain prisoners throughout the seventeenth and eighteenth centuries. In 1789 Louis XVI caused unrest by sacking his minister Necker, and fears began to grow that the king might disband the National Assembly. Rioting began on 12 July and the Paris Commune was formed the following day, as was the National Guard, commanded by Marquis de Lafayette. The Bastille was stormed on 14 July in order to obtain munitions for the fighting that was taking place throughout France.

))))▶ *French Revolution, Louis XVI of France*

BATISTA, FULGENCIO (1901–73)

Cuban dictator. Batista twice ruled Cuba, the first time (1933–44) as an effective reformer, the second (1952–59) as a brutal dictator. During his eight-year absence from government, there was an upsurge in corruption and a breakdown of public services. Batista's return to power was welcomed, until he embezzled huge sums from Cuba's booming economy and suppressed the press and Congress. Fidel Castro's long guerilla campaign finally toppled him in 1958.

))))▶ *Fidel Castro*

BAY OF PIGS INVASION (1961)

Fidel Castro became prime minister of Cuba in 1959. His government was Communist and the regime he established was seen as a threat to world peace by the USA. On 17–20 April 1961, some 1,500 US-sponsored Cuban exiles attempted to invade Cuba and seize power from Castro. The invasion was badly planned, however, and Castro's ill-equipped militia was able to defend the Bay of Pigs, where the landings took place. Adding insult to injury, in 1962 Castro demanded a ransom of $53 million worth of food and medicine from the US government in return for most of the prisoners.

))))▶ *Fidel Castro*

BEATLES (1960)

English pop group of the 1960s. Formed in Liverpool in 1960 by guitarists John Lennon, Paul McCartney and George Harrison, the Beatles were later joined by the drummer Richard Starkey or Ringo Starr. They made their first record in 1963, and by the mid-1960s 'Beatlemania' was rife among screaming teenage girls on both sides of the Atlantic; opinion-formers in the world of 'serious' music were scarcely less enthusiastic about the work of the group's songwriting duo, Lennon and McCartney. In the second half of the decade the group made more ambitiously experimental music. The group broke up in 1970, Lennon and McCartney enjoying some success in their solo careers; John Lennon was murdered in a New York street in 1980.

BECKET, ST THOMAS (c. 1117–70)

English martyr. Thomas Becket was born in London, educated in Bologna and Auxerre before becoming chancellor in 1155 and Archbishop of Canterbury in 1162. A close friend of the King Henry II, he had lived a worldly life but once appointed archbishop he became a fierce supporter of the rights of the clergy. He objected strongly to the claim that clergy found guilty by a bishop should be handed over to the state for punishment. His close friendship with Henry turned into bitter enmity and he was exiled a number of times. He returned to Canterbury in 1170 and was murdered in his cathedral on 29 December by knights from Henry's court. He was proclaimed a martyr at once and canonized in 1173. His shrine in Canterbury Cathedral is a famous place of pilgrimage for Christians. His feast day is 29 December.

ABOVE: The murder of St Thomas Becket in Canterbury Cathedral at the hands of killers hired by his former patron, King Henry II.

RIGHT: The German composer Ludwig van Beethoven.
BELOW: Bedouin children in a marketplace in the Middle East.

BECQUEREL, (ANTOINE) HENRI (1852–1908)

French physicist. Although Marie and Pierre Curie are popularly regarded the parents of radioactivity, there was another scientist who was making similar discoveries contemporaneously. Antoine Henri Becquerel had discovered that radiation was emitted from uranium salts and it was, partly, his work that inspired the Curies. The three of them shared the Nobel Prize for Physics in 1903.

)))▶ *Marie Curie*

BEDOUINS

Nomads of the Middle East. The Bedouins are Arabic-speaking nomads, usually animal herders, who tend to live in the deserts of Arabia, Iraq, Syria and Jordan during the rainy seasons, moving back to the cultivated lands of the countries during the drier months of the summer. Each of the Bedouin tribes has e a leader called a Sheikh who is assisted by a tribal council, usually made up of elders of the tribe.

)))▶ *Nomads*

BEETHOVEN, LUDWIG VAN (1770–1827)

German composer. Born in Bonn, and groomed by his singer father to be exhibited as a keyboard prodigy in the manner of the young Mozart, Beethoven had to assume responsibility for his family from his mother's death in 1787. In 1790 he met Joseph Haydn, who eventually agreed to take him on as a student in Vienna. A performing pianist of some renown and a well-regarded composer, Beethoven was by 1802 increasingly afflicted by deafness. His works, however, betrayed none of his depression, his third symphony, the *Eroica* (1804,) setting new standards in ambition and enterprise – standards only extended in the six further symphonies which followed. Considered by many to be Europe's greatest-ever composer, Beethoven also produced important choral music, concertos and sonatas; the 'late quartets' written from 1817 onwards were works of unprecedented depth and dark emotion.

)))▶ *Wolfgang Amadeus Mozart, Joseph Haydn*

BELISARIUS (6TH CENTURY)

Byzantine leader. With the fall of the Roman Empire came the Byzantine Empire (AD 395–1453), also known as the Eastern Roman Empire because it inherited much of Roman culture, but was based at Constantinople (Istanbul). Under Emperor Justinian I, General Belisarius scored many victories for the Byzantine Empire. He recovered North Africa from a tribe known as the Vandals in 533 AD and defeated the Visigoths and Ostrogoths in Spain and Italy respectively.

))))➤ *Byzantium, Justinian*

BELL, ALEXANDER GRAHAM (1847–1922)

Scottish inventor. Alexander Graham Bell demonstrated the telephone for the first time in 1876 in the United States. The inventor was Scottish-born, but moved across the Atlantic to Canada in 1870, with his family. He invented the telephone by assembling together and perfecting various devices invented by others.

BEN-GURION, DAVID (1886–1973)

Born in Poland, Ben-Gurion emigrated to Palestine in 1906. He was expelled by the Turks during World War I and recruited Jews to join the British Army. In 1919 he founded a socialist party and headed the Jewish Agency in 1935. He led the Mapai Party from 1930 and moulded it into the main party of Yishev during British rule. He became prime minister after independence (1948–53) and again (1955–63) encouraging Jewish refugees to enter Israel.

BENEDICTINE ORDER (6TH CENTURY)

Religious order of monks and nuns. St Benedict's (*c.* 480 – *c.* 550) 'The Rule of St Benedict' became the fundamental rule of Western monasticism. It consisted of 73 chapters dealing with spiritual matters, organization, liturgy and discipline. Known as the Black Monks, the regime is simple but not harshly ascetic. The monks helped preserve scholarship and art in worship and liturgy during the difficult years of the second millennium. The abbot is elected and, in spite of an attempt in 1215 to unify the Order, their houses remain autonomous and self-governing but group together in congregations.

))))➤ *Christianity*

BELOW: A Benedictine monk offers his missal to his abbot.

BENIN (15TH–18TH CENTURIES)

African kingdom. The kingdom of Benin flourished in the area that is now Nigeria. It was ruled over by the king, or Oba, who was responsible for the many rituals and ceremonies to ensure the gods provided sufficient rainfall and good harvests. Human and animal sacrifices were made at such festivals. Foreigners began to trade with Benin in the nineteenth century and the Oba was involved in providing slaves from his kingdom to European nations.

))))➤ *Slavery*

BENTHAM, JEREMY (1748–1832)

English philosopher and social thinker. As political economist and pamphleteer, Bentham was the pre-eminent voice of utilitarianism, which calls for measures calculated to produce 'the greatest happiness of the greatest number'. His implied indifference to the feelings of the individual led to his being reviled by the generation of Romantics which followed him, though many of the social reforms he proposed were in themselves commendably humane.

))))➤ *Romanticism*

BERING, VITUS (1680–1741)

Danish navigator. He entered the navy of the Russian tsar Peter the Great and in 1724 was sent to explore the water routes between Siberia and North America. Having taken supplies overland, Bering sailed from Kamchatka into what is now the Bering Sea. He continued north through a channel now named Bering Strait into the Arctic Ocean. Fog prevented him from sighting the North American continent but his voyage proved that it is not joined to the Asian continent. In 1741 he set sail for North America, sighted its coastline and landed on Kayak Island.

))))▶ *Peter the Great*

BERLIN AIRLIFT (1948–49)

Large-scale airlift of supplies to West Berlin. The city was divided into British, French and American occupation zones (West Berlin) and a Soviet zone (East Berlin) at the end of World War II, but as relations worsened between East and West, the Soviets set up a blockade. The West responded with 272,000 flights delivering supplies every day from 24 June 1948 to 12 May 1949. The Soviet Union conceded defeat and reopened the borders.

))))▶ *Berlin Wall, Cold War*

BERLIN WALL (1961–89)

Wall that divided East and West Berlin. Between 1949–61 about 2.5 million East Germans defected to West Germany. To stop this exodus, the East German authorities built a 47-km (29-mile) wall on 12 August 1961. About 5,000 East Germans managed to cross it, but about the same number were caught. Over 100 people were killed attempting the escape. The Wall remained a symbol of division until it was dismantled following the collapse of the East German Communist regime in 1989.

))))▶ *Cold War, Iron Curtain*

BERLIN, CONGRESS OF (1878)

International meeting between European powers. Otto von Bismarck chaired the conference, called primarily to halt Russian expansion in the Ottoman (Turkish) Empire. Among other deals, Bosnia and Herzegovina were assigned to Austria-Hungary and the boundary lines between Greece and Turkey were redrawn. The resulting treaty totally changed the political map in Eastern Europe.

))))▶ *Otto von Bismarck*

BIBLE

The Christian Bible is a library of books (from a Greek word meaning 'books') of many different styles. The Christian Bible had taken its present form by the second century AD. The Christian Bible contains the Old and New Testaments; for Christians, the New Testament is most important. It contains four gospels (accounts of Jesus's life and teachings) and a number of letters from the early years of the Church. The Gospels are very different from one another but they all focus on Jesus as the Messiah who brings freedom from sin and the possibility of eternal life to those who follow him. It is the only written source for knowledge of Jesus. Christians interpret the Bible differently but all accept that the Gospels represent Jesus as revealing God's love for the world. It is the central resource and inspiration of the Christian faith. The Christian Old Testament corresponds to the Jewish (Hebrew) Bible.

))))▶ *Christianity, Judaism*

ABOVE: The cover of the tenth-century Echternact *Bible.*
LEFT: A former symbol of suppression, hatred and division: the ramparts of the Berlin Wall in East Berlin.

BIKO, STEPHEN (1946–77)

Founder of South Africa's Black Consciousness Movement. In 1968 Biko became the first president of the South African Students' Organization, aiming to increase black self-esteem and consciousness, spreading into communities throughout South Africa (1970s). Biko was considered a danger to the apartheid government and was repeatedly arrested. His death in custody in 1977 caused an outcry.

)))▶ *Apartheid, Nelson Mandela*

BILL OF RIGHTS (1789)

The first 10 amendments of the United States Constitution. The opponents of the Constitution maintained it held itself open to tyranny by central government and demanded a Bill of Rights to protect individual citizens. The First Congress of the United States (1789) proposed 12 Constitutional amendments. The first two were not ratified, amendments 3–12 were, comprising the Bill of Rights, signed by Frederick Muhlenberg, Speaker of the House and President of the Senate, John Adams.

)))▶ *United States Constitution*

BISMARCK, OTTO VON (1815-98)

Premier of Prussia (1862–90) and chancellor of Germany (1871–90). Bismarck ruthlessly set about bringing the German states under the Prussian Crown of William I, through provoking wars and making strategic

alliances. The Franco-Prussian War (1870–71) was a humiliating defeat for France and William I was crowned Emperor of Germany. But it was Bismarck, his 'Iron Chancellor', who was the true leader of Europe. Under him German industry boomed, radical social reforms were introduced and the country acquired foreign colonies. Bismarck was sacked by his arch enemy, William II, in 1890.

BLACK HOLE OF CALCUTTA (1756)

In 1756 the Nawab of Bengal attacked the East India Company's operations centre. He took 146 British prisoners in the process. On 19 June he chose to incarcerate them all in the dungeon at Fort William, which measured just 90 sq m (300 sq ft). Unfortunately, due to neglect rather than intent, between 43 and 123 (history has it somewhat confused) prisoners failed to survive the ordeal and the incident became known as the Black Hole of Calcutta.

)))▶ *British East India Company, Seven Years War*

BLACK MONDAY (1987)

Nickname for Monday 19 October 1987, when US stock market prices fell steeply, precipitating sharp declines in other stock markets, notably in London and Tokyo. By the end of the day the Dow–Jones Industrial indicator of prices had fallen over 500 points, reducing the value of stocks by 22.5 per cent. The crash was blamed on the USA's lack of leadership in international trade, weaknesses in the economy and overreactions triggered by computerization. By the year-end all lost ground was recovered.

BLAIR, TONY (b. 1953)

Prime minister of Great Britain (since 1997). First elected to parliament in 1983, Blair rose swiftly through the Labour Party to become leader in 1994, following the death of John Smith. His modernizing influence has seen Labour move to the political centre, rejecting state socialism and embracing market competition along the way. New Labour's landslide victory in the 1997 election ended 18 years of Conservative rule. Since then he has overseen devolved assemblies in Scotland and Wales, abolished hereditary peerage in the House of Lords and signed a peace agreement in Northern Ireland, leading to the country's self-rule.

FAR LEFT Otto von Bismarck, Prussian prime minister and Chancellor of Germany.
BELOW LEFT: British prime minister Tony Blair and wife Cherie pose in front of the Labour Party's election campaign bus.
BELOW: Louis Bleriot perfected the powered monoplane, which he used to make the first Channel crossing in 1909.

BLENHEIM, BATTLE OF (1704)

Battle during the War of the Spanish Succession. On the left bank of the River Danube lies a German village named Blenheim, which was in Bavaria at that time. It was here that the battle took place on 13 August 1704. Allied forces, under the leadership of John Churchill, 1st Duke of Marlborough (1650–1722) scored a decisive victory over combined French and Bavarian forces, helping to turn the tide of the fortunes of the war.

))▶ *War of the Spanish Succession*

BLÉRIOT, LOUIS (1872–1936)

French aviator. Louis Blériot was the first person to fly across the English Channel, or *La Manche* ('The Sleeve') as the French call it. He did so in 1909 in a machine designed and built by himself. Blériot was a skilled aviation designer and he did much to hasten the evolution of the aeroplane. He pioneered the monoplane shape and devized means of operating ailerons by cable and pulley.

BLITZ (1940–41)

Aerial attack on Britain by the Germans during World War II. The initial push by the invasion forces of Germany during World War II was called the *Blitzkrieg* ('lightning war'). The British borrowed part of the name to describe the period of heavy bombing by the German Luftwaffe which began in 1940.

German air raids were unrelenting for the first 18 months of the war and occurred all over Britain. During that period 44,641 men, women and children were killed, with a further 52,352 seriously wounded. London and other cities were razed to the ground in parts, resulting in the evacuation of many – especially children – to rural areas.

))▶ *Blitzkrieg, World War II*

BLITZKRIEG (1939)

When the Germans initiated World War II they had developed a new strategy for land warfare which they called *Blitzkrieg* ('lightning war'). The name described the approach very well – to strike quickly and hard, with an element of surprise. They used combined ground and airborne forces with state-of-the-art technology.

))▶ *World War II*

CALAIS DOUVRES

JUILLET BLÉRIOT 1909

BLOODY SUNDAY (1972)

Day on which demonstrators were killed by British army in Northern Ireland. On Sunday 30 January 1972, British soldiers shot at a crowd of 300,000 Catholic demonstrators in Londonderry and killed 13 people. The authorities claimed the dead were 'gunmen' although weapons were never found on them. Subsequent inquiries have been inconclusive. The Irish Ambassador in London was recalled to Dublin and the British embassy in Dublin was burned down. The year following Bloody Sunday showed a sharp increase in sectarian violence, with the Irish Republican Army (IRA) finding many new recruits among nationalists who now turned to direct action to expel British troops.

BODHIDHARMA (c. AD 500)

A teacher in the Ch'an tradition, ('Zen' in Japanese) 28th in line from the Buddha, Bodhidharma arrived in China from India c. AD 520. He attempted to teach the Emperor Wu the truth of 'Emptiness' but failed. He spent nine years meditating facing a wall. Ch'an is the general term for meditation in Chinese Buddhism. Bodhidharma's teaching when fused with Taoism produced the distinctive form of Ch'an. Few historical details known about him. He is usually portrayed with an appearance of fierce concentration.

))))▶ *Buddhism, Taoism*

BOER WAR (1899–1902)

Campaign for control of South African territories between Great Britain and the Boers (South Africans of Dutch descent). Horatio Herbert Kitchener was chief-of-staff to the British forces in South Africa between 1900–02, under Lord Roberts. There had already been a South African War between the British and the Boers in 1881, principally over gold and diamond mines in the area known as the Transvaal.

The Boers were descended from Dutch colonials and had occupied the region since the establishment of the Dutch East India Company in 1652, but had become marginalized by the decline in power of the Netherlands, leading to the sale of Cape Town and its environs to Britain in 1814. Things came to a head once more in 1899 following an attempt by the British Cape Colonials to inspire a revolt against the Transvaal president, Kruger, by the non-Boer immigrants of the area, *uitlanders*, who were treated as second-class citizens by the Boers.

LEFT: A funeral procession for those who fell during Bloody Sunday in 1972, when 13 Irish demonstrators were gunned down by British soldiers in Northern Ireland.

ABOVE: The Dutch-descended Boers in action.

Instead the Boers retaliated by invading British territory.

The Boer War lasted for three years. Ultimately the British defeated the Boers, largely because they outnumbered them. However, Kitchener, resorted to the tactic of interring Boer women and children in concentration camps to counter Boer guerrilla activity. Some 26,000 women and children died.

))) *Boers, Dutch East India Company, Lord Kitchener*

BOERS (1652)

Huguenot or Dutch settlers in Southern Africa. Jan van Riebeeck of the Dutch East India Company established a shipping station on the Cape of Good Hope (1652). By 1707, 2,000 Dutch, German and French settlers made up the settlement. It prospered, but the Boers were hostile to the native Africans, relying on them as a source of slaves. The Cape colony became a British possession (1806) but British policy led to the Great Trek (1835–43), seeing the Boers move north into Natal and the Transvaal. Gold was discovered (1867) and influxes of British immigrants led to the Boer War (1899–1902).

))) *Boer War*

BOHR, NIELS (b. 1922)

Danish physicist. The element at 107 on the Periodic Table is known as Bohrium. It is named after Niels Bohr who did much for our understanding of atoms. In 1975 he shared the Nobel Prize for Physics with two other scientists for devising an atomic nucleus model.

))) *Nobel Prize*

BOLÍVAR, SIMÓN (1783–1830)

South American soldier and statesman. Bolívar fought against the Spanish in Venezuela and in 1813 captured Caracas. Royalist forces drove him into exile but in 1817 he returned, established a

government and was elected president. In 1819, having ended royalist rule in Colombia, he was proclaimed president of the combined territory. He defeated a resurgent Spanish force in 1821, thus ensuring Venezuelan independence.

Bolívar's vision of a united South America drove him to secure independence for what are now Ecuador, Peru and Bolivia. He died disillusioned, having failed to pacify contending factions, but is today revered as 'the Liberator'.

BOLSHEVIKS (1903–52)

Political and military group that seized power in Russia in 1917. The Bolsheviks, meaning 'one of the majority', originated in 1903 under the leadership of Vladimir Ilyich Lenin. From the beginning the party was highly centralized, disciplined and professional. The group insisted that party membership of the Russian Social Democratic Workers Party should be restricted to professional revolutionaries. By 1912 the group was still small despite its high-profile leader. In 1917 after the February Revolution that signalled Lenin's return to Russia, the Bolsheviks had gained control of the key worker councils in Petrograd and Moscow. This assured Russia's exit from World War I. After the October Revolution the Bolsheviks suppressed other political rivals and took power. They became the Russian Communist Party of Bolsheviks in 1918 and the All Union Communist Party of Bolsheviks in 1925. The term disappeared when they were renamed the Communist Party of the Soviet Union in October 1952.

))) *Vladimir Ilyich Lenin, Nicholas II of Russia, Russian Revolution, World War I*

ABOVE: Simón Bolívar, otherwise known as 'the Liberator', freed South American countries like Venezuela, Colombia, Ecuador, Peru and Bolivia from the clutches of Spanish colonial rule.

BONAPARTE, NAPOLEON (1769–1821)

Emperor of France (1804–14 and 1814–15).
Napoleon Bonaparte was born in Corsica. He was
commissioned in the army in 1785, but he welcomed the
French Revolution in 1789. Bonaparte fought in the
Revolutionary Wars, to great acclaim at Toulon in 1793,
but was forced into retirement. Recalled to crush a
Royalist rebellion in 1795, he was made a general in 1796
and fought against the Austrians in Italy. He carried the
war to Egypt, hoping to conquer India, but his fleet was
defeated at the Battle of the Nile by Horatio Nelson.

Spotting his chance in domestic political turmoil,
Bonaparte returned home in 1799 and toppled the ruling
Directory, making himself dictator. Bonaparte reformed
French government, law and finances. In 1804 he was
created Emperor, but in 1803 began the Napoleonic
Wars. In 1814 he abdicated after the Battle of Leipzig,
returning in 1815 to be defeated finally at Waterloo.

))))▶ *Napoleonic Wars, Admiral Horatio Nelson, Battle of
Waterloo, Duke of Wellington*

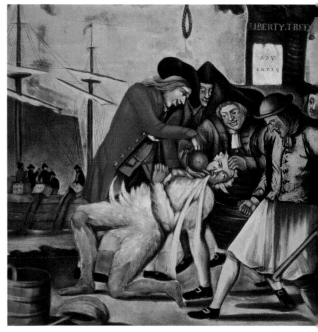

BOSTON MASSACRE (1770)

Conflict between American colonials and British
forces during the American Revolution. On
5 March 1770 an event occurred that fuelled anti-British
feeling in American colonies. In Boston crowds were
voicing their resentment at the presence of British soldiers
when the commanding officer ordered his troops to fire
into the crowd. Five were killed in the 'Boston Massacre'.

))))▶ *American Revolution*

BOSTON TEA PARTY (1773)

Protest against British taxation by the people of
Boston. The American colonists resented British
measures such as the Navigation Acts, which subordinated
American to British commercial and industrial interests,
the imposition of a stamp tax (1765) and later a tea tax.
At the Boston Tea Party on 16 December 1773,

*LEFT: Napoleon Bonaparte, Emperor of France and skilled military
commander, disrupted European political infrastructure with his
nationalist ideas.*
*ABOVE: The Boston Massacre of 1770 fuelled anti-British feelings among the
American colonialists. This picture is entitled* Bostonians Force-Feeding the
Excise Man.

protesters, dressed as Native Americans, dumped British tea into Boston Harbour. This was a prelude to the American Revolution.

)))▶ *American Revolution*

BOUDICCA (c. AD 30-62)

Queen of the Iceni tribe of Britons. Married to King Prasutagus of the Iceni tribe, Boudicca is the most famous of the Celtic queens. Prasutagus died (AD 61); Boudicca and her daughters were flogged and raped by Roman soldiers. She led the Icenis against the Romans, sacking Colchester, St Albans and London, killing 70,000. She was only stopped when reinforcements were called from Wales to assist the Romans. Boudicca was said to have poisoned herself rather than be captured.

BOURBON DYNASTY

One of Europe's most powerful ruling families. Descended from Louis IX, King of France (1226–70), through his grandson Louis I, Duke of Bourbon (1327–42), a title inherited from his mother.

Bourbons ruled France (1589–1792, 1814–48), Naples and Sicily (1735–1861), and Spain (1700–1868, 1870–73, 1874–1931, 1975–), and lesser dukedoms such as Lucca and Parma.

Henri IV of France (1553–1610), son of Antoine de Bourbon, inherited the title. His descendants ruled France until 1792 when Louis XVI was executed during the French Revolution. Louis XVIII was restored in 1814, followed by his brother Charles X (1824–30), who was toppled in the Revolution of 1830.

In 1700 Charles II of Spain died childless. The title passed to his great-nephew, Philip of Anjou, succeeding as Philip V. He was grandson of Louis XIV of France, who had married Charles's sister, Marie-Thérèse. In 1713, following the War of the Spanish Succession, the Treaty of Utrecht forced Philip to give up any claims to the French throne.

Philip V's third son, Charles, seized Naples and Sicily in 1734. In 1759 he succeeded to the Spanish throne, handing over Naples and Sicily to his younger son Ferdinand.

)))▶ *Louis XIV of France, Louis XVI of France*

BOXER REBELLION (1900)

Uprising against foreign influence in China. At the end of the nineteenth century European and American cultures were beginning to pervade that of China. Chinese nationalists formed a society known as the I ho ch'uan ('Righteous Harmonious Fists'), nicknamed the 'Boxers' by Europeans.

In 1900 the Empress Tz'u-hsi (c. 1834–1908) instigated the Boxer Rebellion. The European and US embassies were besieged in Beijing. On 14 August an international punitive force captured Beijing, liberating the legations. However, thousands of missionaries and Chinese Christian converts had been murdered by the Boxers and China agreed to pay an indemnity.

BRAHMA

Hindu god. Brahma is the creator god in Hindu belief, one of the triad (with Shiva and Vishnu). He was one of the most significant gods in the Vedic tradition, but has since become less widely worshipped.

)))▶ *Hinduism, Shiva, Vishnu*

BRANDENBURG GATE (1788)

Monumental gateway in Berlin, Germany. Built between 1788 and 1791, the Brandenburg Gate was designed by Carl Gotthard von Langhans and topped with Gottfried Schadow's famous *Quadriga* statue, depicting a winged woman – Victory – in a chariot drawn by four charging horses. This was stolen by Napoleon's troops in 1806, but recaptured and replaced in 1814. International politics intervened again during the Cold War: when the Berlin Wall went up in 1961, the gate was left marooned in the no-man's-land between the city's eastern and western sectors. Its reopening in 1989 resonated profoundly throughout Germany and beyond.

)))▶ *Berlin Wall, Napoleon Bonaparte, Cold War*

BRANDT, WILLY (1913–92)

German political leader. A Social Democrat, Brandt was elected mayor of West Berlin (1957–66) where he came to international attention over his handling of the Berlin Wall crisis. The main objective of his political career (he was West German foreign minister, 1966–69, and chancellor, 1969–74) was his

Ostpolitik (eastern policy) – a desire to improve relations with East Germany and the Soviet Union. Brandt was forced to resign after the discovery of an East German spy in his government.

)))▶ *Berlin Wall, Cold War*

BRAUN, WERNHER VON (1912–77)

German engineer. Wernher von Braun was the mind behind the development of the V1 and V2 rockets for Adolf Hitler during World War II. Braun went on to develop the Saturn rockets for the US Apollo missions of the 1960s and 70s.

)))▶ *World War II*

ABOVE: Willy Brandt, a Social Democrat and former German chancellor, is best remembered for his efforts to improve East-West relations between Germany and the Soviet Union at the height of the Cold War.
ABOVE RIGHT: The Brandenburg Gate, Berlin's landmark monument. The statue crowning the gate was temporarily stolen by Napoleon Bonaparte before being returned to the German people in 1814. During the Cold War years, the gate remained uneasily located between the city's eastern and western sectors.

BREST-LITOVSK, TREATY OF (1918)

Nine months before the end of World War I the Treaty of Brest-Litovsk was signed between Russia, Germany and their allies. Russia agreed to recognize the independence of various Eastern European nations, but ultimately the Russians became one of the winning allies, so the treaty was annulled.

)))▶ *World War I*

BRETTON WOODS CONFERENCE (1944)

International Monetary Conference held at Bretton Woods, New Hampshire, USA, 1–22 July 1944, under the presidency of Henry Morgenthau, US Secretary to the Treasury. At the conclusion of the conference an Agreement was published, providing for the creation of the World Bank for Reconstruction and Development and the opening on 1 March 1947 of the International Monetary Fund, designed to assist the smooth working of trade, to prevent crises and to preserve exchange stability.

)))▶ *International Monetary Fund*

BRINKMANSHIP

US foreign policy of pushing opponents 'to the brink'. As US Secretary of State (1953–59) at the beginning of the Cold War, John Foster Dulles developed 'brinkmanship' to influence negotiations, particularly with the Soviet Union. He would threaten full-scale nuclear attack as a deterrent to any opposition to American interests.

BRITAIN, BATTLE OF (1940)

Aerial battle between the British RAF and the German Luftwaffe during World War II. Having successfully invaded France, Belgium and Holland during the Blitzkrieg, Adolf Hitler set his sights across the Channel. British forces had evacuated mainland Europe and he knew that they presented a considerable threat to his plans for the Third Reich while they had time to muster support and strength.

Hitler had an invasion plan for Britain called *Seelowe* ('Sea Lion') but he chose to launch an air attack first to weaken and intimidate British defences. Despite considerable advantage, including 50 per cent more aircraft, the Luftwaffe ultimately lost the Battle of Britain (July–October 1940) due to inferior intelligence.

)))➤ *Blitzkrieg, World War II*

BRITISH EAST INDIA COMPANY (1600)

English commercial company chartered by Queen Elizabeth I in 1600 and given the monopoly of trade between England and India. Its first trading posts were established in India in Bombay and Madras provinces. It competed with the Dutch, French and Portuguese. Under Charles II the Company acquired sovereign rights in addition to its trading privileges and the Company became in effect the ruler of much of India. In 1813 the Company's monopoly of Indian trade was abolished, however, and in 1858, following the Indian Mutiny, its powers and possessions were assumed by the Crown. The Company was dissolved in 1874.

)))➤ *Dutch East India Company, French East India Company*

ABOVE: *The Bretton-Woods Conference was held to attempt to resolve fluctuations in trading standards and to create a unified International Monetary Fund. Here India's Agent-General, Girja Shankar Bajpai, signs the agreement.*

BRITISH EMPIRE (1670–1997)

Phrase used to describe the worldwide colonies, protectorates and territories administered by the British government. Wanting to compete commercially and militarily with France, British colonies were established in the Americas and the West Indies by 1670. The Hudson Bay Company was active in Canada and the East India Company established trading posts in India in 1600.

The first British settlement in Africa was made (1661) at James Island on the Gambia River. Although the slave trade was abolished, over the period 1807–33, this was one of the driving forces behind colonizing the Caribbean and the Americas. The Seven Years' War that ended in the Treaty of Paris (1763) left Britain dominant in India and Canada. Although Britain lost its 13 colonies in America in 1783, new settlements were established in Australia (1788) and there was considerable growth in Canada.

Following the Napoleonic Wars Britain acquired Trinidad, Ceylon, Tobago, Mauritius, St Lucia and Malta. Singapore was acquired in 1819. New Zealand became British (1840), followed by Fiji, Tonga and Papua. Following the Indian Mutiny the British Crown replaced the East India Company and acquired Burma (1886) and the Punjab (1849). The Suez Canal was completed (1869) allowing British influence to be extended in Arabia and the Persian Gulf. Cyprus was occupied (1878), the Malay States (1880s) and Hong Kong (1841). In Africa Britain acquired Egypt (1882), Sudan (1899), South Africa (1910).

Limited self-government was encouraged, particularly in Canada, Australia, New Zealand and Natal. At the outbreak of World War I, Britain declared war on Germany on behalf of the whole empire but in 1918 many of the dominions signed independent peace treaties and joined the League of Nations as equals. In 1931 the Statute of Westminster recognized many of them as independent countries within the British Empire. In 1939 they made their own Declarations of War. Following World War II independence was granted; India (1947), Sri Lanka and Burma (1948) and Ghana became the first African colony in 1957. After the 1960s the majority of the former colonies had been granted self-government. The last British colony, Hong Kong, was returned to the Chinese (1997).

)))➤ *Indian Independence*

BRUSILOV OFFENSIVE (1916)

Russia entered World War I in August 1914. As the Russians mobilized their forces to defend their ally Serbia the Germans declared war on them. By 1916 the Russians were in the thick of it and launched their Brusilov Offensive against the Ukraine in June. The Ukraine had been united with Russia since 1785 but had become occupied by Austro-Hungarian forces. Under commander Alexai Brusilov the Russian army attacked the Eastern Front (4 June – 10 August), pushing back the enemy frontline to a point called the Pripet Marshes. Eventually, though, the Russian attack was blunted by the arrival of German reinforcements.

))))➤ *World War I*

BUDDHISM

Buddhists consider their religion to consist of the Three Jewels: the Buddha, the Doctrine he taught, and the Order (Sangha) of monks and nuns he founded. For the Buddhist, Buddhism has no beginning and no end – for the world has no beginning or end. The Buddha taught that salvation depends on one's own efforts alone. He did not deny the existence of gods but regarded them as mortal. The Buddha taught the Middle Way. If one is to escape from karma (all actions have a consequence and lead to samsara – rebirth) then one has to achieve Enlightenment.

In his first sermon he taught the Way of Enlightenment is the Middle Way between self-indulgence and self-torture and he taught the Four Noble Truths. These are: suffering; the origin of suffering; the elimination of suffering; and the path leading to the elimination of suffering. Even 'pleasure' is suffering because it does not last; 'unsatisfactoriness' is a better term because it implies imperfection and impermanence. The first

three Noble Truths analyze the human condition, the fourth teaches a way out of 'unsatisfactoriness'. That consists of morality, meditation and wisdom; the foundation of all morality being generosity.

All Buddhists keep at least five moral rules: not to kill, steal, be unchaste, lie or take intoxicants. There are different schools of Buddhist thought with two main divisions Theravada, more accurately Hinayana (Small Vehicle) and Mahayana (Great Vehicle). Buddhism declined in India, birthplace of the Buddha, but expanded north into Tibet; east into China and Korea; and south-east into Sri Lanka, Burma and Thailand.

))))➤ *Siddhartha Gautama, The Buddha*

BUNKER HILL, BATTLE OF (1775)

Battle which took place at Boston, Massachusetts, during the American Revolution. The Battle of Bunker Hill – 17 June 1775 – was actually fought atop the nearby Breed's Hill in Charlestown which was later engulfed as a suburb of Boston. The battle was won by the British, but they suffered such heavy casualties that the outcome was seen as a moral victory for the American rebels. The British had 1,054 dead or wounded, as compared with 450 for the colonials.

))))➤ *American Revolution*

BUSH, GEORGE JNR (b. 1946)

43rd president of the United States (since 2001). Son of George Bush Snr (41st US president). Bush pipped Democrat Al Gore to the post in one of the most controversial elections in American history, becoming president despite losing the popular vote by 500,000 (out of 105 million cast). Bush was governor of Texas (1995–2000) and a former businessman (he owned an oil company and the Texas Rangers baseball team).

))))➤ *George Bush Snr, President*

BUSH, GEORGE SNR (b. 1924)

Former US president (1989–93). His long political career included stints as ambassador to the UN, director of the CIA and vice president (1981–89) to Ronald Reagan. As president he invaded Panama (1989) and sent American troops to the Persian Gulf War in 1991. He also signed a number of nuclear disarmament agreements with the Soviet Union. Bush was beaten by Democrat Bill Clinton in the 1992 election.

))⏵ *George Bush Jnr, President*

BYRD, RICHARD (1888–1957)

American explorer and aviator. Byrd's claim to have made the first flight over the North Pole was overturned by navigational experts, but in 1929 he made the first flight over the South Pole. He mounted altogether four expeditions to Antarctica, during which vast amounts of territory were mapped and many discoveries made. On his second expedition (1933–35) he conducted meteorological and auroral researches while living alone in a shack for five months. From 1955 to 1956 Byrd headed Operation Deep-Freeze, an Antarctic expedition organized by the USA in connection with the International Geophysical Year.

BYZANTIUM (c. 658 BC)

Ancient Greek city, founded *c.* 658 BC on the European side of the Bosporus and occupying part of modern Istanbul. It became a leading port and distribution centre, especially in the grain trade, thanks to its excellent harbour, strategic location between the Black and Mediterranean Seas and abundant fishing grounds.

Destroyed by the Persians in the fifth century BC, Byzantium was rebuilt in 479 BC by the Spartans, who for the next 100 years were in repeated contention with Athens over control of the city. It was forced to recognize Macedonia suzerainty under Philip II and his son Alexander the Great (fourth century BC) and underwent later attacks and subjugation

BELOW: American explorer and aviator Richard Byrd became the first man to fly over the South Pole by airplane.

by the Scythians, Celts, Syrians and Romans. In AD 326 Constantine the Great, having defeated his co-emperor Licinius, started rebuilding the city, which in 330 was inaugurated as the capital of the Roman Empire and renamed Constantinople. The new city became the sole capital of the Byzantine Empire, the eastern Roman empire, in AD 359. Until its fall to the Turks it was a powerful city, which preserved Greek culture and Roman law during the Dark Ages and acted as a bulwark of Christendom against Muslims and barbarians.

))⏵ *Alexander the Great, Constantine*

CABOT, JOHN (c. 1450–99)

Italian navigator and explorer. A former trader in eastern spices, Cabot had by 1496 taken up residence in England and persuaded Henry VII to sanction a westward voyage across the Atlantic. He sailed from Bristol with a crew of 18 and landed on what he believed to be north-eastern Asia in 1497. His landfall, probably in Maine or Nova Scotia, was the first recorded on the North American mainland by Europeans. Cabot found evidence of human habitation but saw no inhabitants. He died on a later voyage bound for Japan, which he believed to lie south of his previous landfall.

CAESAR, AUGUSTUS (63 BC – AD 14)

First Roman Emperor, and adopted son of Julius Caesar. Augustus won the Battle of Actium and secured absolute power across the Roman world.

Born Gaius Octavius, he married Caesar's niece and became his heir as Gaius Julius Caesar Octavianus. Following Caesar's murder in 44 BC he formed the Second Triumvirate with Mark Antony and Lepidus. Bitter civil war followed as they wiped out their main rivals at Philippi in 42 BC and then fought amongst themselves.

Actium left Octavian the victor in 31 BC. Back in Rome he was awarded the title Augustus (meaning 'majestic'), and an exceptional portfolio of positions, leaving him in control of the army and legislation. With support from his friend Agrippa, and his wife Livia, he reformed abuses of power, improved public services, erected public buildings, and settled frontiers with a system of garrisons, governorships and buffer states. On his death, Augustus's powers passed to his stepson Tiberius.

))▶ *Battle of Actium, Julius Caesar, Romans, Triumvirate*

CAESAR, JULIUS (100–44 BC)

Dictator of Rome and general. Caesar, a senator, loathed the dictator Sulla who wiped out democratic opposition in 82 BC. Caesar wooed the Roman public with hand-outs, and was made Governor of Spain in 61 BC.

In 60 BC Caesar formed the First Triumvirate with Pompey and Crassus. In 58 BC he began his Gallic war, which secured vast new territories and earned him a spectacular reputation. In 55 and 54 BC he made two brief forays into Britain.

In 49 BC, Caesar returned to Rome, his power at its peak. Hostilities broke out between him and Pompey. In 48 BC, Pompey was defeated at Pharsalus, and then murdered in Egypt. Caesar began a relationship with Cleopatra and had a child, Caesarion. In 46 BC he was made dictator, and in 45 BC defeated Pompey's sons in Spain. Fears that he planned to make himself king led to his murder by Brutus and Cassius in 44 BC in Rome.

))▶ *Augustus Caesar, Romans, Triumvirate*

LEFT: John Cabot (far right), a Genoese merchant and explorer, tried to find a short cut to Asia, and accidentally discovered the coast of Newfoundland instead, paving the way for future seafaring and the conquest of North America. ABOVE: Augustus Caesar, adopted son of the great Julius Caesar, secured victory at the Battle of Actium and joined forces with Lepidus and Mark Antony to form the Second Triumvirate upon Caesar's death.

CALIFORNIA GOLD RUSH (1848–49)

One of the most massive migrations in history. On 24 January 1848 James Marshall discovered gold at the Sutter's Mill in Sacramento. When it became public knowledge 'the rush' began, with more than 90,000 people making their way to California in the following two years, either by land or sea, travelling around Cape Horn or as far south as Panama. Their intention was not to settle in California but to take the gold; they became known as 'the 49ers'. The census of 1850 showed 90 per cent of the newly discovered California's population were male, with 73 per cent between the ages of 20 and 40.

CALIGULA (AD 12–41)

Third Roman Emperor, notorious for cruelty. Succeeding his great-uncle Tiberius in AD 37, Gaius Caesar was initially popular as son of the famous general Germanicus, earning the nickname Caligula as a child for wearing miniature military boots (*caligae*). His tolerance and liberal behaviour soon gave way to mental instability, and his belief in his own divinity. Stories of incest and perversion abounded. In AD 41 he was murdered by the Praetorian Guard.

))))➤ *Romans*

CALIPHS (AD 632–1258)

Rulers and leaders of the Muslim community. When Mohammad died in AD 632, the caliphate was established, its leader being the caliph – 'successor' or 'successor of the Messenger of God'. The first caliph, Abu Bakr, was succeeded by Umar ibn al-Khattab, then Uthman and Ali, all known as orthodox, 'perfect' or 'rightly guided' caliphs. The leaders of Damascus and Baghdad also took the title, as did Cordoba and Egypt. The Ottoman sultans claimed the title in 1517 and used it until 1924. Muslims believe that no caliph is legitimate unless he is a direct descendant of the Prophet Mohammad.

))))➤ *Islam, Prophet Mohammad*

RIGHT: Jean Calvin helped preserve the structure of the Church, troubled by internal schisms, by arguing in favour of its 'union with Christ'.

CALVIN, JEAN (1509–64)

Leader of the Protestant Reformation in Europe. Calvin was born in Noyon, Picardy, and studied at Paris, Orleans and Bourges. In Paris he experienced a change in religious outlook. Encouraged by the work of people like Martin Luther he began to write and teach. He was soon forced to leave Paris. In 1536 he published *Institutes of the Christian Religion* and soon settled in Geneva before having to flee to Strasbourg. In 1541 he returned to Geneva and remained there until his death. In *Ecclesiastical Ordinances* Calvin displays a grasp of the importance of structure and discipline for the Church's survival in difficult conditions. He argued that at the heart of Christian life lies 'union with Christ', salvation being dependent entirely on God's grace. The Bible focused attention on Jesus Christ and was vital in reforming every aspect of the Christian life and faith. Calvin's teaching was hugely influential in Western Christianity.

))))➤ *Bible, Martin Luther, Protestantism, Reformation*

CAMPAIGN FOR NUCLEAR DISARMAMENT (CND)

Global campaign to rid the world of nuclear weapons. Funded by members and supporters, CND aims to change government policies, to eliminate British nuclear weapons, to stimulate public debate on alternatives to the nuclear cycle, and to empower people to engage in work for a nuclear-free world in co-operation with other UK and international groups. CND is part of Abolition 2000, a network with the main aim of eliminating nuclear weapons globally.

CAMPANELLA, TOMMASO (1568–1634)

Italian philosopher and theologian. Born at Stilo, Italy, Campanella became a Dominican monk in 1583. He touched on areas considered by the Inquisition to be heretical. He was imprisoned in 1599 for heresy and conspiracy against Spanish rule after leading a revolution against Spanish rule in southern Italy, being released in 1626. He took refuge in Paris in 1634. His most famous work is *City of the Sun* (*c.* 1602), a vision of the ideal society, which shows the influence of Plato and Thomas More. Campanella had sympathy with the views of Nicolas Copernicus and Galileo Galilei (whom he met in later life).

))▶ *Nicolaus Copernicus, Galileo Galilei*

CANUTE (c. AD 995–1035)

Viking king of England, Denmark and Norway. In 1013, Sweyn, King of Denmark, invaded England with his son, Canute. In 1014 Sweyn died. Canute was forced to leave, returning with a powerful army. In 1016 he defeated Edmund Ironside, son of the English King Ethelred II ('the Unready'). Canute was proclaimed King of England and married Ethelred's widow. He faced opposition but used Anglo-Saxon laws to establish a beneficial reign. In 1018 his brother Harold, King of Denmark, died and Canute took the Crown. In 1027 he forced the Scots to pay him homage, and in 1028 he conquered Norway.

))▶ *Vikings*

CAPONE, AL (1899–1947)

Famous American gangster, nicknamed 'Scarface'. Born in Brooklyn, Alphonse Capone received three scars on his face from an insulted girl at school. Capone moved to Chicago

RIGHT: Al Capone, the infamous Chicago gangster, nicknamed 'Scarface'.

(1920) and took over the gangster empire of his uncle during the period of Prohibition. In 1929 he masterminded the St Valentine's Day Massacre, gunning down seven men. He was sentenced to 11 years in Atlanta prison; he was transferred to Alcatraz in 1934, remaining there until 1939. He died in Miami from syphilis.

CARLOS I OF PORTUGAL (1863–1908)

Penultimate king of Portugal. Nineteenth-century Portuguese history was rocked by invasions during the Napoleonic Wars, civil war and political feuds. Under Luis (1861–89), republicanism increased in popularity while Portuguese imperialists saw their ambitions in Africa restricted by Britain. Governments were unable to solve Portugal's problems, allowing republicans to gain ground in towns. Appointed premier in 1906, Joao Franco, failed to unite rival monarchists and was suspected of siphoning public funds to Carlos, and plotting. In 1908 Carlos and his son Luis were assassinated in Lisbon – an event celebrated by republicans who toppled his younger son, Manuel II, in 1910.

CARNARVON, LORD (1866–1923)

Egyptologist. George Edward Stanhope Molyneux Herbert, 5th Earl of Carnarvon, a keen amateur Egyptologist, was the sponsor whose money made possible Howard Carter's historic excavations in the Valley of Kings. If his popular fame has outlasted that of the archeologist himself, that is because his death so soon after Carter's discovery of Tutankhamen's tomb in 1922 led to fevered speculation that he had fallen victim to the pharaoh's curse.

))▶ *Ancient Egypt, Tutankhamen*

CAROLINGIAN EMPIRE (AD 768–987)

Dynasty of Frankish kings, characterized by a revival of Roman literacy, architecture, the decorative arts in gold and silver, painting and mosaics. Named after Charles I (Charlemagne).

The Empire extended from western France to the Elbe in Germany, and from Denmark to the Mediterranean.

The Empire was the first centralized Christian power in Western Europe, leading to the papal title 'Holy Roman Empire'.

Churches and monasteries were founded, and encouraged to improve education and literacy. A new form of standard handwriting ('Carolingian minuscule'), a programme to revise the Bible, and copy and archive surviving classical texts led to the Carolingian Empire becoming a centre of learning, enhancing the prestige of its rulers, preserving the Latin language, and attracting scholars, for example Alcuin of York who met Charlemagne in AD 781 and became head of the palace school.

Architecture enjoyed a renaissance. In AD 805, the Palatine chapel at Aachen was consecrated. Based on an octagon and dome, it was modelled on and influenced by surviving monuments of the ancient world. Nothing like this had been built in the West for centuries. Others revived the basilican style, while all the buildings were embellished with mosaics and frescoes.

)))➤ *Alcuin, Charlemagne, Holy Roman Empire*

CASAS, BARTOLOME DE LA (1474–1566)

Spanish missionary and historian. Ordained a priest in 1510, he worked throughout his life to improve living conditions in South America and abolish slavery. The New Laws (for humanitarian treatment of indigenous people in Spanish colonies) were adopted in 1542. He became bishop of Chiapa in 1544, working again for the abolishment of slavery and among the natives of Guatemala. Bartolome de la Casas also wrote *Historia de las Indias*.

)))➤ *Slavery*

CASTRO, FIDEL (b. 1926)

Cuban leader (since 1959). Castro (with his brother Raul and Che Guevara) fought a guerilla campaign against the dictator, Batista. On taking power, he transformed Cuba into the first Communist state in Latin America, with Marxist reforms of industry and agriculture. He forged close ties with the Soviet Union, and survived political crises with the USA, including the Bay of Pigs invasion and the Cuban missile crisis. A new constitution in 1976 created a National Assembly with Castro as president. The long US economic blockade and the end of large Soviet subsidies have ruined the economy and left Castro isolated. He introduced limited free enterprise following anti-government demonstrations in 1993.

)))➤ *Bay of Pigs Invasion, Che Guevara, Cuban Missile Crisis*

CATHERINE THE GREAT (1729–96)

Russian empress. A German princess, Catherine's husband Peter succeeded in 1762, but was quickly deposed and murdered for his insanity and despotism. Catherine was made ruler in his place and was very popular throughout her reign. However, she depended on aristocratic support, which prevented reforms for peasants and led to a series of revolts.

Catherine extended Russia's territories by partitioning Poland and, in the Crimea during wars with the Turks, establishing a base on the Black Sea. Catherine always encouraged an interest in European culture, wrote a history of Russia, collected art, painted, and corresponded with Voltaire. Her affairs were notorious.

BELOW: Catherine the Great became Empress of Russia after her husband's life was claimed in a military coup. During her rule, Russia's empire extended its boundaries considerably.

CAVOUR, COUNT CAMILLO DI (1810–61)

Italian statesman. Cavour was premier of Sardinia (1852–59, 1860–61): his main achievement was to unify Italy under the rule of Victor Emmanuel II, King of Sardinia and the first king of united Italy (1861–78). During the mid 1800s, Italy was split by the wars of Risorgimento as different factions and foreign powers battled it out. The kingdom was formed when the separate states of Tuscany, Modena, Parma, Bologna and Romagna voted for union with Sardinia in 1861.

)))▶ *Victor Emmanuel II*

CEAUCESCU, NICOLAE (1918–89)

Communist leader of Romania. Ceaucescu was a Communist youth movement member, imprisoned in 1936 and 1940. He escaped from prison in 1944 and served as secretary of the Union of Communist Youth (1944–45), minister of agriculture (1948–50) and deputy minister of the armed forces (1950–54). He succeeded Gheorghiu-Dej as leader (March 1965), head of state (1967) and president of Romania (1974). He was shot by a firing squad, along with his wife, having been convicted of mass murder and other crimes in Timisoara (1989).

)))▶ *Communism*

CHAMBERLAIN, NEVILLE (1869–1940)

British politician. He became prime minister in 1937, following two stints as Conservative chancellor. Chamberlain was responsible for the policy of 'appeasement' towards Hitler: this resulted in the 1938 Munich Pact that abandoned Czechoslovakia to Germany. On his return to London he announced that he had achieved 'peace in our time', then resigned when World War II broke out the following year.

)))▶ *World War I*

CHANNEL TUNNEL (1994)

Rail connection beneath the English Channel, connecting England with France. The tunnel is 50 km (31 miles) long and runs between Folkestone and Sangatte (near Calais), with a journey time of 35 minutes. There are three tunnels, two for rail traffic and one for services and security. It accommodates coaches and cars.

CHAPLIN, CHARLIE (1889–1977)

English actor. South-London-born Charlie Chaplin became one of the brightest stars of the silent cinema in his unforgettable persona – half-hilarious, half-melancholy – of the bowler-hatted, cane-wielding, splay-footed 'tramp'. A co-founder of the United Artists' studio, aimed at giving creative actors more control over their work, he directed several classic films, including the scathing social satire, *Modern Times*.

CHARGE OF THE LIGHT BRIGADE (1854)

Infamous event during the Crimean War. Technology was forcing officers to rethink their strategies for effective warfare in the field of battle by the middle of the nineteenth century. Soldiers still wore brightly coloured uniforms, for example, making them easy targets for long-range rifles. The Battle of Balaclava (25 October 1854) involved a foolish charge by a British cavalry unit, the Light Brigade. Their leader, Lord Lucan, gave the order for them to ride their horses along the North Valley right into the firing lines of entrenched Russians artillery. There were 673 soldiers involved in the charge and 272 ended up as casualties. The Light Brigade would probably have been completely decimated had the French cavalry not come to its aid.

))▶ *Battle of Balaclava, Crimean War*

CHARLEMAGNE (AD 742–814)

King of the Franks from AD 768, succeeding his father Pepin the Short, and Holy Roman Emperor from AD 800. He answered the pope's request for help in Lombardy against the Saxons

BELOW: Charlie Chaplin, one of the world's best-loved comedians, in his classic 'disguise'.

and by AD 804 had conquered Saxon territory, while extending his control across northern Italy and Bavaria to areas of modern Austria and Croatia. A campaign against the Muslims in Spain foundered in the Pyrenees, but Charlemagne had established the first major Christian state in western Europe since the Roman Empire, famous for its art, architecture, monasteries and learning. He reformed law, weights and measures, and coinage.

))▶ *Carolingian Empire, Holy Roman Empire*

„Charlie"

CHARLES I OF ENGLAND (1600–49)

King of England 1625, executed 1649. Frustrated by parliament's refusal to grant money, Charles dissolved it in 1629, resorting to taxation of coastal districts. This provoked outrage, fuelled by resentment at his religious policy, regarded as pro-Catholic, and brought to a head when he imposed an English prayerbook on Scotland. Parliament was recalled in 1640 but dissolved when it refused money until grievances were settled. The Scots invaded and parliament met again, outlawing Charles's excesses. In August 1642 Charles challenged parliament to war, leading to his final defeat at Naseby in 1645. Continued plotting led to the trial condemning him to death.

))) *Charles II of England, Oliver Cromwell, English Civil War*

CHARLES II OF ENGLAND (1630–85)

King of England, son of Charles I, restored in 1660 after the Commonwealth. Recalled from exile, Charles made a triumphant entry to London, but spent much of his reign secretly planning to establish himself as a Catholic absolute monarch, accepting French money in support of his naval wars with the Dutch. Parliament forced Charles to back down. In 1678 fears of a 'popish plot' led to further legal restrictions on Catholics. His marriage to Catherine of Braganza was

ABOVE: Charles I of England (seen here with his queen, Henrietta Maria) was tried and beheaded – an event which sent shock waves through Europe.

RIGHT: Charles II of England was proclaimed King of England during the Restoration.

childless, but Charles was notorious for his numerous mistresses and illegitimate children. He was a great supporter of the arts and scientific discovery.

))) *English Civil War, Restoration*

CHARLES III OF FRANCE (AD 879–929)

King of France from AD 893–922. Charles III (known as 'the Simple') lost power in AD 897 after civil war. The death of his rival, Eudes, in AD 898 restored him but he was controlled by Eudes' brother, Robert. Normandy was created following the defeat of the Vikings ('Northmen') by Robert in AD 911. Charles granted their leader Rollo part of northern France. In AD 922 he was deposed in favour of Robert, but killed Robert in AD 923, before being imprisoned during intrigues against Robert's successor.

))) *Normans*

CHARLES IX OF FRANCE (1550–74)

King of France from 1560, son of Henri II. He succeeded his brother François II as king at the age of 10, and his Italian Catholic mother, Catherine de Medici, ruled as regent for a decade. Henri II had persecuted French Protestants (Huguenots), but Charles was influenced by their leader, the French admiral Gaspard de Coligny. Terrified, Catherine made Charles order the St Bartholomew Massacre from 24 August to 3 October 1572. Around 25,000 Huguenots were killed.

))) *Huguenots, Medici Family*

CHARLES II, HOLY ROMAN EMPEROR (AD 823–77)

King of France from AD 843 and Holy Roman Emperor AD 875. Son of Louis I 'the Pious' (d. AD 840), Charles II (known as 'the Bald') and his brothers wrangled over their inheritance until the Carolingian Empire was divided at Verdun (AD 843). Charles ruled western and northern France, constantly buying off Viking raiders. The relative stability of his kingdom led the pope to make Charles Holy Roman Emperor. In AD 877 he died after an unsuccessful war in Italy. His kingdom was split amongst his descendants.

))➤ *Carolingian Empire, Holy Roman Empire, Vikings*

CHARLES V OF FRANCE (1337–80)

Regent from 1356–60, King of France 1364, during the Hundred Years' War with England. Charles V (known as 'the Wise') stuck to the terms of the 1347 Treaty of Calais with England, but challenged the transfer of his rights in Aquitaine. Initially, he concentrated on controlling power struggles with his barons and dealing with mercenary bands ravaging the countryside.

When war with England resumed, Charles engaged the English in small-scale skirmishes and started eroding English territory. He regularized taxation, encouraged military training, introduced pay, and created a system for maintenance of defences. An alliance with Castile brought naval support, and he founded a French navy.

))➤ *Hundred Years' War*

CHARLES VI, HOLY ROMAN EMPEROR (1685–1740)

Holy Roman Emperor from 1711. Charles claimed the Spanish throne in 1700. In 1711 he succeeded to his brother's titles in Austria, costing him support in the War of the Spanish Succession. From 1716–18 Charles seized territory in Eastern Europe from the Ottoman Empire, but by 1740 he had lost most gains. Hopes that his daughter Maria Theresa could succeed him as Empress of Austria were compromised by the War of the Austrian Succession.

))➤ *War of Austrian Succession, War of Spanish Succession*

CHARLES VIII OF FRANCE (1470–98)

King of France from 1483. Charles's sister Anne and her husband, Pierre de Bourbon, ruled as regents due to Charles's youth, ill-health and stupidity. Establishing his power under the influence of court favourites, Charles gave up territory in order to pursue his claim to the kingdom of Naples. His expensive campaign of 1494–95 led to his being crowned in Naples, but he was forced to fight at Fornovo to escape, dying during plans for another campaign.

))➤ *Bourbon Dynasty, Italian Wars*

CHARLES XII OF SWEDEN (1682–1718)

King of Sweden from 1697. Early military success in The Great Northern War against Denmark, Poland and Russia led to a catastrophic defeat at Poltava in 1709, destroying Swedish forces. Charles fled to Turkey, returning to Sweden in 1715. He started a war against Norway but was killed during the siege of Fredriksten in 1718. An absolute monarch, Charles was a highly skilled soldier concerned with moral leadership and strategy, as well as sound administration and reform.

))➤ *Great Northern War*

CHAUCER, GEOFFREY (c. 1345–1400)

English poet. A courtier in the royal household, first of Edward III and after that of Richard II, Geoffrey Chaucer is now known as the greatest poet of the English Middle Ages. His most famous work, the *Canterbury Tales* – begun around 1387 but never completed – purports to be the stories told by a motley group of men and women upon a pilgrimage, to while away the journey. Both sexes are represented, and every class from a courtly knight to a humble ploughman. The tales vary accordingly in style, and even more in taste, ranging from the racy memoirs of the Wife of Bath to the parson's pious sermon. Chaucer's own offering, ironically, is a rhymed romance so execrably bad that he is eventually ordered to stop, and make way for another storyteller.

))➤ *Edward III of England*

ABOVE: Geoffrey Chaucer, medieval chronicler, poet and social satirist.

CHENG HO (c. 1371–1435)

Chinese admiral, explorer and diplomat. Cheng Ho (or Zheng He) first set sail, on the emperor's orders in 1405, with 62 ships laden with gold and other treasures, and on this and six subsequent voyages his fleet reached destinations as far flung as Southeast Asia, India, east Africa, the Persian Gulf and Egypt. His missions extended Chinese maritime and commercial influence and encouraged the emigration that was the basis of Chinese colonization in South East Asia.

CHERNOBYL (1986)

Nuclear disaster. In April 1986 two explosions at a nuclear power station in Chernobyl, Ukraine, destroyed the central reactor and removed a protective roof weighing some 1,000 tonnes. Thirty-one people died immediately, but it is reckoned that tens of thousands will die from cancers as a result of exposure to radiation contamination over the following few decades.

CH'IN DYNASTY

In the seventh century BC the Ch'in (Qin) dynasty became powerful in western China, increasing power by taking western territory. Ch'in was isolated from eastern power struggles, developed the rules of law and farming reform, and exploited diplomacy and subterfuge to divide rivals. In 221 BC Ch'in unified China under Shih Huang-ti, an absolute ruler who ended feudalism, suppressed knowledge and forced millions to build the Great Wall of China. The Ch'in dynasty collapsed on his death in 206 BC.

))))▶ *Chou Dynasty, Great Wall of China*

CHOU DYNASTY

The Chou (Zhou) dynasty ruled China from around 1050–255 BC, and defined Chinese society across a period of great advances in writing, philosophy, technology, agriculture and communications. The Chou were rivals of the Shang. A long period of intermittent skirmishing led to an all-out campaign to seize Shang territory. By c. 1050 BC, the Chou had taken control of all China.

To control such vast territory, a system of feudal states was established which remained effective until the feudal lords began to pursue their own ambitions, at the expense of the emperor's, by the eighth century BC. Thereafter, the empire fragmented further into small units fighting amongst one another, and forming alliances.

Art benefited from this diversity, with regional styles being developed. The political chaos led to the development of regional capitals and defences, but also allowed the Ch'in Dynasty to seize the initiative and wrest supreme control in 221 BC.

))))▶ *Ch'in Dynasty*

CHRISTIANITY

The origins of Christianity lie with the life, death and resurrection of Jesus. Christians themselves regard the origins as stretching back into covenants made with Israel by God documented in the (Christian) Old Testament. There is a vast diversity within Christianity but all believe that in some way Jesus reveals the love and forgiveness of God, and through him, humans and God

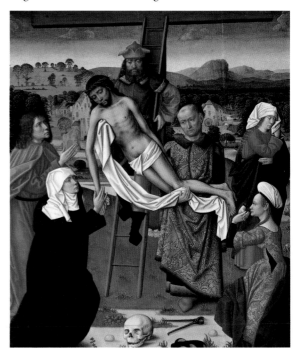

RIGHT: *The crucifixion and deposition of Jesus Christ of Nazareth, one of the central events in Christianity.*

can be reconciled. It is believed that Jesus is the Messiah, the Christ from which 'Christianity' comes, probably first used about AD 40. Christianity moved away from its Jewish roots, accelerated by the destruction of the Temple in Jerusalem in AD 70.

Christian beliefs are: Jesus was fully man and fully God; that Jesus's life reconciled God to human beings; followers of Jesus feel the Holy Spirit confers on them special gifts; that, as Christians, they are, in some sense, members of the Body of Christ. These views, traditionally, led to the formation of doctrines of the Incarnation, Atonement and Trinity.

Initially a small movement, it was held in suspicion for centuries and, at times, heavily persecuted. In fact persecution strengthened the developing Church. Once Constantine became Emperor in the early fourth century, the situation eased and under Theodosius I (Emperor 379–95) Christianity became the official religion of the Roman Empire.

As the faith grew and spread divisions arose between Eastern and Western Churches, a particular issue being the primacy claimed by the bishop of Rome. After the Great Schism in 1054, the next major disruption was the Reformation in the sixteenth to seventeenth centuries with the Reformed Churches dividing further on issues of doctrine and practice. The Catholic Church continues to regard itself as the prime Church and while the different churches often work together, ecumenically, there are still few examples of organized unity. The Protestant churches sought greater autonomy and self-government reflecting the recognition of individualism and the breaking up of the type of community values represented by the Catholic Church.

The development of Christianity has included immense contributions to art, education, architecture and learning as well as concern for the sick, the poor and the dying. The religion marks great events in the life of Jesus and some of the saints (those who have been exemplary in faith and practice). Prayer and worship are fundamental to the Christian life. The Christian principle should be the pervasive manifestation of love (agape) in practice; life will then be transformed.

))))▶ *Great Schism, Jesus Christ, Protestantism, Roman Catholicism*

CHURCHILL, WINSTON (1874–1965)

British statesman. Churchill was first elected to parliament in 1900. During World War I he was in charge of the admiralty (1911–15), but resigned after the failed Dardanelles campaign. His political career was similarly chequered: he served in both Liberal and Conservative cabinets, including Chancellor of the Exchequer (1924–29). Churchill replaced Chamberlain as prime minister in 1940 and is best remembered for his outstanding leadership during World War II. Labour won the post-war election in 1945, but Churchill was again prime minister from 1951–55. He wrote many biographies and memoirs and won the Nobel Prize for Literature in 1953.

))))▶ *Dardanelles Campaign, World War I, World War II*

CISTERCIAN ORDER (1098)

Order of White Monks named after the motherhouse at Citeaux; founded in 1098 by St Robert of Molesme. A more rigorous form of the existing Benedictine Order. Bernard, abbot and founder of Clairvaux (1190–53) is its most famous son. The Order spread rapidly; by 1200 there were 500 houses across Europe. Cistercian life was rigorous: houses were built in secluded places; strict rules on diet and silence were imposed; and manual labour was given a prominent position. They became important agricultural pioneers. Their organization was influential over other monastic orders, becoming compulsory for others after 1215. Today they are particularly strong in the USA.

))))▶ *Benedictine Order*

ABOVE: Winston Churchill, one of Britain's most influential statesmen.

CIVIL RIGHTS MOVEMENTS (1955–63)

American social reform movement that secured legal rights for black Americans. Following the American Civil War and the freedom of black slaves, the Jim Crow Laws created separate white and black societies in America. Although the Supreme Court in 1896 established the principle of separate but equal rights, it was not until the 1950s that this was seriously challenged. In 1954 the Supreme Court banned school segregation and in 1955 the Civil Rights Movement began after Rosa Parks, a black woman in Alabama, refused to move to the back of a bus. Several civil protest movements were created, notably the Reverend Dr Martin Luther King's Southern Christian Leadership Conference, The Student Non-Violent Co-ordinating Committee and the Congress of Racial Equality. Non-violent protests came to a head in 1963 with the March on Washington. This led John F. Kennedy and Lyndon Johnson to push through many civil rights laws. As a result of their protests the Civil Rights Act of 1964 banned discrimination in many areas. The Voting Rights Act 1965 guaranteed black citizens the right to vote and the Housing Bill 1968 banned discrimination in housing. By the time King was assassinated (4 April 1968) black militants, such as the Black Panthers, had moved away from non-violent action and were behind the rioting in many major cities. This period marked the end of the Civil Rights Movement but continuing anti-discrimination policies, supported by the courts, have established many of the rights that lay at the heart of the movement.

))))▶ *Martin Luther King*

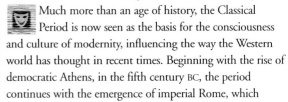

ABOVE: In the 1960s, TIME Magazine dedicated its front cover to Martin Luther King, one of the brightest stars of the Civil Rights Movement.

CLASSICAL PERIOD (c. 500 BC – AD 400)

Much more than an age of history, the Classical Period is now seen as the basis for the consciousness and culture of modernity, influencing the way the Western world has thought in recent times. Beginning with the rise of democratic Athens, in the fifth century BC, the period continues with the emergence of imperial Rome, which developed the civilization it found in the conquered Greek cities. The 'classic' principles of balance, order and restraint find their ultimate expression in Athens' Parthenon – though they can be discerned in everything from poetry to sculpture. Although later Greek artists sacrificed these principles in pursuit of more complex forms, the Romans spurned such 'effeminacies' in favour of a return to severer symmetries. Essentially a humanistic approach, emphasizing man's ability to impose regular forms on unco-operative nature, classicism was out of kilter with the religious values of the Middle Ages. Its rediscovery between the fourteenth and fifteenth centuries would be the key to the European Renaissance; it has underpinned our tastes and attitudes ever since.

))))▶ *Acropolis, Neoclassicism, Renaissance*

CLEMENT VII, POPE (1478–1534)

Born Guilio de Medici in Italy, he was pope from 1523–34. He allied himself with François I of France against the Holy Roman Emperor, Charles V, who sacked Rome in 1527 and took Clement prisoner. Eight thousand people were killed in the Sack of Rome. Clement managed to escape to Orvieto. The sacking of Rome is often regarded as the event that brought the Renaissance to an end. Clement was indecisive and his failure to deal with the English Henry VIII's divorce from Catherine of Aragon hastened the Reformation in England. The antipope, Clement VII (d. 1394) was elected by French cardinals in 1378, so beginning the Great Schism and the Avignon Papacy.

))))▶ *Charles V, Great Schism, Henry VIII of England, Sack of Rome*

CLINTON, BILL (b. 1946)

Former US president (1993–2001). First elected Arkansas governor in 1976, he defeated George Bush in 1993. Clinton's battles with a Republican-dominated Congress meant he was unable to pass healthcare reforms, although he did increase the minimum wage. Foreign policy successes included restoring relations with Vietnam and a role as peacemaker in Bosnia and Northern Ireland. But his presidency was dogged by scandal, including the Whitewater Case and his affair with Monica Lewinsky. Clinton was the first sitting president to testify before a grand jury and he narrowly avoided impeachment after committing perjury. His wife, Hillary Rodham Clinton, is Senator of New York.

)))➤ *George Bush Snr, President*

CLIVE, ROBERT OF PLASSEY (1725–74)

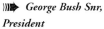

Following the incident known as the Black Hole of Calcutta, in which many Britons died, the British were after the blood of the Nawab of Bengal, Suraj-ud-Dowlah. Robert Clive had been lieutenant-colonel and governor of Fort St David since 1755 and he was appointed the task of tackling the Nawab. In February 1757, with 1,900 men, he defeated the Nawab's army, of 36,000 men, outside Calcutta. Clive has become known as one of the best military leaders of his age, although his later career was dogged by charges of corruption.

)))➤ *Black Hole of Calcutta*

CLEOPATRA (c. 70 – 30 BC)

Queen of Egypt and mistress of Julius Caesar and Mark Antony. Daughter of Ptolemy XII, descended from one of Alexander the Great's generals, Cleopatra became queen in 51 BC with her brother, Ptolemy XIII. In 48 BC she was deposed but when Caesar arrived he restored her. They became lovers, Cleopatra bearing him a son, Caesarion, accompanying him to Rome. She returned to Egypt after his assassination but in 41 BC she became Antony's mistress, by whom she had three sons. After the Battle of Actium she fled home, followed by Antony, to commit suicide with a fatal bite from a poisonous snake.

)))➤ *Battle of Actium, Mark Antony, Julius Caesar*

ABOVE LEFT: Cleopatra, the last queen of Egypt, was romantically linked with both Julius Caesar and Mark Antony, two of Ancient Rome's greatest generals. Her myth has endured throughout history.
ABOVE: US President Bill Clinton enjoyed two terms in office.

COLD WAR (1945–89)

Term given to the political and economic struggle between the capitalist, democratic Western powers and the Soviet Union. The Cold War began after World War II and continued (with a brief respite during détente) until the break-up of the USSR.

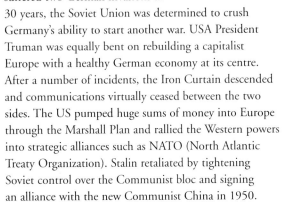

The first stand-off came during the post-war division of Germany. With 20 million dead and having suffered two German invasions in 30 years, the Soviet Union was determined to crush Germany's ability to start another war. USA President Truman was equally bent on rebuilding a capitalist Europe with a healthy German economy at its centre. After a number of incidents, the Iron Curtain descended and communications virtually ceased between the two sides. The US pumped huge sums of money into Europe through the Marshall Plan and rallied the Western powers into strategic alliances such as NATO (North Atlantic Treaty Organization). Stalin retaliated by tightening Soviet control over the Communist bloc and signing an alliance with the new Communist China in 1950.

'Hot wars' broke out in Korea and Vietnam as the US tried to stop the spread of Communism in south east Asia in the 1950s and 60s. The nuclear stand-off reached its peak during the Cuban Missile Crisis. There were various flashpoints during the 1970s and the 80s, such as the Soviet invasion of Afghanistan, but the world had outgrown the superpower clash. The Cold War had proved costly to both the Soviet and US economies and Mikhail Gorbachev's huge concessions on arms reduction, the withdrawal of Soviet troops from Afghanistan and the demise of Communism in the Soviet Union signalled the end.

))) *Cuban Missile Crisis, Mikhail Gorbachev, Iron Curtain, Korean War, Marshall Plan, North Atlantic Treaty Organization, Joseph Stalin, Harry S. Truman, Vietnam War*

ABOVE: Two iconic figureheads of the Cold War in the 1960s: US President John F. Kennedy and Russian prime minister Nikita Kruschchev.

COLONIALISM (1415–1945)

Political control over an alien territory. Although the Egyptians, Babylonians, Persians, Venetians, Greeks and Romans were colonial powers in ancient times, Vikings and others during the medieval period, modern European colonialism was led by Spain, Portugal and Great Britain. The Portuguese set up trading posts around the world but were driven out by the Dutch and English. In the Americas, Spain dominated most of South America whilst the British and French settled in North America. Although the British and French lost most of their colonies in the nineteenth century, the colonizations of Africa by the British, French, Belgian, Germans and Portuguese were virtually completed by 1914. Britain controlled India, Canada, Southern Africa and Ceylon largely as a result of winning European wars. The Russians colonized Central Asia, permanently absorbing many states and cultures. The Americans extended their colonization of North America, as well as strategic positions in the Pacific and Caribbean, whilst the Japanese were engaged in the colonization of the mainland and islands of the Far East. The two global wars of the twentieth century led to the collapse of colonialism and decolonization after 1945. By the 1970s the colonial Empires were all but gone. Nineteenth-century colonialism claimed to bring Third World countries, as they are now known, all the benefits of Western civilization, including administration, economic growth and protection. In exchange cultures were destroyed and in certain cases whole peoples exterminated. Britain was the most successful of the colonizing powers controlling 20 per cent of the world's land and 400 million people in 1900.

))) *British Empire, Pilgrim Fathers*

COLOSSEUM (AD 80)

Roman amphitheatre. Inaugurated in AD 80, the Flavian Amphitheatre or Colosseum was built to accommodate the gory entertainments the Romans loved: gladiators and wild animals would die here in their hundreds before audiences of up to 40,000. The policy of keeping the urban populace content with a dole of 'bread and circuses' is often associated with the Empire's later decadence and decline, but was actually the Roman way from the beginning. By the first century BC, indeed, almost every second day was a public holiday in the imperial capital.

))) *Romans*

COLUMBUS, CHRISTOPHER (1451–1506)

Italian navigator. Columbus achieved fame by sailing west across the Atlantic Ocean in search of a route to Asia and instead making landfall on an island in the Caribbean Sea, the first recorded European to reach America.

As a youth his travels and studies convinced him that Asia could be quickly reached by sailing west.

He moved to Spain around 1485 and after long persistence persuaded Queen Isabella and Ferdinand V of Castile to support an exploratory voyage. Three small ships set sail in August 1492. The crew feared that they would sail off the edge of the Earth but after some difficulties the fleet struck land, probably on San Salvador or Samana Cay.

On three subsequent voyages, Columbus landed in Central and South America, led a party ashore at the mouth of the Orinoco River and established several colonies, often in the face of hostility from the natives.

)))▶ *Conquistadors, Ferdinand and Isabella of Spain*

COMMONWEALTH GAMES (1954)

International sporting tournament. Although the British Empire gradually disintegrated in the second half of the twentieth century, it suited both the newly independent states and Britain itself to maintain harmonious relations. A 'commonwealth' of nations was accordingly formed, organized around diplomatic and commercial agreements. The British Empire Games, first held in 1930, were clearly rendered obsolete by the dissolution of the Empire, but a similarly conceived Commonwealth Games seemed the perfect way of preserving the old ties in a spirit of friendly competition. Featuring athletics, boxing, swimming, shooting and all the major Olympic sports, the games have been held four-yearly since 1954, midway between Olympiads.

)))▶ *British Empire, Olympic Games*

COMMUNISM (1785)

Socialist movement based on the teachings of Karl Marx. Communism pre-dates Karl Marx as it was first advocated by Plato when he suggested that everyone should share in the production and use of goods and services. Joseph-Alexandre-Victor Hupay de Fueva first advocated more modern Communism in 1785. The manifesto of the Communist Party (1848) written by Karl Marx and Friedrich Engels coined the phrase 'working men of all countries unite'. By 1912 Marx's parties had formed in nearly all of the industrialized nations. The first Communist government came to power in Russia in 1917 with Lenin as head, later being replaced by Stalin. Several other Communist governments in Eastern Europe, China (1949), Cuba (1959) and others in Africa were supported at some stage by Russia. In August 1991 the Communist system collapsed where it had begun, in Russia, when a coup led by Communist Party hardliners failed.

)))▶ *Karl Marx*

ABOVE: Sixteenth-century Italian navigator Christopher Columbus, the first recorded European to reach America. LEFT: In ancient times, the Colosseum provided a focal point for the Roman populace to come and witness the bloody entertainment of gladiatorial combat.

COMMUNIST REVOLUTION

Overthrow of capitalism by a workers' uprising. For hundreds of years forms of Communism, such as sharing common land, existed in many societies. It was the Industrial Revolution in the nineteenth century that created the new 'working' classes. They often lived and worked in terrible conditions and great poverty, while the industrialists enjoyed great wealth. A number of socialists and revolutionaries of the day advocated a communal solution to this misery.

It was German philosopher and writer Karl Marx who first wrote about Communist revolution in his *Communist Manifesto* (1848). In it he

claimed that the overthrow of the property-owning class by the working class was a natural progression of history. Marx believed that the proletariat must seize control of the economy in order to achieve a classless society. In the twentieth century Marxist thinking was behind the Communist Revolutions in Russia, China, Vietnam and Yugoslavia, among others.

))))> *Communism, Karl Marx*

COMTE, AUGUSTE (1798-1857)

French philosopher and 'Father of Sociology'. He was secretary to the Comte de St-Simon (1818) and began delivering lectures (1826), leading to publication of *Course of Positive Philosophy*. He suffered breakdown in 1827 and from 1832–42 studied at Ecole Polytechnique. Comte published *System of Positive Polity* in 1854 but is best remembered for his *Law of the Three Stages*.

ABOVE: The impassive features of Mao Zedong, a founder and leader of China's Communist revolution.

RIGHT: A haunting photograph of undernourished concentration camp victims looking through the barbed wire fence of their prison.

CONCENTRATION CAMPS (1939–45)

Concentration camps were nothing new by the time of World War II but the Nazis, under Adolf Hitler, took them to a new extreme in terms of the brutality meted out to those incarcerated.

Hitler intended to rid his Third Reich of all those people whom he viewed as either a threat or sub-human by race or nature. Those sent to concentration camps included homosexuals, gypsies, vagrants and Jews. Another Austrian Nazi, Adolf Eichmann (1906–62), became the architect of Hitler's extermination system, building death camps. The most infamous of these concentration camps were Auschwitz, Belsen, Dachau, Maidanek, Sobibor and Treblinka.

In the concentration camps prisoners were subjected to appalling conditions and treatment. Many were worked to death as slaves. Some were experimented on before execution. Over six million died in these camps. The majority – around four million – were exterminated in gas chambers, disguised as showers, and by other means.

))))> *Adolf Hitler, Nazi Party, World War II*

CONCORD, BATTLE OF LEXINGTON AND (1775)

First battle in the American Revolution. On 19 April 1775 the British General Gage sent a small number of troops to sieze an illegal military store at Lexington, Massachussetts. The local militia were defending their store, though. Shots were fired and the American Revolution was underway. The outcome of the battle itself was inconclusive.

))))> *American Revolution, Battle of Bunker Hill*

CONCORDE (1976)

Supersonic Anglo-French aircraft, which entered passenger service in 1976. Famed for its stylish elegance, it has a maximum cruising speed of 2,179 kph (1,176 knots), twice that of any other longhaul aircraft. A Concorde tragically crashed soon after take-off near Paris in July 2000, killing over 200 people.

CONFEDERACY (1861–65)

Government of the South during the American Civil War. A provisional government (1861) followed by a permanent one (1862) governed the 11 states, led by Richmond, Virginia; Jefferson Davis was president and their constitution was adopted March 1861. Failing to force European powers into an alliance by withholding cotton exports, and struggling with high inflation, lack of financial reserves, manpower and materials shortages caused by Union blockades, the Confederacy surrendered in 1865 to the North.

)))➤ *American Civil War*

CONFUCIANISM

Eastern religion. The word 'Confucius' is used to refer to the teaching of K'ung Fu-Tzu or to any traditional values in Chinese society. Confucius was a social reformer, an educator and communicator of knowledge. His teaching forms a religion as well as a philosophy expressing itself in very different terms from Western religions. Morality was inseparable from the rites, rituals and responsibilities of family life and social relations; parents and ancestors were a key element. The Gold Rule of K'ung Fu-Tzu was 'Do not impose on others what you do not desire'. The followers of K'ung Fu-Tzu are devoted to the pursuit of moral wisdom and sincere intentions.

)))➤ *Confucius*

CONFUCIUS (552–479 BC)

K'ung Fu-Tzu's (Confucius) teaching focused on loyalty, humanity, integrity, filial devotion, personal self-restraint and respect. He derived his sense of mission from Heaven (T'ien), which he regarded as having a positive moral force. He was sceptical, however, of many of the traditional beliefs and practices of his day. Ritual action, particularly with regard to ancestors and family, was important as was human solidarity across social and class boundaries. His teachings are found in the *Analects*, his recorded conversations with his disciples. He is reputed to have had 3,000 disciples, often being regarded as the great teacher of East Asia. His philosophy is silent on the existence of God and the after-life but he did regard Heaven as his protector and the author of virtue that was in him.

)))➤ *Confucianism*

ABOVE: Confucius (seated, far right), founder of the religion Confucianism, regarded the worship of one's own ancestors as a principal tenet of spiritual devotion.

CONQUISTADORS

Discoverers, explorers and settlers who established the Spanish Empire in America between about 1492 and 1550.

As soon as Christopher Columbus returned to Spain with news of his discoveries in the New World, Spaniards began to migrate there, settling in the Caribbean islands, Central America, Mexico and later in the western coasts and highlands of South America. The first migrants were nearly all from south-western Spain and came from all sectors of Spanish society except the higher nobility. They are now known as conquistadors, that is, conquerors of the indigenous people. Their aim was to acquire wealth and return to Spain but many chose to remain in the New World, which offered benefits such as plentiful labour.

The conquistadors often exercised great brutality in subduing the local populations and they and the missionary priests who accompanied them spread not only their spirituality and culture but also deadly diseases such as smallpox.

))))➤ *Christopher Columbus, Hernan Cortés, Francisco Pizarro*

CONSTANTINE (c. AD 285–337)

First Christian Roman Emperor. Proclaimed at York in AD 306, Constantine engaged in civil war to wrest total control of the Empire, succeeding in AD 324. A great victory at Rome in AD 312 was attributed to divine intervention. In AD 313 under the Edict of Milan, Constantine legitimized Christianity, recognizing its potential to unify the Empire and provide him with new supporters. In AD 325 he supervized the first council of the Church, at Nicaea. He founded the eastern imperial capital at Constantinople.

))))➤ *Christianity*

LEFT: Spanish conquistadors established and managed a vast empire in the Americas for Spain. Many never returned home, choosing to settle down in the New World instead.

CONSTANTINOPLE

Former capital of the Eastern Roman and Turkish Empires, now known as Istanbul. It was founded by Constantine the Great, the first Christian emperor, on the site of the ancient city of Byzantium and became the seat of the imperial government in AD 330. Like Rome, Constantinople was built on seven hills and its elaborate fortifications enabled it to resist a succession of sieges. It was twice captured by the armies of the Fourth Crusade (1203–04), then by the Greeks in 1261 and finally fell to the Turks in 1453, when it became the capital of the Ottoman, or Turkish, Empire.

))))➤ *Constantine, Ottoman Empire*

COOK, CAPTAIN JAMES (1728–79)

British naval officer, explorer and cartographer. Cook made three great voyages in the Pacific Ocean and North American coastal waters adding greatly to knowledge of the peoples, natural history and geography of these regions and disproving the existence of a 'Great Southern Continent'.

On Cook's first voyage, a circumnavigation of the globe (1768–71), he observed the transit of Venus from Tahiti, providing mathematicians with astronomical observations. Cook circumnavigated and mapped both islands of New Zealand and made landfall at Botany Bay on the south-east coast of Australia, whence he sailed north-east, charting that coastline. Cook's second voyage twice crossed the Antarctic circle, reaching the record latitude of 71° 11'S and circumnavigating Antarctica although never sighting it. The third voyage sailed through the Bering Strait but failed to find a Pacific entrance to the North-West Passage. Cook's insistence on a proper diet virtually eradicated scurvy from his voyages.

LEFT: A marble bust of Constantine, the first Christian Roman emperor. RIGHT: The Spanish conquistador Hernán Cortés stumbled on the mountainous route leading to Tenochtitlán, the fascinating Aztec capital governed by Montezuma, on one of his many expeditions.

COPERNICUS, NICOLAUS (1473–1543)

Polish astronomer. Anthropocentrism had led people to believe that the Earth must be at the centre of the Universe ever since the Ancient Greeks first suggested it. Nicolas Copernicus was the first to suggest that the Earth and other planets actually revolved around the Sun. Copernicus was still slightly wrong, as he believed that the Sun was the centre of the Universe, but his theory introduced the idea of the Solar System.

CORN LAWS (12TH TO 19TH CENTURIES)

Regulations governing the export and import of grain and twelfth-century penalties imposed on exporting grain without a license. By 1394 exports were freely allowed but by 1663 heavy duties were imposed on imported grain. The Bounty Act of 1673 and Corn Bounty Act of 1689 were passed; by 1773 exports were again forbidden. There was controversy over the laws with different interests demanding protection between 1791–1846. In 1838 the Anti-Corn Law League persuaded British prime minister Robert Peel to repeal the laws (1846).

CORTÉS, HERNÁN (1485–1547)

Spanish explorer and conqueror of the Aztec Empire of Mexico. In 1518 Cortés commanded an expedition to Mexico, founded a settlement in Yucatán and marched inland to the capital of the Aztec empire

at Tenochtitlán. The Aztec ruler Montezuma welcomed Cortés, believing him to be Quetzalcoatl, the legendary god-king. However, Montezuma was killed when the Aztecs revolted. For 10 years Cortés continued his military expeditions to quell rebellion and extend Spanish rule in Mexico and Honduras.

)))➤ *Aztecs, Montezuma, Tenochtitlán*

COSSACKS (15TH CENTURY)

Russian fighters and farmers. Forming semi-independent states these people fled from serfdom, fighting off the troops of the tsars. They formed villages and farmed their lands, paying few taxes and providing additional cavalry resources for the Russian armies. During World War I the Cossacks lost their privileged existence in the Russian Revolution and turned solely to farming. During World War II they assisted the Russians in pushing back the Nazi forces, mostly serving as cavalry.

)))➤ *Russian Revolution, World War I, World War II*

COUNTER-REFORMATION (16TH TO17TH CENTURIES)

Movement for revival and reform in the Catholic Church in the sixteenth and early seventeenth centuries. The reforming elements within the Catholic Church were, generally, not dependent on the Reformation and largely rose from within the Church itself. The religious orders of Augustinians, Carmelites and the Jesuits owed nothing to Protestantism which became the spearhead of the Counter-Reformation in Europe, America and the East (1562–63). The Council of Trent (1545–63) affirmed the supremacy of the pope over those who sought conciliation with Protestants and the Church emerged with greater vigour and a new liturgy. The Church embarked on a development of architecture, music and ritual and missionary zeal inside and outside Europe. Poland and Germany returned to Rome and in 1622 the Sacred Congregation for the Propagation of the Faith was founded to co-ordinate the missionary enterprise. The movement helped harden the division between Catholic and Protestant that was not resolved until the Treaty of Westphalia in 1648.

)))➤ *Reformation, Roman Catholicism, Treaty of Westphalia*

CRÉCY, BATTLE OF (1346)

First battle in the Hundred Years' War. On 26 August 1346 Edward III of England skilfully defeated Philip VI of France, at Crécy-en-Ponthieu in Northern France, by attacking cavalry with his infantrymen.

)))➤ *Battle of Agincourt, Hundred Years' War, Battle of Poitiers*

CRIMEAN WAR (1853–56)

War between Russia against England, France and Turkey. In 1853 Russia invaded the Balkans, with a view to accessing the Mediterranean sea. Considerable mistrust in Russian ambitions by Britain and France led to their intervention. An Anglo-French expedition force was sent to the Crimea, in the Ukraine, to attack Savastopol on the Black Sea.

Britain and France declared war on Russia in 1854 and laid siege to Sevastopol in September. There followed a series of battles which saw heavy losses on both sides. They included the battles of Balaclava, Inkerman and Alma. The Crimean War was characterized by negligent mismanagement at the War Office, leading to a long, drawn-out campaign and the loss of far more British and French lives than necessary. The war was ended by the Treaty of Paris in 1856.

))))➤ *Battle of Balaclava, Charge of the Light Brigade, Florence Nightingale*

CROMWELL, OLIVER (1599–1658)

English soldier and statesman. A Puritan, Cromwell entered parliament in 1628. He led parliamentary forces against Charles I in the Civil Wars, finally calling for the king's execution in 1649. After the Commonwealth was set up, Cromwell led expeditions to put down Irish and Scottish rebellions, and defeated Charles II (1951). He dissolved parliament and set up a protectorate, with himself as Lord Protector (1653–58), though he refused parliament's offer of the Crown. Cromwell restored England to its former glory as a leading European power under Elizabeth I through a series of trade wars and commercial treaties. Though a committed Puritan, Cromwell's rule was one of religious tolerance. The protectorate collapsed when his son Richard attempted to

succeed him on his death and the army and parliament struggled for power. His body was dug up and posthumously executed in 1661.

))))➤ *Charles I of England, Charles II of England, English Civil Wars, Restoration*

CRUSADES (1096–1281)

Series of military expeditions from Western Christianity to Syria and Palestine in twelfth and thirteenth centuries. Some argue they continued until 1464, so traditionally the number is eight. The aim was, in theory; to secure the Christian sites allowing proper access to them.

The First Crusade (literally meaning 'cross-marked') was instigated by Pope Urban II in 1095 and was the most successful. The Crusaders captured Jerusalem in 1099. Succeeding crusades were less successful. The Third Crusade included the English king Richard I and much folklore has developed around his absence from England and the activities of his brother King John. In truth the Crusades emphasized the division between Eastern and Western Christianity and reinforced the ideological divide between Islam and Christianity. *The Song of Roland* captures the spirit: 'Christians are right, pagans are wrong' (or at least Western Christians are right). Western Christianity was to become identified with military force and power; it was Christians who sacked Constantinople. The era, however, remains in the public mind as a glorious period of Renaissance and the Arab civilization and civilizing tendencies were ignored.

))))➤ *Christianity, Richard I of England*

CUBAN MISSILE CRISIS (1962)

Cold War confrontation between the US and Soviet Union. After the unsuccessful Bay of Pigs invasion to oust him by US-backed Cuban exiles, Fidel Castro began acquiring weapons from the Soviet Union.

LEFT: The Thin Red Line of the 93rd Highlanders repel the Russian cavalry during the Battle of Balaclava in the Crimean War.
ABOVE: Oliver Cromwell, Lord Protector.

RIGHT: Polish-born scientist Marie Curie studied the nature of uranium rays and discovered the elements polonium and radium.

In 1962, Soviet missiles with nuclear warheads trained on American cities were secretly stationed in Cuba. US spy planes detected these and President Kennedy demanded their removal. After six tense days – during which the world came close to nuclear war – the Soviets agreed to dismantle the missile sites. In return, the USA removed its own nuclear missiles from Turkey.

))))➤ *Bay of Pigs Invasion, Fidel Castro, John F. Kennedy*

CUBISM (20TH CENTURY)

Early twentieth-century artistic movement. Arguably the decisive move in which modern art broke free from the representational traditions of several centuries, Cubism was originated in Paris around 1907 by the joint genius of Georges Braque (1882–1963) and Pablo Picasso. Rejecting the old arts of perspective and foreshortening by which an illusion of depth and distance was given, they sought to show subjects, not as they were passively perceived but as they were known to be – from several sides at once, though in a two-dimensional plane. The nudes of the Spanish painter Picasso – boxy, angular, and seemingly wrenched out of shape – are perhaps the best-known cubist works today.

))))➤ *Modernism, Pablo Picasso*

CULTURAL REVOLUTION (1966–74)

Great Proletarian revolution in China. Mao Zedong favoured more Communist ideals than his contemporaries. Wishing to remake Chinese society he found that factions opposed him in the party and army. Unpractised as a ruler or economist, his early policies failed. He proposed the Cultural Revolution to drive opponents out of government and the army. The Red Guard started rebellions and demonstrations targeting Mao's rivals. The Cultural Revolution had dire consequences within China and on foreign affairs. Tension mounted with the USSR, as Mao denounced their invasion of Czechoslovakia. By April 1969, the Maoists appeared to have gained control of the party and the country, but many of the influential figures were moderates. Mao remained distrustful of

bureaucracy and Confucianism but brought China back on to the world stage with membership of the United Nations and diplomatic relations were re-established with America and Japan. Mao died in 1976 and the struggle between moderates and radicals re-emerged.

))))➤ *Confucianism, Mao Zedong*

CURIE, MARIE (1867–1934) AND PIERRE (1859–1906)

Polish scientists; pioneers in the study of radiation. In fact, they shared the Nobel Prize for Physics with Henri Becquerel, in 1903, for the discovery of radiation. They discovered the radioactive elements polonium and radium in pieces of pitchblende, managing to isolate samples in 1902. Marie went on to win the Nobel Prize for Chemistry in 1911 for her continued work in the field.

))))➤ *Henri Becquerel*

CUSTER, GEORGE ARMSTRONG (1839–76)

US leader against the Native American Indians. During the American Civil War, George Armstrong Custer became the youngest brigadier general in the Union army. By the close of the war he had made it to major general, earning him the moniker 'General Custer'. In fact he was relegated to captain when hostilities ceased. In the post-war period he was charged with keeping Native American tribes in check, eventually being killed by Sioux warriors at the Battle of Little Bighorn, 1876.

))))➤ *Battle of Little Bighorn*

CYRUS THE GREAT (d. c. 530 BC)

King of Persia (559–530 BC). Cyrus was renowned as a wise and just ruler, who significantly expanded the Persian Empire during his reign. He founded the Achaemenid dynasty and conquered much of Asia Minor, Babylonia, Syria and the Iranian plateau.

))))➤ *Babylonia, Persia*

D-DAY (1944)

Allied offensive during World War II. On 6 June 1944, between 6.30 and 7.30 a.m., the Allied invasion of Normandy was launched against the Germans. A vast American and British invasion force arrived at various beaches between the Orne and St Marcouf.

The Germans put up fierce resistance on D-Day to defend Hitler's 'Fortress Europe' but eventually the Allied forces breached their lines and the way was opened for victory. The term 'D-Day' referred to the first day of the invasion, with subsequent days listed as D+1, D+2 and so on – 'D' being an abbreviation for 'Day'.

To ensure the success of the D-Day landings, artificial harbours called 'Mulberry harbours' were constructed on the English coast and towed across the Channel. They enabled the Allied forces to unload vital military equipment for the campaign. Soldiers were delivered to the beaches in landing craft that ferried them from ships anchored out to sea.

))))▶ *World War II*

DADAISM (20TH CENTURY)

Artistic movement. As promulgated by the Romanian poet Tristan Tzara (1896–1963), German painter and sculptor Hans Richter (1888–1976) and the French writer and artist Hans Arp (1886–1966), Dada was a doctrine of outrageous absurdity and subversive clowning. Arising in neutral Zurich at a time when the rest of Europe was convulsed by the turmoil of World War I, Dadaism was defiantly frivolous, its chief concern to debunk the old artistic pieties. The name Dada, French for 'hobby-horse', was allegedly the first word found when a dictionary was opened and the Dadaist aesthetic generally rejoiced in the random, the strange conjunctions and juxtapositions to be found in nonsense verse and whacky collages. Though in itself short-lived, its irreverent spirit would prove lastingly influential in modern art.

))))▶ *Modernism*

LEFT: A war veteran pays tribute to those who fell on D-Day, 6 June 1944. BELOW: His Holiness the 14th Dalai Lama fled Tibet after the invasion of the Chinese in 1959.

DAGUERRE, LOUIS (1786–1851)

French scientist. Along with fellow Frenchman and colleague, Joseph Niépce (1765–1833), Louis Daguerre has been credited with the invention of photography. His 'daguerreotype' process was invented in 1838, but it was one of various techniques being developed by scientists at the time due to the discovery of light-sensitive chemicals. Niépce had produced the first primitive photograph in 1826, but the daguerreotype process offered a saleable photographic product to the waiting public.

DALAI LAMA (b. 1935)

Tibetan religious leader. Born Lhamo Thondup at Takstera in Northern Tibet, Tenzin Gyatso was identified as the 14th Dalai Lama when he was four years old. He assumed temporal power when he was 15 but had to flee

Tibet because of the Chinese invasion in 1959. He has lived in the West since then. The Gelig (Geluk) School of Buddhism in Tibet developed a line of Dalai Lamas (almost Buddhist saints). He has written 40 books teaching a message of love, compassion and non-violence. He was awarded the Nobel Peace Prize in 1989. He is referred to as 'Gyalwa Rinpoche' by Tibetans ('Precious Eminence').

))) *Buddhism*

DALÍ, SALVADOR (1904–89)

Spanish artist. Dalí rose to prominence in Paris in 1929 as a disciple of the Surrealist movement, though the movement's founder André Breton (1896–1966) was from the first suspicious of his real artistic motives. Appalled at what he saw as his follower's indecently unbohemian commercial sense, Breton accorded him the almost-anagrammatical nickname, 'avida dollars', and his subsequent reputation has been dogged by a feeling that he was too good at self-promotion. Yet, whatever his final status, Dalí's strange surrealistic dreamscapes of the 1930s, his lobster telephones and melting watches, did make his works undoubted popular hits of twentieth-century art.

))) *Surrealism*

DANEGELD (AD 991–1016)

Tax that originated in Anglo-Saxon England. These tax payments are thought to have commenced in AD 991 and continued through to 1016. Unlike a 'heregeld', or annual tax, levied to pay Danish mercenaries, the Danegeld was a tax levied to buy off Danish invaders during the reign of Ethelred II ('the Unready'). The tax was revived by the Normans under William the Conqueror.

))) *Anglo-Saxons,*
Vikings

BELOW: The Dardanelles strait was the scene of many naval battles between British and Turkish fleets.

DARDANELLES CAMPAIGN (1915–16)

Unsuccessful Allied campaign during World War I. Britain declared war on Turkey at the close of 1914. The strait known as the Dardanelles, where the Sea of Marmara spills into the Aegean, became a hot-spot of bitter fighting. In April 1915, under the command of Sir Ian Hamilton, a joint British, Australian, New Zealand and French force landed on the Gallipoli peninsula. The Turks proved a formidable foe and the Allied forces became entrenched. The beleaguered survivors were eventually withdrawn in January 1916. Some 36,000 Commonwealth troops were lost at Gallipoli. The majority were ANZAC (Australian and New Zealand Army Corps) troops.

))) *World War I*

DARK AGES (AD 476–800)

Early Middle Ages in Western Europe. After the fall of Rome a collapse in the trade and communication infrastructure across Europe emerged. Barter replaced money, towns and cities declined, and roads became overgrown. Feudalism emerged with lords ruling a small state by force of arms. Self-sufficiency replaced trade and the more ambitious warlords carved out larger kingdoms, but these often collapsed when the leader died. Many historians suggest that the period AD 500–1000, marked by a lack of written records, is a more accurate measure of the Dark Ages because little is known of this time. Europe at this time was comparatively primitive. Eventually loose confederations became kingdoms but government was weak. The Church was fragmented but, by the ninth century, European unity began to re-emerge, based on the Roman legacy. The period drew to a close with the coming of the Vikings and Magyars in the tenth century.

)))➤ *Feudalism, Magyars, Vikings*

DARWIN, CHARLES (1809–82)

English naturalist, evolutionist and writer, known for 'Darwinism'. The son of Dr Robert Darwin and the grandson of Erasumus Darwin, author of *Zoonomia, or the Laws of Organic Life*, Charles Darwin set off on HMS *Beagle* in 1831 as a naturalist studying evolution, to the west coast of South America on a five-year voyage. On his return in 1836 he began working on his books and is renowned for his writings on evolution and for his evolutionary theories. Two major works, *On the Origin of Species by Means of Natural Selection* (1859) and *The Descent of Man, and Selection in Relation to Sex* (1871) subsequently had a huge impact on the thoughts of future scientists, as well as future developments.

BELOW: English chemist, Humphry Davy, responsible for the isolation of six of the chemical elements named in the periodic table. He was also responsible for the invention of the eponymous safety lamp.

Darwin was also interested in the natural phenomena and wrote *Variation in Animals and Plants under Domestication* (1868) which, amongst other things, was a study of the role of earthworms in the fertility of soil.

DAVY, HUMPHRY (1778–1829)

English inventor. Davy discovered six of the elements in the Periodic Table. He isolated four of the six alkaline earth metals in group II – barium, calcium, magnesium and strontium – and two of the six alkali metals from group I – potassium and sodium. He used electrolysis to obtain samples. Davy also invented a miners' lamp that used a gauze to prevent ignition of firedamp: a mixture of methane and air.

DE GAULLE, CHARLES (1890–1970)

French general and statesman. De Gaulle was an army officer in World War I and, while in exile, head of the French Resistance during World War II. A checkered political career followed, including stints as president and provisional head of state. De Gaulle became president (with a new constitution that strengthened the role) in 1958. He was determined to resolve the crisis created by the civil war in Algeria (a French colony) and in 1962, he negotiated Algeria's independence. De Gaulle's high spending on nuclear defence, among other things, sparked demonstrations by workers and students in 1968 that nearly brought down his government. He resigned the following year.

)))➤ *World War II*

ABOVE: Charles de Gaulle on the cover of TIME magazine. De Gaulle became leader of the French troops during the German occupation of France. He was head of the provisional French government from 1944–46.

DE STIJL (1917)

Artistic movement, from the Dutch 'The Style'. De Stijl was the name of the journal established in 1917 by Dutch painters Piet Mondrian (1872–1944) and Theo van Doesburg (1883–1931) and, consequently, of the artistic style it promoted. Characterized by clear colour and geometric shapes, it is most famously exemplified by the bold blocks of Mondrian's own paintings – as playful as they are austere – but it also influenced the firm outlines of much modern architecture.

DECLARATION OF INDEPENDENCE (1776)

Document proclaiming the independence of 13 North American British colonies from Great Britain. On 19 April 1775 war broke out between Britain and her colonies in North America. The Declaration of Independence was the culmination of a conflict that had begun as a protest against restrictions imposed on the states by Britain. The Declaration states the grievances that the colonies had and is the foundation of the Bill of Rights of the US Constitution. On 7 June 1776 Richard Henry Lee, a Virginian delegate of the Continental Congress, proposed a motion of independence. A committee was appointed that included Thomas Jefferson and Benjamin Franklin to prepare a declaration in line with Lee's suggestions. It was unanimously adopted on 4 July and officially endorsed by Congress on 2 August. It resolved that 'these united colonies are and of right ought to be free and independent states'.

)))➤ *American Revolution, Bill of Rights, Benjamin Franklin, Thomas Jefferson, United States Constitution*

DEMOCRACY

System of government in which the people rule (through their elected representatives). Democracy had its roots in the Ancient Greek city-states, but the modern concepts of universal suffrage, democratic government and political equality sprang from the American and French Revolutions.

In Ancient Greece, all the citizens (except women and slaves) were part of the governing assembly and could be elected to official posts. This system gave way to oligarchy and was not to re-emerge for another 2,000 years. Present-day democracy began when medieval European rulers sought approval of their policies from different groups – the gathering of these groups were the early forms of parliament.

Thinkers such as Jean-Jacques Rousseau developed the idea of a social contract between a ruler and the people, in which the natural rights of people could not be taken from them. Such ideas had a huge impact on British government, and the revolutions in America and France from which sprung key documents that shaped Western democracy, the American Declaration of Independence (1776) and the French Declaration of the Rights of Man (1789). Political democracy was established in most Western countries by the nineteenth century.

Since the mid-twentieth century, most political systems have described themselves as democracies, even when operating a one-party system and not stressing individual rights, fundamental tenets of Western democracy. This has led to a clash of definitions: socialism maintains that true democracy lies in economic equality and public ownership of wealth. Multi-party democracy has flourished with the collapse of Communism in Eastern Europe and the fall of a number of dictatorships in Latin America and Africa.

)))➤ *American Revolution, Communism, Declaration of Independence, French Revolution, Socialism*

ABOVE: The signed American Declaration of Independence document.

DÉSCARTES, RÉNE (1596–1650)

French philosopher. Born at Les Hayes near Poitiers in France Déscartes attended a Jesuit college then (probably) the University of Poitiers. He joined the army and served in France and the Netherlands. He settled in Paris (1613) then moved to the Netherlands in 1628 where he remained until 1649 when he went to teach in Sweden, where he lived for the rest of his life. He wrote *Discourse on Method* (1637) in Part IV of which is his famous dictum *Cogito, ergo sum* ('I think, therefore I am'). He argued that if God is perfect then God must exist otherwise God would not be perfect (ontological argument). His other works *Meditations on First Philosophy* (1641) and *Principles of Philosophy* (1644).

DÉTENTE (1960s–70s)

Improved relations between US and the Soviet Union in the 1960s and 70s. Détente reached its height in agreements over the limitation of nuclear arms, such as the Helsinki Accords (1975). The Soviet invasion of Afghanistan in 1979 and Ronald Reagan's anti-Soviet stance brought an end to this period.

DIASPORA, JEWISH

The dispersion of the Jews (diaspora is a Greek word) began with the Assyrian and Babylonian deportations in 722 and 597 BC; Jews spread throughout the Mediterranean world and into Armenia and Iran. After the destruction of the Second Temple (AD 70) and the Bar-Kochba revolt (AD 132–135), Jewish religious life was kept alive through academics, Jewish schools and the synagogue. Today there are large numbers of Jews outside Israel, in the USA, Australia and South Africa. Support for the state of Israel has become a strong focus for the Jewish Diaspora communities.

DIAZ, BARTHOLOMEW (c. 1450–1500)

Portuguese navigator. Diaz was the first European to sail round the Cape of Good Hope in 1487. In command of an expedition to explore the west coast of Africa, he sailed to the south of the continent and made landfall at Mosselbaai about 320 km (200 miles) east of the Cape. His voyage opened up the sea route from Europe to the Far East although it fell to Vasco da Gama to complete the first successful passage to India.

))》 *Vasco da Gama*

ABOVE: Bartholomew Diaz was the first to sail around the Cape of Good Hope.
LEFT: The seventeenth-century French philosopher Descartes conducts a demonstration at the court of Queen Christine of Sweden.

DICKENS, CHARLES (1812–70)

English novelist. Born the son of a navy clerk, Dickens' family fell on hard times when his father was made redundant from his job. In 1824 he was arrested for debt and sent to the Marshalsea Prison – a setting in Dickens' later novel *Little Dorrit* (1855–57) – while Charles himself had to work long hours in a London blacking factory. These experiences, and the insights they afforded him into the lives of the impoverished middle class, would inform the fictional work which Dickens, by now a journalist, began writing in his early twenties. Beginning with the brief comic anecdotes of *Sketches by Boz* (1833–36) he would continue to publish serially in popular magazines, though works like *Oliver Twist* (1837–39), *David Copperfield* (1849–50) and *Bleak House* (1852–53) would ensure his lasting place among Britain's pre-eminent writers.

DIET OF WORMS (1521)

Hearing at which Martin Luther defended his views. Pope Leo X condemned Luther's 41 propositions in June 1520 and excommunicated him the following January. Frederick III, Luther's Prince of Saxony, arranged with the Holy Roman Emperor Charles V a hearing at Worms. He defended his beliefs but was outlawed as a heretic by the Edict of Worms in May 1521.

))) ➤ *Martin Luther, Maximilian I of Germany*

DISNEY, WALT (1901–66)

American animator and producer. Walter Elias Disney, Chicago-born creator of Mickey Mouse, worked for several years as a commercial artist before setting up his own animation studio. Mickey was in fact there from the beginning, in Disney's first independently-produced films *Plane Crazy* and *Steamboat Willie* (both 1928). Made in 1937, *Snow White and the Seven Dwarfs* initiated an entirely new cinematic genre – the feature-length cartoon: it was followed by a long series of classics, including *Fantasia* (1940), *Dumbo* (1941) and *Bambi* (1942). In the decades that followed, Disney and his corporation would populate the consciousness of the world with a host of unforgettable characters: the original Disneyland theme park, opened in 1955, was Disney's personal brainchild.

BELOW: Minnie Mouse at Eurodisney, the European equivalent of Walt Disney's brainchild, the Disneyland theme park.

DOME OF THE ROCK (AD 687)

Built on the site of the Jewish Temple in AD 687, sometimes called the 'Mosque of 'Umar' after the Caliph who inspired its building. The third most important city in Islam, Jerusalem is special because of the story of the Prophet Muhammad's 'Night Journey' (al-Isra') and Ascent. The angel Jibreel woke the Prophet one night and took him through the seven heavens on a winged horse. There he met all the prophets and led them in prayer; he was taken to different heavens and saw Paradise and Hell, the glory of Allah (God) and the universe. The rock in the Dome of the Rock marks the spot from which the Prophet ascended, the Rock split with the Prophet leaving his footprint on it.

))) ➤ *Islam, Prophet Mohammad*

DOMESDAY BOOK (1086)

William the Conqueror's survey of England. Despite much public resentment, William carried out his survey of England using seven or eight teams of commissioners, each of whom covered all of England with the exception of the northern areas. The survey resulted in 'Great Domesday' covering all counties with the exception of Norfolk, Suffolk and Essex, which were covered in 'Little Domesday'. The survey contained information about the estates of the king and his tenants, gathered from formal sessions held with sheriffs, barons and representatives from each of the villages. The Domesday Book is kept at the Public Record Office in London.

)))➤ *William I of England*

DOMINICAN ORDER (1215)

Religious order of monks. Known as 'Friars Preachers' or 'Black Friars,' the Order is committed to preaching and study. Founded by St Dominic (1170–1221) in 1215, the monks practise corporate poverty and live by begging. The Order spread rapidly. In 1475 the pope (Sixtus IV) revoked the rule on corporate poverty and allowed the Order to have property and receive income. Chief interests are education and theological study with St Thomas Aquinas being one of its greatest products. Monks were often involved in the Inquisition; they were known as 'watchdogs of orthodoxy' and were heavily involved in missionary activity. The constitution of the Order balances central authority and decentralization.

)))➤ *St Thomas Aquinas, Inquisition*

ABOVE: The Domesday Book.
RIGHT: The typical habit of a Dominican friar.

DOMINO THEORY

US foreign policy after World War II. Also called the Domino Effect, the theory was that non-Communist countries would topple over (into Communism) like dominos in a line when next to a neighbouring Communist country. President Truman first used this to justify sending military aid to Turkey and Greece in the 1940s. The theory gained greatest popularity in the 1950s and 60s when a number of American presidents (from Eisenhower to Kennedy) used it as an argument for military involvement in South East Asia, particularly during the Vietnam War. The theory was revived in the 1980s to describe the threat perceived from leftwing unrest in central America.

)))➤ *Harry S. Truman, Vietnam War*

DRAKE, SIR FRANCIS (c. 1540–96)

English navigator and explorer, first British seaman to circumnavigate the globe. He sailed from Plymouth in 1577, crossed the Atlantic, sailed through the Strait of Magellan and, after a 52-day storm, continued up the Pacific coast of North America. Then he sailed across the Pacific and Indian Oceans and rounded the Cape of Good Hope. Queen Elizabeth I knighted him for his achievement and his booty of Spanish gold and ships.

))))▶ *Elizabeth I of England*

DREADNOUGHT (1906)

Ship commanded in the Anglo-French wars of the mid-eighteenth century by Admiral Edward Boscawen (1711–61), nicknamed 'Old Dreadnought'. Also the name of a type of battleship launched in 1906 in response to the expansion of the German navy. The original *Dreadnought* displaced 17,900 tons and had a speed of 21 knots, obtained from coal- and oil-fired boilers and turbines. It was heavily armoured and powerfully equipped with 10 12-inch long-range naval guns.

DUAL ENTENTE (1893)

Franco-Russian Alliance signed by France and Russia in 1893. In 1907 the alliance was joined by Britain, becoming the Triple Entente. Then in 1911 the Triple Entente became a military alliance as the threat of war loomed large. It formed the basis for the Allied Powers who entered World War I against the Central Powers – Germany and Austria-Hungary. The Russian Revolution of 1917 saw the end of the Triple Entente.

))))▶ *Triple Entente, World War I*

DUTCH EAST INDIA COMPANY (1602)

Commercial company incorporated in 1602. Its monopoly extended from the Cape of Good Hope to the Strait of Magellan, with sovereign rights in whatever territory it acquired. The Company's headquarters was Batavia (now Jakarta, Indonesia). Through war with Spain (1605–65), the Company gained control of Indonesia, the Malay Peninsula, Japan, Ceylon (Sri Lanka) and the Malabar coast of India. It drove the English from the Malay Archipelago and the Moluccas, and established the first European settlement in southern Africa. At its greatest power in 1669 the Company deployed 10,000 soldiers and 40 warships. The Company went into liquidation in 1799.

))))▶ *British East India Company, French East India Company*

ABOVE: The Elizabethan sea dog, Sir Francis Drake.

EASTER RISING (1916)

Republican uprising against the British government in Ireland. The revolt, also known as the Easter Rebellion, began on 24 April, Easter Monday. The plan was for a nationwide uprising by a number of organizations, but due to a series of mishaps, it only took place in Dublin. The leaders Patrick Pearse and Tom Clarke – with about 1,800 men – seized the Dublin General Post Office and other strategic points in the city centre. There was fighting for a week while British troops put down the insurrection and the leaders were all executed. Although the uprising itself had been unpopular, the executions fuelled the Irish cause and the government collapsed.

EDDINGTON, ARTHUR (1882–1944)

English astronomer and physicist. Einstein's theory of relativity was published in 1905, but it required tangible some proof to become popularly accepted. Arthur Eddington conducted pioneering work on atomic theory. In 1919 he obtained proof that Einstein was right. Einstein had argued that light should be attracted by gravity and Eddington was able to show that light passing the sun was indeed pulled off course by its gravity.

)))➤ *Albert Einstein*

EDICT OF NANTES (1598)

Edict that ended the French wars of religion, signed by Henri IV. Huguenots were allowed freedom of worship (except in certain towns), civil equality, fair justice, the power to hold certain fortified towns as their own, and given a state subsidy to support troops and pastors. Louis XIV revoked it in 1685.

)))➤ *Huguenots, Louis XIV of France*

EDISON, THOMAS ALVA (1847–1931)

American inventor. Edison first made his fortune by selling a machine he had invented in 1869 that used a paper 'ticker' tape for sending electrical information on stocks and shares. With the proceeds, Edison established his industrial research laboratory that served him for the rest of his life. In the laboratory he had a team of dedicated technicians who would try things out time and time again until an idea was perfected into a working prototype. His most celebrated invention was the electric light bulb.

RIGHT: Thomas Edison invented the first commercially viable electric bulb.

EDWARD I OF ENGLAND (1239–1307)

King of England from 1272; son of Henry III. Nicknamed 'Longshanks' for his height, Edward was influenced by Simon de Montfort who led the barons against Henry III's rule. Edward was reconciled to Henry and fought Simon in the Barons War, killing him at Evesham in 1265. He acceded while on crusade. Edward believed in government and taxation by consent, creating the first parliament in 1295 and reforming feudal abuses. He conquered Wales between 1282–84, after Llewellyn's uprising, creating his son Prince of Wales in 1301. Wars in Scotland were indecisive despite removing the coronation stone from Scone to London, and defeating William Wallace in 1305.

))) *Parliament*

EDWARD III OF ENGLAND (1312–77)

King of England from 1327, son of Edward II and Isabella. In 1330, Edward executed his mother's lover, Roger Mortimer, securing control for himself. He defeated the Scots at Halidon Hill in 1333, establishing a puppet king, John Balliol. In 1337 he began the Hundred Years' War against France, claiming the French Crown. With his son Edward, the 'Black Prince', he secured great victories at Crécy in 1346, and Poitiers in 1356, exploiting the advantage of English longbowmen over mounted knights. In 1360 he recovered Aquitaine but after 1369 he lost all French lands except Calais. His financial needs strengthened parliament's control.

))) *Battle of Crécy, Hundred Years' War, Battle of Poitiers*

EIFFEL TOWER (1889)

Paris landmark. Built for the World's Fair of 1889, the Eiffel Tower still dominates the Paris skyline: in its day it was the tallest building in the world. Minus its (later) radio antenna, the tower is almost 300 m (1,000 ft) high and some 6,300 tonnes of wrought iron were used in its construction. A proselytizer for wrought-iron construction, Alexandre Gustave Eiffel (1832–1923) built everything from bridges to churches, all over the world, yet this great tower remains far and away his most enduring achievement.

))) *Empire State Building*

LEFT: King Edward II of England was overthrown by his wife, Isabella and her lover, Roger Mortimer.
ABOVE: The Eiffel Tower, one of Paris's enduring attractions.

EINSTEIN, ALBERT (1879–1955)

Swiss-born mathematician. Albert Einstein's work in mathematical physics astounded the world. Prior to Einstein's theories, human understanding of gravity and other physical phenomena had been based on Newtonian laws.

Einstein published his own theories, based on mathematical formulae, that demonstrated relationships between time, light, mass, gravity and space. Unlike Newton's laws, however, they could not be easily proven by experimentation, even though they worked on paper. Other scientists, such as Arthur Eddington, eventually began to show that Einstein was correct in his assertions.

Einstein's best-known theory is his theory of general relativity, published in 1905. It shows that motion and mass have relative, rather than absolute, characters, because of interdependence between matter, time and space. His famous formula $E = mc^2$ demonstrates that mass and energy are equivalent.

))⯈ *Arthur Eddington, Isaac Newton*

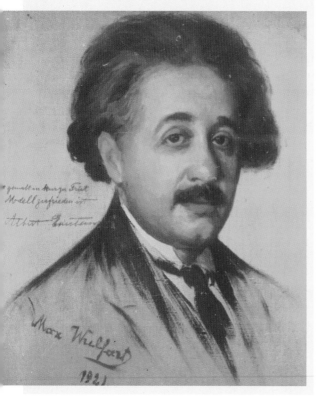

EISENHOWER, DWIGHT (1890–1969)

American general and US president (1953–61). Commander of US forces during World War II, 'Ike' Eisenhower was appointed supreme commander of the Allied forces and planned the cross-channel invasion of France on D-Day. He organized NATO's defence forces after the war, then won the 1952 presidential election. Despite ending the Korean War, he continued Harry S. Truman's Cold War policy and the Eisenhower doctrine committed the USA to containing Communism in the Middle East. He won a second term with ease in 1956. Civil rights were coming to the fore and Eisenhower sent federal troops to Little Rock, Arkansas, to enforce a court-ordered school desegregation.

))⯈ *Cold War, D-Day, Presidents, Harry S. Truman, World War II*

LEFT: Albert Einstein formulated theories about the nature and structure of the Universe which permanently changed our view of cosmology.
ABOVE: General Dwight Eisenhower commanded the Allied forces in Italy during World War II and was later elected 34th US president.

EL ALAMEIN, BATTLES OF (1942)

During World War II North Africa presented a new theatre of battle for both Allied and Axis powers. Desert fighting was something not previously experienced in the campaign. The frontline moved westward and eastward along the Barbary Coast as each side waxed and waned, but El Alamein, in northern Egypt, proved to be the strategically decisive spot. Both Battles of El Alamein (July and October–November 1942) were won by the Allies, largely thanks to shorter supply lines than Erwin Rommel's.

))➤ *Erwin Rommel, World War II*

ELIZABETH I OF ENGLAND (1533–1603)

Queen of England 1558, daughter of Henry VIII by Anne Boleyn. Highly intelligent and fluent in several languages, Elizabeth established an archetype of Protestant monarchic power.

Declared illegitimate after Anne's execution, Henry's will restored Elizabeth to the succession after Edward VI and Mary I. Mary imprisoned her in 1554, believing Elizabeth was involved in plots against her.

Elizabeth's accession was followed by the 1559 Religious Settlement, enforcing Protestantism.

She depended on William Cecil, later Lord Burghley, chief secretary from 1558–98, but spurned all potential suitors, including her favourite, Robert Dudley, Earl of Leicester. Her heir remained her cousin Mary, Queen of Scots, but Elizabeth's spies uncovered plots by Mary's circle to kill her. In 1587, Elizabeth executed Mary, leaving Mary's son James, as heir.

In 1588, the destruction of Philip II's Spanish Armada by weather and English naval commanders was a triumph but Spain remained a problem, and an Irish rebellion followed in the 1590s. Elizabeth died in 1603, one of the longest-serving and most effective rulers England had known.

))➤ *Philip II of Spain, Spanish Armada*

ELIZABETH II OF ENGLAND (b. 1926)

Queen of the United Kingdom since 1952, and Head of the Commonwealth. Daughter of George VI and Elizabeth, now the Queen Mother. Elizabeth served during World War II in the ATS. In 1947 she married her cousin Philip Mountbatten, created Duke of Edinburgh, succeeding to the throne while on a tour of Kenya. They have four children: Charles, Prince of Wales (b. 1948), Anne (b. 1950), Andrew (b. 1960) and Edward (b. 1964). The reign has been characterized by great changes in the image of the monarchy, while the queen has remained fervently committed to the duties of her position, despite the marital problems of her children.

EMPIRE STATE BUILDING (1931)

US landmark. On its completion in 1931, the Empire State Building became the first man-made structure to surpass the Eiffel Tower in height, though several other buildings have overtaken it in recent decades. As remarkable as its scale, however, was the rapidity of its construction from prefabricated sections of steel and concrete – the entire project took less than two years from start to finish. The building was consciously conceived as an advertisement for these modern building methods, and it remains for many round the world the quintessential 'skyscraper'.

LEFT: Queen Elizabeth I of England.

ENIGMA MACHINE (1940s)

During World War II it became essential that military information be sent in code form to prevent the enemy from gaining the intelligence they needed to counter an operation. The Germans did this by inventing a special machine that encrypted signals into a complex and indecipherable code – the Enigma code. Eventually the code was broken by a chance event: a depth-charged German U-Boat was captured that contained an Enigma coding machine set up for transmission.

))))➤ *World War II*

ENLIGHTENMENT (c. 1700)

Intellectual movement. Breaking the hold of a religious authority already weakened by the two-fold traumas of Renaissance and Reformation, a new spirit of free enquiry can be seen to have arisen from around 1700 onwards. Though its origins lay earlier, in the philosophy of René Déscartes and in the scientific discoveries of Sir Isaac Newton, the Enlightenment was very much an eighteenth-century phenomenon. For it was then that, emboldened by these advances, French *philosophes* like Voltaire (1694–1778) began berating the Church for its 'superstition', Jean-Jacques Rousseau denouncing the enslavement of individuals by laws and governments. The prototypical Enlightenment project was the great *Encyclopédie* (1751–80), edited by Denis Diderot (1713–84) and Jean d'Alembert (1717–83), which attempted to set down and summarize all human knowledge. None of its contents was new: what was truly radical was the implication that it was possible for an individual to apprehend everything on a rational basis – henceforth there would be no ineffable mysteries, the preserve of priests; no God-given authority, the traditional justification for monarchs. While the Enlightenment's values of intellectual and political freedom would find their ultimate expression in the French Revolution of 1789, conservatives would see the ensuing Terror as confirming their most nightmarish fears.

))))➤ *René Déscartes, Neoclassicism, Isaac Newton, Jean-Jacques Rousseau*

ENTENTE CORDIAL (1904)

Unofficial alliance between France and Great Britain. Britain became a component of the Triple Entente, along with France and Russia, in 1907, seven years before the outbreak of World War I. In 1904 Britain and France made an agreement called the Entente Cordiale (French for 'Friendly Agreement') to show goodwill between nations as a prelim. The Entente Cordiale recognized British interests in Egypt and French interests in Morocco, with a mutual understanding that each would be left to their own devices.

))))➤ *Dual Entente, Triple Entente, World War I*

ESTATES-GENERAL

French national assembly. Also known as the states-general, the assembly consisted of the clergy, nobles and commons, but it was never as powerful as the English parliament. The monarchy maintained financial control and royal power continued to grow in France. There were long periods when the estates-general was not convened – between 1614 and 1789, when Louis XVI finally assembled the estates in desperation over the country's financial situation. When the commons or third estate renamed itself the National Assembly in 1789, the act sparked off the French Revolution.

))))➤ *French Revolution, Louis XVI*

ETHNIC CLEANSING

Purging an area of an unwanted ethnic group. Although ethnic cleansing is associated with the former Yugoslavia, in particular Bosnia and Herzegovina, deportation, mass murder and genocide has featured in European history for many centuries. The Jews suffered from ethnic cleansing in Spain, Great Britain and Germany in the 1930s and 40s. The Armenians suffered

RIGHT: A bronze Etruscan head.
BELOW: The prolonged conflict in Bosnia-Herzegovina, formerly Yugoslavia, resulted in countless 'ethnic cleansing' atrocities.

at the hands of the Turks at the end of the nineteenth century. Following the break up of Yugoslavia, Bosnian Muslims suffered at the hands of the Serbs from 1992, forcing the UN to deploy troops to protect six safe areas in the region. To date many of those responsible for ethnic cleansing have not been brought to trial despite widespread world condemnation of the massacres that claimed the lives of up to 250,000 people and displaced 2.3 million. In 1996 the International Criminal Tribunal for the former Yugoslavia indicted 50 Bosnians for massacring civilians during the war, including Radovan Karadzic, the President of the Bosnian Serb Republic and General Ratko Mladic, his military commander. By 1997 the tribunal had indicted 74 people; 54 Serbs, 17 Croats and three Muslims, the first time an international court has tried someone for war crimes since World War II.

ETRUSCANS (800–283 BC)

Ancient Italian civilization. It is unknown whether the Etruscans were descended from migrants of Asia Minor or were native Iron Age people. By the middle of the seventh century BC, the Etruscans had begun to settle in Italy from the Alps to the Tiber River. The aristocracy controlled Etruscan society and most of their cities had an independent status, forging links through marriage. By the fifth century BC their expansion had been stopped as the Greeks, Romans and Carthaginians

united against them. The Romans captured the city of Veii in 396 BC, marking the beginning of Rome's conquest. The Romans captured most of central and southern Italy and then turned their attention to the northern cities of Caere Tarquinia and Vulci. All attempts to ally with the Gauls against the Romans failed. At their height they had immense military strength but it was not well co-ordinated due to the independence of the city-states. Little is known about religion but it is believed that they worshipped animal gods and many of their deities became the well-known Roman ones, such as Venus and Apollo. Etruscan art was similar to that of the Greeks and many of their buildings were constructed of wood and brick.

))))➤ *Romans*

EUROPEAN COAL AND STEEL COMMUNITY (1952)

Authority controlling Europe's coal and steel industries, operative from 1952. Its signatories were Belgium, France, West Germany, Luxembourg, Italy and the Netherlands. The ECSC supranational authority had wide powers and oversaw a period of great expansion in both industries and a doubling in internal trade in five years, thanks partly to the abolition of customs barriers. ECSC production grew to about 20 per cent of total world production by 1974. Once considered 'basic' industries, however, coal and steel began to decline from the 1970s on and in the 1980s faced increasing competition from imports of coal from outside the Community, e.g. Eastern Europe.

In 1957 the six members of the ECSC signed the Treaty of Rome, which established the European Economic Community, and in 1967 the EEC, ECSC and Euratom, the European Atomic Agency, were amalgamated as the European Community (EC). By 2000 the EC numbered 15 members.

))))➤ *European Economic Community, Treaty of Rome*

EUROPEAN COMMISSION

Civil service of the European Union. Twenty members, or commissioners (including a president and several vice presidents), head the European Commission, with at least one commissioner from each country in the Union. With a staff of 15,000, the Commission is the EU's largest body. Its job is to implement the various treaties and rules laid down by the council of ministers, which is the real decision-maker. The Commission also administers the EU's agricultural policies and regional development programmes, as well as preparing acts put before the European parliament.

)))➤ *European Union*

EUROPEAN ECONOMIC COMMUNITY

Association of European countries established to promote economic unity. The EEC was set up to develop a 'common market' for member states at the end of World War II, as well as to create political stability. It was formally established by the Treaty of Rome (1957) and the original members were France, West Germany, Italy, the Netherlands, Belgium and Luxembourg. Its primary goal was to eliminate internal tariff and customs barriers and this was so successful that trade between EEC members quadrupled from 1958 to 1968. In 1967 the EEC joined together with the European Coal and Steel Community and the European Atomic Energy Community to form the European Community or EC. One of the main goals of the EC was to integrate its members' economies into a single market without frontiers, with a common currency and central bank. The EC does now have its own currency, the Euro, though not all EU members have voted to join this.

)))➤ *European Coal and Steel Community, European Union*

EUROPEAN UNION

Name given to the European Community since the Maastricht Treaty. The new title reflects the greater links between members of this organization, which includes most of the countries of Western Europe. The EEC was primarily concerned with economic integration, but the EU also works towards unified action in security and foreign policy as well as judicial matters. The EC grew out of the efforts of such statesmen as Jean Monnet and Robert Schuman of France and Paul Henri Spaak of Belgium, who envisioned a unified Europe.

The success of the EEC's trade liberalization in the 1960s–80s made its members open to greater integration. In 1991 members signed the Treaty on European Union or the Maastricht Treaty, which promised greater economic and political union. The treaty officially created the European Union (in 1993) comprising the European Community (the renamed EEC), the Council of Ministers, the European Parliament (directly elected by voters) and a court of justice. Maastricht strengthened the parliament, called for the creation of an EU central bank and common currency, and took steps towards a joint defense policy. The European Economic Area, an enormous free-trade zone larger than the common market, was established in 1994.

Full members now include Austria, Belgium, Britain, Denmark, Finland, France, Germany (originally West Germany), Greece, Ireland, Italy, Luxembourg, the Netherlands, Portugal, Spain and Sweden. The Maastricht Treaty paved the way for other European countries to join the EU. Austria, Finland, and Sweden – all members of the European Free Trade Association (EFTA) – became members in 1995.

)))➤ *Maastricht Treaty*

ABOVE: The European Union flag.
LEFT: European Economic Community headquarters.

EXPRESSIONISM (1901–30)

Artistic movement. A potent force in European – and especially German – art, between 1901 and 1930, expressionism found its establishing inspiration in the anti-impressionist rebellion of artists like Vincent van Gogh (1853–90) and Paul Gauguin (1848–1903); the Norwegian artist Edvard Munch (1863–1944), creator of *The Scream* (1893) was another influence. While astonishingly original in form and technique, impressionism had in fact been deceptively conservative in its aims: the faithful recording of nature as it presented itself to the eye of the artist. Van Gogh's attempts to look beyond the representational surface to a (generally tragic) emotional reality may have had little in common with the exotic distortions of Gauguin's increasingly primitivist South-Sea vision. Both, however, were concerned to transcend what they saw as the passivity of the impressionist approach – a concern which growing numbers of younger painters soon found themselves sharing. The French *Fauves*

BELOW: Expressionism found its anti-impressionist voice of rebellion in the works of painters like Paul Gauguin.

('wild beasts') were led by the charismatic figure of Henri Matisse (1869–1954): their work was characterized by intensely bright and clashing colours which scorned traditional realism. More violent still were the canvases of the German *Die Brücke* ('The Bridge') school, whose leader was Ernst Ludwig Kirchner (1880–1938). In their frenzied fragmentation of line and colour, his works seemed to aspire to the condition of mental breakdown. The Nazis' suppression of expressionism as 'degenerate' led to its dissemination abroad as artists went into exile: thus, in the decades following his flight to London in 1938, the Austrian genius Oskar Kokoschka (1886–1980) did much to promote the expressionist cause in Britain.

))))➤ *Impressionism, Modernism*

FALKLANDS WAR (1982)

Campaign between Britain and Argentina over ownership of the Falkland Islands. The first British settlers arrived at the Falkland Islands, in the South Atlantic, in 1765. The islands had been named after Lord Falkland, treasurer to the British navy, at the end

of the seventeenth century. In 1766 France sold West Falkland to the Spanish, who ejected the British in 1770–71, and named the islands *Islas Malvinas*. However, British sovereignty was not ceded and the islands became a solely British settlement from 1833 when the last of the Argentines – Spanish descendants – were expelled.

On 2 April 1982 Argentina invaded the Falkland Islands. The United Nations Security Council called for a withdrawal but it was ignored. Britain immediately dispatched a task force of army, navy and airforce personnel to launch an offensive against the Argentineans. The task force took some days to reach the islands, giving the Argentineans time to bring reinforcements in preparation for the battle ahead.

The Falklands War proved to be a fierce conflict. Argentine troops outnumbered British, but the British had the advantage of superior technology. Eventually, between 14–15 June 1982, the Falklands were returned to British rule. A thousand Argentinean and British troops died in the campaign, before the Argentine force, of 12,000, ultimately surrendered.

Argentina still holds with its claim on sovereignty over the Falklands. In 1990 it created a new state, Tierra del Fuego, and claimed the Falkland islands and other British-held South Atlantic Islands to be part of it. An agreement on oil rights in surrounding waters was signed in 1995.

))))➤ *Margaret Thatcher*

ABOVE: A British paratrooper opens fire on enemy lines during the Falklands War.
RIGHT: Michael Faraday proved the connection between magnetizm and electricity by moving a compass needle along an electrical current.

FARADAY, MICHAEL (1791–1867)

British physicist and chemist. Initially an assistant to Humphry Davy, Michael Faraday was a pioneer of electromagnetic investigation. He was the first to show that electrical energy can be translated into motive force, by building a prototype electric motor. Conversely, he demonstrated that motive force could be converted into electricity – magnetic induction – by inventing the dynamo. Faraday also pioneered scientific understanding of electrolysis by enunciating the appropriate laws.

FASCISM

Form of government that puts the glory of the nation or state before the individual. Fascism advocates rule by an authoritarian leader who personifies the nation's ideals, opposes democratic and socialist movements, and embraces racism, such as anti-semitism, and military aggression. The term was first used by

BELOW: Queen Isabella of Spain.

Benito Mussolini for his National Fascist Party, founded in 1921. It has been used to describe other forms of right-wing nationalism, such as Hitler's National Socialism and the Franco regime in Spain. Fascist regimes have existed for varying periods in other countries, including Austria, Argentina and Greece.

Fascism was at the height of its popularity between 1919 and 1945. A combination of factors, including the after-effects of World War I, unemployment, the Depression of the 1930s and the rise of Communism, turned fascist ideas into a political force. The movement found support from a range of groups, including the discontented working and middle classes, and the powerful capitalist class. Fascist leaders exercised state control over all areas of economic activity, but protected the interests of the capitalists. Special police forces were used to instill fear in the population and to control behaviour and dissent.

The movement usually took hold in countries that were economically under-developed or had a tradition of strong authoritarian rule. Mussolini's Fascist Party promised modernization and appealed to the national pride among Italians, crushed after World War I. German National Socialism was more racist and attracted the bankers and industrialists by its anti-Communism and by its promise to rebuild the German economy.

))))▶ *Dictatorship, Francisco Franco, Adolf Hitler, Benito Mussolini*

FERDINAND (1452–1516) AND ISABELLA OF SPAIN (1451–1504)

Ferdinand was King of Aragon in his own right from 1479, and King of Castile through his marriage to Isabella, adding Naples by war in 1504.

Castile passed to their daughter on Isabella's death, but her husband, Philip of the Netherlands, ruled as regent until his death in 1506, when Ferdinand assumed it, passing an intact inheritance to his grandson Charles V, Holy Roman Emperor, in 1516.

The reign saw the final expulsion of Islam from Spain in 1492, and the unification of Spain as a Catholic nation. Administration was centralized although the regions retained their identities. Feudal power was suppressed, parliamentary influence declined, and magistrates appointed by the monarchs replaced local officials. Any Jew or Muslim failing to convert was expelled, costing Spain talent. A Papal Bull established the Inquisition to enforce Catholic orthodoxy. Ferdinand and Isabella funded Christopher Columbus's 1492 voyage seeking a westerly route to Asia, but the discovery of America led to Spanish power being widely established thanks to the papal allocation of territory in the New World.

))))▶ *Christopher Columbus, Inquisition*

FERDINAND, ARCHDUKE FRANZ (1863–1914)

Heir to the Habsburg crowns of Austria and Hungary, through his uncle, Emperor Franz Josef I, after the suicide of his cousin Rudolf in 1889, and his father's death in 1896. Highly committed to the monarchy, he acted against the nobility who challenged imperial authority, but he was also prepared to consider reform. He was profoundly opposed to Serbian nationalism and visited Sarajevo in Bosnia on 28 June 1914, the anniversary of the end of Serbian independence. He and his wife, Sophia, were assassinated there by Serbian nationalists, 'The Black Hand', triggering events leading to the outbreak of World War I.

))))▶ *World War I*

FEUDALISM (8TH – 14TH CENTURIES)

Political and military system in Western Europe. Feudalism represented the granting of fiefs (land) by a lord to a vassal in return for his personal loyalty. The early Frankish kingdoms in the eighth century established the practice and it spread with the Frankish conquests into northern Italy, Spain, Germany and the Slavic kingdoms. After the Normans conquered England in 1066 it was adopted there and in Scotland and Ireland. Crusader knights brought it to the Near East. Military service was central to feudalism but, by the thirteenth century, payments had replaced this. By the fourteenth century it was no longer a political or social force. The feudal system was also used to describe the triangular social hierarchy adopted in the Middle Ages, in which the monarch stood at the top and the serfs at the bottom, little more than slaves.

FIVE-YEAR PLANS

Strategic programmes to develop the Soviet economy. Stalin initiated the first five-year plan (1928–33) to speed up the industrialization of the Soviet economy and to collectivize agriculture. This led to riots as peasant farmers withheld crops and famine ensued. Nonetheless, five-year plans formed the basis of the

ABOVE: The rise of feudalism in the Middle Ages involved landowners granting land to their serfs in return for their loyalty and service.
RIGHT: The US automobile manufacturer Henry Ford sitting in his first prototype model of a car.

USSR's economic policy as it developed light and heavy industry in a primarily agricultural country. Similar plans were carried out in other Communist countries and in some developing nations.

◗ *Joseph Stalin*

FLEMING, ALEXANDER (1881–1955)

Scottish scientist. In 1941, during World War II, commercial production of penicillin began. The theatre of war was the perfect setting to show how remarkable this antibiotic was at combating bacterially infected wounds. Alexander Fleming was the man behind the discovery of penicillin. He had been researching pathogenic *Staphylococci* bacteria and noticed that a mould called *Penicillium notatum* secreted a substance that inhibited growth in the bacteria. He won the Nobel Prize for Medicine in 1945.

FORD, HENRY (1863–1947)

American industrialist and automobile pioneer. In 1903 he founded the Ford Motor Company and in 1908–09 developed the famous Model T vehicle (discontinued after sales of 15 million in 1927). In 1913 he began using standardized interchangeable parts and assembly line methods of manufacture, which became widespread practices throughout American industry, greatly increasing productivity. A pacifist, Ford visited Europe in 1915–16 to try to end the war. During World War II the Ford Company manufactured 8,000 bombers.

◗ *World War II*

RIGHT: St Francis of Assisi.

FOX, GEORGE (1624–91)

Founder of the Quakers. Fox preached to an enormous crowd at Pentecost 1652, the date when The Religious Society of Friends is traditionally considered to have begun. Fox had remarkable energy and vision, teaching the Holy Spirit could come directly to people without the mediation of Church or scripture. The origin of the term 'Quaker' possibly derives from the Spirit of God making people tremble or 'quake'. Originally a term of abuse, it is now a familiar name for the Religious Society of Friends.

FRANCIS OF ASSISI, ST (c. 1181–1226)

A native of Assisi and born into a wealthy family, Francis was led to a complete change of lifestyle when, after hearing at Mass Jesus's commission (*Matthew* 10:7-19) in 1209, he founded the Franciscan Order. It was based on joyous worship of Christ and poverty. Francis, in 1214, travelled to Palestine to convert the Muslims but failed. The Order was approved by Innocent III and tradition says that on 14 September 1224 he received the stigmata on his hands and feet. Traditionally kind and gentle to animals, he is believed to have created the first 'crib scene' now familiar at Christmas time in Christian homes and churches.

FRANCO, FRANCISCO (1892–1975)

Spanish dictator (1939–75). As army general, Franco led the Nationalist rebels to victory in the Spanish Civil War (1936–39). With help from a fascist Italy and Nazi Germany, Franco invaded Spain from Morocco and established a corporate state. He kept Spain officially out of World War II, although he sent aid to the German side, and in 1947 he declared Spain a kingdom and himself regent. In 1969 he named Prince Juan Carlos as his successor.
))))➡ *Spanish Civil War, World War II*

FRANCO-PRUSSIAN WAR (1870–71)

Otto von Bismarck (1815–98) became chancellor of the Northern German Federation – Prussia – in 1867. He had ambitions to annex parts of northern France in creating a German Empire. In 1870 Bismarck put forward a German candidate for the Spanish throne which had become vacant at that time. It was a strategic move designed to provoke the French emperor Napoleon III (1808–73) into declaring war.

The Franco-Prussian War began in the same year and lasted until 1871. The Battle of Sedan in the Ardennes, France, saw Napoleon III surrender to Bismarck's army, which then laid siege to Paris. Eventually the Treaty of Frankfurt was signed in May 1871. The result was that France surrendered Alsace and Lorraine to Prussia, as well as paying a large indemnity. Bismarck became Imperial Chancellor of Prussia. In the same year, William I became emperor of all Germany.
))))➡ *Otto von Bismarck*

FRANKLIN, BENJAMIN (1706–90)

American scientist. Franklin was a man of many talents. He played an active role in the American Revolution by enlisting the help of the French on the colonial side, and became president of Pennsylvania in the post-war years, championing anti-slavery sentiments. He was also a scientist; fascinated by electricity, he showed that lightning is electrical by using a wet kite line to conduct lightning into an electrical cell. He invented the lightning conductor as a result, and explained electrical flow by distinguishing between negative and positive electricity.

FREDERICK II OF DENMARK (1534–88)

King of Denmark and Norway from 1559. The reign was defined by the northern Seven Years' War with Sweden, which started in 1563 over competition for supremacy in the Baltic. Frederick's plan was to conquer Sweden and unify all three countries. In this he comprehensively failed and, in 1570, peace secured Sweden's independence. Thereafter, Frederick exploited and improved Denmark's control of access to the Baltic to raise money to rebuild the country. He provided facilities for the astronomer Tycho Brahe.

))))◆ *Seven Years' War*

LEFT: Frederick the Great, King of Denmark and Norway, is approached by a petitioner with a letter.

FREDERICK II OF PRUSSIA (1712–86)

Prussian ruler and conqueror. Frederick II of Prussia (Frederick the Great) was son of Frederick William I of Prussia, a ruthless and successful ruler. Frederick was highly educated. At this time, Germany consisted of numerous autonomous states. In 1740 Frederick succeeded and started to seek more territory. By 1745 the empire had been forced to hand over Silesia and Glatz. In 1756 he attacked Saxony, leading to the Seven Years' War and victory for Prussia. In 1772 he secured part of Poland in an agreement with Russia. Frederick was a highly efficient administrator, organizing agricultural, educational and industrial improvements.

))))◆ *Prussia, Seven Years' War*

FRENCH EAST INDIA COMPANY (1664)

Commercial company established in 1664. Its first trading post was founded in Bombay in 1675 and its main base at Pondicherry in 1676. The company's operations were extended to China and Persia. Reorganized with the American and African French colonial companies in 1719 as the Compagnie des Indes, it suffered successive losses except in India, where it prospered. French control was limited to southern India between 1751 and 1761. The Company's operations were suspended in 1769 and its capital turned over to the French Crown. A new company established in 1785 failed to survive the French Revolution.

))))◆ *British East India Company, Dutch East India Company, French Revolution*

FRENCH REVOLUTION (1789–99)

In the latter half of the eighteenth century the common people of France were growing increasingly resentful of the of the way they were being treated. They lived under a regime of absolute monarchy and were subjected to feudal laws which kept them in poverty whilst those in high society lived in the lap of luxury.

The French Revolution began on 5 May 1789, when Louis XVI attempted to increase taxation. His states general (political and religious leaders) formed a National Assembly and tried to establish constitutional control at a meeting in Versailles, sensing the unrest of the population. Further repressive measures taken by Louis finally provoked a mob in Paris to storm the Bastille Prison on 14 July. The mob freed seven prisoners and killed the governor and most of the garrison before razing the building to the ground.

In 1791 the National Assembly drew up a constitution ending feudalism, which Louis XVI accepted under duress, as a prisoner. 1792 saw France at war with Austria, but the revolution remained on course. The National Convention then declared France a republic and abolished the monarchy.

A mob stormed the Tuileres palace and Louis, with his wife Marie Antoinette and family, were guillotined for treason in 1793. A Reign of Terror, led by Maximilien Robespierre lasted until he was overthrown in 1794. A Directory then held power until Napoleon became dictator in 1799.

))))➧ *Storming of the Bastille, Louis XVI of France, Marie Antoinette of France, Maximilien Robespierre*

ABOVE: European crowned heads began to roll during the French Revolution. This picture depicts the execution of Louis XVI at the guillotine.
RIGHT: Sigmund Freud, father of psychoanalysis.

FREUD, SIGMUND (1856–1939)

Austrian neurologist and founder of psychoanalysis. In 1873 he graduated from Sperl Gymnasium and joined the University of Vienna. In 1882 he trained with the psychiatrist Theodor Meynert and Hermann Nothnagel at the General Hospital in Vienna and was appointed lecturer in neuropathology in 1885. Freud opened a clinical practice in neuropsychology in Vienna and continued this work for almost 50 years, studying hysteria, psychological disorders, human bisexuality, erotogenic zones, free association, resistance and unconscious thoughts. In 1895 he wrote *Project for a Scientific Psychology* (published in 1950, 11 years after his death). Freud has been called 'the most influential intellectual legislator of his age'.

))))➧ *Carl Jung*

GAGARIN, YURI (1934–68)

Russian cosmonaut and first person to travel in space. In 1961 Gagarin rode aboard the satellite Vostok I on a single orbit of the Earth at 27,400 km/h (17,000 mph) between 180 and 327 km (112 and 203 miles) above the Earth's surface. Gagarin was killed in the crash of a test aircraft.

))))➤ *Space Race*

GALEN, CLAUDIUS (c. AD 129 – c. 199)

Ancient Greek physician. The field of medicine in Ancient Greece was one of superstition. Galen became the first person to attempt a theoretical framework for the workings of the body. He experimented on animals and humans alike to find out as much as he could. He made many discoveries simply because no one else had ever looked. His theories of the Four Humours were followed for centuries.

))))➤ *Ancient Greece*

GALILEI, GALILEO (1564–1642)

Italian scientist. Galileo Galilei pioneered the modern method of scientific investigation by experimentation. He is thought to have been the first to notice that a pendulum swings at a constant frequency even though its arc decreases with gradual loss of momentum, and therefore noted its value for timekeeping. Galileo showed Aristotle was wrong by demonstrating that objects of different weight but the same density will fall at equal rates (allowing for air resistance) by dropping objects from the tower at Pisa. He also discovered the parabolic flight paths of projectiles, which was of practical importance in ballistics warfare.

))))➤ *Isaac Newton*

GAMA, VASCO DA (c. 1460–1524)

Portuguese explorer and navigator, first European to reach India by the sea route around Africa. He sailed in July 1497 from Lisbon with four ships and was out of sight of land for over 13 weeks before sighting Natal. Mutiny on board, opposition on land, an outbreak of scurvy and fierce storms impeded his progress, but he reached the Malabar coast of India in May 1498. With a subsequent voyage, da Gama founded colonies in southern Africa, broke the Muslim monopoly on trade with India and established Lisbon as the centre of the European spice trade and a world power.

GANDHI, INDIRA (1917–84)

Indian politician. Daughter of India's first prime minister Jawaharlal Nehru, she herself served two terms as prime minister (1966–77 and 1980–84). Her government became increasingly authoritarian. When faced with questions over the validity of her re-election in 1975, she declared a state of emergency, suspending civil rights and imprisoning her opponents. She was defeated in 1977, mainly due to her unpopular programme of social and economic reforms. Gandhi was re-elected in 1980, but assassinated four years later by her Sikh bodyguards following her use of troops to attack the Golden Temple in Amritsar, the Sikhs' holiest shrine. Her son Rajiv succeeded her as prime minister.

))))➤ *Sikhism*

GANDHI, MAHATMA (1869–1948)

Indian political and spiritual leader. Called 'the Mahatma' ('great-souled'), Gandhi fought for Indian independence from Great Britain through a policy of non-violence or passive resistance. In 1915 he returned to India from South Africa, where he had been a human-rights lawyer defending the country's Indian community, and became leader of the Indian National Congress party. He denounced Western dress and customs, aiming to lead a simple spiritual life. He preached religious tolerance and advocated the end of India's caste system. Gandhi organized

LEFT: Galileo Galilei perfected the lens of the refracting telescope and exploited the phenomenon of the pendulum as a time-keeping device.

civil disobedience and hunger strikes, and was imprisoned a number of times by the British authorities, including a spell during World War II when he refused to co-operate. He was a major influence in the negotiations for independence in 1947, but was deeply distressed by the religious partition of the country into Pakistan and India. Violence broke out between Hindus and Muslims and Gandhi was assassinated by a Hindu nationalist.

GARIBALDI, GIUSEPPE (1807–82)

Italian soldier. Garibaldi was responsible for most of the victories of the *Risorgimento* (Nationalist movement), the most famous of which was conquering Sicily and Naples in 1860 with his army of Redshirts. This contributed to the formation of the kingdom of Italy under Victor Emmanuel II. Before that, his political beliefs had led to his exile in South America where he fought as a mercenary. Garibaldi was a master of guerilla warfare: he fought against Austria (1848–49), led two unsuccessful campaigns to overthrow papal rule in Rome, served in the Austrian War of 1866 and helped France fight the Franco-Prussian War (1870–71).

)))➤ *Franco-Prussian War, Victor Emmanuel II*

ABOVE: Giuseppe Garibaldi drove the Neapolitan army contingent out of Sicily and played a crucial role in the unification of modern-day Italy.

BELOW: A sixth-grader shows Bill Gates the computer she uses at a school in Harlem, New York City.

GARRAT, BILLY 'THE KID' (1859–81)

Notorious gunfighter. Reputedly killing 27 men, he led a life of theft and lawlessness, often with gangs of men. In 1880 he stood trial for murder and sentenced to hang, but escaped, killing two men, and remained at large for three months when he was shot dead (aged 21).

GATES, BILL (b. 1955)

American businessman, co-founder in 1975, chairman and chief executive of the Microsoft Corporation, which introduced such innovations as MS-DOS, the operating system for the IBM personal computer, and Microsoft Word software. Gates' technical brilliance and business acumen have made him unimaginably wealthy (£37.5 billion in 2001). The US government, however, laid monopoly charges against Microsoft.

GENERAL AGREEMENT ON TARIFFS AND TRADE (GATT) (1947)

Treaty signed in Geneva in 1947 by 23 non-Communist nations to create an international forum for expanding multilateral trade and settling trade disputes. GATT members agreed to treat all other members equally and to strive to abolish all non-tariff trade barriers. In 1994 the World Trade Organization superseded GATT, extending the original mandate to include trade in services, intellectual property rights and investment and, since February 1997, the liberalization of the telecommunications trade.

GENETIC ENGINEERING

When James Watson (b. 1828) and Francis Crick (b. 1916) discovered the chemical structure of DNA (deoxyribonucleic acid) in 1953, the way was opened for genetic engineering to become a part of progress in the biological sciences. Genetic engineering is done by a technique known as gene splicing, which involves the cutting and rejoining of genes, just like lengths of film. As all living things use the same basic molecule – DNA – for coding this means that sections of gene can be transplanted from one species to another totally unrelated species, thereby arriving at new species with unique traits.

GENEVA CONVENTION (1949)

International treaties protecting civilians sick and wounded in war. Henri Dunant, founder of the Red Cross, established the Convention for the Amelioration of the Wounded in Time of War (1864). It stated that places dealing with the wounded should not be captured or destroyed, the wounded of all sides should be treated equally, civilians aiding wounded should be protected and the Red Cross symbol should be recognized. Adopted by most great European powers and other states it was extended (1906). During World War II many conventions were abused, leading to four new conventions, approved in Geneva on 12 August 1949.

))))➤ *World War II*

GEORGE III OF ENGLAND (1738–1820)

King of Great Britain and Ireland from 1760. Grandson and successor of George II, following the death of his father, Frederick. George sought supportive prime ministers, initially depending on his old tutor, the Earl of Bute, forced to resign after ending the Seven Years' War on unfavourable terms. Lord North's pro-George administration of 1770–82 foundered on the loss of the American colonies in the Revolution. George's appointment of Pitt the Younger led to the erosion of royal power over government. Later years were taken up with the French Revolutionary and Napoleonic Wars, and the regency of the future George IV during George III's later periods of dementia.

))))➤ *American Revolution, Regency, Seven Years' War*

RIGHT: George III of England.

GERMAN DEMOCRATIC REPUBLIC (1949)

Official name of East Germany. Established in 1949 from the former Soviet occupation zone, East Germany was a satellite state of the USSR. The Berlin Wall was built in 1961 to halt the flow of refugees to West Germany and as leader (1971–89) Eric Honecker presided over one of the most politically repressive police states in the Soviet bloc. In 1989, Honecker was ousted, the hated secret police disbanded and the borders were reopened. Reunification with West Germany occurred the following year.

))))➤ *Berlin Wall, Cold War*

GHENGIS KHAN (1162–1227)

Mongol ruler and conqueror. Born in central Asia near Lake Bailal, inheriting lands controlled by his father, Yesukei, stretching from the River Amur in the west to the Great Wall of China in the east. In 1206 he was awarded the name Genghis Khan ('Mighty Ruler'). China refused him tribute so in around 1212 he invaded north China, following this with more wars of conquest, which extended his power west and south to northern India.

BELOW: The Battle of Gettysburg was decisive in the outcome of the American Civil War.

BOTTOM RIGHT: Egypt's ancestral glory is evident from monuments like the Sphinx and the Pyramids of Giza, the last of the world's ancient wonders.

By 1227 his dominions extended from Persia and the Black Sea in the west to Korea and parts of China in the east. He left no permanent form of government but the Mongol Empire continued to grow, becoming the largest in history.

))))➤ *Mongols*

GETTYSBURG, BATTLE OF (1863)

Battle during the American Civil War. The Battle of Gettysburg took place to the north-west of Baltimore in Pennsylvania on 1–3 July 1863. The defeated Confederates suffered heavy losses and it proved a turning point in the war. With a Union win at Vicksburg in the same week, the Confederacy remained on the defensive for the remainder of the conflict.

))))➤ *American Civil War, Confederacy, Abraham Lincoln*

GIZA, GREAT PYRAMID OF (2600 BC)

Egyptian monument. One of a cluster of monuments at Giza which includes the slightly smaller (and younger) pyramids of Khafre and Menkaure as well as the figure of the Sphinx, the Great Pyramid was one of the Wonders of the Ancient World. Built around 2600 BC, as a tomb for the Pharaoh Khufu,

it still seems extraordinarily imposing today, possibly the most massive single building ever constructed. Standing at just under 150 m (492 ft) in height, and measuring over 200 m (656 ft) on each side at the base, it has been calculated to contain some 2.3 m (7.5 ft) blocks of stone.

))))➤ *Hanging Gardens of Babylon, Wonders of the Ancient World, Sphinx*

GOBIND SINGH, GURU (1666–1708)

Tenth guru of Sikhism. He emphasized martial values in defending religious freedom. At Baisakhi (a festival) in 1699 he inaugurated the Khalsa (community) characterized by the wearing of the 'Five Ks' and a code of conduct. He then assumed the name 'Singh' (lion), as do all male members of the Khalsa, females take 'Kaur' (princess). At his death he ordered Sikhs to accept the book, the *Adi Granth* (Guru Granth Sahib) as the final 'living' guru.

))))➤ *Sikhism*

GOERING, HERMANN WILHELM (1893–1946)

Prime minister of Germany from 1933 and Nazi leader. Goering had been a flying ace in World War I, and built up the Luftwaffe as commissioner for aviation before World War II. He also directed the construction of the concentration camps. The failure of the Luftwaffe over Britain led to his expulsion from the Nazi party. He poisoned himself, having been sentenced to death for war crimes at Nuremberg.

))))➤ *Concentration Camps, Nazi Party, World War I, World War II*

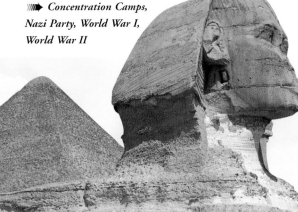

GOLD STANDARD (1816)

System wherein money may be exchanged, on demand, for gold. It existed to facilitate settlement of international transactions and to stabilize foreign exchange rates and domestic money supply. Most countries adopted it between 1816 (UK) and 1900. After the Great Depression nearly all relinquished it, believing that devaluing their currencies in foreign-exchange terms would boost their exports. Once most countries had followed suit, none retained any competitive advantage. Gold is now more of a commodity than a standard.

))))▶ *Great Depression*

GORBACHEV, MIKHAIL (b. 1931)

Last president of the USSR (1988–91). Gorbachev's policies of *glasnost* ('openness') and *perestroika* ('restructuring') radically altered Soviet society. They also led ultimately the break-up of the USSR and downfall of Communism in Eastern Europe. In 1991 hard-liners attempted to overthrow Gorbachev, and by the end of the year he resigned as president, following the formation of the Commonwealth of Independent States led by Boris Yeltsin which had left him out of a job.

))))▶ *Communism, Boris Yeltsin*

GOTHIC

Architectural, literary and artistic style. To begin with the derogatory label attached by Renaissance architects to what they saw as the barbaric irregularities of medieval style, the term was afterwards enthusiastically taken up by adherents of romanticism. Reacting against the certainties of Enlightenment thought, its unquestioning faith in the boundless possibilities of reason and science, they were attracted by an artistic outlook which seemed to suggest that life still had its unfathomable mysteries. Hence the vogue for horrific 'gothic novels' – all ancestral curses and mad monks – and, increasingly, for neo-medievalism in architecture. If neoclassicism,

LEFT: Mikhail Gorbachev, former president of the Soviet Union, is best remembered today for his policies of Perestroika and Glasnost which were partly responsible for bringing an end to Communism in Russia.
BELOW: The buttressed façade of a church in typical Gothic architectural style.

in its perfect symmetries, suggested man's ability to impose his order on an untidy nature, the riotous disorder of the old cathedrals – with their crazy spires, their tortuous stonework, their grotesque gargoyles – represented its exact opposite. For later connoisseurs like John Ruskin the architectural anarchy that the gothic appeared to reveal suggested construction as a collective effort by a workforce of skilled craftsmen left free to be creative. This contrasted all too starkly with the degradation of labour in the mechanization of the industrial age: where the Enlightenment had regarded the old cathedrals as symbols of subjection, now they could be seen as a symbol of liberation.

))))▶ *Arts and Crafts Movement, Romanticism*

BELOW: A 1930s cartoon conveys the misery and poverty experienced by Americans during the Great Depression, their most severe economic slump.

GREAT DEPRESSION (1929–39)

Severest economic depression. It began in the USA but spread to become a worldwide economic slump, hitting European countries most indebted to the USA, including Great Britain and Germany. Germany had six million unemployed. In the USA 11,000 banks failed and unemployment rose to between 12 and 15 million. Manufacturing output by 1932 was 54 per cent of 1929 levels and world trade had fallen by half. Countries were imposing tariffs and quotas on foreign imports. It directly led to the rise of Adolf Hitler in Germany, who ended the depression by public work projects and the expansion of the munitions industry.

))))➤ *Prohibition*

GREAT EXHIBITION (1851)

Trade fair held in London, May–October 1851. Ostensibly an international exhibition to display the achievements of all nations, the Great Exhibition inevitably ended up a shop window for the products of Britain's own Industrial Revolution. Held in a specially constructed 'Crystal Palace', the exhibition, its committee chaired by Albert, the Prince Consort, served only to highlight the enormous lead British industry still had at the time over its nearest competitors on the continent and in North America.

))))➤ *Industrial Revolution*

GREAT FIRE OF LONDON (1666)

Worst fire in the history of London. The fire began in a baker's premises in Pudding Lane and an easterly wind exacerbated the flames, causing it to rage for two days. It was extinguished at one point but then it enflamed itself again at the Temple, causing some houses to be blown up by gunpowder. The fire destroyed most of the civic buildings of London, including 13,000 houses, 87 churches and St Paul's Cathedral. Many of the refugees, made homeless from the fire, fled the city by boat on the River Thames, travelling to Hampstead, Highgate and Moorfields.

))))➤ *Plague*

GREAT SCHISM (1378)

The 'Great Schism' refers to two unrelated events: the excommunication by Rome in 1054 of the Patriarch of Constantinople, and the disputed elections of Urban VI. The doctrinal reason for the excommunication merely set a seal on the rift between the Eastern and Western church that had lasted for centuries. The papal schism in the Western church (1378–1417) arose from the disputed election of Urban VI. Disaffected cardinals elected Clement VII, a cousin of the French king, who took up residence in Avignon. In 1409, the two sides met, disagreed and created a third pope at Pisa. In 1415 at the Council of Constance the Pisa pope was deposed; the Roman pope, Gregory XII resigned. The Avignon pope took refuge in Spain where his successor finally repudiated claims in 1429.

))))➤ *Clement VII, Urban VI*

GREAT TREK (1835–40s)

Migration of the Boers from the Cape of Good Hope. Following the emancipation of the Boers' slaves (1833), and the return of land to African tribes (1836), Boer families moved north in order to escape British control. The Voortrekkers, as they were called, led by Pieter Retief and Andries Pretorius, settled in Natal (1838–39). Their defensive encampments proved too powerful for the Zulus and the Boers were able to settle on the east coast.

GREAT WALL OF CHINA (7TH CENTURY BC)

The only human-built construction able to be seen from orbit. The defensive construction began on the 'Square Wall' in the northern part of the kingdom from earth and stone, terminating at the shores of the Yellow Sea. The Great Wall, through several centuries and different leaders, was constructed from castles and fortifications of the several different Chinese kingdoms, mainly to protect them from threats of invasion. The first Ch'in Emperor, Shih Huang-ti saw the unification of China.

))))▶ *Ch'in Dynasty, Mongol Empire*

GREENPEACE (1971)

International organization founded in British Columbia. This non-violent organization is dedicated to preserving endangered species of animals, preventing environmental abuse and heightening environmental awareness. It was first formed to oppose US nuclear testing on the island of Amchitka (Alaska). Campaigns have included the protection of endangered

LEFT: Chinese tourists walk along the Great Wall of China, the only man-made construction visible from outer space.
BELOW: Che Guevara, Cuban revolutionary and writer, joined forces with the Castro brothers in the 1960s and formed a guerilla movement to depose Batista.

whales and seals, the end of nuclear weapon testing and the stopping of the dumping of toxic chemical and radioactive materials at sea. The majority of staff are volunteers.

GREGORIAN CALENDAR (1582)

Reform of the Julian calendar also known as the new style calendar. Proclaimed by Pope Gregory XIII in 1582, this is a solar dating system that is now in general use and involved advancing the Julian calendar by 10 days after 4 October 1582, making the following day 15 October and not 5 October. It was adopted by Italy, Portugal, Spain and Catholic Germany (1583), Protestant Germany (1699), England (1752), Sweden (1753), Japan (1853), China (1912), the Soviet Union (1913) and Greece (1923). The Gregorian calendar is said to capable of remaining accurate to within one day in 20,000 years.

))))▶ *Julian Calendar*

GUEVARA, ERNESTO 'CHE' (1928–67)

Cuban revolutionary. Argentine-born doctor and political activist, Ernesto 'Che' Guevara joined Cuban brothers Fidel and Raul Castro in their guerilla campaign to overthrow Fulgencio Batista. He was Castro's chief lieutenant in the revolution (1956–59) and served as minister of industry (1961–65) in the new

government. He left Cuba to train revolutionaries in Africa and Latin America, but was caught and executed by the Bolivian army in 1967.

))))▶ *Fulgencio Batista, Fidel Castro*

GULF WAR (1991)

War ostensibly fought over territory, although the real agenda was ownership and control of oil reserves. On 2 August 1990, Iraq, under the leadership of Saddam Hussein, invaded and annexed Kuwait. The move was provoked by a dispute over a shared oilfield.

Iraq found itself isolated, facing a coalition of 28 nations prepared to take action on behalf of Kuwait, and spearheaded by USA. All had vested interests in maintaining supplies of crude oil to their respective countries. Over the next five months troops piled into Saudi Arabia in preparation for an offensive. By January 1991 there were 500,000 US, 42,000 UK, 15,000 French and 20,000 Egyptian troops, plus smaller forces from other nations.

The United Nations Security Council authorized the use of military force on Iraq if it didn't withdraw from Kuwait by 15 January. It didn't, and action began the following day. The Gulf War lasted for six weeks and was an easy victory for the Allies. The Iraqi army and strategic targets were subjected to overwhelming bombardment from 'smart' weaponry that totally outclassed anything the Iraqis had to offer. Kuwait was liberated and the war was over by 28 February.

))) ➤ *Saddam Hussein, United Nations*

GUPTA EMPIRE (AD 320–550)

India's classical age. From AD 320, Chandragupta I founded the Gupta dynasty after conquering neighbouring states. His grandson Chandragupta II (AD 375–413) expanded the Empire to incorporate all of India north of the Narmada River. The Empire flourished

ABOVE: The 1991 Gulf War in Kuwait was given the most intensive media coverage of any event in world history.
RIGHT: The German printer Johann Gutenberg revolutionised the printing process by devising a system for using individual types of characters movable within a frame.

for 160 years as the centre of Hinduism, music, art and literature. Notably, Sanskrit became the universal language of the subcontinent. Whilst Rome was in decline, the great masterpieces of Indian literature, including the epic *Mahabharata*, were being composed. Buddhist monks established magnificent temples along the Silk Road and converted millions of Chinese to the faith. Gupta culture influenced countries as far afield as Cambodia and Vietnam. By the end of the fifth century, reeling under the attacks of the White Huns, who had followed in the footsteps of the Mongol invaders, the Gupta Empire broke up, finally disappearing by the middle of the sixth century. The Empire has been compared to Hellenism in terms of its influence.

))) ➤ *Buddhism, Hinduism*

GUSTAVUS ADOLPHUS OF SWEDEN (1594–1632)

King of Sweden from 1611. A skilled strategist, Gustavus faced war with several countries simultaneously. He reformed and modernized his armies, negotiated peace with Denmark, fought Russia in 1617, and then Poland, securing an advantageous settlement in 1629. His purpose thereafter was to dominate Baltic trade, and intended to do this by controlling Protestant German states, entering the Thirty Years' War in 1631 to do so, but was killed at the Swedish victory of Lutzen in 1632.

))) ➤ *Thirty Years' War*

GUTENBERG, JOHANN (1400–68)

German printer. Though it is said to have been in use much earlier in China – and even, it has been claimed, in Minoan Crete – the invention of printing in the West is generally attributed to Johann Gutenberg. Working in Mainz with various partners, Gutenberg developed a printing press with movable type, finally producing the first ever printed edition of the Bible.

))) ➤ *Printing*

his marriage in 1477 the Low Countries, Burgundy, and later Spain and her possessions, while a treaty in 1491 secured the eventual passing of Hungary and Bohemia to the Habsburgs.

Under the Emperor Charles V (r. 1519–56), Habsburg power was at its peak but the lands were divided between him and his brother Ferdinand, who took Austria, Hungary and Bohemia.

The Habsburgs struggled to control such vast dominions, especially as nationalist and ethnic consciousness developed during the nineteenth century. This led to the Serbian nationalists assassinating Franz Ferdinand, archduke of Austria-Hungary in 1914.

))))➤ *Holy Roman Empire, Archduke Franz Ferdinand*

HABSBURG EMPIRE (1273–1918)

European royal family which dominated European history for five centuries until 1918, named after the family castle Habsburg ('Hawk's Castle') in Switzerland.

Serious power began with Rudolf I, a Habsburg, elected king in Germany in 1273. Rudolf conquered Austria, which thereafter became the most important part of the Hapsburg possessions. He and his successors were dukes of Austria, becoming archdukes in the fifteenth century.

Frederick III, a descendant of Rudolf, was created Holy Roman Emperor in 1452. Although the title was elective, under the Habsburgs it became effectively hereditary until the Empire came to an end in 1806. His son, Maximilian I (r. 1493–1519), secured through

HADRIAN, EMPEROR (AD 76–138)

Roman Emperor from AD 117, succeeding Trajan. Hadrian abandoned Trajan's conquests and fixed the Empire's frontiers, touring the provinces and frontier armies, encouraging discipline and instigating Hadrian's Wall in Britain. A lover of Greek culture, he modelled his villa at Tivoli on architecture from around the Roman world, and designed the extant Pantheon in Rome, one of the most celebrated buildings of antiquity.

))))➤ *Ancient Rome*

HAIG, GENERAL SIR DOUGLAS (1861–1928)

Commander-in-chief of Allied forces during World War I. General Sir Douglas Haig's command has been severely criticized, due to the heavy losses resulting from some of his policies. Haig oversaw the Somme offensive of 1916. It was a success for the Allies, but 600,000 lives were lost. The fruitless Passchendale offensive of 1917 saw a further 400,000 die. Haig's command was taken by Frenchman Ferdinand Foch (1851–1929) in 1918, who launched the final Allied offensive, winning the war.

))))➤ *Battle of the Somme, Passchendale, World War I*

HALLEY'S COMET (1682)

Comet first sighted in 1682 by British astronomer Edmund Halley (1656–1742). Halley's Comet completes its eccentric orbit once every 76 years. Halley correctly predicted that it would return in 1758, having deduced that earlier sightings in 1531 and 1607 had been the same comet.

HAN DYNASTY (206 BC – AD 220)

Chinese imperial dynasty and golden age of Chinese philosophy. Founded by Liu Pang (256–195 BC), replacing the Ch'in dynasty, there are three distinct periods, each of which ended in disorder and rebellion. In the early years Chinese control spread into Vietnam and Korea. The Chinese silk industry grew; porcelain, paper, water clocks and sundials were extensively traded. Confucianism was the state religion; poetry, mathematics, medicine and philosophy flourished. The last Han emperor abdicated in AD 220.

HANDEL, GEORGE FRIDERIC (1685–1759)

German-born English composer. Born in Hallé, Saxony, the son of a barber, Handel became organist in the cathedral there before taking a position at the court of the Elector of Hanover. When his patron ascended the English throne as George I in 1714, Handel naturally moved to London – though he had in fact made several previous attempts to launch a career in England. As an operatic composer there, Handel enjoyed variable success; not until he began writing oratorios did he achieve real popularity. In this new genre, however, he was hugely successful, and his *Messiah* (1742) has been beloved of audiences ever since.

HANGING GARDENS OF BABYLON

Semi-legendary monument in ancient Mesopotamia. Not strictly 'hanging', the gardens of the royal palace in Babylon were raised up on cleverly constructed tiers of terraces on the roof, and irrigated by water brought from the nearby River Euphrates. Supposedly built by King Nebuchadnezzar II in around 600 BC, or by Queen Sammuramat some two centuries earlier, there has as yet been no certain archeological proof that the gardens ever actually existed, but several classical writers testify to their immense scale and spectacular appearance.

)))➤ *Great Pyramid of Giza, Wonders of the Ancient World*

HANNIBAL (247 – c. 182 BC)

Carthaginian general in the three Punic Wars fought between Rome and the Phoenicians of Carthage, North Africa. The Second Punic War was precipitated by the siege of the Roman town of Sagantum (Sagunto), Spain, by Hannibal. Hannibal took his army overland to Italy in 218 BC, and won a series of campaign battles, but failed to take Rome. He poisoned himself following a Roman victory in Carthage.

)))➤ *Phoenicians, Punic Wars*

LEFT: A prancing horse and rider: image from a Han dynasty tomb in China.

HASTINGS, BATTLE OF (1066)

Decisive battle in the Norman Conquest of England, 14 October 1066. Immortalized in the Bayeux Tapestry, the Battle of Hastings marked the end of the Anglo-Saxon era and the beginning of the Norman era in England. William I, Duke of Normandy, took his army across the Channel and met the army of King Harold II (*c.* 1020–66) at Senlac, just north of Hastings. The French army won and William ('The Conqueror') became king of England. Harold was killed in the battle.

))⟩⟩ *William I of England*

HAYDN, FRANZ JOZEF (1732–1809)

Austrian composer. Educated as a chorister at St Stephen's Cathedral, Vienna, Haydn became a jobbing musician as a young adult. His appointment to the service of the Esterházy household in 1761 was something of a breakthrough. As musical director responsible for the composition and performance of chamber, orchestral, operatic and choral music, he was perfectly placed to develop his native genius. A great composer in his own right, Haydn also had a profound influence on those in the generations that followed, establishing the basic forms of both the string quartet and the classical symphony.

HEISENBERG, WERNER (1901–76)

German physicist. In 1927 Heisenberg drew up the 'uncertainty principle' of quantum mechanics, which states that an atomic particle cannot have a measurable position and momentum simultaneously, because at nanoscale the very act of measuring will disturb the particle so as to nullify the measurement.

))⟩⟩ *Quantum Theory*

HENRI II OF FRANCE (1519–59)

King of France from 1547. From 1526–30 Henry and his elder brother François (d. 1536) were imprisoned by the emperor Charles V as ransom for the freedom of their father, François I, after his defeat. On accession, Henry II continued the war, eventually making peace due to the cost, and the distraction of fighting Protestantism in France through organized persecution. He was killed after a tournament accident.

))⟩⟩ *Holy Roman Empire*

HENRY V OF ENGLAND (1387–1422)

King of England from 1413, son of Henry IV. Henry fought successfully against Welsh rebels led by Owen Glendower, during his father's reign. On accession he immediately acted on his ambition to restore England's power over France. In 1415 he invaded France, winning a devastating victory at Agincourt when English longbow men decimated French mounted knights. A second expedition in 1417 led to the surrender of Rouen in 1419, and his marriage with Catherine, daughter of Charles VI of France, in 1420. By this, Henry became heir to the French throne. However, the war continued and Henry died on campaign in 1422.

))⟩⟩ *Hundred Years' War, Battle of Agincourt*

HENRY VIII OF ENGLAND (1491–1547)

King of England 1509, son of Henry VII and Elizabeth of York whose union had ended the Wars of the Roses. The reign was defined by Henry's quest for a male heir, which led to the introduction of the Protestant Church, and the strengthening of England's international influence.

Highly intelligent, Henry was a talented sportsman and musician, becoming heir after his elder brother, Arthur, died in 1502. Henry married Arthur's widow, Catherine of Aragon, who bore him Mary (afterwards Mary I of England). Advised by Thomas, Cardinal Wolsey, Henry played Spain and France off against each

FAR LEFT: The influence of Austrian composer Franz Josef Haydn can still be felt today in quartet and classical symphony orchestral arrangements.

LEFT: Werner Heisenberg's Uncertainty Principle has become fundamental to understanding quantum physics.

other, making and breaking alliances, seeking to increase England's influence. The pope's refusal to annul the marriage to Catherine so Henry could marry Anne Boleyn led Henry, helped by his adviser Thomas Cromwell, to declare himself head of the Church in England. In 1533 he married Anne, and proceeded to dissolve monasteries and confiscate their wealth.

Anne bore Henry a daughter (afterwards Elizabeth I), but in 1536 Anne was executed for being unfaithful. Henry married Jane Seymour who died in 1537 after bearing a son (afterwards Edward VI).

To strengthen England's Protestant connections, Cromwell arranged for Henry to marry the German Anne of Cleves in 1539. Revolted by her, Henry divorced Anne and executed Cromwell, marrying Catherine Howard in 1540, and executing her for adultery in 1542. In 1543 he married Catherine Parr who survived him.

))) *Elizabeth I of England, Mary I of England*

HENRY THE NAVIGATOR (1394–1460)

Prince of Portugal, patron of navigation and exploration. He established the first school for navigators in Europe and made improvements to shipbuilding. He made no voyages himself but directed many important expeditions along the west coast of Africa, hoping to find a sea route to India and the Far East to secure trade. Henry's navigators reached Madeira (1420), Ras Nouadhibou (1441) and the mouth of the Gambia River (about 1446).

HEROD THE GREAT (c. 72–4 BC)

Ruler of Judaea, established as king by Octavian (Augustus) in 31 BC, as part of his policy of ruling certain regions through pro-Roman puppet monarchs. Herod restored the cities of the region, and began the reconstruction of the Great Temple in Jersualem.

LEFT: King Henry VIII.

However, he jealously guarded his power through massacres of rivals, including some of his family, and the entire Hasmonean dynasty. He is attributed with the Massacre of the Innocents in an effort to wipe out Jesus.

))) *Augustus Caesar*

HERTZ, HEINRICH (1857–94)

German physicist. Heinrich Hertz did much to develop the understanding of electromagnetic radiation. He discovered radio waves, as predicted by James Clerk Maxwell, and also discovered that heat and light are all part of the same electromagnetic spectrum, but at differing wavelengths or frequencies – the two being inversely proportional.

))) *James Clerk Maxwell*

HIJRAH (AD 622)

Hijrah means 'emigration'. The Muslim calendar (AH = al-Hijrah) dates from AD 622 when the Prophet Muhammad emigrated from Mecca to Medina at the invitation of its citizens. Originally called Yathrib, Medina was renamed Medinat al-Nabi ('the City of the Prophet'). It was there that the Prophet organized the Muslims into a religious community before returning to Mecca in AD 630. The event is celebrated as New Year's Day in the Islamic calendar.

HILDEGARD OF BINGEN, ST. (1098–1179)

Medieval mystic and visionary. Hildegard entered a Benedictine community around 1116 and in 1136 became abbess. She recorded her visions, which condemn contemporary vice and prophesy disaster. Hildegard was an accomplished author, artist and composer. She believed men and women were equal in their work for God.

))) *Benedictine Order*

HILLARY, SIR EDMUND (b. 1919)

New Zealand mountaineer and Antarctic explorer. A strong climber, in 1953 he joined the British Mount Everest Expedition, led by John Hunt. On 29 May he and Sherpa Tenzing Norgay became the first known climbers to reach the summit, for which he was later knighted. In 1955, as leader of the New Zealand part of the British Commonwealth Trans-Antarctic Expedition led by Vivian Fuchs, he crossed the continent by snow tractor, the first to cross overland since Robert Scott in 1912. Hillary's Himalayan Trust has built schools, hospitals and airstrips for the Sherpa people and planted new forests.

))))➤ *Captain Robert Scott*

HINDENBURG (1937)

German-built airship that burst into flames on landing at Lakehurst New Jersey, in 1937, killing 36 of its 92 passengers and crew. The airship was 245 m (804 ft) long. She was inflated with 190 million litres (6.7 million cubic ft) of oxygen gas which, being 14.4 times lighter than air, gives more lift than other non-flammable gases such as helium but is highly explosive. The *Hindenburg* had made 10 transatlantic crossings in ordinary commercial service in 1936.

HINDUISM

The word 'Hindu' derives from a Sanskrit work 'sindhu', the name given to the River Indus. It was later applied to the land of India and the religion of its peoples. Hindus also go by the name 'Santana Dharma' ('eternal way of life'). There is no traceable founder nor a moment of origin, which gives rise to a huge diversity of practice based on the difference of linguistic, social, geographic and cultural backgrounds of the Indian people.

There are some common features across this diversity. These include: an acceptance of the importance of the four *Vedas* ('Knowledge'). These are sacred texts traditionally handed down by word of mouth over thousands of years. Other texts such as the *Ramayana* and the *Mahabharata* are less important, but the *Bhagavad Gita* ('Song of the Blessed Lord') which is part of the *Mahabharata* is beloved by many Hindus.

There is an acceptance of karma – the belief that all actions have consequences. Attachment to actions results in being caught up in samsara, the continuous cycle of birth and re-birth. The transcendence of this cycle is moksha ('liberation'), achieved when the person realizes the union between atman, the individual spirit present in all life, and Brahman, the Supreme Spirit. In order to attain moksha one has to follow one's dharma ('that which sustains or upholds'). This means, roughly, to complete one's duty, do what is intrinsic to oneself, i.e. live a true religious life.

There are many schools of Hindu philosophy which re-interpret the basic principles but for most Hindus their religious life is expressed in worship of devas and devis (gods and goddesses) from the well-known – Krishna, Rama, Sita, Vishnu, Ganesha, etc. to the individual spirits that inhabit water holes and trees.

In the Hindu ideal, everyone belongs to one of four varnas. A varna determines a person's social status and responsibility. They are, in descending order, brahmins, kshatriyas, vaishyas and sudras. This is no longer a rigid division in contemporary Hinduism but reflects the broad division of labour. In practice, Hindus associate themselves with jati (castes or sub-castes). This has led to some groups being termed 'outcastes' although the Indian government in its intention to achieve social equality prefers the title dalit ('oppressed').

Hinduism is a set of practices and tradition that has evolved over 5,000 years. Hindus in the villages (80 per cent of the population) live their lives through regular propitiation of village duties, celebrating rites of passage, worship and pilgrimage.

ABOVE: Hinduism is one of the world's most fascinating religions, accounting for approximately 14 per cent of world faith. This is Il al-Bhairab, the Hindu god of terror.

HIROHITO (1901–89)

Emperor of Japan from 1926. Hirohito ruled Japan throughout its wars of aggression in Manchuria, China, and then World War II from 1941. Real power lay with Hideki Tojo, general and premier between 1941–44, with Hirohito playing only a reluctant role. By the end of the war Hirohito favoured unconditional surrender. After the dropping of atomic bombs on Hiroshima and Nagasaki in August 1945 he made the first public address by a Japanese emperor, announcing the surrender. The US-controlled post-war reconstruction of Japan retained Hirohito as a figurehead.

))))➤ *Hiroshima, Nagasaki*

HIROSHIMA (1945)

Japanese city destroyed by the first atomic bomb. On 6 August 1945 US president Harry S. Truman ordered the bombing of Hiroshima when the Japanese army refused to surrender unconditionally. The bomb destroyed most of the city, killed tens of thousands of people instantly and caused many more casualties over time from radiation sickness. Three days later a second bomb was dropped on the port city of Nagasaki and the

BELOW: Following unconditional surrender by the Japanese at the end of World War II, Emperor Hirohito was the first Japanese monarch to renounce his divinity. He is seen here standing underneath the Japanese flag.
BELOW RIGHT: Adolf Hitler, surrounded by his henchmen, delivers the nefarious Nazi Party salute to the crowds.

Japanese surrendered. Estimates of the number of dead for both cities range between 200–250,000. Hiroshima has been rebuilt, though an area was left in its bombed state to create the 'Peace City' memorial.

))))➤ *Nagasaki, Harry S. Truman*

HITLER, ADOLF (1889–1945)

Nazi leader. Hitler was born in Austria, spending his early years in poverty in Vienna and Munich. In his mid twenties he served in World War I as a volunteer and began developing fascist ideas to satisfy his anger at the treatment of Germany after the war. By 1921 he was leader of the National Socialist German Workers Party, which he abbreviated to 'Nazi Party'. Hitler used the Nazi Party as his vehicle for nurturing hatred toward races and creeds that he blamed for the humiliating plight of the German people. By 1933 he had become chancellor of a Nazi–Nationalist coalition. 1934 saw the suppression of the Nationalist contingent and Hitler became Fuehrer. Hitler led the Anschluss with Austria in 1938 and whipped Germany into a frenzy of nationalism in the preparation for World War II. Throughout the war he remained the driving force behind the German campaign, but committed suicide when he realized that the Central Powers were facing defeat.

))))➤ *Anschluss, Concentration Camps, Fascism, Nazi Party, World War II*

HITTITES (2000–1200 BC)

Ancient people who dominated Syria and Asia Minor 2000–1200 BC, the Hittites rank after the Egyptians and Assyrians in importance among the civilizations of the Middle East. According to *Genesis*, they were the followers of Heth, son of Canaan. They are best remembered for their hieroglyphics and cuneiform script.

)))) *Assyrians*

HO CHI MINH (1890–1969)

President of North Vietnam (1954–69). Minh was the leader of the Vietnamese nationalist movement for nearly three decades. After spending time in Moscow, he returned to Vietnam in World War II to found the Communist Viet Minh (1941), the Vietnamese independence movement. His army fought the Japanese when they invaded the country, and drove out the French colonial regime in the Indochina War (1946–54). The Geneva conference in 1954 divided Vietnam in half, and Minh became the first president of North Vietnam. Peace did not last and he lived to see the start of war against the US-backed government of South Vietnam.

)))) *Vietnam War*

HOLOCAUST (1933–45)

Name given to the persecution and extermination of the Jews during World War II. The 'final solution of the Jewish problem' inspired by Adolf Hitler and the Nazi regime in Germany, killed six million Jews. The Ashkenazi, or North European Jews, suffered particularly in the genocide, with the Jewish population of Poland being virtually exterminated. During that period Jews were taken into slave labour, used for medical experiments and identified and humiliated in public through the wearing of a yellow star. Herded on to trains and taken to concentration camps such as Auschwitz and Treblinka, the systematic killing of Jews, plus homosexuals and gypsies, continued until the very end of World War II. The profound shock of the event was an important element in the foundation of the state of Israel in May 1948. The Holocaust Memorial (Yad Vashem) in Jerusalem is a potent sign of that period.

)))) *Concentration Camps, Adolf Hitler, Nazi Party, World War II*

HOLY ROMAN EMPIRE (9TH CENTURY)

Territory ruled by Franks and afterwards Germans from the beginning of the ninth century until 1806. Regarded as the Christian revival of the Roman Empire in the West, it remained one of the most powerful forces throughout medieval Europe. The term 'Holy Roman Empire' dates from the mid-thirteenth century, but the title 'Holy Roman Emperor' is a modern one.

In AD 800 Charlemagne was given the title 'Emperor' by Pope Leo III as a reward for his services to Christian rule. In AD 912 the Frankish title lapsed with the death of Louis IV. In AD 962 the title passed to the German kings through Conrad, Duke of Franconia. Thereafter the title remained elected by German princes (the electors) until 1806 though in practice the title tended to pass through dynasties, principally the Austrian Habsburgs from the fifteenth century, and became synonymous with that line of descent though it was always identified with the German nation.

The emperor controlled extensive lands in Central and Northern Europe, stretching from France across Germany to Austria and beyond, and including Switzerland and northern Italy. The papal origins of the title gave way to a conflict over leadership of Christian Europe. The papacy regarded the Empire as its secular form, and saw itself as the basis of imperial authority, while the emperors attributed their power to military strength and political success, for which they were answerable to God.

By the sixteenth century the effects of the Reformation reduced imperial power and influence when a number of German principalities became Protestant. This enhanced the autonomy of the German electors. The Thirty Years' War (1618–48) had a catastrophic effect on Germany, leaving the imperial title little more than a label.

The end came with Napoleon who tried to

ABOVE: Emperor Charlemagne.

RIGHT: The US magician Harry Houdini, originally a circus and vaudeville performer, found fame with death-defying escapology acts.
BELOW: The Hudson's Bay Company was set up to monopolise fur trade in the region around the Hudson River.

absorb the imperial title into his portfolio. Francis II, the last emperor, changed his title to 'Emperor of the Austrians' to deny it to anyone else, finally bringing it to an end in 1806 to guarantee that no-one could usurp it. The concept of German imperial identity was revived with the nineteenth-century 'Second Reich', and then by Hitler's 'Third Reich'.

▶ **Charlemagne, Habsburg Empire, Thirty Years' War**

HOME RULE (1870)

Movement by Irish nationalists to secure self-government. The modern movement began in 1870 and its vocal leader Charles Stewart Parnell unified the Irish Parliamentary party and publicized the cause. Prime Minister Gladstone was converted and introduced the first Home Rule Bill (1886) but it failed to pass; the second bill (1893) was defeated by the House of Lords. This defeat led to the rise of revolutionary factions, seeking alternatives to constitutional means to achieve self-government. It was a long wait until the third bill (1912), and when it was passed, Protestant Ulster threatened civil war. The Lords excluded Ulster, but the bill was interrupted by World War I. After years of conflict the fourth bill (1920) gave a form of home rule to the six counties of Northern Ireland, though they remained part of Britain. The Anglo-Irish treaty in 1921 recognized the 26 southern counties as the Irish Free State.

HOUDINI (1884-1926)

American magician and escapologist. Houdini's career started as a trapeze artist and from 1882 he performed in New York vaudeville shows. In 1900 he started to perform his escapology act, freeing himself from ropes, handcuffs, straight-jackets, locked containers and chains, often whilst submerged in water. He

was skilled at manipulating locks and had physical strength and agility. He wrote *The Unmasking of Robert-Houdin* (1908), *Miracle Mongers and Their Methods* (1920), *A Magician Among the Spirits* (1924).

HUDSON'S BAY COMPANY (1670)

English corporation formed in 1670. It enjoyed a monopoly in fur trade throughout the Hudson's Bay region. The Company also had power to establish laws, erect forts and maintain warships. A clash with the French over the fur trade was finally settled when the British conquered Canada in 1763. In 1821 the company merged with its great rival, the North West Fur Company of Montreal. It lost its monopoly in 1859 but remained the most important Canadian fur company.

HUGUENOTS

From French *Hugues* ('confederate'), French Calvinist Protestants whose rivalry with Catholics in the form of the House of Guise led to the French Wars of Religion (1562–98). There had been increasing persecution under Henri II (1547–59). Their leader, Henri of Navarre, succeeded to the throne in 1589. In spite of being a Huguenot, he reportedly said, 'Paris is worth a Mass,' to justify taking control of the capital. He then converted to Catholicism. He did grant important concessions to the Huguenots in the Edict of Nantes (1598). After 1630, there was another Huguenot rebellion and Louis XIV revoked the freedoms agreed in the Edict (1685) with consequent persecution and emigration. On 24 August 1572 the slaughter of Huguenots in Paris was ordered by King Charles IX, this became known as the St Bartholomew's Day Massacre. Two days before, an attempted assassination of the Huguenot's leader, Admiral Coligny, had failed; this led to even more fervent civil war.

))))➤ *Edict of Nantes, Louis XIV of France*

HUMANISM (14TH CENTURY)

Philosophy emphasizing the dignity and worth of the individual. The term is used to describe a cultural and literary movement in Western Europe in the fourteenth and fifteenth centuries. It was also very much involved in reviving the study of Greek and Roman classics. Leading figures in the movement included Dante, Giovanni Boccaccio, Francesco Petrarch and Pico della Mirandola. The movement was influenced by the arrival of scholars fleeing the Turks after the fall of Constantinople. These figures strove to discover and preserve classical works and translate them, particularly as printing had just been invented, as well as promote the study of classical art. Gradually the movement extended into theology and education and became very influential in the Reformation period. In England classical scholars such as Grocyn, Linacre, Fisher and Erasmus established humanism in the universities of Oxford and Cambridge. Humanism paved the way for Elizabethan culture and literature.

))))➤ *Petrarch*

HUME, DAVID (1711–76)

Scottish historian and philosopher. Hume developed the notion that people can know nothing outside of their own experiences and perceptions, arguing that we cannot be certain of cause and effect even if we have experienced it before. He rejected scientific laws, argued that the concept of right or wrong was not rational and contributed to economic theory that influenced Adam Smith. His *History of England* described the intellectual and economic forces that played a part in history.

RIGHT: The philosopher David Hume argued that human beings cannot be certain of anything outside of their own experiences and senses.

RIGHT: *Saddam Hussein, seen in this poster, first came to the world's attention with his ruthless invasion of Iran in 1988.*
BELOW: *Christiaan Huygens.*

HUNDRED YEARS' WAR (1337–1453)

Series of conflicts fought over the sovereignty of Gascony, now in south-west France. At the time it was part of the kingdom of England, according to the English, but the French had other ideas. Rivalry between kingdoms had existed for many years, so the fighting was more an extension of past disagreement than something new. The war began when England feared that France might assist the Scottish, with whom England had been in conflict. Edward III claimed the crown of France.

Initially fighting went in favour of the English. The naval Battle of Sluys (1340) and the land battles of Crécy and Poitiers were all English victories. But the balance of power began to shift and from 1369 the French had the upper hand in proceedings.

By the time Edward III died in 1377, England was holding only Calais, Bordeaux and Bayonne in the north. A stalemate situation remained while both sides half-heartedly fought one another until 1415. Henry V invaded France and won the Battle of Agincourt on 25 October. Henry gained France and married French princess Catherine of Valois.

Joan of Arc launched the French counteroffensive with the siege of Orleans (1429). It continued following her execution, until France had regained all of her territory – including Gascony – by 1453, except Calais.

))⇒ *Battle of Agincourt, Battle of Crécy, Edward III of England, Henry V of England, Joan of Arc, Battle of Poitiers, Battle of Sluys*

HUSSEIN, SADDAM (b. 1937)

Iraqi dictator. Saddam Hussein came to prominence and power as a politician in 1968. Like all dictatorial figures he had a ruthless nature and suppressed opposition to his ambitions. By 1979 he had worked his way to the presidency. He presided over the Iran–Iraq War of 1980–88. During the conflict Hussein persecuted the Kurdish rebels of Northern Iraq.

In 1990 Hussein annexed Kuwait, resulting in an offensive by a coalition force, led by USA (1991). He lost the Gulf War, but remains Iraqi president.

))⇒ *Gulf War*

HUYGENS, CHRISTIAAN (1629–95)

Dutch physicist and astronomer. Huygens built the first pendulum clock, based on the principle observed by Galileo. He was also the first person to suggest that light might be thought of as waves, rather than particles; although it has since been shown to behave as both. As an astronomer Huygens did much to improve the telescope, invented by Hans Lippershey (1570–1619), and discovered the rings of the planet Saturn.

))⇒ *Galileo Galilei*

IMPRESSIONISM (1860s)

Artistic movement. The enormous influence of Claude Monet, and the enduring popularity of his work, has to an extent obscured the true technical and visionary variety of impressionist art. Monet was one of a number of French painters who, from the 1860s onwards, were coming to question the values of the established academic tradition. Contemporaries like Pierre-Auguste Renoir (1841–1919) and Alfred Sisley (1839–99) had also been growing increasingly impatient with the old conventions: in particular the concentration on narrative or dramatic scenes (often taken from the ancient myths) in which natural reality was strictly secondary. Like the painters of the Barbizon School, they felt that nature was far too important to be left in the 'background'. Their ambition was neither to capture some timeless essence or emotion nor to trace the physical contours of any scene, but to record the immediate sense-impression it made on the beholder.

Although to uninformed eyes vague and dreamy, lacking in clear definition and outline, the canvases of

BELOW: Edouard Manet's paintings (such as this one entitled Sur La Plage) *questioned the values of nineteenth-century artistic establishments and tried to capture the the impressions of the fleeting moment on canvas.*

the impressionists were in fact believed by their creators to be more scientifically accurate for that: an elaborately worked-out theory of colour actually underpinned their apparent daubings. Joined by a growing number of fellow spirits, including Camille Pissarro (1830–1903) and Paul Cézanne (1839–1906), Edgar Degas (1834–1917) and Edouard Manet (1832–83), they began to come together for the first time as a self-conscious school.

In 1873, works by Pissarro, Monet, Renoir, Cézanne and Sisley were all rejected from a major establishment exhibition: paradoxically, it was to be the making of the movement. Though to start with a school of landscape-painting, impressionism was soon taking on every sort of contemporary subject: Manet and Degas in particular were quintessentially urban, indoor painters.

))))➤ *Barbizon School, Modernism, Claude Monet*

INCAS (1100–1572)

Native South American Andean Empire. Originally from Peru they settled in the Valley of Cuzco. The tribe's eighth ruler enlarged the Empire in the early fifteenth century. In the next 30 years successive rulers extended it 4,000 km (2,500 miles) north to south and 800 km (500 miles) east to west, the population rising to 16 million. In 1525 the Empire was divided between Huáscar and Atahualpa, who prevailed in 1532 but the Spanish under Francisco Pizarro arrived. The Incas viewed them as demi-gods and Pizarro, through political skills and treachery, captured Atahualpa. In return for a room of gold, the Spaniards promised his release but on 29 August 1533 Atahualpa was strangled after converting to Christianity. Manco Capac, brother of Huáscar, took the throne, revolted against the Spaniards, was defeated and assassinated. The Spaniards, bringing an end to the Inca Empire, beheaded the last heir to the Inca throne, Tupac Amaru, son of Manco Capac.

)))➤ *Conquistadors, Francisco Pizarro*

BELOW: Sikh and Hindu students take to the streets of Lahore, shouting anti-Pakistan slogans and brandishing weapons during their fight for Indian independence in 1947.

consulting elected Indian councils. During the war anti-British agitation continued. By 1945 Gandhi and other leaders had been released. India and Pakistan were established as independent countries in 1947.

)))➤ *British Empire, Mahatma Gandhi, World War II*

INDIAN MUTINY (1857)

Native uprising against the British in India. The uprising is named the Indian Mutiny, the Sepoy Rebellion or the Mutiny Revolt, since the British saw it as a mutinous betrayal. The catalyst was the introduction of a new – paper – rifle cartridge. Muslims believed it to be sealed with pig fat, and Hindus with the fat of cows, thereby causing offence to their respective beliefs. The uprising was quelled but it led to the end of the East India Company.

)))➤ *British East India Company*

INDIAN INDEPENDENCE (1947)

Creation of modern-day India and Pakistan. Political riots and uprisings became intense in India after World War I, Gandhi calling the Indian people to counter British repression with passive resistance. During the 1920s and 30s civil disobedience led to the imprisonment of Gandhi and nearly 30,000 Indian nationalists. Despite autonomous legislative bodies being established (1935), when World War II broke out the Viceroy of India declared war on Germany without

ABOVE: Modern-day Peruvians dressed in replicas of the traditional attire worn by the ancient Incas from the Valley of Cuzco.

INDO-PAKISTAN WAR (1965)

Border war between India and Pakistan. On 14 August 1965 a Pakistani force crossed into Indian territory in an attempt to annex Kashmir as a province of Pakistan. India immediately dispatched an army to block the Haji Pir pass. A second Indian force launched a counteroffensive by crossing the border into Lahore. The tank battles that ensued were extremely fierce. Both sides suffered heavy losses of personnel and military equipment. A treaty – the Tashkent Agreement – was signed in 1966.

INDUS VALLEY CIVILIZATION
(2400–1500 BC)

Ancient civilization of northern India resulted from waves of migration by Aryan peoples who settled in the Indus Valley and created great cities. The magnificence of their remains suggests a high degree of culture. The petty kingdoms were eventually subjugated by the Persians under Darius.

))))➤ *Persia*

INDUSTRIAL REVOLUTION
(18TH–19TH CENTURIES)

Term applied to the economic developments that, from *c.* 1760 to 1830, transformed Britain from a primarily agricultural country to a primarily industrial one. It also denotes the social effects of this great change and its worldwide impact.

The Industrial Revolution was made possible by a series of inventions, especially in the textile industries, such as the flying shuttle, spinning jenny, spinning frame and power loom. Increasing mechanization had several consequences: domestic industry based on human labour gave way to the factory system; productivity was increased; further invention was encouraged; a division of labour occurred; management became more specialized; and marketing required new flair.

A common factor in industrialization everywhere was the advent of new sources of power other than water – first steam, then electricity – to drive machines and later also for locomotion. In Britain roads were improved, a network of canals was built and in 1825 the first railway was opened. The iron industry was transformed by the substitution of coke for charcoal in smelting. Existing materials such as iron and glass acquired new uses and further materials were discovered or created, particularly chemicals.

A sense prevailed that nature had finally been conquered. Work in factories attracted innumerable people to towns, where for at least a generation many suffered hard and unhealthy conditions, owing to over-crowding and lack of sanitary facilities.

ABOVE: The advent of the Industrial Revolution in the late nineteenth century saw a dramatic growth in technology and productivity.

Social change also revolutionized political life, by the replacement of the great landowners as the dominant class by the industrialists, and by the creation of an independent labour movement.

INNOCENT III (1160–1216)

Italian pope. Born Lotario dei Conti de Segni in Agnoni, Italy, Innocent III was pope from 1198 to 1216. His papacy is considered to represent the high point of temporal and spiritual supremacy of the Roman See. He excommunicated King John for refusing to recognize Stephen Langton as Archbishop of Canterbury in 1212. He convened one of the great councils of the Church, the Fourth Vatican Council in 1215. Innocent was the first pope to call himself 'Vicar of Christ'. During his papacy, clerical celibacy became more widespread, the chalice was withheld from the laity at mass, and confession was introduced. Persecution became the duty of Catholic kings.

INNOCENT IV (d. 1254)

Italian pope. Born Sinibaldo Fieschi in Genoa and trained in canon law at Bologna, Innocent reigned as pope from 1243–54. It was his unscrupulous use of power through the exercise of patronage that brought the struggle between the Emperor Frederick II and the papacy to a climax. The Council of Lyons in 1245 was devoted to measures against the Emperor. Innocent's time as pope was a symbol of the papacy's lack of interest in reform.

After the death of Frederick (1250) he sought to establish papal rule in Sicily. He established the permanent Inquisition as permanent in Italy.

)))) *Inquisition*

INQUISITION (1232)

Roman Catholic tribunal for prosecuting heresy, it was first created on a temporary basis by Pope Gregory IX in France and Germany in the thirteenth century. The Inquisition in general was established by Gregory IX in 1232 with inquisitors being mainly Dominican and Franciscan monks. The office has been redesigned and renamed over the centuries and in 1965 it became the Congregation for the Doctrine of the Faith.

In Spain the Inquisition was centred in Tarragossa in Aragon. This was superseded by the Spanish Inquisition founded by papal bull (1478) and set up in 1480. It was concerned to investigate the orthodoxy of Jews (1492) and Muslims of Castile (1502) who had been forced to accept the Christian faith. Sixteen permanent tribunals were eventually created in Spain between 1500–1640. In the first 10 years it burnt 2,000 people and punished 15,000 others. It played a major role in the extermination of Islam from Spain in the fifteenth to seventeenth centuries. The Inquisition was extended to Portugal,

Goa (1560), Brazil, Peru (1570) and Mexico (1571). It was finally abolished in Spain in 1834. The Inquisition represented the end of the easygoing ways of the past and the start of a regime of repression.

INTERNATIONAL MONETARY FUND (1947)

Specialized agency of the United Nations, established in 1947 after the Bretton Woods Conference, to support economic development, promote international monetary co-operation, facilitate international trade and payments, eliminate foreign trade restrictions and flatten out exchange-rate fluctuations. It also provides advice on economic and fiscal policy and technical assistance for central banks. Membership is open to all sovereign nations. Each member may borrow from the Fund's pool of resources to ease temporary balance-of-payments difficulties.

)))) *Bretton Woods Conference*

IRANGATE (1986)

US political scandal during Reagan's administration. Also know as the Iran-contra affair, the incident involved the secret government selling of arms to Iran to provide funds for the Nicaraguan contra rebels. Congress had prohibited aid to the contras and the US had called for a worldwide ban on sending arms to Iran, so the discovery violated a number of laws. The chief negotiator was Oliver North, and his boss at the National Security Council, John Pointdexter, was also put on trial. No evidence could be found to directly link either President Reagan or Vice-President George Bush, although both men were thought to be aware of the arrangements.

)))) *Ronald Reagan*

LEFT: *Oliver North taking his famous oath during the Irangate scandal.*
ABOVE: *International Monetary Fund offices in Washington, D.C., USA.*

IRON CURTAIN (1945)

Political and military barrier put up by the Soviet Union after World War II to seal itself off from Western Europe. Although the term had been in use before, it was popularized by Winston Churchill's speech in 1946: 'From Stettin in the Baltic to Trieste in the Adriatic an iron curtain has descended across the continent.' The Berlin Wall in 1961 reinforced the concept, which largely ceased to exist following the 1989 fall of Communism in both the USSR and its satellite states. The bamboo curtain has also been used to describe the barrier between Communist China and other countries.

)))))▶ *Berlin Wall, Cold War*

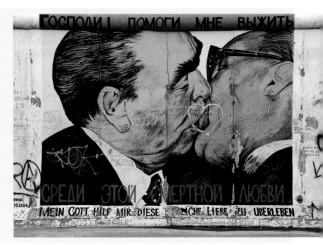

ISLAM

Based on the revelations given to the Prophet Muhammad in the seventh century, Muslims ('submitters [to God, Allah]') believe Islam has always existed and there have been many revelations of God (Allah) to all the prophets before Muhammad, who is the last and final prophet. The revelations to Muhammad are collected together in the Qur'an which is believed to be the word of Allah. Islam calls for complete surrender and submission to Allah through the acceptance and practice of the Qur'an and Sunnah (Tradition) of the Prophet in daily life. The word 'Islam' appears in the Qur'an and means' entering into peace and security with Allah through obedience to him'. There are six articles of faith in Islam: there is only one God; everyone is accountable to God on the Day of Judgement; believe Allah's messengers; believe the prophets who delivered the messages; believe in Allah's angels; and believe in Allah's pre-knowledge of human action. These beliefs are practised through: the statement of faith (Shadadah) 'There is no God but Allah and Muhammad is the messenger of God'; the five daily prayers; zakat (the obligation to support the poor and needy); siyyam (to keep the month-long fast of Ramadan by abstaining from food, drink and sexual relations between dawn and sunset); and hajj (pilgrimage to Mecca once in a lifetime). There are well over one billion Muslims in the world, and, although there are two main groupings, Sunni (around 90 per cent) and Shiah (10 per cent), the fundamental principles of Islam are common to all.

)))))▶ *Hijra, Prophet Muhammad*

ABOVE: A street poster depicts Communist leaders during the iron-curtain era when Europe was split into the USSR-backed East and the US-backed West. BELOW: Muslims at prayer facing Mecca.

ITALIAN WARS (1494–95)

In 1494 Charles VIII of France invaded Italy and claimed the throne of Naples. He arrived at Florence on 17 November and expelled Piero di Medici from office. Charles moved on to Rome, reaching it on 31 December, forcing the pope to take refuge in the Castle of St Angelo. On 22 February 1495 Charles had reached Naples itself. The King of Naples, Alfonso II, had fled, leaving the throne in the charge of his son Ferrante, who assumed the title Ferdinand II. Charles ousted him and crowned himself King of Naples on 12 May. The tables turned in July however, when Ferdinand II reconquered Naples, assisted by the Spanish fleet under Gonzalo de Cordova. Charles was now up against a coalition force between Milan, Venice, Spain and the Holy Roman Emperor. He won the Battle of Fornovo, but ultimately lost the Italian Wars.

)))》 *Charles VIII of France, Holy Roman Emperor*

IVAN III OF MOSCOW (1440–1505)

Grand Prince of Muscovy (Moscow) from 1462; known as 'the Great'. Ivan refused to pay tribute to the Tatar leader, Grand Khan Ahmed. He then expelled the Tatars, annexed Novgorod, Yaroslavl and Rostov land, and recaptured Ukrainian territory from Poland and Lithuania. Centralizing control over his possessions gave meaning to Ivan's imperial ambitions, which developed when he married Sophia Palaeologus, niece of Constantine XI, the last emperor of Byzantium. Ivan named himself Tsar of all Russia, and introduced the Russian imperial device of the double-headed eagle. He granted life tenure of lands to servants on condition of loyalty to the grand prince. Ivan made Muscovy a significant force on the European stage.

)))》 *Byzantium, Tatars*

BELOW: Ivan the Terrible, the Grand Duke of Muscovy, brought the borders of his principality to the Urals, the mountain range dividing Europe and Siberia.

IVAN IV OF MOSCOW (1530–84)

Tsar of Russia from 1547; known as 'the Terrible'. Crowned at the age of 17 Ivan IV was subjected to squabbles amongst the nobility (boyars), and he learned to loath them. Despite starting his reign by introducing reforms he degenerated after 1564 into ruthless and suspicious despotism, thereby founding the tsarist style of autocratic rule, for example the sacking of Novgorod. He instituted a secret police force, which operated through summary arrest, torture and execution. He extended his territories to the Caspian Sea and east into Siberia. He instituted trading with England and made overtures of marriage to Elizabeth I. In 1580, Ivan killed his son in a fit of temper. He remained in penance until his death.

)))》 *Elizabeth I of England*

JACKSON, THOMAS J. (1824–63)

American general during the American Civil War; earned the nickname 'Stonewall' for his tenacious leadership of the Confederates at the battle of Bull Run in July 1861. Jackson served in the Mexican War (1846–48) before becoming professor of military tactics at Virginia Military Institute. After several notable campaigns he was accidentally shot by his own men at Chancellorsville, having defeated Hooker's army.

)))➤ *American Civil War*

JACOBITES (1688–1745)

Supporters of the exiled House of Stuart. William of Orange dethroned James II of England in the Glorious Revolution of 1688. In the next 60 years Jacobites made five attempts to restore the Stuarts to the throne. James II (March 1689) landed in Ireland but his Irish/French army was defeated by William at the Battle of the Boyne (July 1690). A second French invasion failed (1708). The final rebellion (1745) found Charles Edward Stuart temporarily victorious until he met the Duke of Cumberland at the Battle of Culloden. He was defeated; the revolt and the Stuart cause ended forever.

JAINISM

Jainism is one of the oldest religions in India although there are communities worldwide. It has an estimated following of four million people. 'Ahimsa' or 'non-violence/not hurting' is the central, paramount principle of Jainism and has characterized its history. Jainism believes that if one follows the teachers as 'Fordmakers' then one can cross the fjord from death and rebirth and reach salvation. Mahavira ('great hero') is often called the founder of Jainism; he lived in the fifth to sixth centuries

ABOVE: A Jain deity.

ABOVE RIGHT: Thomas Jefferson drew up the Declaration of Independence on 4 July 1776 and set a new precedent in world politics.

in the Ganges valley in India, dying at the age of 72 after over 40 years of teaching. For nearly 1,000 years Mahavira's teaching was passed on by word of mouth before being written down.

JEFFERSON, THOMAS (1743–1826)

Third US president (1801–1809). He founded the Democratic party and held a number of political roles, including governor of Virginia and vice-president. Jefferson was a leading exponent of Enlightenment, an eighteenth century movement that emphasized social progress and the possibilities of rational and scientific thought. His writing formed the basis of the Declaration of Independence (1776), the document which renounced allegiance to the British crown and formed the basis for the new US government.

)))▶ *Declaration of Independence, Enlightenment*

JENNER, EDWARD (1749–1823)

British physician. Jenner established the principle of vaccination by demonstrating that someone inoculated with cowpox would become immune to smallpox. Cowpox is related to smallpox but far less virulent, so the lesser disease can be used to stimulate the body into producing the right antibodies.

JERUSALEM

Capital of State of Israel. Captured by King David (*c.* 1000 BC), its origins go back to 1800 BC and it was the site of Solomon's Temple (*c.* 950 BC). Jerusalem was destroyed by the Babylonians in 587 BC and partially restored by Nehemiah in 445–433 BC. Herod the Great carried out a re-building programme. In AD 70 the Temple and city were destroyed by the Romans under Titus. Only the Western Wall remains today of the old city. After the Bar Kochba revolt (AD 132–135) it was renamed 'Aolia Capitolina' by Hadrian and all Jews were expelled.

BELOW: A devout Jewish man worships by the Wailing Wall in Jerusalem.

For Christians Jerusalem is the city of Jesus's death and resurrection. The Jewish–Christian church existed there until the exile under Hadrian. The Christian centre of the city is the Church of the Holy Sepulchre (purported to be built over the burial place of Jesus). Jerusalem is a potent Christian symbol as a place of pilgrimage.

Jerusalem is not mentioned in the Qur'an but is the third most important city for Muslims. Muhammad's Night Journey took place in Jerusalem and Jerusalem was originally (before Mecca) the direction of Muslim prayer. The 'al-Aqsa' mosque and the Dome of the Rock were erected on Temple Mount after the Muslim invasion of AD 614 and the capture of Jerusalem in AD 638. Muslims were tolerant of Jews and Christians in Jerusalem until 1009 when many Christian buildings were destroyed. Saladin overthrew the Crusaders, who had captured Jerusalem and respected religious differences.

)))▶ *Crusades, Dome of the Rock, Herod the Great, Islam, Judaism*

JESUITS (1540)

Catholic Society of Jesus. Ignatius Loyola, a former soldier, who recognized in military organization and discipline a power that could be harnessed for the benefit of the Church and Christ, formed the Jesuits in 1540. The Jesuits became the 'evangelists of the sixteenth century Counter-Reformation' (Hugh Trevor Roper). They were clerics in community under vows but were not obliged to sing the divine office. As the spearhead of the Counter-Reformation they became feared and admired for their learning, vision and energy as well as their uncompromising attitude to heresy. Officially called the 'Society of Jesus' and approved by the pope in 1540, they carried no arms. As the Jesuit movement grew, they travelled far and wide – not just in Europe but also to India and China and the Caribbean.

))))➤ *St Ignatius Loyola, Counter-Reformation, Roman Catholicism*

JESUS CHRIST (c. 6 BC – AD 31)

Born in Bethlehem to Mary and Joseph and raised in Nazareth in Galilee (Israel), Jesus was a wandering teacher in the north of Israel who visited Jerusalem only once or twice. Jesus gained a reputation for healing and exorcism and challenging the religious

authorities. He appeared to possess insight into the reality and Fatherhood of God. He ate and drank with the outcasts in society and taught forgiveness, compassion and humility, and the nearness of the rule of God to human life. Jesus gathered a group of 12 disciples around him encouraging them to go and preach that the Kingdom of God was at hand. After a ministry of three years he came to be regarded as a religious and political troublemaker.

He was betrayed by one of his disciples, arrested, deserted by his followers, tried by religious authorities and then Pontius Pilate the Roman governor, condemned him to death on a cross in public. He died and was buried. After that a number of his disciples had visions and experiences that led them to believe that God had raised Jesus, God's son, from the dead. Jesus was the Messiah. It is on this story that the Christian Church and Christianity rest.

))))➤ *Christianity, Judaism, Pontius Pilate*

LEFT: An image of Jesus Christ.
ABOVE: Joan of Arc.

JOAN OF ARC (1412–31)

French heroine. Seventy-two years into the Hundred Years' War between England and France there came a French heroine named Joan of Arc to the rescue of a France largely held by English forces. In 1429 she met Charles VII of France (1403–61) at Chinon and convinced him that she was on a divine mission to save France. He gave her permission to go to battle and with her army she managed to raise the Siege of Orleans. Her army defeated the English at the Battle of Patay, and her victory led to the coronation of Charles on 17 October.

Joan's efforts marked the turning point in the war, eventually leading to a French victory in 1453. In 1430, in an attempt to take Paris, Joan was captured by the enemy. She was tried and found guilty of witchcraft and heresy. Her sentence was death by burning and her execution took place in Rouen marketplace on 30 May 1431. She was canonized in 1920.

BELOW: Pope John Paul II resides at the Vatican in Rome.

JOHN PAUL II (b. 1920)

Polish pope. Born in Wadowice, near Krakow, Poland, Karol Wojtyela moved to Krakow when he was 18 and studied Polish language and literature at university. During World War II he worked in a factory and in 1946 was ordained, gaining a doctorate at Rome in 1948. He continued to lecture at universities in Poland before becoming a bishop in 1958 and Archbishop of Krakow in 1963. After becoming a cardinal in 1967, he was elected pope in 1978. He travelled extensively throughout the world, the first non-Italian pope for centuries, surviving an assassination attempt in 1981. He has been keen to re-establish and re-affirm traditional Catholic values on social, political and theological matters.

⟫⟫ *Roman Catholicism*

JUDAISM

The origins of Judaism are set out in the Tanakh (the Hebrew Bible). It is believed God entered into a covenant with the Jewish community through Abraham and then Moses. The Jews were chosen by God, giving them extra responsibilities to live in accordance with God's law.

The central event in Judaism was the revelation made by God to Moses after he had led the Israelites out of Egypt. When they eventually entered the Promised Land the area was divided into 12 for the 12 tribes of Israel. 'Jew' and 'Judaism' derive from Judah, one of the 12 sons of the patriarch, Jacob.

Jewish beliefs and practices are rooted in the Tanakh: the Torah (teaching), the Nevi'im (prophets) and Kethuvim (writings). The Talmud (to study), compiled in the early centuries of the Common Era, is divided into the Mishnah (teaching) and Gemara (completion). Another literary tradition is the midrash (collections of rabbinic interpretations).

Key beliefs include the Oneness of God, the Shema (hear), a daily prayer containing a clear statement that the Lord is One God. The Torah includes the mitzvot (commandments) that cover every aspect of life. To study the Torah is a sacred task and central to religious life. Humanity is created in the image of God and therefore creation has to be treated responsibly. Sin and forgiveness are a part of life and God can always be restored to broken people and relationships. Jews have always looked for the Kingdom of God on Earth; this has been connected with the coming of a Messiah (Anointed One). Traditionally this belief is that the Messiah will be revealed, all Jews will be gathered into Israel from exile, the Temple will be re-built and there will be eternal peace.

There are different traditions in Judaism: the Orthodox, Hasidic (pious), Progressive (including Liberal and Reform) which re-interprets traditional Jewish beliefs and practices, and Masorti (or Conservative) often characterized as being between Orthodox and Progressive.

Judaism is a practical religion. Boys are circumcized on the eighth day and are

BELOW: A rabbi circumcises a Jewish infant at a traditional ceremony.

Bar-Mitzvahed before they are 13 (girls in some traditions have a Bat-Mitzvah). The keeping of Shabbat (Sabbath) is central to the pattern of Jewish life. It is a day of worship and peace reflecting the day God rested from creation. While Jews vary enormously in religious practice, these three aspects of life will be followed to some degree by all religious Jews. Not all Jews follow the food laws (Kashrut – fitness) but most identify with Israel. Attendance at the synagogue varies but the regular cycle of festivals mean that Jewish heritage and tradition are never far from even non-practising Jews. Judaism is a religion of the family – the family of the Jewish community and the individual Jewish family. There are around 15 million Jews in the world today.

➤ *Abraham, Jewish Diaspora, Torah*

JULIAN CALENDAR (AD 43–1582)

Established by Julius Caesar, also known as the old Style Calendar. It replaced the Roman Republican calendar and was devised by Sosigenes, an Alexandrian astronomer, who made each of the 12 months 30 or 31 days long, except February which had 28 days except in every fourth year (a leap year) when it had 29. Over-estimation of 11 minutes and 14 seconds, culminating in a shift of about 10 days had occurred by 1582 when the Gregorian calendar was introduced.

))))➤ *Julius Caesar, Gregorian Calendar*

JUNG, CARL (1875–1961)

Swiss psychologist and psychiatrist. Forming an alternative school to that of Sigmund Freud, Jung had studied at the University of Basel and in Paris. He worked at the University of Zurich as a physician and lecturer from 1900–13, becoming Professor of Psychology at Federal Polytechnic University of Zurich

(1933–41) and University of Basel (1943). He developed the theories of introverts, extroverts and the unconscious mind, and wrote *Modern Man in Search of a Soul* (1933) and *Memories, Dreams, Reflections (1962).*

))))➤ *Sigmund Freud*

JUSTINIAN (c. AD 482–565)

Eastern Roman (Byzantine) emperor from AD 527, who succeeded his uncle Justin I. Justinian's ambition was to restore the Roman Empire's territories. Through his generals Belisarius and Narses he recaptured North Africa, and parts of Italy and Spain, restored northern frontiers and held back the Persians. He centralized his rule, broke down the power of bureaucrats, and sought Christian unity, but most importantly, he revised and collated Roman law. He built many churches, including St Vitale in Ravenna, and Santa Sophia in Constantinople.

))))➤ *Romans*

LEFT: Carl Jung.
ABOVE: The Byzantine emperor Justinian (seen here in the centre of the image) aimed to restore the Roman Empire's former territories.

KANT, IMMANUEL (1724–1804)

Famous German philosopher in the theory of knowledge, ethics and aesthetics. In 1740 he studied at the University of Königsberg, working as a private tutor until 1755 when he became a university lecturer. Famous works were *Critique of Pure Reason* (1781) and *Critique of Practical Reason* (1788). His main philosophical studies were centred on the 'idealists' and the 'materialists' and the relationship of mind and matter, thus bringing forth a new development in philosophical thought.

KENNEDY, JOHN F. (1917–63)

35th US president (1961–63). At 43 Kennedy was the youngest ever president. Many of his domestic reforms, such as civil rights and extra spending on education and welfare, stalled in Congress. His time was spent dealing with foreign affairs, including the Bay of Pigs invasion, the Cuban missile crisis (1962) – the peaceful outcome of which was a personal triumph for Kennedy, and increasing the number of US military advisers to South Vietnam to 16,000 (1963). Kennedy was assassinated while campaigning for a second term.

⟩⟩⟩⟩ *Bay of Pigs Invasion, Cuban Missile Crisis, Presidents*

KEPLER, JOHANNES (1571–1630)

Mathematician and astronomer. Johannes Kepler devised three laws to explain the motion of the planets around the Sun. The first was that the Sun marks one focus of a planet's elliptical orbit. The second was that the radius of a planet sweeps out an equal area over equal time. The third was that the square of the period of a planet is proportional to the cube of its mean radius. He supported Copernicus's heliocentric theory of the Solar System.

⟩⟩⟩⟩ *Nicolaus Copernicus*

KEYNES, JOHN MAYNARD (1883–1946)

English economist, financier and journalist. Keynes studied at Eton and Cambridge then worked in the India Office, examining pre-World War I Indian finance. He was an economic adviser at the Versailles Peace Conference and wrote *The Economic Consequences of the Peace* (1919) and *The General Theory of Employment, Interest and Money* (1936). In 1944 he was the Chief British Representative at the Bretton Woods Conference and negotiated the 1945 loan from the USA to Britain.

⟩⟩⟩⟩ *Bretton Woods Conference*

KHOMEINI, RUH ALLAH, AYATOLLAH (1902–89)

'Ayatollah' means 'signs of God' and contemporary ayatollahs are the caretakers for the Imam who will return at the end of time. In Shiite hierarchy there were 12 imams the last of whom disappeared. The application of the title 'Ayatollah' appears to depend upon the personality and charisma of the scholar as well as recognition by the community. Ayatollah Khomeini was the main opponent of the Shah of Iran before the Shah's overthrow; exiled in 1964 until finally returning in 1979. After the revolution in 1978–79 Khomeini was recognized as Vilayat Faqih – the supreme representative in Iran of the Hidden (12th) Imam. His opposition to the West and his promotion of his form of Islam has had a powerful bearing on the portrayal of Islam in the West.

ABOVE LEFT: Immanuel Kant emphasized the critique of knowledge as the way to get to the bottom of philosophical conclusions.
LEFT: John F. Kennedy.

BELOW: The Ayatollah Khomeini opposed the Shah of Iran who was later overthrown and exiled in the USA.

KING, MARTIN LUTHER (1929–68)

US non-violent black leader. Son of an Ebenezer, a Baptist Church pastor, King was ordained in 1947, became pastor of the Dexter Avenue Baptist Church in Montgomery (1954) and received a PhD in theology (1955) as well as heading the Montgomery Improvement Association, formed to boycott the segregation of the city's buses. In 1957 he was awarded the Spingarn Medal by the National Association for the Advancement of Coloured People and was voted President of the Southern Christian Leadership Conference in 1958. He visited India the following year to study Gandhi's non-violent protest techniques, holding a non-violent protest against discrimination in 1961. He was arrested in 1963 during campaigns for desegregation in Alabama, received the Nobel Peace Prize in 1964, being the youngest ever recipient, regarding it as a tribute for the Civil Rights Movement. Making a stand against the Vietnam War, believing money could have been used to combat poverty and condemning the violence of war, he planned the Poor People's Campaign, marching on Washington (1968). His influence led to the Civil Rights Act (1964) and the Voting Rights Act (1965).

))))▶ *Civil Rights Movement, Vietnam War*

KITCHENER, HORATIO HERBERT (1850–1916)

British military commander during the Boer War and World War I. The Boer War was brought to a successful conclusion for the British by their commander-in-chief, Lord Horatio Herbert Kitchener, who assumed his role in the war from 1900. Victory was won, in part, by the invention of concentration camps which resulted in the deaths of 26,000 Boer women and children. Kitchener spearheaded the campaign for volunteers at the outbreak of World War I and was British war minister. He died in 1916 onboard a ship which was hit by a mine and sank.

))))▶ *Boer War, World War I*

KMER ROUGE (1975–79)

Communist rulers of Cambodia. Cambodia was granted independence by France in 1953. Pol Pot, an urban radical and Communist, became Secretary General of the party in 1963. With a war raging in Vietnam, the Cambodian monarch, Sihanouk, attempted to keep the country out of the war. A right-wing military coup, led by the US-backed General Lon Nol, overthrew Sihanouk in 1970 and the Kmer Rouge fought a civil war that finally defeated Lon Nol after the capture of the capital, Phnompenh. During the next four years at least 1.7 million Cambodians were killed as intellectuals were massacred and minorities wiped out. Buddhism was suppressed and the Kmer Rouge began attacking neighbouring countries, including Vietnam, Thailand and Laos. After a rebellion in 1978, the Vietnamese invaded and eventually Pol Pot was arrested in 1997 and sentenced to life imprisonment for his crimes. The rebels took power after January 1979.

))))▶ *Communism, Pol Pot*

KNIGHTS OF ST JOHN (11TH CENTURY)

Christian soldiers dedicated to protecting pilgrim travellers. In the eleventh century there was considerable ill feeling between Christians and Muslims in the Middle East. Christians on their pilgrimage to Jerusalem from Europe had to be well protected. In 1048 St John's Hospital was established in Jerusalem by Christian merchants from the Amalfi coast. This hospital lent its name to the Knights of St John or the Order of St John: Christian soldiers dedicated to protecting pilgrims.

))))▶ *Crusades*

KNIGHTS TEMPLAR (1119–1314)

Religious military order. A group of knights, led by Hugues de Payens, vowed to devote themselves to the protection of pilgrims at risk from marauding Muslim bandits in the Holy Land. They

were supported by Baldwin II, King of Jerusalem, and given the former Jewish Temple as their base. They numbered 20,000 at their height, and had many fortresses in Palestine. They became wealthy and were used as bankers by kings and pilgrims. In 1307, with the help of Pope Clement V, King Philip IV of France imprisoned the Templars in France and their property was confiscated by various states.

⟫➤ *Crusades*

KOHL, HELMUT (b. 1930)

German political leader. Kohl was a conservative politician and head of the Christian Democratic Union (CDU). As chancellor of West Germany (1982–90) he pressed for the country's reunification with East Germany following the collapse of the USSR. In 1990 his government signed a treaty to unify the two countries' economic and social-welfare systems and called the first all-German parliamentary elections since 1932. Kohl was duly elected Chancellor of the Federal Republic of Germany (1991–94), but he was voted out by dissatisfaction with the tax increases and cuts in government spending that were needed to pay for unification.

LEFT: Helmut Kohl, former German chancellor.

LEFT: The Knights Templar vowed to protect Christian pilgrims in the Holy Crusades from attacks by Muslim bandits on their way to the Holy Land.

KON-TIKI EXPEDITION (1947)

In 1947 Thor Heyerdahl (b. 1914), a Norwegian anthropologist and explorer, with a crew of five successfully sailed 6,920 km (4,325 miles) from Callao, Peru, to the Tuamotu Islands of Polynesia on a balsa raft named the *Kon-Tiki*. The 101-day voyage was undertaken to prove that native South Americans could have migrated to Pacific islands around AD 500. The raft was modelled after those used by ancient Peruvians and made from nine large logs 9–14 m (30–46 ft) long, lashed together with rope. It was named after the Inca high priest and sun king. The voyage gave credibility to Heyerdahl's conjecture without conclusively proving it.

KOREAN WAR (1950–53)

War between North and South Korea. At the close of World War II, Korea was occupied by Japanese forces. Russian and US troops entered Korea and accepted the surrender of the Japanese. They then divided the country in two, at the '38th parallel' due to their divided political interests. North Korea and South Korea were strictly isolated from one another in post-war years.

North Korea effectively became a republic of the USSR, as it had a Soviet-backed provisional government installed which was dominated by Korean Communists trained in Moscow. South Korea meanwhile was being set up with a pro-US government and then named itself the Republic of Korea in 1948. North Korea responded by naming itself the Democratic People's Republic of Korea and Soviet troops departed.

With the lines firmly drawn between the two new countries, tensions began to rise. In 1950 North Korea invaded South Korea with a view to reuniting the two areas of territory under one Communist banner. The North Koreans were backed by their Communist neighbour, China. South Korea quickly found defence support from the United Nations and all-out war began.

Still holding on to a small area of territory in the south-east of the Korean peninsula, known as the Pusan perimeter, the South Koreans, with the support of US

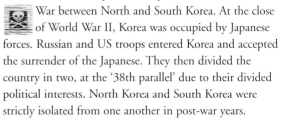

reinforcements, managed to begin pushing their way northward. By October 1950 the Chinese had become directly involved in the warfare and things reached a stalemate position. Negotiations for a truce began in 1951 but an armistice was not reached until 1953.

KRISTALLNACHT (1938)

'Night of broken glass', symbolizing the shattering of Jewish existence in Germany. When news of the shooting in Paris of German diplomat Ernst vom Rath by a Polish-Jewish student, Herschel Grynszpan, reached Hitler, he ordered massive Nazi attacks on Jewish persons and property throughout Germany. A thousand synagogues were burned or damaged, 7,500 businesses, hospitals, homes, schools and cemeteries were ransacked and looted, killing 91 and leading to the arrest of 30,000 male Jews aged 16–60.

)))⏵ *Adolf Hitler, Holocaust*

KHRUSHCHEV, NIKITA (1894–1971)

Premier of the USSR (1958–64). Krushchev rose rapidly in the Communist Party, directing the second five-year plan and the Red Army's southern front during World War II. He became the Soviet agricultural expert when he was charged with restoring agricultural production after the war. After Stalin's death Krushchev was appointed head of the Communist Party, but he denounced Stalin and demoted many of his supporters. He was made Soviet premier on the resignation of Bulganin in 1958, until he himself was deposed in 1964 following accusations of political error over the Cuban missile crisis. He was dropped from the party in 1966.

)))⏵ *Cuban Missile Crisis*

KU KLUX KLAN (1866 AND 1915 ONWARDS)

Terrorist organization. Taking its name from the Greek word for 'circle', it was established by Confederate soldiers but became an underground resistance movement aiming to restore white supremacy and terrorize non-whites in the southern states of America. Originally led by the Confederate General, Nathan Bedford-Forrest, their first Grand Wizard, they dressed in robes and sheets to prevent Federal troops from identifying them. White supremacy had been achieved by the 1870s and the Klan diminished. In 1915 a new Klan arose to counter what they saw as a change in the ethnic character of America as a result of immigration. Membership peaked in the 1920s with four million members being opposed to Jews, Roman Catholics and all foreigners. It resurged in the 1960s and was responsible for shootings and bombings in the south. Lyndon Johnson renounced the organization on nationwide television. The Klan is still active having strong alliances with right-wing extremists and neo-Nazis.

KUOMINTANG (1911)

Chinese name for the Nationalist People's Party. The party was founded by Sun Yat-sen, a revolutionary leader who overthrew the Manchu dynasty in 1911 and set up a republican government. In the 1920s sharp divisions arose between the right-wing and the Communist elements in the party. Leader of the right-wing faction, Chiang Kai-shek, threw out the Communists in 1927 and began a campaign to unify the whole country under Kuomintang. The nationalist regime was finally defeated by Mao Zedong in 1949 and Kuomintang supporters (an estimated two million people) withdrew to the island of Taiwan, which was fortified with US economic aid. Chiang Kai-shek continued to rule until his death in 1975.

KUBLAI KHAN (1216–94)

First Mongol Emperor of China from 1259. Kublai Khan, grandson of Genghis Khan, inherited an empire reaching from the Black Sea to the Pacific Ocean. His main preoccupation was conquering the rest of China. He founded the Yuan dynasty, declaring himself Chinese Emperor. He founded a new capital at Cambaluc (Beijing), and in 1276 conquered the Sung dynasty capital at Hangchow. By 1292 all of China was under his control, though he failed to conquer Japan. Benign and religiously tolerant, Kublai Khan opened China to foreigners, encouraged art and trade, and established Buddhism.

)))⏵ *Mongols*

LASCAUX

Site in France at which important cave-paintings were found. Stumbled upon in 1940 by boys looking for their lost dog, this cave in the Dordogne turned out to be a treasure-house of prehistoric art. Bison, deer, wild horses and cattle career across the roof and walls of the cave: captured in all their grace and strength by mysterious artists 15,000 years ago. While most of the images had literally been painted with mineral pigments obtained from the Earth, some were engravings, scratched into the rock. Though their purpose is obscure, they are widely assumed to have served a ceremonial function as part of hunting rituals or fertility rites.

LEAGUE OF NATIONS (1919)

Organization established for international co-operation. In an attempt to prevent another world conflict, a covenant was drawn up by Allied Powers at the Paris Peace Conference (1919) covering collective security, dispute arbitration, open diplomacy and armament reduction. New members were assimilated during the 1920s; the League's headquarters were based in Geneva with the aim of preserving the covenant established in the peace treaties following World War I. A series of failures to maintain this status quo during the 1930s forced the League to cease its activities during World War II, being replaced in 1946 by the United Nations.

)))) *United Nations, World War I*

LEIPZIG, BATTLE OF (1813)

Battle during the Napoleonic Wars. Napoleon Bonaparte began to see his fortunes change in 1812 when his army was forced to pay a high price in casualties for tackling the tenacious Russians at Borodino. Napoleon's army struggled on for another year, however, before outright defeat was experienced, at Leipzig in Saxony, on October 1813. Napoleon was finally beaten by a coalition force of Prussians, Austrians and Russians at the Battle of Nations (or Leipzig).

)))) *Napoleon Bonaparte, Napoleonic Wars*

LENIN, VLADIMIR ILYICH (1870–1924)

Russian revolutionary and political theoretician. Lenin created the Soviet Union and headed its first government (1917–24). After the failure of the 1905 revolution, he spent time in exile where he wrote many revolutionary pamphlets, including *State and Revolution*, his most important contribution to Marxist political theory. Lenin adapted Marxism to Russian conditions to create Leninism. In 1917 the Bolsheviks came to power and Lenin was finally able to put his theories into practice, although civil war broke out between 1918–21.

BELOW: The tenth meeting of the League of Nations at Geneva.
RIGHT: Vladimir Lenin changed the face of Imperial Russia by ensuring all businesses became property of the State.

After the war Lenin introduced the New Economic Policy, which returned the Soviet Union to a market economy, at the same time insisting on single party rule.
))⟩➤ *Bolsheviks, Karl Marx*

LENINGRAD, SIEGE OF (1941–44)

Campaign during World War II. On 1 September 1941 the Germans laid siege to the city of Leningrad (St Petersburg) in Russia. Hitler had stated that he wanted to 'wipe Leningrad from the face of the Earth' – but he hadn't reckoned on the tenacity of the city's inhabitants. An estimated one million people lost their lives in the siege, but despite this the city was not taken and remained in Russian hands when the siege ended on 27 January 1944.

BELOW RIGHT: Leonardo da Vinci's work and ideas are representative of the Renaissance movement which originated in fifteen-century Italy.

LEONARDO DA VINCI (1452–1519)

Italian artist and scientist. The ultimate 'Renaissance man', a master of many different disciplines and skills at once, Leonardo is most famous as painter of the mysterious *Mona Lisa* (*c.* 1504). Other paintings, like his *Last Supper* (1498) and *The Virgin of the Rocks* (*c.* 1508), are held in equal regard by modern experts, among whom he is widely held to be the greatest Western artist of all time. Unfortunately, much of his output has been lost, having been executed on long-degraded plaster surfaces, while his sculpture, admired in his day, has similarly vanished. Often the form of his finished work can only be guessed at from the preparatory drawings he left behind, but even these rough sketches are treasured today as priceless masterpieces. Leonardo's range of interests outside the realm of art was all but endless. The thoughts recorded in his extensive notebooks cover everything from anatomy to aeronautics (he designed at least one flying machine), from crop-irrigation to military engineering.
))⟩➤ *Renaissance*

LEPANTO, BATTLE OF (1571)

Battle between the Ottoman Empire and the Holy League in which galley warships were used in warfare for the last time. The Battle of Lepanto between the Ottomans and Christian Holy League took place on 7 October 1571. Although the Christians managed to break Muslim seapower, the campaign was inconclusive.
))⟩➤ *Ottoman Empire*

LINCOLN, ABRAHAM (1809–65)

16th US president (1861–65). Lincoln steered the Union to victory in the American Civil War and abolished slavery. Known as Honest Abe, he was a member of the state legislature from 1832–42 and elected as a Republican president in 1860. His main goal was to stop the southern Confederate states seceding from the Union, which they duly did on his election. The first outbreak of civil war came when Lincoln refused to evacuate the federal garrison at Fort Sumter, Charleston in South Carolina, and the Confederates opened fire. Lincoln had difficulty finding a competent general, but he finally put Ulysses S. Grant in command, who eventually brought the war to an end. In his Gettysburg Address, Lincoln called for equality for all men and freedom for slaves. He was re-elected the following year with a large majority and proposed reconciliation with the South. Five days after General Lee's surrender, Lincoln was shot by a Confederate sympathizer.

))))▶ *American Civil War, Confederacy, Battle of Gettysburg, Slavery*

LINDBERGH, CHARLES (1902–74)

American aviator, first person to make a non-stop solo flight across the Atlantic. Lindbergh took off in his single-engine monoplane *Spirit of St Louis* from Long Island on 20 May 1927 and landed at Le Bourget Airport near Paris 33 hours and 32 minutes later, thereby claiming a $25,000 prize. In 1933 Lindbergh surveyed over 48,000 km (30,000 miles) for transatlantic air routes and landing fields. The kidnap and murder of his baby son attracted nationwide attention.

LISTER, JOSEPH (1827–1912)

English surgeon. Joseph Lister (1827–1912) was the first person to introduce sterilization procedures into his operating room. He sprayed phenol (carbolic acid) on to wounds and heated instruments before use so that the environment was as antiseptic as possible. He was influenced by the work of Louis Pasteur.

))))▶ *Louis Pasteur*

LEFT: Former US president Abraham Lincoln.
ABOVE: Charles Lindbergh made the first solo flight across the Atlantic.

LITTLE BIGHORN, BATTLE OF (1876)

Battle between white settlers and Native American Indians. The battle has become legendary in US folklore for being such a decisive victory for the Indians. Under the leadership of General George Armstrong Custer a group of outnumbered US troops faced the wrath of the Sioux tribe at the Little Bighorn river in Montana on 25 June 1876. The Sioux were led by chiefs Crazy Horse and Sitting Bull. Custer and all his men were killed.

)))➤ *George Armstrong Custer, Sitting Bull, Battle of Wounded Knee*

LIVE AID (1985)

Fund-raising rock concert. Shocking reports of the unfolding famine in Ethiopia appeared on British television during 1984, as a result of which Irish rock musician Bob Geldof organized 'Band Aid', a group of fellow stars from Britain and Ireland recording a Christmas single for the benefit of the victims. 'Do they Know it's Christmas?' became the best-selling record in history. Geldof went on to put together a multinational concert for the following summer: simultaneous shows took place in London and Philadelphia on 13 July 1985. Edited together, and broadcast worldwide, 'Live Aid' is believed to have raised more than $100 million and has done much to shape the idea of modern 'telethon' fundraising for all sorts of charities.

BELOW: Sir Bob Geldof launched Live Aid, a fund-raising rock concert in aid of starving children in Ethiopia.

LIVINGSTONE, DAVID (1813–73)

Scottish doctor, missionary and one of the foremost explorers of Africa. From 1840 Livingstone made several expeditions into regions where no European had ever been, including crossing the Kalahari Desert. In 1855 he followed the Zambezi River to its mouth in the Indian Ocean, thereby discovering the Victoria Falls. In 1866 he led an expedition to discover the sources of the Nile and Congo Rivers. His explorations resulted in a revision of all contemporary maps. Moreover, his concern over the maltreatment of indigenous Africans by Arabs and Portuguese contributed to the abolition of the slave trade.

)))➤ *Slavery*

LOMBARD LEAGUE (1164)

During the twelfth century the Holy Roman Emperor Frederick Barbarossa (1123–90) made a claim of sovereignty over all Italy, which was then divided into provinces. The northern province of Lombardy took a lead in countering his claim by forming an alliance of towns and cities prepared to fight for their independence in 1164. Supported by Milan and Pope Alexander III (1105–81), the Lombard League took up arms against Frederick in 1179 at the Battle of Legnano, beating him. They went on to hold off sovereignty claims by Otto IV (*c.* 1182–1218) in 1214 and Frederick II (1194–1250).

LONGBOAT (c. 300 BC)

Viking sea vessel. This was a double-ended sail and oar ship that could range from between 14 and 23 m (45 and 75 ft) in length and carried one square sail. It was used predominantly by the Vikings during the ninth century, but was also subsequently used by the French, English, German and Dutch.

)))➤ *Vikings*

LOUIS XIV OF FRANCE (1638–1715)

King of France from 1643, also known as the Sun King. During his minority, power was wielded by Cardinal Mazarin who faced Spanish-backed opposition from the nobility for his exclusion of them from office. Louis' marriage to Maria Theresa of Spain in 1660 brought peace.

Louis took firm control of government in 1661, choosing effective ministers to reform finances and the armed forces. These enhanced his territorial ambitions but William III of England led European resistance against him in the War of the League of Augsburg (1689–97). Louis saw the importance of image, creating a performance of monarchical grandeur and sophistication at Versailles. The latter part of his reign was beset by defeats in the War of the Spanish Succession (1702–13).

)))) *Versailles*

LOUIS XVI OF FRANCE (1754–93)

King of France from 1774, and married to Marie Antoinette. Attempts to tax nobles were wrecked by Marie Antoinette's support of aristocrats, leading to dismissal of ministers like Necker. France backed the American War of Independence, causing further financial trouble and popularizing liberty. In 1788 Necker was reinstated, demanding the recall of the estates-general (parliament: nobles, clergy and commons) in 1789 for the first time since 1614. The commons declared themselves the National Assembly, a revolutionary act followed by the storming of the Bastille.

Louis and his family were brought to Paris but they escaped. Recaptured, they lost control as the new government took France into the Revolutionary Wars with Prussia and Austria. Louis sought aid from other monarchs but was executed on 21 January 1793.

)))) *Storming of the Bastille, French Revolution*

ABOVE: *Louis XVI of France.*
LEFT: *Louis XIV of France.*

LOUISIANA PURCHASE (1803)

The province of Louisiana was colonized by the French in the early eighteenth century; it was ceded to the Spanish in 1762 and returned to France in 1800. President Thomas Jefferson, through his minister, James Monroe, negotiated the purchase of the 2.1 million sq km (1.3 million sq miles) of land from France for $11,250,00. The Louisiana Purchase was intended to provide growing room and ease tensions between settlers and France. The US doubled in size.

LOYOLA, IGNATIUS ST (1491–1556)

Fouder of the Jesuits. Inigo de Recalde de Loyola was born in the Basque province of Spain. He served in the army and was seriously wounded at Pamplona in 1521. After recovery he spent some time reflecting on how to help the Church. He visited Rome and Jerusalem, riding into the Holy City on a donkey. He published the first draft of his great work *The Book of Spiritual Exercise* in 1523. He and six companions took vows of poverty, chastity and obedience at the Church of Montmartre in 1534. He called for the greater glory of God under the obedience of the pope. He became the founder and first General of the Society of Jesus in 1540. Ignatius was canonized in 1622.

))))▶ *Counter-Reformation, Jesuits, Roman Catholicism*

BELOW Martin Luther (centre) reformed the German Christian Church and became one of the founders of Protestantism in Europe. One of his main objections to the Catholic Church was its sale of indulgences to the devout.

LUTHER, MARTIN (1483–1546)

Born at Eisleben, Luther was the founding father of the German Reformation. Ordained in 1507, he was appointed professor of scripture at Wittenberg in 1512. In 1517 he posted his '95 Theses' on the door of Wittenberg Cathedral, objecting to the selling of indulgences by the Church. After debating his views with Catholic theologians he was censored by the pope in 1520. At the Diet of Worms the Emperor Charles V asked him to recant; Luther refused unless scripture could persuade him. Concerned for Luther's safety the Elector of Saxony gave him protection.

In 1525 Luther married and the security of home life became a great strength to him. Luther was not to argue his case in the systematic way of the other great reformer, Jean Calvin. He argued passionately and occasionally paradoxically, with pastoral concerns at the forefront of his mind. His main theological emphasis lay on the importance of scripture and salvation. Through faith alone can a person attain salvation. Faith is the means by which a person can receive all that Christ offered by his death. Lutheranism spread rapidly across Europe, particularly in Scandinavia, Iceland, Prussia and the Baltic States.

))))▶ *Jean Calvin, Diet of Worms, Reformation*

MAASTRICHT TREATY (1991)

Historic document signed by members of the European Community (EC) in the Dutch city of Maastricht. The city was put on the map when it hosted an important summit between the 12 members of the EC, convened to accelerate their economic and political integration. The resulting treaty, officially called the Treaty on European Union, granted European citizenship to citizens of each member country. This allowed greater freedom for people to move between countries in order to live, work or study.

))))⯈ *European Union*

MACARTHUR, DOUGLAS (1880–1964)

US commander during World War II. General Douglas MacArther was commander of the US forces in the Far East until spring 1942. He then helped plan the defeat of Japan as commander in the south-west Pacific. VJ (Victory over Japan) Day came on 2 September 1945.

))))⯈ *World War II*

MACHIAVELLI, NICCOLO (1469–1527)

Italian statesman and writer. Born in Florence, Machiavelli came to prominence when the Florentine Republic was proclaimed in 1498. He was involved in diplomatic negotiations with France,

---

the Vatican and Germany. Machiavelli reorganized the defence of Florence (1503-06), preferring to rely on local conscripts rather than mercenaries, as had been the tradition. He was imprisoned in 1512 when the Medici gained power and the republic was dissolved. He wrote *The Prince* (1532) in which he stated that 'a ruler should not be bound by ethics and should only be concerned with power'. He based much of his theory on the contemporary ruler Cesare Borgia.

))))⯈ *Medici Family*

MAFEKING, SIEGE OF (1899–1900)

Siege during the Boer War. The city of Mafeking was besieged by the Boers on 12 October 1899. The city was being held by British troops under the command of Lord Baden-Powell. He managed to hold the Boers off until a relief column arrived to defend the besieged town. Ultimately the Boer republics were annexed by the British.

))))⯈ *Robert Baden-Powell, Boer War*

MAGELLAN, FERDINAND (c. 1480–1521)

Portuguese navigator and explorer. Magellan was the first European to cross the Pacific Ocean, which he named, and the first person to circumnavigate the Earth – since on his westward voyage he passed the easternmost point he had reached earlier. His voyages helped to confirm the notion of the world as a sphere, demonstrated that the world's oceans were linked, and enabled estimates of the size and shape of South America and the true vastness of the Pacific. His great voyage (1519–21) was plagued by misfortunes, including mutiny, scurvy and near-starvation. Magellan was killed by Philippine islanders.

ABOVE: Propagandistic literature in favour of the Maastricht Referendum.
RIGHT: Ferdinand Magellan was the first explorer to circumnavigate the globe.

MAGNA CARTA (1215)

Charter granted by King John of England to the English barons. Also called the Magna Charta, this was a list of human rights drawn up by the barons to guard against the misuse of royal power. The charter guaranteed feudal rights and defined the judicial system: no freeman should be arrested, imprisoned or punished except by the judgement of his peers or by the law of the land. The king originally refused to sign the charter, but was forced to do so at Runnymede.

MAGYARS

Nomadic people. Originally a Finnish or Siberian tribe, they originated from Ugric and Turkic stock. The Magyars became subjects of the Chazars but became independent in the early ninth century. Árpád led the Magyars against the Bulgars, the Walachians and the Moravians and ruled Hungary until the late tenth century. They were able to subjugate the Huns, Avars and Slavs in the area and incorporated the Pechenegs into their armies. Their military strength was crushed at the Battle of Lechfeld (AD 955) but they continued to raid far into Europe. They are now the largest ethnic group in Hungary and speak the Hungarian language, Magyar.

))))▶ *Árpád, Huns*

MAHARAJAS (1st CENTURY BC)

Title given to the ruler of one of the principal states of India. It is believed that the Kushans first introduced the title during the first century BC, preferring the more elaborate title of 'Great King' to that of simply 'King'. The term 'Maharaja' refers to a Hindu prince ranked above a 'Raja'. Candra Gupta I is said to have been the first ruler to take the title of 'Maharajadhiraja', meaning 'Great King of Kings', during the Gupta period (AD 320–540). Also spelled Maharajaj, nowadays it is used to refer to someone in an administrative rank in India.

MAKKAH (ALSO MECCA)

Birthplace of the Prophet Muhammad, the last messenger of Islam. Mecca was a busy trading centre, buying and selling goods and the worshipping of idols was commonplace. Muhammad received messages from Allah that Meccans found disturbing. He was exiled in AD 622, called the Hijrah (migration). He returned in 630. In the centre of Mecca is the Ka'ba ('cube'). The Ka'ba marks the spot, Muslims believe, where Ibrahim was willing to sacrifice his son, Ishmael. Today two million Muslims make the pilgrimage (Hajj – to set out with purpose) to Mecca each year, a basic requirement for all Muslims to perform once in their lifetime. Muslims face Mecca when praying; it is the earthly focus of Islam.

))))▶ *Islam, Prophet Muhammad*

MALCOLM X (1925–65)

Black American militant leader, born Malcolm Little. Whilst imprisoned in 1946 he was converted to the Black Muslim faith and on his release in 1952 changed his name to Malcolm X. He became an effective speaker for the Nation of Islam and founded 'Muhammad Speaks' (1961). He rejected integration and racial equality; left the organization (1964) to form his own religious organization and reaffirmed his conversion to orthodox Islam. He was shot dead by three Black Muslims.

))))▶ *Civil Rights Movement, Martin Luther King*

ABOVE: The Magna Carta as granted by King John to his barons in 1215.

MANCHURIA

European name for the north-eastern region of China. From 1937 the Japanese invaded China as part of their empire expansion, having already set up a puppet state in Manchuria in 1932. The Chinese military commander, Chiang Kai-shek (1887–1975), received assistance from Britain and the USA from 1941. At the end of the war in 1945 Soviets occupied Manchuria. The Manchuria region was eventually returned to Chinese control after Japanese settlers were expelled.

))))➤ *World War II*

MANDELA, NELSON (b. 1918)

South African Black Nationalist and Statesman. Mandela joined the African National Congress in 1944, becoming one of its leaders in 1949. He was tried for treason but acquitted in 1961, but was jailed again in 1962 for five years. Whilst imprisoned he was tried for sabotage, treason and violent conspiracy and in 1964 was sentenced to life imprisonment, incarcerated at Robben Island Prison until February 1990. In

March he was made Deputy President of the ANC, replacing President Tambo in July. For his work to end apartheid he was awarded the Nobel Peace Prize in 1993 and the following year won South Africa's first all-race elections and established The Truth and Reconciliation Commission. He retired from politics in 1999.

))))➤ *Apartheid, Stephen Biko*

MANHATTAN PROJECT

US project to develop the atomic bomb. The US initiated the Manhattan Project under strict secrecy. Leading project members were Enrico Fermi (1901–54) and J. Robert Oppenheimer (1904–67). Tests were completed at Los Alamos, New Mexico. Two atom bombs were dropped on Japan – on Hiroshima (6 August 1945) and Nagasaki (9 August 1945). Surrender was signed on 2 September.

))))➤ *Hiroshima, Nagasaki, World War II*

LEFT Nelson Mandela, one of the leaders of the African National Congress (ANC). BELOW: The Maori Wars were fought in New Zealand between European settlers and native Maoris who were perceived to be uncultured savages.

MAO ZEDONG (1893–1976)

Founder of the People's Republic of China; Chinese leader (1949–76). Mao Zedong has been described as the 'architect of the new China'. A founding member of the Chinese Communist Party in 1921, he became a dedicated Communist and expert soldier. After heading the famous Long March in 1934–35 (a 9,700-km/15,520-mile trek) Mao became the Communist Party leader.

In 1949 Mao became the Communist Party Chairman and declared the People's Republic of China. Under Mao's radical reforms all land was distributed to the peasants, farms run communally and industry controlled by the State.

Two of Mao's national campaigns, 'The Great Leap Forward' (1958) and the 'Cultural Revolution' (1966), failed in advancing China. They led to the collapse of the economy and the execution of millions – and widespread unrest resulted.

MAORI WARS (1845–48, 1860–70)

Two wars fought between Maoris and British settlers. The first settlers arrived in New Zealand in 1815 and in 1841 the country became a colony of Great Britain. By 1845 the Maoris began to revolt against the loss of their tribal lands. The First Maori War became known as the Flagstaff War, because the first act of defiance from the Maoris came with the chopping down of the Union flag on a pole at a settlement on North Island. Uprisings began again in 1860. The most famous encounter of the Second Maori War was at Gate Pah in 1864 when the British attacked a Maori stockade. Although the stockade fell, the British had lost three times as many men as the Maoris. Permanent peace was finally established in 1870.

))))➤ *Maoris*

MAORIS

Polynesian people of New Zealand. The Maoris arrived in New Zealand from other Pacific islands over a period of 500 years to 1350. Maori culture was well developed before the arrival of the Europeans in the late eighteenth century. In 1840 Great Britain and Maori Chiefs signed the Treaty of Waitangi that established British rule. Conflicts arose between the Maoris and Europeans, after which most Maori land was confiscated. As a result of the wars and European diseases, the Maori population rapidly declined. However, in the twentieth century the Maori population recovered and their arts, culture and politics continue to flourish.

)))➤ *Maori Wars*

MARATHA WARS (1775–82, 1802)

Two wars between the British and the Maratha princes of southern India. Maharashtra is a state in western-central India, dominated by the Maratha people, of Indo-European origin. The Marathas were organized into a loose confederacy under the leadership of various Hindu princes. The Marathas warred victoriously with the Mogul Empire – a situation which brought them up against the British in 1775. The Second Maratha War saw the Marathas defeated by Arthur Wellesley (later Duke of Wellington) and the collapse of Maratha power.

)))➤ *Duke of Wellington*

MARATHON, BATTLE OF (490 BC)

Battle in the Persian Wars. The Persians landed at Marathon, situated 20 miles from Athens, in an attempt to lure the Greeks towards this landing site while a second force landed elsewhere and took Athens itself. The strategy worked, but despite being vastly outnumbered by the Persians, the Greeks drove them back into the sea then turned back to face the second force, which had landed at Phalerum. It was a great victory for the Greeks.

)))➤ *Ancient Greece, Persian Wars*

MARCONI, GUGLIELMO (1874–1937)

Italian physicist. In the late 1890s Guglielmo Marconi developed radio communications, or the 'wireless' as it became known. He perfected the system by 1897 and was able to raise the funds to establish a communications company which was transmitting between England and France by 1899. Transatlantic transmissions were possible by 1901 and the wireless would soon become a vital piece of kit in shipping and warfare communications.

MARIE ANTOINETTE OF FRANCE (1755–93)

Queen of France and daughter of Maria Theresa of Austria. Marie Antoinette was married to Louis XVI at the age of 15. The marriage was happy, but Marie Antoinette's frivolity damaged the French monarchy in the face of demands for liberty. She supported nobles in their resistance to taxation. During the Revolution her steadfastness kept the royal family together but her scheming, and attempts to secure intervention by her brother, the emperor Leopold II, ended chances of a settlement. In October 1793, she followed her husband to the guillotine.

)))➤ *French Revolution, Louis XVI of France*

MARNE, BATTLES OF THE (1914 AND 1918)

Campaign during World War I. The First Battle of Marne (6–9 September 1914) saw the Germans make an offensive move, only to be defeated by French and British troops under French general Joseph Joffre (1852–1931). The Second Battle of Marne (15 July– 4 August 1918), told a similar story, only with the addition of US troops on the Allied side.

)))➤ *World War I*

ABOVE: Guglielmo Marconi produced the precursor of the radio, a type of wireless telegraph. He had been much influenced by Hertz's theories of electromagnetic waves.

MARSHALL PLAN (1948–52)

Programme of US financial aid to rebuild Europe after World War II. Officially known as the European Recovery Programme (ERP), it was called the Marshall Plan after the US secretary of state, George Marshall. The US pumped $13 billion into Europe to revitalize agriculture and avert mass starvation. It also had its own well-being in mind: the USA needed a buoyant Europe to buy its products and wanted to counter Soviet influence in the region.

)))➤ *World War II*

MARX, KARL (1818–83)

Founder of Marxism. Marx published *The Communist Manifesto* in 1848. He was critical of the way in which the capitalist classes used religion to mute the revolutionary capabilities of the working classes. There are characteristics of Marxism that apply to religion. The working class were, for this German Jew, the Chosen People whose pilgrimage through the wilderness would end with entry into the Promised Land – a just, fair society. Passive contemplation was, for Marx, an unreal abstraction. Marx both captured and formulated the spirit of the age when traditional social structures and the authoritarianism of religion were under siege.

)))➤ *Communism, Marxism*

MARXISM (1844)

Doctrines of Karl Marx and Friedrich Engels. Arguably Karl Marx created his own vision of Communism in 1844 following a period as editor of a Cologne newspaper. Marxism has come to mean the political doctrines of the Soviet Union (1917–91) and other Communist or Socialist countries. Although complex and revised by many other writers, Marxism encompasses views on class, economics, art, capitalism, materialism and dialectics. Marx believed that the class struggle would lead to a classless society where those who use their energies to create would benefit directly from what they have achieved. Capitalism was the last stage before this would happen.

)))➤ *Karl Marx, Communism*

MARY I OF ENGLAND (1516–58)

Queen of England from 1553. The Catholic eldest daughter of Henry VIII, by Catherine of Aragon, Mary succeeded after the early death of Edward VI, suppressing the Protestant attempt to place Lady Jane Grey on the throne. Committed to restoring the Catholic Church, Mary's marriage to Philip II of Spain annihilated support, provoking a Protestant rebellion led by Sir Thomas Wyatt. Persecutions and executions followed, while her loveless and childless marriage foundered. In 1557–58, Mary joined Spain in war against France, only to lose Calais, England's last French possession.

)))➤ *Henry VIII of England, Philip II of Spain*

MARY, QUEEN OF SCOTS (1542–87)

Queen of Scotland within a week of birth, on the death of her father James V. While Mary was brought up in France for protection, her mother, Mary of Guise, ruled as regent. In 1558, Mary married François, the French dauphin. He became king in 1559, but she returned to Scotland after his death in 1560. Mary then married Henry, Lord Darnley, who fathered her son, the future James VI of Scotland (I of England). Mary married the Earl of Bothwell soon after Darnley's murder, in which Bothwell was implicated, in 1567. Mary's Catholicism and behaviour alienated her from the

LEFT: Karl Marx.
ABOVE: Mary I of England.

Protestant nobility in Scotland. Fleeing to England for help, Elizabeth I (her cousin) imprisoned Mary, where she became the centre of Catholic plots against Elizabeth. She was executed in 1586.

)))◆ *Elizabeth I of England*

MAXIMILIAN I (1459–1519)

Holy Roman Emperor and German king from 1493. Through marriage and war he greatly increased imperial possessions. His marriage to Mary, heiress of Charles the Bold of Burgundy, in 1477 added the Low Countries. In 1495, at the Imperial Diet at Worms the imperial princes resisted any attempts by Maximilian to reform the imperial chamber and taxation, forcing Maximilian to introduce commissions of his own to deal with these. In 1496 he married his son Philip I to Joanna, daughter of Ferdinand and Isabella of Spain. Philip and Joanna's son, the emperor Charles V, inherited Spain in 1516.

Maximilian pursued inconclusive wars in France, Switzerland and Italy, in a futile attempt to revive a universal empire in the west and make himself pope, though his war against Hungary in 1506 improved the imperial claim to the throne there.

)))◆ *Ferdinand and Isabella of Spain, Holy Roman Empire, Diet of Worms*

MAXWELL, JAMES CLERK (1831–79)

Scottish mathematician. James Clerk Maxwell studied the phenomenon of electromagnetic radiation. Maxwell devised equations that demonstrated the relationship between electricity, magnetism and light. He went on to study the nature of colour vision and, in 1861, produced the first colour photograph that used a three-colour process, in the same way that the human eye receives and interprets visual images on the retina.

MAYA (1500 BC – AD 1519)

Native American civilization. The Mayans settled in present-day Mexico, Guatemala, Honduras and El Salvador. Before AD 200 they had been an agricultural people but began to build temples, palaces and pyramids and develop writing and astronomy. They made paper and were great sculptors and architects. At the height of the Mayan civilization the population had reached two million

across their 40 cities. Whether war or the exhaustion of the land was to blame by AD 900 the civilization was in decline. The Mayans abandoned most of their temples and returned to their agricultural life. During the tenth century the Toltecs had taken over the most important city of the Mayans, Chichén Itzá. When the Spanish arrived in the sixteenth century they easily overcame the remnants of the Mayan civilization but independent communities still existed until 1901. Their writing was not deciphered until the mid-twentieth century, shedding light on their religion, rituals, mathematics and astronomy.

MAYFLOWER (1620)

Ship in which the Pilgrim Fathers travelled to the New World. Captain Christopher Jones was in charge of this 66-day transatlantic journey. It is thought that the 180-tonne sailing ship had three-masts, was 30.48 m/100 ft in length and 7.92m/26 ft wide. The ship had two decks and galley and quarters for a crew of 30.

)))◆ *Colonialism, Pilgrim Fathers*

MAZZINI, GUISEPPE (1805–72)

Italian revolutionary. An advocate of Italian unification, Mazzini joined the revolutionary Carbonari society in 1827. He was exiled to France where he founded the Young Italy (Giovine Italia) Society. Mazzini returned to Italy for the 1848 revolution and headed a republican government before its overthrow the following year. The nationalist movement (Risorgimento) was taken over by monarchists such as Camillo di Cavour, and Mazzini took no pleasure in the creation in 1861 of a unified Italian kingdom rather than a republic.

)))◆ *Camillo di Cavour*

ABOVE: A Mayan stone relief carving fails to yield clues about this civilization's mysterious decline.

MECCA (SEE MAKKAH)

MEDICI FAMILY

 Ruling family of Florence. Medici power began with Giovanni di Medici (1360–1429), a banker. His son, Cosimo (1389–1464), was expelled by the ruling oligarchy. Returning in 1434, he became the model for Machiavelli's *The Prince* through his manipulation of republican government to wield supreme power over the city. Like Cosimo, he patronized art, further embellishing Florence, and was a poet. His great-granddaughter was Catherine di Medici (1519–89), mother and regent of Charles IX of France.

Following Lorenzo's death, Charles VIII of France invaded Italy to seize Naples, and exiled the Medici, damaging their power in Florence even though they came back in 1512. Medici power now lay with Lorenzo's son, the pope Leo X (in office 1513–21), and nephew, the pope Clement VII (in office 1523–34), until a descendant of Giovanni di Medici, Cosimo (1519–74), revived the family fortunes. Granted Siena by the emperor, he was created First Grand Duke of Tuscany in 1569, establishing a dynasty lasting until 1737.

))))➤ *Charles IX of France*

MENDELEYEV, DMITRI (1834–1907)

Inventor of the Periodic Table of chemical elements. In 1869, Dmitri Mendeleyev published the periodic table he had devised for the chemical elements. Chemically similar elements were grouped in vertical rows, yet the elements appeared in order of relative atomic mass (RAM) in periods. Mendeleyev correctly predicted the discovery of elements to fill the vacant spaces.

ABOVE: Cosimo di Medici.

RIGHT: The Creation of Man *panel inside the Vatican's Sistine Chapel is a magnificent example of Michelangelo's artistic genius.*

METHODISTS

Protestant religious offshoot. The founder of the Methodists, John Wesley (1703–91), was an Anglican priest who tried hard not to allow Methodism to break from the Church of England. His message of hope and personal salvation was increasingly popular and, with his brother Charles (1707–89), John made many trips to America. It was in 1738 that John and Charles both received separate revelations confirming the power of their faith. John Wesley travelled for 52 years, preaching 40,000 sermons. The term 'Methodist' comes from the methodical order of life – fasting twice a week and two services on Sundays. Methodism gave rise to other splinter groups after Wesley's death, of which only the Salvation Army survives.

))))➤ *Protestantism*

MICHELANGELO (1475–1564)

Italian sculptor, architect, painter and poet. Michelangelo Buonarroti, born in Florence, was one of the key figures in that city's leadership of the Renaissance under the patronage of wealthy nobleman Lorenzo di Medici (1444–92). Though it was his work in stone that first brought him fame, with such statues as the great *Pieta* of 1498–49 and the superb *David* of 1501–04, his awesome powers as a painter are revealed in the marvellous frescoes he created on the ceiling of the Sistine Chapel in the Vatican, 1508–12. His greatest monument, however – in size, as well as vision – is the great Cathedral of St Peter, Rome, which he completed.

))))➤ *Renaissance*

MIDDLE AGES (5TH–15TH CENTURIES)

European history from the collapse of Rome to the Renaissance. Italian Humanists describing the 1,000 years between the fifth and fifteenth centuries introduced the term. After Alaric had sacked Rome in AD 410, the early Middle Ages, or Dark Ages, saw a period of fragmentation and incessant war. By the tenth century the era of migrating Barbarians had ended and trade and commerce began to revive. Strong cultural and economic forces shifted power from the Eastern Mediterranean to Western Europe. Agriculture had developed and the population expanded rapidly. By the thirteenth century gothic architecture and sculpture, politics and religion dominated society, including the works of Thomas Aquinas. In this century medieval society saw the growth of the Secular State and the emergence of the monarchies of Spain, France and England. After the Black Death in the 1340s the expansion of trade and finance transformed the European economy and paved the way for the Renaissance period.

)))) *Thomas Aquinas, Dark Ages*

BELOW: The Middle Ages was a violent period in history, but it also cultivated gentler pursuits like the art of courtly love.

MIDWAY, BATTLE OF (1942)

Sea battle between the USA and Japan during World War II. The battle took place in June 1942 in the Pacific Ocean. The war in the Pacific had been turning in favour of the Japanese until the USA decisively defeated them off Midway island. Japanese naval air superiority was destroyed in a single day, marking the turning point of the conflict.

)))) *World War II*

MING DYNASTY (1368–1644)

Last native Chinese dynasty. Founded by Chu Yuan-Chang, who ruled as Hung-wu, following the fall of the Mongol Yuan dynasty the Ming dynasty united China for nearly 400 years. The Ming bureaucracy had over 20,000 positions, from ministers to police chiefs. It was a structured society that saw the population rise from 60 to 150 million. His successors extended the empire but by the sixteenth century they were under pressure from the Mongols and the Japanese.

)))) *Mongols*

MISSOURI COMPROMISE (1820)

Agreement for regulating slavery in the USA. In 1818 Missouri applied for statehood. As slave owners this would have tipped the balance between the 11 slave and 11 free states. The Compromise allowed them statehood provided no slaves would be allowed to enter Missouri and those there would be gradually freed.

)))) *Slavery*

MITTERRAND, FRANÇOIS (1916–96)

President of France (1981–95). Mitterand founded the French Socialist Party in 1971 and beat Giscard d'Etaing in 1981 to become the first socialist president. After introducing some left-wing economic policies such as nationalizing key industries, Mitterand abandoned them in 1983 after France's worsening financial situation. From then on he adopted a free-market approach and generally ruled as a centrist. The socialists lost their majority in 1984 and Mitterand was forced to form a government with a right-wing prime minister, Jaques Chirac. In 1988 he defeated Chirac to run for another seven-year term, in which he focused on promoting European unity.

MODERNISM (20TH CENTURY)

Movement in twentieth-century literature, art and architecture. Arguably no more than a catch-all phrase for the many and varied artistic upheavals of the early part of the twentieth century, modernism can nevertheless be seen to have certain distinguishing features. Like the Impressionists, concerned to achieve an art that was more true to the life of the immediately experienced moment than anything produced by the conventional realism or romanticism of the nineteenth century, writers like England's Virginia Woolf (1882–1941) and the Irish genius James Joyce (1882–1941) experimented with techniques such as 'stream of consciousness'.

Paradoxically, this had the effect of breaking up traditional narrative and logical coherence, hence the notoriously difficulty of works by American writers based in Europe like T. S. Eliot (1888–1965), Ezra Pound (1885–1972) and Gertrude Stein (1874–1946), and the over-simplifying view that modernism was the mere rejection of all that had gone before in art and literature. Straddling these two worlds, English novelist and painter Percy Wyndham Lewis (1882–1957) was influential both as practitioner and critic. On the continent and in America, meanwhile, architects like Le Corbusier (1887–1965) and Frank Lloyd Wright (1867–1959) sought to encapsulate the new anti-romantic principles in the spare, stripped-down austerity of their designs.

))))➤ *Impressionism, Romanticism*

MOGUL EMPIRE (1526–1857)

Indian empire, which ruled from 1526 until the dethronement of the last emperor by the British in 1857. The emperors were called Moguls (Mongols) as descendants of Tamerlaine.

Babur, a Central Asian Chaghtai Turk, founded the Empire in 1526. Akbar greatly expanded its frontiers and laid the foundations of economic growth. The Empire reached its greatest extent, encompassing almost the whole subcontinent, under Aurangzeb.

The Mogul emperor occupied a position of supreme power but close relations were maintained with Hindu society and officialdom. The Moguls excelled in manuscript illustration, painting and architecture, notably the Taj Mahal, built by Shah Jahan.

))))➤ *Aurangzeb, Akhbar, Babar, Tamerlaine*

MOHENJO DARO (2000 BC)

Ancient city in India. Mohenjo Daro, along with Harappa, were the largest cities in the world at their height in around 2000 BC. Situated in the Indus Valley, Mohenjo Daro was the hub of the Hindu religion in ancient times.

))))➤ *Hinduism*

MONET, CLAUDE (1840–1926)

French painter. The founder of Impressionism, which took its name from the title of one of his pictures, *Impression: Sunrise* (1872), Monet was also the most doctrinaire in his adherence to the movement's scientific principles. Though he started out, surprisingly, as a caricaturist, his mentor Eugène Boudin (1824–98) quickly converted him to landscape-painting *plein-air* (in the open air), a genre to which he would maintain unswerving loyalty thereafter. Even as his work became ever more widely respected from the 1890s onward, Monet's own artistic focus appeared to narrow: his last years' work were dominated by a series of giant canvases of waterlilies recorded in his garden at Giverny, outside Paris.

))))➤ *Barbizon School, Impressionism*

LEFT: La Promenade *by Claude Monet, the founder of Impressionism.*

MONGOLS (1196)

Tribal people. By 1196 Temujin had eliminated most of his rivals among the Mongols and became Genghis Khan. Under his leadership the Mongols would carve out one of the largest land empires in history, from the Caspian Sea to the South China Seas. In 1214 he crossed the Great Wall of China and defeated the Manchus. After Peking had surrendered he razed it to the ground and turned westward to conquer Afghanistan and Persia. He died in 1227 but the Mongols continued their conquests. Mongol rule in China continued as the Yuan dynasty despite the rest of the Empire fragmenting.

))))▶ *Genghis Khan, Kublai Khan*

MONROE, MARILYN (1926–62)

American film star. Born in Los Angeles, Norma Jean Mortenson became a photographic model at the age of 20, after which a series of small movie parts led quickly to stardom in films like *Gentlemen Prefer Blondes* (1953) and *Some Like it Hot* (1959). Though increasingly uncomfortable with her type-casting as giggly dumb blonde, she struggled to make an impact in more serious roles, while her marriages to baseball star Joe di Maggio and playwright Arthur Miller both ended unhappily. Her suicide saw her stereotyped again, this time as iconic victim of Hollywood's destructive hunger for youth and beauty, and this is how her image has come down to later generations.

MONROE DOCTRINE (1823)

Formulation of US policy in the Western Hemisphere. Attempting to safeguard US interests in preventing European countries from re-establishing colonies in the Americas, President James

BELOW LEFT: Marilyn Monroe and Laurence Olivier in The Prince and the Showgirl.

BELOW: Montezuma, the last great Aztec emperor, was first tricked and then taken hostage by Hernán Cortés, the Spanish conquistador.

Monroe established a justification for US expansion. The doctrine was used in the late nineteenth century to exert control over the Panama Canal. After World War II the US declared that 'an attack on an American nation was an attack on all nations', and later used it to keep Communism out of Latin America.

))))▶ *Panama Canal, World War II*

MONS, BATTLE OF (1914)

Early battle of World War I. An Allied force of British and French troops launched an offensive against the invading German army at Mons. However, French reinforcements failed to arrive as planned. In panic the French troops at the frontline abandoned their position, leaving the British vulnerable to encirclement by the Germans.

))))▶ *World War I*

MONTEZUMA II (1466–1520)

Last Aztec emperor of Mexico, from 1503. He regarded the coming of the Spanish warrior and conqueror, Cortés, as the arrival of a god. To please Cortés, Montezuma offered him gifts, which only stimulated the Spaniards' greed. Realizing the truth, Montezuma invited Cortés to his lake capital, Tenochlitlán. Cortés seized Montezuma as a hostage but his soldiers lost control and embarked on massacring the inhabitants. In the confusion as Aztec forces attacked Cortés and his men, Montezuma was killed.

))))▶ *Aztecs, Hernán Cortés, Tenochtitlán*

MOORS (7TH CENTURY)

After the Arab conquest of the Berbers, a period of inter-marriage and development created a new group of peoples who settled in North Africa and conquered Spain. After settling here they were gradually expelled by the Christians between the eleventh and seventeenth centuries. The Umayyad dynasty ruled Muslim Spain for three centuries. Particularly notable was its greatest ruler, Abd-ar-Rahman III. They returned to inhabit Morocco, Algeria and Mauritania. Historians also describe the Arabic-speaking Berbers who lived in towns in North Africa as Moors and, more generally, the inhabitants of the Turkish Barbary States.

MORE, ST THOMAS (1478–1535)

Chancellor to Henry VIII and scholar. A twice-marrried lawyer, More published *Utopia* in 1516 gaining him a European reputation for scholarship. In 1529 he became Lord Chancellor but was unable to support Henry VIII's drive for a divorce. He resigned, refused to recognize the king as head of the English Church and was imprisoned in the Tower of London where he wrote *Dialogue of Comfort against Tribulation*. After 15 months he was beheaded in 1535 and his head displayed on Tower Bridge. He was made a saint in 1935.

)))) *Henry VIII of England*

MORMONS (1830)

Common name for the Church of Jesus Christ of Latter Day Saints. Founded in 1830, Mormons do not accept the traditional Christian belief in the Trinity, believing Father, Son and Holy Ghost are three separate beings. The Church was founded by Joseph Smith (1805–44) in Fayette, USA, after receiving authority from God in a vision in 1820. *The Book of Mormon: Another Testament of Jesus Christ* was published in 1827 and is used alongside the Bible. There are around 10 million members worldwide. The family is a central focus for Mormons and healthy living is encouraged with coffee, tea and alcohol being discouraged.

ABOVE: Samuel Morse, inventor of the Morse code, was also credited with building the first electric telegraph in 1835.

MORSE, SAMUEL (1791–1872)

US inventor. The telegraph was invented by Samuel Morse in 1838. It was an electrical system that transmitted on/off signals along a wire, from one location to the next. To make his invention practicable Morse adopted Alfred Vail's (1807–59) system of long and short signals that coded for the letters of the alphabet, which became known as Morse code. A short signal was called a 'dot' and a long one a 'dash'.

MOTHER THERESA (1910–97)

Albanian-born founder of the Order of the Missionaries. 'Mother Teresa of Calcutta' joined the Institute of the Blessed Virgin Mary in Ireland in 1928 and then travelled to India to work as a teacher. She studied nursing and founded the Order in 1948, adopting Indian citizenship. In 1963 she was recognised for her services to the people of India and was awarded, in 1971 the first Pope John XXIII Peace Prize and in 1979 the Nobel Peace Prize. The Order has continued serving the disadvantaged since her death in 1997, numbering 1,000 nuns operating 60 centres in Calcutta and 200 worldwide.

MOZART, WOLFGANG AMADEUS (1756–91)

Austrian composer. The archetypal child prodigy, Mozart was playing the piano by the age of four and had written his first composition by the time he was six. Where many such stars prove unable to negotiate the difficult passage to adult achievement, however, Mozart went from strength to strength with a string of major works. In addition to several important concertos, for piano and for other instruments, his symphonies won the admiration of the great Franz Josef Haydn. A master of every sort of chamber and choral music, his crowning achievements were perhaps achieved in the field of opera, where creations like *Don Giovanni* and *The Magic Flute* remain acknowledged masterworks.

))))▶ *Franz Josef Haydn*

MUHAMMAD, PROPHET (AD 570–632)

Muhammad, the last of Prophets in the Muslim religion, was of the family of Banu Haskim in the tribe of Quraysh. At the age of 25 he married Khadija, his employer, with whom he had two sons and four daughters. In AD 611 he received a message from

Jibril insisting he 'recite' (Iqra). Over the next 22 years he received a number of messages, which form the Qur'an. Muhammad's messages were not well received in Mecca where he lived and in AD 622 he left (called 'the Hijra') for Yathrib (now called 'al-Madina). In AD 630 Muhammad returned, purged idols and images from Mecca. He died in AD 632.

ABOVE: A fifteenth-century Persian manuscript showing the prophet Muhammad being escorted to Paradise by the angel Gabriel.
ABOVE RIGHT: Benito Mussolini, leader of the Fascist Party in Italy, became Aldolf Hitler's principal ally during World War II.

Called the 'Seal of the Prophets', his message, Muslims believe, is the true, final and uncorrupted Word of God (Allah). Muhammad was unlearned, a human being (not a god) and not without sin. He is, however, a living commentary on the Qur'an. He is not the founder of Islam as Muslims believe Islam has always been; Muhammad is the final revelation.

MUNICH AGREEMENT (1938)

Pact signed by Germany, Italy, France and Britain in which Czechoslovakia was forced to surrender its Sudetenland region to Hitler. Britain and France, still recovering from World War I, were desperate to avoid confrontation with Germany and agreed on this policy of appeasement in return for Hitler's promise not to claim any other territory. The Munich pact was nullified when German troops marched into Czechoslovakia in March 1939 and claimed the rest of the country.

))))▶ *World War II*

MUSSOLINI, BENITO (1883–1945)

LA TRIBUNA ILLUSTRATA

LA STORICA VISITA DEL DUCE AL FÜHRER

Italian dictator (1922–1943). Mussolini was the leader (Il Duce) of Italian Fascism, which he founded in 1919. His Blackshirt militia, supported by landowners and industrialists, terrorized socialist and peasant groups. He formed a coalition government in 1922 and by 1926 had created a totalitarian, single-party state. Mussolini invaded Ethiopia (1935–36), but the Italian army suffered many defeats in World War II, which they entered in 1940 in support of Germany. Mussolini was forced to resign from the Fascist Council in 1943. With German help he set up a republican government in northern Italy, but was captured in 1945 and executed by the partisans.

))))▶ *Facism, World War II*

NAGASAKI (1945)

Japanese city destroyed by an atomic bomb. Nagasaki was a major shipbuilding city, chosen as the target for a second atomic bomb dropped on Japan in World War II. The city was bombed three days after Hiroshima, while the Japanese were still debating their response to the first bomb. Nagasaki's size and geography led to a smaller loss of life and destruction, even though the bomb dropped on the city was significantly more powerful.

⮞ *Hiroshima*

NANAK, GURU (1469–1539)

First Sikh Guru and founder of the Sikh religion. Nanak married and had two sons, after which he became pre-occupied with a spiritual quest. In 1499 he experienced God's call. He went on to teach that God is 'One and eternal'. One can meditate on God's name to master the impulses and passions of life but above all one must trust the guru (spiritual teacher). He composed hymns, now contained in the *Adi Granth*. He also taught irrelevance of caste – inner purity was vital.

⮞ *Sikhism*

NANKING, TREATY OF (1842)

Treaty that ended the First Opium War. The treaty established Hong Kong as a temporary British colony and opened four ports for European trading.

⮞ *Opium Wars*

NANSEN, FRIDTJOF (1861–1930)

Norwegian explorer and statesman. Nansen made the first crossing of Greenland. Study of Arctic currents convinced him that a ship frozen into the ice would drift over the North Pole. He attempted this in the ship *Fram* but slowness of drift forced Nansen and a companion to strike out for the Pole by dog-sled. They reached 86°14', a new record. Nansen became a Nobel laureate for his work following the Russian Revolution.

NAPOLEON III (1808–73)

Last emperor of France, from 1851–70. Nephew of Napoleon I, Napoleon III grew up with a romantic interest in liberal causes. In 1836, he led a revolt against French monarchy. In 1848 he was created president of the new French Republic, but in 1851 declared himself emperor. He encouraged industrial and financial modernization, built railways, allied France with Britain, and supported Italian unification. He compromised popularity by supporting the pope and sending an army to Mexico to collect debts. Leading France into the Franco-Prussian War was unpopular and a republic was declared when Napoleon was captured at Sedan in 1870. He died in England.

⮞ *Franco-Prussian War*

NAPOLEONIC WARS (1803–15)

Series of campaigns fought between Europe and France. Napoleon Bonaparte had been a general in the French Revolution from 1796 and overthrew the ruling Directory in 1799. He made himself dictator and, in 1803, launched a campaign with the aim of conquering the whole of Europe.

LEFT: The Battle of Nanking in 1937.
ABOVE: Napoleon III.

LEFT: French and Austrian armies occupy Edelsberg bridge near Vienna during the Napoleonic Wars.

In 1808 Napoleon invaded Spain, but failed to take Portugal, due to assistance from the Duke of Wellington. He again defeated the Austrians at Wagram (1809) and by 1812 was ready for an invasion attempt on Russia. Napoleon managed to defeat the Russians at Borodino but casualties were high, leaving him with a diminished army. Then came the Battle of Leipzig, October 1913, where a coalition force of Prussians, Austrians and Russians won a decisive victory.

Napoleon's army found itself attacked from the east and south by an international war machine. Despite a skilful defence of France, Napoleon was forced to abdicate in April 1814, bringing the Napoleonic Wars to an end.

))))▶ *Battle of Austerlitz, Napoleon Bonaparte, Battle of Leipzig, Admiral Horatio Nelson, Battle of Trafalgar, Battle of Waterloo, Duke of Wellington*

NASSER, ABDEL (1918–70)

President of Egypt (1956–70). Nasser was the driving force behind the 1952 coup to oust King Faruk. He then negotiated a treaty with the British to end their 72-year occupation of Egypt. His policy of non-alignment brought conflict with the British and the USA, who withdrew finance for the Aswan Dam. In order to raise money for the project, Nasser nationalized the Suez Canal, which led to an armed response from France, Britain and Israel. The three countries were forced to withdraw by the USA, but a UN force remained. Tensions erupted again in 1967 when Israel attacked Egypt in the Six-Day War, occupying the entire Sinai Peninsula.

))))▶ *Six-Day War, Suez Crisis*

Until 1805 warfare remained at sea, giving Napoleon the chance to reform France and prepare it for the campaign ahead. In 1804 he crowned himself Emperor Napoleon I and assumed absolute power over his nation. The naval Battle of Trafalgar (1805) was a victory for the British under Admiral Horatio Nelson, ensuring that Napoleon's ambition to conquer Britain was thwarted.

The first land battles came in 1805 when Russia and Austria declared war on France. Napoleon devastated their forces at the battles of Ulm and Austerlitz. By 1806 Napoleon had western Germany and Italy under his control and Prussia was pushed into action.

Before Russian assistance could arrive, Napoleon took on the Prussian army at the battles of Jena and Auerstadt, both on 14 October 1806, defeating it easily. When the Russian army finally arrived, Napoleon and Tsar Alexander I reached stalemate at the battles of Friedland and Eylau. Russia and France became unwilling and distrustful allies, blockading trade with Britain.

NATIVE AMERICAN INDIANS

 Indigenous people of America. Prior to the arrival of the Europeans, 90 million people inhabited the Americas, with 10 million north of Mexico. It is believed that these peoples came from Siberia during the Paleolithic period. By the seventeenth century the Americas had been infiltrated by Europeans in their thousands. Systematically, the Native Americans were dislocated, driven off their native lands, slaughtered and, on rare occasions, absorbed into the new European society.

For the fledgling United States the Native Americans were considered a danger to human life and an inhibition to the expansion of their country. By 1830 the Indian Removal Act had been passed and their removal from areas designated for settlers had become commonplace. The Allotment or Dawes Act (1887) attempted to parcel out communally owned reservation land to individual Indians but many found themselves landless as speculators snapped up the 160-acre allotments. As far as the settlers and frontiersmen were concerned, the indigenous people needed to be slaughtered in self-defense. By the mid nineteenth century Indian territories, or reservations, had been set aside in some of the least habitable parts of the country, inciting the Plains Indian Wars, which eventually saw the slaughter of the Sioux tribe. By the 1890s settlers had reached the Pacific Ocean and as far as the government was concerned Native Americans were now wards of the USA.

By the 1990s Native Americans accounted for less than one per cent of the US population. They still have 56 million acres of reservation land. Notable Native American leaders include Tecumseh (d. 1813), leader of the Shawnee, Geronimo (d. 1909), Apache chief, and Sitting Bull (d. 1890), Sioux chief.

⫸ *George Armstrong Custer, Battle of the Little Bighorn, Sitting Bull, Trail of Tears*

NAWAB

Ruling Indian princes. In 1756 Siraj-ud-Dawlah, the nawab or viceroy of Bengal, seized Calcutta and imprisoned several British in a dungeon called the Black Hole of Calcutta. In January 1757 Robert Clive recaptured Calcutta and in June decisively defeated the nawab at Plassey, thus securing British power in India.

⫸ *Black Hole of Calcutta, Robert Clive, Battle of Plassey*

NAWAL EL SAADAWI (b. 1930)

Egyptian feminist, author of classic work on women in Islam *The Hidden Face of Eve*. She was dismissed from Egyptian Ministry of Health in 1972 because of political activities; arrested 1987 and only released after assassination of President Sadat. She wrote copiously on Muslim women in Islamic society notably in *Women and Sex* (1972).

NAZI PARTY (1933–45)

German political party. The abbreviated name of the National Socialist Party, the Nazis governed Germany under the brutal dictatorship of Adolf Hitler from 1933 to 1945. The Party ideology included state control over the individual, enforced by violent repression, and racism, a policy that resulted in the deaths of, among others, six million Jews in concentration camps. The party was banned in Germany after World War II, though neo-Nazism gained some popularity following reunification and groups have also sprung up in other countries.

⫸ *Concentration Camps, Adolf Hitler, World War II*

ABOVE LEFT: Native American Indians lost their lands and culture to European settlers. Nowadays they account for less than one per cent of the entire US population.

ABOVE: A uniform bearing a swastika, the symbol of the Nazi Party.

BELOW: *A stone relief image depicting the Egyptian queen Nefertiti; she is seen here offering libations to the gods.*

NAZI-SOVIET PACT (1939)

Treaty of non-aggression between Germany and the Soviet Union. The secret pact was signed a few days before the outbreak of World War II and divided Eastern Europe into separate German and Soviet spheres of influence. This enabled Hitler to invade Poland from the east and partition the country. The pact dissolved when Germany invaded the Soviet Union in 1941. Until 1989, the USSR denied the pact's existence as it was evidence of its annexation of the Baltic States.

))))➤ *Nazi Party, World War II*

NEFERTITI (c. 1360–30 BC)

Egyptian queen. As wife of the heretic pharaoh Amenophis IV (Akhenaten), Nefertiti helped lead the religious revolution replacing traditional Egyptian gods with the Sun-god, Aten. Nefertiti is best-known for the carved reliefs depicting her and her husband with their daughters in intimate

settings, and the remarkable portrait bust found in the regime's new capital at Akhetaten. Mystery surrounds her fate, and she has been linked to the obscure figure, Smenkhare, her husband's short-lived successor. Her daughter Ankhesenamun was married to Tutankhamun, owner of the celebrated tomb at Thebes.

))))➤ *Akhenaten, Ancient Egypt, Tutankhamun*

NEHRU, JAWAHARLAL (1889–1964)

Prime minister of India (1947–64). Nehru led the socialist wing of the Congress party and was second only in influence to Gandhi, though his approach to politics was more secular. He was imprisoned many times during the fight for Indian independence and became the new republic's first prime minister.

Nehru isolated Western powers with his foreign policy of nonalignment and finally drove the Portuguese out of Goa. His daughter was Indira Gandhi, who also became prime minister.

))))➤ *Indira Gandhi, Mahatma Gandhi, Indian Independence*

NELSON, ADMIRAL HORATIO (1758–1805)

British hero of the Napoleonic Wars. Horatio Nelson joined the navy at the age of 12. He fought in the Revolutionary Wars against France, losing his right eye and arm in action. During that time he climbed the ranks and had considerable military success. His greatest moment came with victory against the Napoleonic fleet at Trafalgar in 1805, by which time he was serving as admiral. He was hit by sniper fire and died on board HMS *Victory*.

))))➤ *Napoleonic Wars, Battle of Trafalgar*

NEOCLASSICISM

Artistic and architectural movement. The most immediate impulse to this eighteenth-century movement may have been a spate of significant archeological finds, and the insight these offered into the extraordinary achievements of classical civilization. Yet the neoclassical spirit would not have proved so profoundly important, had it not appealed to a developing Enlightenment sensibility which saw in the strict regularities of classical art an emblem of man's potential to impose form on formless nature, to shape his own existence. In this respect it was a reaction to the spirit of the seventeenth-century baroque, whose extravagant intensity, though beautifully accomplished, hinted at spiritual and emotional transcendence, and loss of control. The German critic Johann Joachim Winckelmann (1717–68) caught the mood of the times with his call for a return to the 'noble simplicity and calm grandeur' of classical art. Revolutionary governments in America and France, meanwhile, associated classicism with the days of democratic Athens and Republican Rome: hence the appeal of the heroic scenes depicted by French artists like Jacques-Louis David (1748–1825) and Jean-Auguste-Dominique Ingres (1780–1867) and by American sculptor Horatio Greenough (1805–52).

))))➤ *Baroque, Enlightenment*

NERO (AD 37–68)

Roman emperor, from AD 54. Vain and ostenta-
tious, Nero took advantage of the fire of AD 64
to clear space for a vast palace in Rome, covering the
expense by fabricating accusations against wealthy men
and confiscating their property. Nero performed in public
as a musician and charioteer, and earned a reputation for
perversion and cruelty. He murdered his mother Agrippina
in AD 59, and his tutor Seneca in AD 65. In AD 68 he was
forced to flee, committing suicide.

)))))➤ *Ancient Rome*

NEW DEAL (1933–39)

Roosevelt's economic reforms. After becoming
president of the US in 1932, Roosevelt enacted a
series of reforms in industry, agriculture, labour, finance
and housing aimed at ensuring that the USA never
suffered again from the ravages of an economic
depression. The New Deal for the 'forgotten man' greatly
extended the government's involvement in the economy.
The sweepig changes were achieved by a series of Acts
over the years, meeting opposition from big business and
other sections at times due to their 'socialist' tendencies.
Nevertheless, New Deal gathered support and was
followed by Truman's 'Fair Deal' policies (1945–53).

)))))➤ *Franklin D. Roosevelt, Harry S. Truman*

NEWCOMEN, THOMAS (1663–1729)

English blacksmith and inventor. Newcomen
worked on improvements to Thomas Savery's
steam engine of 1698 and in 1705, with another English
inventor, John Calley (or Cawley), produced an engine
that used both atmospheric pressure and low-pressure
steam. It was widely adopted in Europe for pumping
water and exported to North America around 1755.
James Watt's engine, which introduced a separate
condenser and air-pump, was patented in 1769 and
by 1790 had replaced the Newcomen engine.

)))))➤ *James Watt*

NEWTON, ISAAC (1642–1727)

Engligh physicist. Newton worked on a theory of
gravitation. It was fundamental to a new way of
looking at the Universe, where counter-intuitive forces

had to be taken into account. Newton realized that every
object must possess its own gravitational pull, which is
proportional to its mass. He also showed that white light
comprises a spectrum of colours by using a glass prism.

)))))➤ *Albert Einstein*

NICAEA, COUNCIL OF (AD 325)

Called by Emperor Constantine to deal with heresy
threatening the unity of the Christian Church.
Most of the 220–250 bishops present were from the
eastern half of the empire, only six attended from the
Western Church. This first ecumenical Council produced
a creed (statement of faith), probably based on the
baptismal creeds of Antioch and Jerusalem, and calculated
the date of Easter. The creed, used frequently today, was
received and agreed by the majority of bishops present.

)))))➤ *Constantine*

ABOVE: Isaac Newton discovers the refraction of light.

NIETZSCHE, FRIEDRICH (1844–1900)

German classical scholar and great thinker. Nietzsche attended Bonn and Leipzig universities, studying classical literature and language. From 1869–79 he was a professor at the University of Basel and whilst there wrote *The Birth of Tragedy* (1872), *Thoughts out of Season* (1873–76) and *Human, All Too Human* (1878). A prolific writer, he continued after his retirement, producing works such as *Thus Spake Zarathustra*, *Beyond Good and Evil*, *On the Genealogy of Morals*, *Twilight of the Idols* and *The Antichrist*.

NIGHTINGALE, FLORENCE (1820–1910)

English hospital reformer; known as the Lady with the Lamp. During the Crimean War she was based in the military hospitals of Turkey, managing to cope with severe overcrowding and the lack of basic necessities. In 1856 the Royal Commission on the Health of the Army was formed, leading to the foundation of the Army Medical School. She established, at St Thomas's Hospital, the Nightingale School for Nurses and in 1907 was the first woman to be awarded the Order of Merit.

))))▶ *Crimean War*

NICHOLAS II OF RUSSIA (1868–1918)

Last tsar of Russia, from 1894. His rule saw Russia ravaged by World War I and Russian society turned upside down by Communist revolutions.

Nicholas II was happily married to the Tsarina Alexandra who dominated him, and who bore him four daughters and one son. Alexandra was heavily influenced by the religious fraud Rasputin.

Nicholas rejected liberal movements in Russia and supported the suppression of any suggestion of socialist revolution or reform. He preferred the support of old-fashioned conservative advisers and politicians. Russia was defeated by Japan in the war of 1904–05, a humiliation leading to the formation of a parliament (*duma*), but it was soon rendered impotent, which Nicholas encouraged.

The outbreak of World War I allowed these problems to be shelved but setbacks and government mismanagement exposed them once more, leading to the Revolution in 1917. Nicholas abdicated, and the family were imprisoned and executed in July 1918.

))))▶ *Bolsheviks, Rasputin, Russian Revolution, World War I*

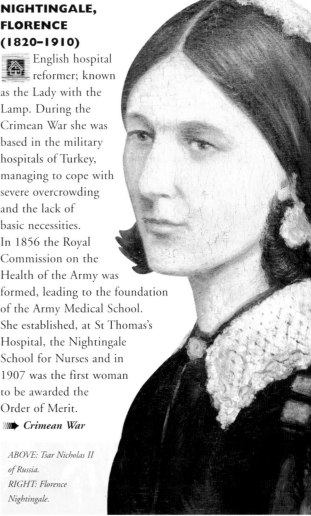

ABOVE: Tsar Nicholas II of Russia.
RIGHT: Florence Nightingale.

NIXON, RICHARD (1913–94)

37th US president (1969–74). Under threat of impeachment over the Watergate scandal, Nixon became the first American president to resign from office. He was vice-president to Eisenhower (1953–61) but lost the presidential election to John F. Kennedy in 1960. He won in 1968 and again in 1972. The Nixon Doctrine called for the US withdrawal from Vietnam and he forged new links with China. Nixon's time in office was cut short by the Watergate scandal, which uncovered many dirty tricks by the Republicans: burglary and wiretapping the Democrats' headquarters (at the Watergate offices); a 'slush fund' for discrediting his political opponents during Nixon's re-election campaign; and the subsequent cover-up operation authorized by the president. The existence of the Watergate tapes (Nixon's taped phone conversations) and his reluctance to release them untampered to the investigating committee led to a likely impeachment. Nixon resigned but was later pardoned by his successor, Gerald Ford.

))))➤ *President, Watergate*

NIVEDITA, SISTER (1867–1911)

Born Margaret Noble, Nivedita became a Hindu nationalist and nun. She became a follower of Vivekananda (a disciple of Ramakrishna) after his visit to London. Moving to India she joined the Ramakrishna Mission devoting herself to social work and establishing a girls' school in Calcutta. She supported the Indian Nationalism Movement.

))))➤ *Ramakrishna*

NOBEL PRIZE (1901)

Prestigious awards given for achievement. Awarded annually and named after the Swedish inventor and industrialist Alfred Bernhard Nobel who bequeathed money in his will (1895) for the purpose. There were five prizes initially: the Nobel prizes for Physics, Chemistry, Physiology or Medicine, Literature, and Peace, and a sixth – Economics – was added in 1969. Nobel stated that the

prizes should be given 'to those who, during the preceding year, shall have conferred the greatest benefit on mankind'. The Nobel Prize takes the form of a medal and the first award was made on the fifth anniversary of the founder's death.

NOBUNAGA, ODA (1534–82)

Japanese feudal warlord. From humble beginnings in the Japanese province of Owari, Nobunaga gradually gained control of the whole region and occupied Kyoto in 1568. By 1580 he was in control of all of central Japan but was assassinated by a vassal before he could unite the whole country.

))))➤ *Warlords*

NOH THEATRE

Japanese dramatic form. Thought to have evolved originally from sacred dance, Noh theatre has little in common with traditional Western drama, its performers' appearance and gestures illustrating and commenting upon, rather than enacting, a basic narrative normally derived from Japanese legend. Dating back to the fourteenth century and earlier, this most solemn and stately of dramatic traditions remains more ritual than entertainment.

RIGHT: The Nobel Prize was named after Alfred Bernhard Nobel who donate part of his fortune to fund the project.

LEFT: Nomadic tribes are always on the move searching for water and more fertile grazing land for their livestock.

weaponry. The Cold War standoff came to an end in 1989 when the USSR fell apart. In the 1990s NATO's role changed to that of peacekeeper with operations in places like Bosnia. Russia opposed applications to join NATO from Eastern European countries, such as Poland, Hungary and the Czech Republic, but all three joined in 1999. By 2001, NATO membership stood at 19.

)))➤ *Warsaw Pact, World War II*

NOMADS

Peoples or tribes that move in search of water, food and grazing land. Nomadic existence has been in evidence since biblical times and continues to this day, principally in Africa and parts of Eastern Europe. Modern-day Nomadic peoples include the Arab tribes, notably the Bedouin, the East African Masai, the Nomadic Pigmy Tribe, the Akka in the Uele Basin and, to a lesser extent, the Aborigines of Australia. Major nomadic tribes in history include the Alans, the Huns, Sarmatians, Scythians and the Mongols led by Genghis Khan. In North America most Native Americans were nomads, including the Blackfoot Cheyenne and Comanche.

)))➤ *Bedouins, Mongols*

NORTH ATLANTIC TREATY ORGANIZATION (NATO) (1949)

Organization set up to implement the North Atlantic Treaty (1949). The treaty established Western Europe's military answer to the Warsaw Pact alliance, led by the Soviet Union. The wartime armies of Britain, France and the USA had been drastically reduced at the end of World War II. In contrast, the Soviets had a huge army in Eastern Europe to reinforce Communist control of the region. NATO's answer was to deploy US nuclear weapons: its numbers were always fewer than the Warsaw Pact's huge ground forces, but NATO had superior

RIGHT: Nostradamus made cryptic predictions about world events up to the year 3797, including that there would be a third world war.

NOSTRADAMUS (1503–66)

French astrologer and self-styled prophet. Born Michel de Notredame in St Rémy, Provence, Nostradamus qualified conventionally enough as a physician in 1519; not until 1547 did he start his second career as foreteller of the future. Two collections of cryptic pronouncements, the *Centuries*, published in 1555

and 1558 respectively, brought him to the admiring attention of King Charles IX of France. He has had his adherents right up to the present day.

NUREMBERG TRIALS (1945–46)

Series of trials in Germany. Under the authority of The London Agreement (8 August 1945), the International Military Tribunal held trials against former Nazi leaders for 'crimes against peace', 'crimes against humanity', 'war crimes' and 'a common plan or conspiracy to commit' the first three counts. At the first session, under General I. T. Nikitchenko, held in Berlin, 24 former Nazi leaders had been charged with the perpe-tration of war crimes. From 30 November all trials were held in Nuremberg under Lord Justice Geoffrey Lawrence. After 216 sessions, three were acquitted, seven imprisoned and 12 sentenced to death by hanging.

)))➤ *World War II*

OLMEC (1500–600 BC)

Pre-Columbian culture of central America. These indigenous peoples lived on the Gulf of Mexico and extended their influence into the Valley of Mexico and south-east into Central America. Their probable capital, San Lorenzo, was destroyed in 900 BC and replaced by La Venta. They were the first people to use stone in architecture and sculpture, creating massive stone heads to adorn their temples and plazas. Olmec writing was the foundation of all South American languages and their culture influenced the whole region for many centuries. Their society was complex and their culture gradually changed over a period of years and at some stage, probably around 600 BC, they ceased to be the dominant influence in the region. They created vast urban pyramids about 30 m (100 ft) high at the centres of their civilization and traded widely. They are particularly remembered for their remarkable art forms, as can be seen at Villahermo.

OLYMPIC GAMES (1896)

Classical Greek – and today international – sporting tournament. In ancient times it was a competition attended by youths from all the cities of Greece, who offered up to Zeus their strength and skills in running, jumping, boxing and throwing. More recently, the idea was revived in a more secular internationalist spirit by the Frenchman

ABOVE: This colossal stone head representing an Olmec ruler was found at La Venta Tabasco, Mexico. RIGHT: The instantly recognizable symbols which today represent the Olympic Games, derived from classical Greek sporting tournaments.

Pierre Coubertin: the first modern games took place in Athens in 1896. Since then they have taken place four-yearly, the number of events rising from 43 to around 300, while the number of participating countries has reached almost 200. Since 1924 there has been a Winter Olympics in intervening years.

)))➤ *Commonwealth Games*

OMAR KHAYYÁM (c. 1048–1122)

Persian poet. A mathematician and astronomer as well as being the author of some 250 brief verses or *robáiyát*, the eleventh-century Persian was destined to become one of the more surprising eminences of nineteenth-century English literature. Rediscovered in the great 1859 translation by Edward Fitzgerald, the *Rubáiyát of Omar Khayyám* would achieve immense popularity in Victorian Britain, and exert enormous influence upon poets.

OP ART (1960s)

Artistic movement. Its name deriving from the optical effects on which it relies for impact (and a punning allusion to the Pop Art current in the 1960s when it had its major vogue), Op Art has its theoretical origins in the work of Josef Albers (1888–1976). His work exploited the reflective properties of different surfaces and was taken up enthusiastically in the 1960s by a generation of artists fascinated by the challenge of adapting to creative ends the sort of optical illusions hitherto dismissed as intriguing tricks. Its leading figures were the British painter and designer Bridget Riley (b. 1931) and Hungarian-born Victor Vasarely (1908–97) and, though now superseded in mainstream art, its influence endures in the fields of textiles and of fashion.

)))➤ *Pop Art*

OPIUM WARS (1839–42, 1856–60)

Two wars between Britain and China over the import of opium. At the start of the nineteenth century opium became big business as a trade commodity in the Far East. Britain used

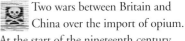

opium produced in British India as currency for imports from China, such as tea, silk and porcelain. However, China closed its ports to British ships, prompting the First Opium War in 1839. Britain won the war three years later. Britain enforced the opening of five Chinese treaty ports and took over Hong Kong as a British Crown colony. The Second Opium War saw Britain and France allied against China. China was forced to expand trade with Europe thenceforth.

ORGANIZATION OF AMERICAN STATES (1948)

Organization formed to foster co-operation, both economic and military, among north, central and south American states. The OAS grew out the Pan-American Union, a defence pact the USA felt was in need of reinforcement at the onset of the Cold War in 1948. Its founding principle was to consider an attack on one American state as an attack on all. The organization aimed to prevent the spread of Communism, and Cuba was suspended in 1961 when a Marxist government came to power. Canada finally joined in 1990. Since the collapse of the Soviet Union, the OAS has focused on encouraging democracy and monitoring elections in its member states.

))))➤ *Communism*

BELOW: Emperor Tao-Kuang reviews his armed forces in Peking. The Opium Wars were fought over the value of opium, which became a much sought-after commodity as the result of British trade with China.

OTTOMAN EMPIRE (1300–1922)

Turkish Muslim empire. At its height it extended from Hungary to Aden and from Algeria to Iran. It was an empire with a talent for war and for minimal government. It was founded by Turks driven from central Asia by the Mongols.

Having overrun Asia Minor, they began their European conquests by seizing Gallipoli in 1355. The Empire quickly recovered from defeat at the hands of Tamerlaine in 1402. In 1453 Constantinople became the third and last Ottoman capital city. Under Suleiman I the Magnificent ('the Lawgiver') Ottoman power was carried to Iraq and throughout much of the Mediterranean. In 1529 Suleiman laid unsuccessful siege to Vienna.

With the Christian counter-offensive starting in 1683 the Turks were gradually pushed back. Turkey fought with Germany in the World War I, losing further territory. Ottoman rule ended in 1922 with the abolition of the sultanate by Mustapha Kemal (Atatark).

))))➤ *Mongols, Suleiman the Magnificent, Tamerlaine*

PANAMA CANAL (1903–79)

By the Hay-Bunau-Varilla Treaty of 1903, Panama granted the USA control of the Panama Canal and five miles of land on either side. The Panama Canal Company was responsible for operating the canal and the land, together with the Canal Zone government, with Balboa Heights as the administrative headquarters for both. Following a treaty in 1977 the Zone was abolished (1979) with ownership remaining joint American-Panamanian until 2000 when Panama resumed control.

PANKHURST, EMMELINE (1858–1928)

Militant woman suffragette. Pankhurst founded the Women's Franchise League (1894), and the Women's Social and Political Union (1903), two members of which (one her daughter Christabel) were imprisoned for assaulting police officers. She was jailed 1908–09 and in the following years was imprisoned 12 times before World War I. She returned to England from campaigns in America in 1926. In 1928, the year of her death, equal votes for men and women were established.

⫸ *Suffragettes*

BELOW: A suffragette medal (c. 1908), containing the photograph of Emmeline Pankhurst. It is decorated with the multi-coloured ribbons associated with the movement.

PARACELSUS (1493–1541)

Swiss medical reformer. Switzerland became a hotbed of medical contention in the sixteenth century due to the rise of Philippus Bombastus von Hohenhiem, known as Paracelsus. He advocated a new approach to medicine. Dismissing traditional notions of bodily humours, he asserted that ailments had specific causes that required treatment with specific chemicals.

PARLIAMENT (1295)

Original legislative assembly of the UK. The English parliament comprises the king or queen, the House of Commons and the House of Lords. There are 650 members of parliament in the Commons, each representing a different part of the country. The word was first used to describe after-dinner conversations between monks in the cloisters.

Parliament traces its roots back to 1295 when Edward I called the first representative meeting between clergy, knights, burgesses and citizens from different counties and cities. The House of Lords developed under Edward III. But it was after the Civil War (1642–51),

when parliament was the revolutionary force against the king, that the modern system was born. The assembly established its control over the executive and judiciary and abolished all royal claim to tax or legislate. The Whig and Tory factions developed and in 1721 Robert Walpole, leader of the Whigs, became the first unofficial prime minister and the real head of government. The Lords' power was diminished by the Parliamentary Act of 1911, and Tony Blair's Labour government eliminated all but 92 hereditary peers. Each session of parliament is opened with a speech by the monarch that contains a list of what the government intends to do in the new session.

)))➤ *Edward III of England, English Civil Wars*

PASTEUR, LOUIS (1822–95)

French chemist. Pasteur discovered that micro-organisms can be destroyed by heat. He published his 'germ theory' in 1865, which put forward the idea that micro-organisms are responsible for fermentation. He demonstrated the application of heat prevents the fermentation process, because it sterilizes the sample. Pasteur also made the important discovery that vaccines for serious diseases, such as rabies, can be produced by weakening the bacterium or virus that causes the illness. This is very useful when a secondary disease, such as cowpox for smallpox, is not available for innoculation.

PAUL III, POPE (1468–1549)

Italian pope (1534–49). He was born Alessandro Farnese at Canino, Italy, educated in Rome and Florence, where he was taught by humanists. He became a cardinal in 1493 although he was not ordained until 1519. Paul III was a reforming pope who encouraged artists and architects (including the completion of the Sistine Chapel by Michelangelo). A report he commissioned, *Concilium de Emendenda Ecclesia* (1538), formed the basis of the Council of Trent (1545). He recognized the Society of Jesus (1540) and in 1542 created the Holy Office of the Inquisition to combat heresy. He excommunicated Henry VIII of England in 1538.

)))➤ *Henry VIII of England, Inquisition, Michelangelo*

PAUL, ST (c. AD 3–65)

Disciple of Jesus. Born at Tarsus, into the tribe of Benjamin, Saul (his original name) was a tentmaker and a Roman citizen. He became an enthusiastic persecutor of Christians, taking an active part in the stoning of Stephen, the first Christian martyr. He was converted to Christianity after receiving a vision of Jesus while travelling to Damascus. He understood his mission as being to take Christianity to the Gentiles and undertook at least three missionary journeys. He was persecuted for his troubles. He wrote a number of letters, mostly to the churches he founded and these form a valuable part of the Christian Bible. He was arrested and taken to Rome for trial (as was his right as a Roman citizen). He probably died there in the Neronian persecution and is honoured, with St Peter, as the co-founder of the Roman Church. He is the most important early Christian theologian.

)))➤ *Bible, Christianity, Jesus Christ, St Peter*

PEARL HARBOR (1941)

Japanese attack on the USA during World War II. While Japanese envoys were holding 'peace talks' in Washington their naval airforce struck a US Pacific naval base called Pearl Harbor, Oahu, Hawaii, on 7 December 1941. Public opinion about entering World War II – which had been against it – was turned on its head in the USA. Some 2,000 US personnel died and the Pacific fleet was severely depleted, sending the Americans into a frenzy of anti-Japanese sentiment. President Roosevelt may have allowed the attack to happen for that very reason.

)))➤ *Franklin D. Roosevelt, World War II*

FAR LEFT: The Houses of Parliament, Westminster, London
ABOVE: St Paul preaches to the unconverted following his own revelation from God.

PEARY, ROBERT (1856–1920)

American polar explorer. Peary made seven polar expeditions, developing the Peary System of Arctic travel, which included Inuit (Eskimo) survival skills and the establishment of supply depots. He crossed northern Greenland and contributed greatly to knowledge of that region, of glaciation and of Inuit ethnology. After three unsuccessful attempts Peary, with his assistant Matthew Henson and four Inuit, reached the North Pole (or near it) on 6 April 1909, having made a final dash with dog-sledges in a spell of fine weather. Dr Frederick Cook claimed to have reached the Pole a year earlier but Peary's records were accepted as genuine.

PEASANTS' REVOLT (1381)

English rebellion against the imposition of Poll Tax. The Poll Tax was imposed in 1381 and the Statute of Labourers started an uprising, centred on south-eastern counties and East Anglia. The revolt, which lasted less than a month, surprised Richard II's government. The Kentish men, led by Wat Tyler, marched towards London and were met by the king at Mile End. While there the group seized the Tower of London and beheaded Archbishop Simon of Sudbury and Sir Robert Hales. After reform promises Richard quelled the crisis in London. In June rebel groups in East Anglia were defeated by Henry le Despenser, Bishop of Norwich.

PEEL, SIR ROBERT (1788–1850)

British prime minister (1834–35, 1841–46) and founder of the Conservative Party. As home secretary, Peel set up the first police force for London (1828), known as Bobby's boys and later, bobbies. In 1829 he introduced Roman Catholic emancipation. Peel resigned as prime minister over his repeal of the Corn Laws (1846). He formed a new third party with his followers that stood between the Liberals and the Conservatives; the majority of Peelites, including Gladstone, later joined the Liberals.

))))➡ *Corn Laws*

ABOVE: During the Persian Wars, the Greeks defended themselves and tried to reclaim their Aegean territory from the invading Persians.

PELOPONNESIAN WAR (431–404 BC)

War between Athens and Sparta. Pericles (*c.* 495–429 BC) was leader of the Athenians, Lysander (d. 395 BC) was a Spartan general. The Spartans grew suspicious of the Athenian's territorial ambitions in 431 BC and war broke out between the two over Peloponnese, the peninsula forming the southern part of the Greek mainland.

The Peloponnesian War lasted until 404 BC. It involved both Athens and Sparta enlisting support from allies and involved most of the Greek world in one way or another. Athens was a seapower and Sparta a landpower, resulting in a protracted war with neither side decisively superior in battle. With the advantage having shifted several times, Sparta eventually gained the upper hand. Lysander succeeded in destroying the Athenian fleet at Aegospotami in 405 BC, and the city of Athens was besieged by land and sea until it ultimately surrendered in 404 BC.

))))➡ *Sparta*

PERÓN, EVA (1919–52)

Wife of Argentine president Juan Perón. During her husband's first term as president, 'Evita' (as she was known) became a powerful political figure in her own right and a champion of the poor. She never held an official government post, but virtually ran the health and labour ministries. She awarded large wage increases to the unions and set up thousands of hospitals, schools and orphanages. Evita helped women get the vote and set up the Peronista Feminist Party in 1949. She was nominated for vice president in 1951, but was opposed by the army. She died of cancer soon after.

PERSIAN WARS (499–479 BC)

Military campaign between the Greeks and Persians. Until 499 BC the Persians had been expanding their empire into the eastern Mediterranean and the Greeks prepared to reclaim their Aegean territory. The Persians made two invasion attempts on the Greek mainland (490 BC and 480 BC) which saw the Greeks succeed in defence. From then the Greeks had the upper hand, pushing the Persians back toward Asia Minor (now Turkey) and ending their heyday. When Persia fought back in 480 BC, intending to take part of the Greek mainland, Greek dominance at sea crushed the Persian fleet. The Persian navy and part of its army withdrew. The remainder of the Persian army wintered in Greece but was eventually defeated by a coalition of Athenians, Spartans and their allies in 479 BC.

)))➡ *Ancient Greece, Persia*

PETER I OF RUSSIA (1672–1725)

Tsar of Russia from 1682, known as 'the Great'. Determined to modernize Russia, Peter, a ruthless man of action, took great interest in developments in industry and science in Western Europe.

From 1696–98, Peter travelled to Holland and England, working as a labourer in the dockyards to master shipbuilding. Back in Russia he promoted education,

hired instructors from the West, started a newspaper, and brought religion under state control. However, the building of the beautiful new capital at St Petersburg was achieved by forced labour. A protracted war against Sweden finally yielded a victory in 1709, winning Russia territory in Finland, Estonia and Lithuania and increased control of the Baltic. Peter died with no heir.

PETER, ST (d. c. AD 62)

Christian saint and disciple of Jesus Christ. Usually regarded as the most senior of the apostles who accompanied Jesus of Nazareth. His original name was Simon but was renamed 'Peter' by Jesus who said he was to be the 'rock' on which he would build his church. Peter is a constant companion of Jesus and is the first disciple to acknowledge Jesus as the Messiah. The Gospels depict him as an impulsive and very human character even to the extent of recording his three denials of Jesus during the last day of Jesus's life. He was married and it appears he may have returned home after the resurrection and ascension of Jesus before becoming the first Bishop of Rome. Tradition says he was martyred there, crucified upside-down. His tomb is in the Church of St Peter in Vatican City.

)))➡ *Christianity, Jesus Christ*

LEFT: Peter the Great, one of Russia's tsars, exploited the skills of craftsmen and engineers to modernize Russia and build the city of St Petersburg, named after him.

ABOVE : St Peter, one of the apostles and founder of the Catholic Apostolic Church, is usually portrayed holding the keys to paradise.

PETRARCH (1304–74)

Italian poet and thinker. One of the great humanists of the fourteenth century, Francesco Petrarca was all but legendary for his learning, but his enduring fame would rest on his more intimate, romantic side. The agonized sonnets he wrote for love of the unattainable beauty Laura were not only profoundly influential in imagery and style but started a fashion for similar sequences expressive of chaste and unavailing love. Shakespeare's sonnets (*c.* 1593) were only the most famous of these: similar sequences were written by English poets such as Sir Philip Sidney (1554–86) and Edmund Spenser (*c.* 1552–99), and by continental geniuses from Pierre de Ronsard (1524–85) to Michelangelo.

)))▶ *Humanism, Michelangelo, Renaissance, William Shakespeare*

PHILIP II OF SPAIN (1527–98)

King of Spain from 1556, succeeding on the abdication of his father, the emperor Charles V. Philip inherited vast dominions in South America, the Low Countries, Naples and Milan, adding Portugal in 1580.

Imports of American bullion caused damaging inflation and England's increasing naval power provided a serious threat to Spain. Philip's childless marriage to Mary I of England ended an attempt to secure England that way. He then resorted to force, a tactic which ended with the Armada's destruction by storms and Elizabeth I's privateers in 1588.

Philip's determination to enforce the Counter-Reformation led to a futile and protracted war with the Netherlands, depriving Spain of Dutch trade and wealth. The Inquisition caused Spain to lose much intellectual and commercial talent.

)))▶ *Elizabeth I of England, Inquisition, Mary I of England, Spanish Armada*

PHOENICIANS (2500–64 BC)

Ancient culture on the east coast of the Mediterranean. Originally a group of city-states, the Phoenicians found themselves under Sumerian and Akkadian control for many years until 1800 BC when Egypt took over the eastern Mediterranean. When the Hittites revolted this gave the Phoenicians the opportunity to take their independence in 1100 BC. From then on their fleets and traders founded many colonies, including Carthage, Rhodes and Cyprus. They traded in wood, linen, cloths, embroidery, wine, metalwork, glass, salt and fish, and it is believed that they invented glass-blowing in the first century BC. Phoenician religion comprised of a variety of gods dominated by the father of the gods, El, and the goddess Astarte. The Phoenician alphabet was later adopted by the Greeks and later still, the Romans.

They were conquered by the Assyrians in the late seventh century BC and became part of the Persian Empire in 539 BC. The leading Phoenician city of Tyre fell to Alexander the Great in 332 BC and they became

LEFT: Francesco Petrarch.
RIGHT: Philip II of Spain.

much more Hellenized, as they were absorbed into the Greco-Macedonian empire. The name Phoenicia disappeared in 64 BC when the country became part of the Roman province of Syria.

))))➤ *Alexander the Great, Hittites, Sumerians*

PICASSO, PABLO (1881–1973)

Spanish painter, sculptor, designer. Born in Málaga, the son of an art teacher, Picasso was destined to change the face of twentieth-century art; his co-founding of Cubism was only one of his vital contributions in everything from sketches to ceramics. His personality was as forceful as his genius. He dominated developments in European art for almost half a century, making Paris his artistic and spiritual home. After the wistful waifs of his early 'blue period' came the distortions of his cubist phase, the crucial insights and techniques of which would remain with him for the great mythological canvases of the 1920s. Perhaps his most famous painting, *Guernica* (1936–69), a denunciation of the horrors of war, was inspired by the German bombing of the basque city in the course of the Spanish Civil War.

))))➤ *Cubism, Modernism, Spanish Civil War*

PILGRIM FATHERS (1620)

Name given to the group of Englishmen who established the first permanent colony in New England. Leaving England because James I would not permit freedom of religion, Separatists and Puritans boarded the *Mayflower* at Southampton, with over 100 travelling aboard a ship designed to take a crew of 30. They had no privacy, sanitary facilities or fresh water and with a lack of fresh fruit and vegetables, many contracted scurvy. They eventually settled in Jamestown, Virginia. The pilgrims drew up the Mayflower Compact, one of the earliest plans for self-government made by European colonists in America.

))))➤ *Mayflower*

PIPER ALPHA DISASTER (1988)

Catastrophe on board an oil platform in the North Sea. An oil fire that melted the rig and escalated out of control caused the death of 167 of the 225 men on board the oil platform at the time. A public enquiry led by Lord Cullen was held after the disaster.

PIZARRO, FRANCISCO (c. 1475–1541)

Spanish explorer and conqueror of Peru. Having learnt of the existence of the Inca Empire on two expeditions (1524–25, 1526–28), Pizarro travelled to Spain to enlist royal aid and in 1531 he sailed from Panama for Peru with about 180 men. He easily subdued the Incas, executed their emperor Atahualpa and founded the city of Lima as the new capital. His greed for gold and silver meant that most examples of Inca metalwork were melted down and thus lost.

))))◗ *Conquistadors, Incas*

PLAGUE (1664–66)

Epidemic that raged through London, killing approximately 70,000. This epidemic began in the St Giles in the Fields area of London and soon spread to the poorer and densely populated areas of Clerkenwell, Cripplegate, Shoreditch, Stepney and Westminster. Because of the lack of quarantine (not established until 1720) this was the worst epidemic in history. The king and his court left London and parliament transferred sessions to Oxford. The Great Fire of London (September 1666) is believed to have assisted in the elimination of the plague from London, although it ceased in other parts of the country without such aid.

))))◗ *Great Fire of London*

PLANCK, MAX (1858–1947)

German theoretical physicist. Modern physics is largely based on the principles of quantum theory – the brainchild of Max Planck, and Einstein's theories of relativity. Quantum theory concerns itself with the relationship between matter and energy at the subatomic or nano scale. Planck suggested that matter and energy were the same within atoms and come in tiny 'packets' called quanta. The theory revolutionized our understanding of subatomic physics.

))))◗ *Albert Einstein*

LEFT: The Spanish explorer, Francisco Pizarro.

PLASSEY, BATTLE OF (1757)

Battle between the British and Indians. In 1756 the Nawab of Bengal, Suraja Dowla, captured Calcutta in defiance of the British. Robert Clive led the army of the East India Company against the Nawab and defeated them at Plassey. Clive was made governor of the area as a result and received many honours for his heroism there.

))))◗ *Black Hole of Calcutta, Robert Clive*

POITIERS, BATTLE OF (1356)

Battle during the Hundred Years' War. The battle was fought at Poitiers, capital of Poitou-Charantes in Western France. It was fought between Edward the Black Prince – Prince of Wales – and King John II of France. Some 3,000 Frenchmen were killed in the battle, which was won decisively by Edward's army on 13 September 1356. King John's son, Philip and 2,000 knights were taken prisoner.

))))◗ *Battle of Crécy, Hundred Years' War*

POL POT (b. 1928)

Self-proclaimed prime minister of Cambodia (1976–79). Pol Pot founded the Khmer Rouge, a radical guerrilla group. In 1975, during Cambodia's civil war, the Khmer Rouge captured the capital city, Phnom Penh. Declaring 'Year Zero', Pol Pot's regime abolished property and money, closed schools, executed professionals and made everyone else slave labourers – and in the process murdered between one and four million people. Vietnamese troops forced the Khmer Rouge out of power in 1979.

))))◗ *Khmer Rouge*

POLO, MARCO (c. 1254–1324)

Italian traveller and author. Aged 17 Polo journeyed to China with his merchant father and uncle, crossing the Pamir Mountains and the Taklamakan and Gobi Deserts, to the court of Kublai Khan at Shangdu, near present-day Beijing. Polo entered Kublai's diplomatic service, acting as his agent

on missions to many parts of the Mongols' empire, including Tibet, Burma, Siberia and Indonesia. He remained in that post for 17 years until 1292. Taken prisoner by the Genoese in 1298, he dictated an account of his travels, imparting in vivid detail the first knowledge available to Europeans about the Far East.

)))➤ *Kublai Khan, Mongols*

POMPEII (600 BC – AD 79)

Ancient Roman city. Founded by the Oscans and Samnites, Pompeii became a Roman colony (80 BC) with a population of 20,000. It was a favoured resort for wealthy Romans. An earthquake damaged the city in AD 63, but when Mount Vesuvius erupted on 24 August AD 79 it buried the city in ash and pumice to a depth of 7 m (23 ft). The heated gas asphyxiated the residents but the city has endured for 17 centuries.

)))➤ *Ancient Rome*

ABOVE: A medieval manuscript depicting Marco Polo's extensive travels throught the Orient.

BELOW: A mural fresco discovered at Pompeii, just outside Naples.

PONTIUS PILATE

Pilate was the Roman governor of Judea at the time of Jesus of Nazareth's death. The Christian Gospels record Jesus's appearance before Pilate who allowed Jesus to be crucified, a Roman method of executing criminals. The Gospels record Pilate's weakness in giving in to the demands of the religious authorities with regard to Jesus, symbolized by his hand washing. Pilate's main concern would have been to keep the peace at the tense time of the Jewish Passover; Jesus would simply have been another criminal to die.

)))➤ *Bible, Christianity, Jesus Christ*

POP ART (1960s)

Artistic movement. The key development of the 1960s, Pop Art was a reaction to the sobriety of earlier artistic schools – and, conversely, a response to the new respect being accorded to popular performers such as the Beatles. Practitioners played with techniques, materials and imagery drawn from the sort of down-market media that the world of fine arts had traditionally despised. Hence Andy Warhol (1928–87) on one occasion famously painted tiered rows of Campbell's Soup tins, while Roy Lichtenstein (b. 1923) worked hard to reproduce the images – and low-budget printing – of the comic strip.

)))➤ *Op Art*

POST-IMPRESSIONISM (1910)

Artistic movement. Not so much a coherent school as a shared instinct to rebel against the impressionist consensus, the radical departure of the 1860s having, by the turn of the century, become a potentially restrictive norm. The three painters generally held up as post-impressionist pioneers – Paul Cézanne (1839–1906), Paul Gauguin and Vincent van Gogh (1854–90) – arguably had little in common other than their wayward originality. The name was coined by British artist and critic Roger Fry for an exhibition he staged in London in 1910 and the concept came to have meaning as ideas

gradually accreted around it. Soon it was clear that the trio could indeed be seen as leading a trend away from impressionism's essentially conservative view of the aims of art as the most faithful possible representation of nature, and towards a new conception of art as expressive of individual creativity.

)))))➤ *Expressionism, Impressionism*

POTSDAM CONFERENCE (1945)

Meeting convened at the end of World War II to organize the administration of post-war Germany. Leaders of the main Allied Powers – US president Harry S. Truman, Winston Churchill (and later Clement Attlee) from Britain and the USSR's premier Joseph Stalin – divided Germany into 'zones of occupation' to be controlled by military forces from each of the delegate countries, plus France. The conference's aims failed in practice due to difficulties among the occupying powers, and the unclear wording of the final declaration.

)))))➤ *Winston Churchill, Joseph Stalin, Harry S. Truman, World War II*

ABOVE: A self-portrait by the post-impressionist Vincent van Gogh.
ABOVE RIGHT: The Pre-Raphaelites drew inspiration from romantic legends. This Rossetti paiting is entitled Joan of Arc Kissing the Sword of Deliverance.

PRE-RAPHAELITES

Artistic and literary movement. Starting life as a secret, quasi-revolutionary 'Brotherhood', Pre-Raphaelitism centred upon three friends from London's Royal Academy: Dante Gabriel Rossetti (1828–82), John Everett Millais (1829–96) and William Holman Hunt (1827–1910). Believing that art had taken a wrong turning towards academicism with the work of Raphael in the late fifteenth century, they sought to recover the simplicity and truth they saw in works by earlier painters like Giotto (1267–1337). This admiration for the medieval heritage at the expense of later periods was a not-uncommon theme in the mid nineteenth century. A talented poet, Rossetti translated a great deal of medieval Italian lyric poetry and strove in his own English verse for the same limpid clarity and sincerity as he saw there. Later critics have tended to find him trite, and compared him unfavourably with his sister, Christina Rossetti (1830–94), whose work shares some of the same values but has far greater depth and power.

)))))➤ *Arts and Crafts Movement, Gothic*

PRESIDENT

Title given to a national leader. The word president comes from the Latin word, *praesidens*, meaning 'one who presides'. The use of the term in a modern sense probably originated in the 1700s in the American colonies. Today the title president refers to the principal office-holder within the national government.

A large majority of the world's countries is led by presidents –140 in all. Presidential leaders usually head a democratic government, but in some cases they are military dictators, and in others their position is largely symbolic. Most presidents lead the administrative arm of government, with the lawmaking arm keeping a check on the their powers.

Presidencies are divided into three types: limited (president's power is curbed); dual (president rules with a prime minister); and unlimited (president has absolute power). There are also non-executive presidents who have a largely ceremonial role, but are given special powers in emergency situations.

PRESLEY, ELVIS (1935–77)

American popular singer. Born in Tupelo, Mississippi, Elvis Aron Presley first sang as a boy in his Pentecostalist Church choir. A record privately made for his mother marked his breakthrough when it was heard by a Memphis music producer. Consciously on the look-out for a white singer who could sing black rhythm and blues, Sun Records' Sam Phillips instantly recognized the raw energy of Presley's singing. The great rock-and-roll success of the 1950s was followed by what many came to see as a long decline, as, under the management of 'Colonel' Tom Parker, Elvis made middle-of-the-road records and starred in mediocre films. His career gained momentum again in the 1970s, when an almost self-parodying version of the star appeared in Las Vegas to

LEFT: Elvis Presley.

delight an audience that had aged along with him. Overweight and groggy with drugs, he died in 1977 at his Memphis home: the house, Graceland, is now a shrine for his still-adoring public.

PRINTING

Technological process for reproducing text. Though seals and signet rings had been used to make impressions in hot wax for many centuries, the first use of printing for making multiple copies of text seems to have taken place in ancient China. By the ninth century AD, Buddhist scriptures were routinely being produced this way. The pages for these scripts were, however, permanently fixed, being carved out of single blocks of wood. By the Middle Ages European printers were using similar blocks for printing holy pictures and simple prayers.

The idea of a system for setting movable type, whose components could be shuffled and recast in different order to produce different texts seems to have come to both Eastern and Western printers at quite an early stage: the difficulty lay in finding a viable way of putting it into practice. Though several printers both in Asia and Europe seem to have tried before him, the first man to have succeeded in perfecting a method of making type this way appears to have been the German Johann Gutenberg, who invented not only a movable metal type but a press suitable for printing it and an ink that could be used on both sides of a single page. All the conditions were thus in place for a proper printed book to be produced: hence the appearance in the 1460s of the Gutenberg Bible.

Other books followed from the presses of printing entrepreneurs like Englishman William Caxton (1422–91), leading to a significant democratization of literature and learning. Like other handicrafts, printing was industrialized in the nineteenth century, with implications not only for news media but literature: the nineteenth-century novelist reached readerships of many thousands, where a sixteenth-century poet might have been read at the most by dozens. Now, thanks to new technologies, the death of the book is widely prophesied: for the moment, however, modern presses, derived from Gutenberg's original invention, are still going strong.

))⯈ *Johann Gutenberg*

PROHIBITION (1919–33)

US ban on the manufacture and sale of alcohol. Although many other countries, including Iceland, Finland, Norway, Sweden and Russia attempted to prohibit the manufacture, sale or transportation of alcohol, it was the American Volstead Act, ratified on 29 January 1919 that is the best-remembered experiment. During Prohibition bootleggers such as Al Capone saw annual earnings of $60 million. By 1932 the Democratic Party had adopted the call for a repeal in order to combat criminal activities and the restriction on individual freedoms. On 5 December 1933 the repeal was achieved and by 1966 all states had abandoned Prohibition.

))))➤ *Al Capone, Great Depression, Wall Street Crash*

PROTESTANTISM

General term for expressions of Christianity arising from the Reformation. The Latin *protestare* means 'to protest' but also 'affirm' or 'avow'. So Protestantism is not negative arising out of a 'protest' against Catholicism; it is a positive affirmation of belief. Protestants stress importance of scripture, that salvation is granted by God's grace, by faith alone and that all believers are 'priests' (i.e. they can all communicate with God directly). They reject the authority of papal supremacy and the sacraments of Catholicism except for baptism and the Lord's Supper. The latter is usually considered to be a memorial meal.

Protestants have stressed the transcendence of God and the sinfulness of human beings; the relative unimportance of the liturgical aspects of worship and that preaching and hearing the Word comes before sacramental faith and practice.

Protestantism has been very divisive and while there may be 500 million Protestants worldwide, there are reckoned to be over 22,000 Protestant sects. This is almost certainly because of the 'private judgement' that is applied to an understanding of scripture and the socio-political environment that has given rise to greater individualism.

))))➤ *John Calvin, Christianity, Martin Luther, Reformation*

Le autorità americane lottano senza tregua perché gli Stati Uniti siano un paese "asciutto", come vuole la legge. E quando scoprono contrabbandi di bibite alcooliche, provvedono subito a pubbliche... esecuzioni. A Zion City, Illinois, in una sola giornata 34124 bottiglie di birra e liquori sono state vuotate nello fogno. (Disegno di A. Beltrame).

PRUSSIA

Former kingdom and state in Germany. The earliest Prussians inhabited the region between the Wisa and lower Niemen rivers. Christianity was established in the mid-thirteenth century by Teutonic Knights. After defeat by Poland and Lithuania in 1410 Prussia was divided. Frederick William secured East Prussia's independence in 1660, strengthened the army and created a navy. The military genius of Frederick II turned Prussia into a major power. At its height under Prince Otto von Bismarck (1815–98) Prussia extended from the Netherlands to the Russian Empire and as far south as Switzerland and Austro-Hungary. The state of Prussia was legally abolished in 1947.

))))➤ *Otto von Bismarck, Frederick the Great of Prussia*

PTOLEMY (AD 90–168)

Greek astronomer. Ptolemy created a model of the Universe that was incorrect but worked so well that it went unchallenged until the arrival of Nicolaus Copernicus. Ptolemy's model had Earth at its centre, as was naturally assumed by people at that time. As well as charting the night sky Ptolemy also charted the lands and seas, becoming the most reliable authority on geography of his time.

))))➤ *Nicolaus Copernicus*

PU YI (1906–67)

Last emperor of China, of the Ch'ing dynasty. Henry Pu Yi, or P'u-i, succeeded as emperor with the name Hsuan Tung in 1908. He was deposed in 1912,

ending two millennia of imperial rule (267 years by the Ch'ing). He was briefly restored in 1917, but throughout continued to live in the palace at Beijing. During the Japanese occupation of Manchuria from 1931–45 he was installed as their puppet emperor of Manchukuo. After World War II he was imprisoned as a war criminal from 1950. Released in 1959, he then worked in a botanical garden.

))))➤ *Ch'in Dynasty, World War II*

PUNIC WARS (264–241 BC, 218–210 BC, 149–146 BC)

Three wars between the Romans and Phoenicians. Before the heyday of the Empire, the Romans had to assert their dominance in the Mediterranean. The Phoenicians were their main enemy; particularly those of Carthage on the coast of North Africa. The First Punic War saw victory for the Romans over the Carthaginians and the annexation of Sicily as part of the Roman Empire when the Carthaginian garrison on the island was forced to surrender by starvation. The war ended under the terms of the Treaty of Catulus.

The Second Punic War was a far more significant campaign, fought in Italy, Spain and Africa. The war involved the Carthaginian leader Hannibal and the Roman general Publius Cornelius Scipio (185–129 BC). The Third Punic War, 149–146 BC, saw Carthage invaded by the Romans. The city was razed to the ground and the population sold into slavery.

))))➤ *Hannibal, Phoenicians, Romans*

ABOVE LEFT: A map of Prussia, a former kingdom and state in Germany.
ABOVE RIGHT: Pu Yi, the last emperor of China became a puppet king in the hands of the Japanese.

QUAKERS (1640s)

Full name 'The Religious Society of Friends'. The origins of the Quakers can be traced to the 1640s. The term 'Quaker' is believed to originate from members expected to 'tremble' before God or, in 1650, George Fox – the first leader – telling a judge to 'tremble' at the Word of the Lord. The Quakers wait for the 'Spirit to speak' in and through them, the 'Inner Light' being as important as scripture. They were persecuted at home and evangelized North America where William Penn, one of the leaders, established Pennsylvania. Another follower, Elizabeth Fry, opened an asylum in 1796. They have become well-known for their pacifism and their refusal to take oaths. There are probably 600,000–700,000 worldwide.

))))➤ *George Fox*

QUETZLCOATL (10TH CENTURY)

Toltec and Aztec god. The legend of Quetzlcoatl was based on a priest king sent into exile in the tenth century. He became revered as a god and legendary ruler and it was believed that he would return, light-skinned and bearded. When Hernán Cortés appeared in 1519 Montezuma II believed he was Quetzlcoatl.

))))➤ *Aztecs, Hernán Cortés, Montezuma*

QUISLING, VIDKUN (1887–1945)

Norwegian fascist. Vidkun Jonsson aided the Nazi invasion of Norway and was made Norwegian premier by Adolf Hitler. He was arrested and shot as a traitor in 1945. 'Quisling' has been adopted by the Norwegians as a word meaning 'traitor'.

))))➤ *Fascism, Adolf Hitler, World War II*

QUR'AN

Islamic religious text. The Prophet Muhammad received the first of many messages from Allah through the Angel Jibril when he was 40 years old. The first message was the first of many surahs (or chapters) now contained in the Qur'an; it was revealed to Muhammad between AD 610 and 632. Muslims believe the Qur'an is Allah's own word, not that of any human being. Muhammad was illiterate and had to learn each revelation (which continued for the next 23 years) by heart; there are 114 surahs of varying lengths. The revelation would be recited ('Qur'an' means 'recite') so it would be remembered. The Arabic of the Qur'an is the finest form of the language and as the Word of God can never be effectively translated into another language. After Muhammad's death the Qur'an was compiled and checked for accuracy by the scribe Zayd Ibn Thabit under the authority of Caliph Uthman. The Qur'an lies at the very heart of Islam, it is the Word of God, the fundamental source of guidance for Muslims and is treated with the greatest respect.

))))➤ *Islam, Prophet Muhammad*

RAIL TRAVEL

Rails, first of stone or wood then of iron, have long been used to reduce friction in locomotion. The first public railway was the Surrey Iron Railway (south of London) utilizing animal power. Early experiments produced locomotives but the first railway line, Stockton to Darlington, opened in 1825 thanks to George Stephenson, whose engine reached a speed of 24 km/h (15 mph). The *Rocket* locomotive, followed in

LEFT: The snake-headed god Quetzlcoatl was revered by the ancient Aztecs and many legends surrounding this deity have been passed down through subsequent generations.

LEFT: *A massive stone head portraying the pharaoh Rameses II guards the entrance to a Sun temple in Luxor.*
BELOW: *Grigori Efimovich Rasputin.*

1829, drawing a coach at 50 km/h (30 mph) on the Liverpool–Manchester line.

This was the general signal for widespread building of railways. In 1846 a British Act of Parliament established a standard gauge for all new railways. In 1948 the various rail companies were nationalized as British Railways. The construction of world railways followed quickly. Electric and diesel traction was developed in the late nineteenth century. In the 1960s Britain's main lines were electrified. High-speed trains such as the Japanese 'Bullet' and the French TGV have reached speeds of over 500 km/h (350 mph). London has the world's largest underground rail system. The top rail-freight countries are the USA, China and Russia. Despite ageing stock and congestion on lines, rail provides fast, efficient and relatively safe travel.

RAMAKRISHNA (1836–86)

Hindu saint who spent most of his life at a temple in Dakshineswar in Bengal. He had a number of visions, becoming convinced that all religions were different paths to the same source. His charismatic personality attracted disciples, the best known being Swami Vivekananda (1863–1902) who was a well-educated law student. He brought Advaita Vedanta, the teaching promoted by Ramakrishna, to Britain and the USA in the late eighteenth or early nineteenth century. There is an order of monks and nuns who follow Ramakrishna's teachings.

RAMESES II (c. 1310–1224 BC)

Egyptian pharaoh from *c.* 1290 BC. A great warrior, Rameses II was third ruler of the nineteenth dynasty which saw Egypt's fortunes reach their last peak. His most famous victory was against the Hittites at Kadesh though their account suggests Rameses was less successful than he claimed. Rameses built extensively throughout Egypt and usurped the monuments of many of his predecessors. Consequently, more buildings and statues bear his name than any other Egyptian ruler. His tomb, and those of his family survive at Thebes, as does his mummy, found in a cache of royal bodies discovered in the nineteenth century.

)))➤ *Ancient Egypt, Hittites*

RASPUTIN (1872–1916)

Mysterious Russian figure associated with the court of Tsar Nicholas II. Rasputin was reputed to be a saint, a mystic and a healer. He achieved fame after apparently healing the Tsar's son who was a haemophiliac. Rasputin became great friends with the Tsarina and was said to exert influence over the Tsar's political decisions. He was assassinated in 1916, but he survived poisoning and being shot, and finally died only when he was thrown into the Neva River.

)))➤ *Nicholas II of Russia*

RASTAFARI

 Rastafari originated with Marcus Garvey (1887–1940) who believed that all black people in the West were oppressed and should seek their homeland in Africa. Garvey predicted that the coronation of an African

king would bring redemption. In 1930 Ras Tafari was crowned Emperor of Ethiopia, claiming the title Haile Selassie (Power of the Trinity). Many saw this as the fulfilment of Garvey's prophecy. The Rastafari religion is not centralised and has no leader, but most believe in the divinity of Selassie, non-violence, and that repatriation to Africa will lead to liberation. In the 1960s protests against black poverty were violently repressed, and Rastafarians gained a bad reputation. In the 1970s they became more of a positive cultural force, contributing to Jamaica's art and music, especially reggae. Recently, the cultural symbols of the Rastafari, such as dreadlocks, have lost their ideological significance and the movement has become more secular.

))))➤ *Haile Selassie*

REAGAN, RONALD (b. 1911)

US president (1981–89). Republican president Reagan was an ex-Hollywood actor. Successful in many areas of domestic policy – his first term saw the American economy flourish – his administration was later marred by the 'Irangate scandal'. Reagan initiated the 'Star Wars' programme, a plan to launch a missile system from outer space.

))))➤ *Irangate, President*

REFORMATION (16TH CENTURY)

Name given to changes in Western Christianity from the fifteenth century. There were many 'reformations' during this period. It was a time of social and political unrest that fuelled a range of religious protests from criticism of papal orthodoxy to discontent with the practices of the Church.

The beginning of the Reformation is usually placed when Martin Luther nailed his '95 Theses' to the door of Wittenberg Cathedral in October 1517. Luther's 'protest' was defended by the Elector of Saxony but there were others protesting. It was 1529 at the Diet of Speyer that the word 'Protestant' emerged, with six German princes protesting at the Emperor's attempt to silence Luther. Ulrich Zwingli (1481–1531) in Switzerland, worked with the state to out-manoeuvre the Catholic Church. Jean Calvin also created a theocracy in Geneva. Calvinist revolution became deeply involved with political change across Europe. Geneva rather than Wittenberg became the centre of the Protestant world and the movement spread rapidly to West Germany, France, the Netherlands and Scotland.

In England the development of the Reformation was uneven. Henry VIII severed connections with Rome in 1534 and by his death there was a Bible in every church and the monasteries were dissolved. Scholastic theology took hold and the brief reversion to the Catholic Church under Mary could not halt change. *The Book of Common Prayer* in 1552 was adopted; and the Church would be governed under the queen and parliament. There were other movements – notably the Anabaptists would wish to abandon all aspects of the medieval Catholic Church and reform a church on New Testament principles.

The Reformation affected every European and forced everyone to make a choice. It touched every facet of life and society and transformed the religious map of Europe, with far-reaching consequences.

))))➤ *Jean Calvin, Henry VIII of England, Martin Luther, Protestantism*

ABOVE: Jamaica is widely considered to be the original home of Rastafari, a movement that was given momentum by leader Marcus Garvey.
LEFT: Former US president Ronald Reagan.

REGENCY (1811–30)

Latter period of George III's reign. George III was intermittently incapacitated by porphyria, called then his 'madness'. After 1811 he became afflicted with blindness and dementia. His son George (after 1820, George IV), a personal and political enemy of his father, became regent. The period was characterized by the introduction of the Prince Regent's love of art and dissolute behaviour, and his friendships with educated and gifted men of the age like Sheridan. The period has given its name to the art and architecture of the late eighteenth and early nineteenth centuries, of which elegance, and revived styles of Ancient Greece are principal features.

)))➤ *George III of England*

REICHSTAG FIRE (1933)

Burning of the Reichstag (parliament) building in Berlin. The fire on the night of 27 February was a turning point in the Nazi party establishing power in Germany. There is still much debate as to whether the Nazis themselves orchestrated the event. They used it to justify the declaration of emergency powers and suppress the Communists, on whom the fire was blamed. The day after the event, Hitler began his dictatorship by suspending the political and personal rights of all German citizens.

)))➤ *Nazi Party*

RENAISSANCE (14TH CENTURY)

Movement in art, architecture, literature and philosophy. Widely held to have started in the city-state of Florence in the fourteenth century, the Renaissance would, in the course of the next 200 years, diffuse throughout the length and breadth of Europe. While the roots of the Renaissance may well have lain in a mercantile boom that saw the European states both increase their consumption of luxuries and extend their commercial horizons through that period, it is to the cultural consequences of the economic revolution that the term is taken to refer.

A new mood of intellectual and artistic confidence meant intellectuals felt more enterprising than they had under the authority of the medieval Church. Renaissance humanism found its inspiration not in the slavish

scholarship of the Middle Ages but in the philosophical ferment of classical Greece. Poets, painters and architects too looked to the classical past to find a way forward. Drawing on the great traditions of ancient epic poetry, the *Divine Comedy* of Dante Alighieri (1265–1321) was not only a magnificent work of literature in its own right: the first major poem to be written in Italian, it broke the intellectual stranglehold of Latin, language of the Church. Architects like Giovanni Brunelleschi (1377–1446) also reinterpreted classical rules for a modern age, while men like Michelangelo, Leonardo and Raphael did the same for the visual arts.

Yet Italy was only the starting-point: the great engraver and painter Albrecht Dürer (1471–1528) took on the task of spreading the Renaissance in his native Germany; Lucas van Leyden (*c.* 1494–1533) came to prominence in the Netherlands. The literature of the period was every bit as exciting, with great humanists like Michel de Montaigne (1533–92), the passionate poetry of Petrarch and his followers, and great comic writing ranging from the work of the riotously scatological Frenchman François Rabelais (*c.* 1490–1553) to Miguel de Cervantes' (1547–1616) mock-epic *Don Quixote*. The unrivalled English writer William Shakespeare belongs unmistakeably to the late Renaissance, as crucial in the history of Western culture as any artist.

)))➤ *Leonardo da Vinci, Michelangelo, William Shakespeare*

ABOVE: The Birth of Venus by Alessandro Botticelli at the Uffizi museum in Florence is emblematic of the vigour and love of beauty celebrated by Renaissance artists.

RESTORATION (1660)

Re-establishment of the English monarchy with Charles II. Following the control of London by General Monck (1659), the Royalist's Convention Parliament called for the restoration of Charles II. Charles issued the Declaration of Breda and returned to England (1660), assuming authority for the nation. This period in history saw the Puritans during the Protectorate, the Cavalier Parliament, the rise of anti-Catholic sentiment, the Whig and Tory factions; the Plague (1665); The Great Fire of London (1666) and the Second Dutch War (1664–67). The Restoration period ended with the Glorious Revolution (1688).

))))➤ *Charles II of England, Great Fire of London, Plague*

RHODES, CECIL (1853–1902)

South African politician. Cecil John Rhodes was born in Britain, so had British sympathies. He became prime minister of Cape Colony in 1890. He harboured ambitions to form a South African federation and a block of British territory running from the Cape of Good Hope, north to Cairo, Egypt. The countries Botswana, Zambia and Zimbabwe, as they are now called, were all annexed between 1885–89 for this purpose, but the plan failed.

RICHARD I OF ENGLAND (1157–99)

King of England from 1189; known as 'the Lionheart'. Richard's mother, Eleanor, incited him and his brothers to rebel against their father, Henry II. Henry died during the revolt but Richard left soon after accession for the Crusades to recapture Jerusalem from Saladin. The campaign ended in truce in 1192, and Richard was captured by Leopold, Duke of Austria, on the way home. A vast ransom secured his release, but he left to fight Philip II in France where he was killed. His chivalry and honour earned him the name 'the Lionheart'.

))))➤ *Crusades, Saladin*

ABOVE: A modern production portraying King Richard III of England.
RIGHT: Cardinal Richelieu orchestrated eighteen-century French domination in Europe behind the ineffectual rule of Louis XIII.
ABOVE RIGHT: The French Jacobin leader, Maximilien Robespierre, as a youth.

RICHARD III OF ENGLAND (1452–85)

King of England from 1483. Edward IV's death in 1483 left Richard, his brother, protector of his nephew, the boy King Edward V. But the enmity of Edward IV's widow, Elizabeth of York and her circle, towards Richard, a competent ruler, led to his coup. Richard declared Edward V a bastard, and himself king. Edward V and his brother were imprisoned in the Tower of London, dying in mysterious circumstances, probably with Richard's knowledge. This lost Richard support, allowing Henry Tudor a chance to claim the throne, defeating and killing Richard at Bosworth Field, and bringing to an end the Wars of the Roses.

RICHELIEU, CARDINAL (1585–1642)

'The Red Eminence', the architect of France's eighteenth-century domination of Europe. Created Bishop of Lucon in 1606 and cardinal in 1622, he became Louis XIII's First Minister of France two years later under the influence of Marie di Medici. He destroyed the Huguenot's political power and established French supremacy by breaking the power of the Habsburgs. In 1635 his support of Gustavus Adolphus and the German Protestant Princes against Austria brought about France's involvement in the Thirty Years' War.

))))➤ *Gustavus Adolphus of Sweden, Huguenots, Medici Family, Thirty Years' War*

ROBESPIERRE, MAXIMILIEN (1758–94)

Leader in the French Revolution. Robespierre was president of the revolutionary Jacobin Club and known for his egalitarian and democratic ideals. After the execution of Louis XVI, he became president of the National Convention, France's new governing body. In an atmosphere of extreme unrest Robespierre's leadership became known as the 'Reign of Terror', characterized by thousands of arrests, executions and massacres. On 28 July 1794, he was seized by soldiers and sent to the guillotine.

)))⮞ *French Revolution, Louis XVI of France*

ROCOCO (18TH CENTURY)

Artistic style. The rococo style was a development of the baroque – and many saw it as representing the inevitable decadence of that movement, given that it took the Baroque's love of intricacy and intensity to what appeared to be absurd extremes. Rococo architects seemed to some to be burlesquing baroque in their mania for elaborate ornamentation, while in the works of French painters like Jean-Antoine Watteau (1684–1721) and, later, Jean-Honoré Fragonard (1732–1806), the sophistication of the seventeenth century seemed to have degenerated into sheer frivolity. The exquisite little porcelains of Etienne-Maurice Falconet (1716–91) could hardly have contrasted more with the heroic sculptures of the neoclassicists who came after him. Yet modern critics have come to appreciate the witty exuberance of these once-despised creations – and to sense an underlying melancholy that gives them more depth than might have been expected.

)))⮞ *Baroque, Neoclassicism*

ROMAN CATHOLICISM

The Roman Catholic Church recognizes the leadership of the pope. The word 'Catholic' means 'universal' and is used to describe other churches, hence the relatively recent addition of 'Roman'. It is the largest Christian tradition with roughly one billion members with three-quarters of them living outside Europe and North America.

The Church traces its origins back to Peter, Jesus's disciple, who, tradition says, was the first Bishop of Rome. It therefore claims the right to hold its own councils. Trent outlined the differences between the Catholic Church and the Protestant reformers; Vatican I asserted the authority and infallibility of the pope; Vatican II moved closer to other Christian churches. Pope John Paul II, however, has re-affirmed the authority of the papacy. The emphasis on the Catholic Church being the only Church has led to persecution of others.

Since Vatican II in the 1960s the Mass, the central act of worship, has been celebrated in the vernacular and the altar (formerly in the east) is now often found in the centre of the church. Strict rules govern membership of the church and only members can receive bread at Mass. Schools and colleges re-enforce Catholic teaching and control is exercised over those allowed to teach in them. There is, however, a healthy debate on theological and ethical issues within the Catholic Church. It has also contributed significantly through art, music, architecture and literature to Christianity as a whole.

The liturgies (worship) within the Church recognize the importance of Mary, the mother of Jesus, and the various saints who have demonstrated God's presence in them. The authority of the Church, that outside the Church there is no salvation, led to criticism, frustrations and eventually the Reformation. The Counter-Reformation strengthened the authority of the papacy and re-vitalized the orders of monks and nuns, in particular the approval given to the Society of Jesus, helping to give new vigour to the Church.

The Catholic Church is highly clericalized, the priesthood is male and Pope John Paul II was the first non-Italian pope for centuries. Opportunities for women are, therefore, limited as they cannot play an effective part in the decision-making of the senior councils of the Church.

)))⮞ *John Paul II*

ROMANOV DYNASTY (1613–1917)

Russian rulers for 300 years. This dynasty provided 17 tsars or tsarinas who ruled Russia until the Revolution of 1917. Descended from Andrey Ivanovich Kobyla, a Muscovite living during the reign of Ivan I, the name was derived from Roman Yurev (d. 1543) whose daughter was the first wife of Ivan IV 'the Terrible'. Her brother's children took the surname Romanov and when Fyodor I, the last ruler of the Rurik dynasty, died in 1598, 15 years of chaos ended with Michael Romanov as the new tsar. Notable Romanovs include Catherine the Great (1729–96) who attempted to westernize Russia and succeeded in making her country a major European power. Alexander I (1777–1825) ruled Russia during the Napoleonic Wars. Alexander II (1818–81) ruled during the Crimean War and led Russia against Turkey, and sold Alaska to the United States (1867). Nicholas II (1868–1918) was the last tsar, deposed by the Russian Revolution. He led Russia to defeat in the Russo-Japanese War (1904) and allowed the Russian economy to become paralysed. During World War I, the failures mounted and he was forced to abdicate. The Bolsheviks held him and his family captive until they were executed on 16 July 1918.

)))⯈ *Bolsheviks, Nicholas II of Russia, Russo-Japanese War, World War I*

ROMANS (753 BC – AD 476)

Rome was founded in 753 BC and gradually the cities of Latium fell under Roman control. The Etruscans were defeated in the fifth to fourth centuries BC and the Samnites in 343–290 BC. The Greek cities to the south were conquered (280–272 BC) as was Cisalpine Gaul (226–222 BC). Rome fought two Punic Wars against Carthage for the possession of Sicily, Sardinia, Spain and North Africa. By 148 BC Macedon had become a province and Greece was added in 146. By AD 117, after having added Gaul, Egypt, Great Britain, Dacia and Mesopotamia, the Empire had reached its greatest expansion, stretching from the Persian Gulf to the Iberian Peninsular.

Gradually the frontiers came under pressure from the Franks, Goths and Parthians. Ultimately the Empire was divided between two emperors in Rome and Constantinople. By AD 410 the Goths had over-run

Greece and Italy and sacked Rome and the Vandals had conquered Italy itself. Britain was abandoned in AD 407 and when the Huns raided Gaul and Italy (AD 451–52) the Empire was virtually unable to defend itself. Each time the Empire contracted Barbarians filled the vacuum. The last emperor was deposed in AD 476 and a Western Roman Empire ceased to exist.

)))⯈ *Ancient Rome, Augustus Caesar, Julius Caesar, Emperor, Hadrian, Punic Wars*

ROMANTICISM

Artistic and literary movement. In reaction to the humanism of Enlightenment thought and the order and restraint of neoclassical art, an aesthetic rebellion swept Europe and America at the end of the eighteenth century. One aspect was a growing taste for the gothic in art and literature, with its hints at mysteries beyond man's comprehension or control. Another was an admiration for bandits, nomads and other such 'free spirits'. The poetry of Lord Byron (1788–1824) offers numerous examples of figures like these – though none fits the romantic outlaw's role as well as the moody, restless poet himself. The paintings of Francisco Goya

ABOVE: The ruins of a Roman ampitheatre provide a glimpse into the incredible heritage left us by this fascinating civilization.

RIGHT: Field Marshal Erwin Rommel defined the logistics for the Blitzkrieg.
BELOW: Lord Byron, one of England's foremost Romantic poets.

(1746–1828) in Spain, and of Eugéne Delacroix (1798–1863) in France are romantic not only in their themes but in an almost reckless technical freedom. But perhaps the most distinctive feature of romanticism was its cult of the feeling individual, which found its first and

most dramatic expression in a novel by German writer Johann Wolfgang von Goethe (1749–1832). His *The Sorrows of Young Werther* (1774) prompted a spate of suicides among young men who identified with its intensely emotional student hero. Yet the cult would find more moderate expression in the idea of the solitary soul happily communing with nature, like the English poet William Wordsworth (1770–1850) in the lake district.

ROME, SACK OF (AD 410)

The Visigoths had migrated west and had become Roman mercenaries in the reign of Theodosius I. Alaric became king when Theodosius died in AD 395. He led the Visigoths to sack Greece and invaded Italy in AD 402. He temporarily allied with Rome again but when Emperor Arcadius died (AD 408) the new emperor, Honorius, broke the pact. Alaric invaded Italy and besieged Rome. He captured it and sacked it in AD 410.
))))▶ *Ancient Rome, Romans*

ROMMEL, ERWIN (1891–1944)

German military comander during World War II, responsible for the strategy of tank warfare. Field Marshal Erwin Rommel was largely responsible for putting tank warfare into practice. He organized spearhead attacks with close-knit packs of Panzers. Having successfully invaded Central Europe and France,

Rommel commanded the North Africa campaign, which he eventually lost due to overstretched supply routes. He ultimately committed suicide.
))))▶ *Battle of El Alamein, World War II*

RÖNTGEN, WILHELM (1845–1923)

German physicist. In 1895, while experimenting with the passage of electricity through gases, Wilhelm Röntgen noticed that his experiment was causing a coated photographic screen to fluoresce. He then discovered that the mysterious rays would pass through some substances but not others. He called them X-rays and began to experiment with photographic plates. X-ray scanning revolutionized medicine by allowing physicians to see inside the body without physical investigation. Röntgen was awarded the Nobel Prize for Physics in 1901.

ROOSEVELT, FRANKLIN D (1882–1945)

32nd US president (1933–45). Roosevelt was the longest-serving US leader. He was elected four times for a 12-year period during the Depression and World War II. In 1933 Roosevelt launched the New Deal, which provided relief for the unemployed and those faced with losing their farms and homes. He later placed heavier taxes on the wealthy and introduced social security. Roosevelt was reluctant to involve the USA in World War II, but after the bombing of Pearl Harbour in 1941 he sent American troops to Europe. Along with Churchill and Stalin, Roosevelt became one of the 'Big Three' Allied leaders during the war.
))))▶ *Great Depression, New Deal, President, World War II*

ROOSEVELT, THEODORE (1858–1919)

26th US president (1901–09). He was Republican president who passed legislation curbing the powers of big corporations in the USA, and introduced food and drug regulations. Roosevelt was very active in international affairs. He helped create the Panama Canal in 1902 and played a central role in ending the Russo-Japanese War.

)))⏵ *Panama Canal, Russo-Japanese War*

ROSETTA STONE

Egyptian artefact. Found in the Egyptian town of Rosetta in 1799 by troops from Napoleon's army on campaign, this black basalt slab was found to bear a quite unique inscription. Like many other similar slabs it bore texts in hieroglyphics (ancient Egyptian pictorial writing) and demotic (the cursive script that followed): what set it apart was that these were followed by a Greek translation. Working with this sample, scholars were at last able to 'crack the code' of Egyptian writing, opening up what had been until then a complete enigma.

)))⏵ *Ancient Egypt*

ROUSSEAU, JEAN-JACQUES (1712–78)

French philosopher. One of the great *Philosophes* of the French Enlightenment – though in many of his theories a prophet of romanticism too – Jean-Jacques Rousseau was actually born in Geneva, Switzerland. Coming to Paris in 1741, he wrote a series of books in praise of the 'natural man', uncorrupted by the institutions of church and society, law and education. 'Man was born free, but is everywhere in chains,' he wrote in his *The Social Contract* (1762). *Emile*, published the same year, was nominally a novel but in fact was a programme of education, imagined a girl brought up unspoiled, in isolation from society and its strictures.

RUSSELL, BERTRAND (1872–1970)

British mathematician and philosopher. Educated at Cambridge, Russell wrote *Principles of Mathematics* (1903), *Problems of Philosophy* (1911) and *Principles of Social Reconstruction* (1917). He wrote *Introduction to Mathematical Philosophy* (1919) whilst imprisoned for pacifist writings, *Marriage and Morals*

RIGHT: Bertrand Russell.

(1929), *An Enquiry into Meaning and Truth* (1940), *History of Western Philosophy* (1946) and *New Hopes for a Changing World* (1951). He was awarded the Order of Merit in 1949 and the Nobel Prize for Literature in 1950.

RUSSIAN REVOLUTION (1917)

Two revolutions resulting in the overthrow of the Russian monarchy. When Russia entered World War I in 1914, the country was on the verge of revolution. Riots broke out in Petrograd (St Petersburg) in February 1917, marking the beginning of the Russian Revolution.

Tsar Nicholas abdicated and a provisional government was established under Prince Lvov. There began a struggle for power between the provisional government and the Petrograd soviet. Vladimir Lenin, who had been exiled in Switzerland since 1914, returned to Petrograd demanding a handover of power to the Petrograd soviet. In July 1917, the Bolsheviks, under Lenin and Leon Trotsky attempted to seize power in Petrograd. But Alexander Kerensky of the provisional government held on to power until November of the same year.

In November 1917, the Bolsheviks began their own revolution. Their military revolutionary committee and Red Guards arrested the provisional government. Lenin, Trotsky and Joseph Stalin emerged as prominent figures in the new government. The Treaty of Brest-Litovsk (March 1918), marked the end of Russia's involvement in World War I. By July the royal family had been murdered and civil war had broken out.

)))⏵ *Bolsheviks, Treaty of Brest-Litovsk, Vladimir Ilyich Lenin, Nicholas II of Russia, Joseph Stalin, Leon Trotsky*

LEFT: Bolsheviks up in arms against the government and the Russian aristocracy during the Russian Revolution of 1917.
BELOW: Beleagured Russian troops in retreat from Manchuria.after Japanese victory at the Battle of Mukden in 1905.

RUSSO-JAPANESE WAR (1904–05)

The north-eastern corner of China, Manchuria, and Korea (then one country), were of territorial significance to both the Russians and the Japanese at the beginning of the twentieth century. For Russia possession of the territory meant an improved land link to the Pacific Ocean; for Japan it would mean a foothold on the mainland of the Eurasian continent. The Russo-Japanese War lasted 1904–05. Japan besieged Port Arthur (Lushun), occupied by Russia, from May 1904 until January 1905. Japan also won the Battle of Mukden, February–March 1905. Russia surrendered and peace came on 23 August.

RUSSO-TURKISH WAR (1877–78)

The Greek War of Independence (1821–29), was fought between the Greeks and the Turks. Allied with Greece during the war were Russia, Britain and France. Conversely, the Crimean War saw Britain and France defend the Ottoman Empire (Turkey) from further pressure by the Russians. The Russo-Turkish War lasted between 1877 and 1878. The Russians compelled Turkey to sign the Treaty of San Stefano in 1878. However, it meant an imbalance of power in Eastern Europe and the other great powers eventually pressured Russia to reach a power compromise at the Treaty of Berlin in the same year.

SADAT, ANWAR (1918–81)

Egyptian president (1970–81). An ex-army officer imprisoned by the British in World War I, Sadat became president in 1970. In 1973 he aligned Egypt's forces with Syria in an invasion of Israel which, though not victorious, did see him triumph as the first Arab leader to regain land from Israel. After the war Sadat pledged peace and made an unprecedented visit to Jerusalem in 1977. His negotiations with Israeli prime minister Menachem Begin culminated in the 1978 Camp David Accords, for which they both received the 1978 Nobel Peace Prize. Sadat was assassinated in 1981.

SAFAVID DYNASTY (16TH–18TH CENTURIES)

Persian clan. In the early sixteenth century the Safavid clan of Persia was at war with the Ottomans in Turkey. Having absorbed some of the western and northern Turkic tribes, they were threatening to expand into Turkey itself. The Ottomans had beaten them back by 1514 and confined them to what is now the Iranian plateau. The best-known king of the Safavid Empire was Abbas I, who encouraged trade with Europeans. The Empire eventually submitted to the Afghans in 1722.

)))⟩⟩ *Ottoman Empire, Persia*

SALADIN (d. 1193)

Sultan of Egypt. Saladin was renowned as an intelligent and just ruler. He began a campaign against the Crusades in 1197 after the Christians attacked a travelling party which included his sister. He declared war on Jerusalem, which by this time was a Christian kingdom. Although Saladin succeeded in capturing the city he did not allow his army to destroy it and loss of life in the skirmish was minimal. Despite this, European forces combined to recapture the city in what became the Third Crusade. They failed to retake Jerusalem, but captured the city of Acre. Peace was reached in 1192, the year before Saladin's death.

)))⟩⟩ *Crusades, Holy Roman Empire*

RIGHT: Japanese Samurai, members of a proud and fierce warrior caste, were virtually wiped out following the Meiji Restoration of 1868.

SALEM WITCH HUNTS (1692)

American witchcraft investigations leading to 19 hangings. In Salem Village, Essex County, in the province of Massachusetts Bay, New England, hysteria broke out after the claims of three young girls that they were possessed by the devil. A West Indian slave named Tituba, Sarah Good and a woman named Osborne were arrested and committed for trial. The three incriminated others in false confessions; a total of 150 were awaiting trial. A special court was set up: 19 were found guilty and hanged. Governor Phips dissolved the court, ordering the remaining accused be released and indemnities to the families of those executed.

SAMURAI (12TH CENTURY–1868)

Japanese warrior caste. Originally the term was used to describe aristocratic warriors in Japan. They dominated Japanese government for over 600 years. Samurai culture incorporated their military skills and codes of conduct or Bushido and Zen Buddhism. They were superseded by a more vibrant merchant

economy and lost their privileges finally in 1871 when feudalism was abolished. The end of the Samurai is usually considered to be when the Meiji Restoration took place (1868) following a Samurai revolt.

)))⟩⟩ *Satsuma Rebellion*

SAN STEFANO, TREATY OF (1878)

Peace treaty signed following the last of the Russo-Turkish wars. The agreement between Prussia and the Ottoman Empire saw significant changes to national boundaries within Eastern Europe. Bulgaria was enlarged and became an independent state; Serbia and Montenegro were given greater territories. The Ottoman Empire was made to pay a large compensation.

)))⟩⟩ *Russo-Turkish War*

SARATOGA, BATTLE OF (1777)

Battle during the American Revolution. George Washington was a military commander before he became the first president of USA. In October 1777, Washington masterminded a crucial victory against the British at the Battle of Saratoga Springs, New York. His rebel army surrounded the British, led by General John Burgoyne, preventing a link up with General William Howe, and turning the war in the favour of the colonists.

)))) *American Revolution, George Washington*

SARGON THE GREAT (c. 2371 BC)

Ruler of Mesopotamia. Sargon changed the method of government of conquered empires. Rather than allowing an empire to continue to be governed by its own people, he appointed his own administrators, limiting the chances of rebellion.

SARTRE, JEAN-PAUL (1905–80)

French philosopher and writer. After wartime service in the Resistance, Sartre became a hero of the French Left, with his partner the feminist Simone de Beauvoir (1908–86), intellectual Paris's dominant presence. In philosophical works like *Being and Nothingness* (1943) as well as in a string of well-regarded novels and plays, he became the figurehead for the then-fashionable philosophy of 'existentialism'. An atheist, he argued that, in a cosmos without a creator, the individual had to make his own way, without reliance on religious or other props.

SASSANID DYNASTY

Rulers of Parthia. Parthia (equivalent to parts of Iran/Persia and Iraq) lay on the eastern borders of the Roman Empire, and was continually involved in a regional struggle for power with Rome. A revival of nationalism led to the rise of Ardashir (Artaxerxes). In AD 224 he defeated the incumbent Arsacid ruler, Artabanos IV, and established the Sassanid dynasty (named after his grandfather Sasan), with himself as King of Kings.

BELOW LEFT: Jean-Paul Sartre.
BELOW RIGHT: Liam Neeson as Oscar Schindler in Stephen Spielberg's Oscar-winning film, Schindler's List.

Rapid success was organized from the capital at Ctesiphon (near Baghdad). A cultural renaissance of Persian tradition followed, including the Zoroastrian religion, and centralization by using Sassanian family members as administrators. In AD 260 the Roman Emperor Valerian I was captured and imprisoned. But Sassanid power was later threatened by the rise of Islam. In AD 637 Muslim Arabs defeated and destroyed the forces of Yazdagird III at Qadisiya.

SATSUMA REBELLION (1877–78)

Medieval Japanese society was hierarchically arranged. Approximately 92 per cent of the population were commoners and eight per cent Samurai. The Samurai were the elite class allowed to carry the famous Samurai sword. In around 1700, the Samurai suffered a financial depression, which marked the beginning of their demise. They were eventually stripped of their role as defenders of the Empire. The Satsuma Rebellion was the last effort of the Samurai to restore their power.

)))) *Samurai, Warlords*

SCHINDLER, OSCAR (1908–1974)

Rescuer of Jews during the Nazi Holocaust. Oscar Schindler was recruited by the German Intelligence Agency to collect information about the Polish. In Krakow he set up a factory, Deutsch Emailwaren Fabrik, but as the Nazi plan for the exter-mination of Jews escalated, he began protecting those working in his factory. He smuggled food and medicines into the labour camp of Plaszow and did everything in his power to keep the Jews out of the concentration camps.

)))) *Nazi Party, World War II*

SCHLIEFFEN PLAN (1905)

German offensive strategy for World War I. The Schlieffen Plan was named after its creator, the German chief of general staff, General Count Alfred von Schlieffen (1833–1913). It was a two-pronged European attack: the idea was to stage simultaneous offensives on France and Russia and to deploy all available resources against the latter when France had been conquered. General von Moltke (1848–1916), altered the Plan before it was put into effect in 1914, resulting in its failure. Adolf Hitler's plans for the conquest of Europe in World War II were inspired by the Schlieffen Plan.

))⟩⟩ *World War I, World War II*

SCHUMAN PLAN (1950)

Post-war economic plan for France and Germany. In the post World War II period, the US and British foreign ministers encouraged French foreign minister Robert Schuman to design a proposal to reincorporate Germany into the new European environment. Schuman drafted a plan calling for a single body to control steel and coal production in France and West Germany. The Schuman Plan was accepted in May 1950, laying the foundation for the European Economic Community.

SCHWEITZER, ALBERT (1875–1965)

Organist and theologian. Schweitzer vowed in 1896 that he would change his life at 30 years of age in order to serve humanity. He qualified as a doctor and in 1913 set out to fight leprosy at Lambarene in Africa, where he remained. He was awarded the Nobel Peace Prize in 1952. His work *Quest of the Historical Jesus* was widely read as it continued the belief current in Protestant theology of his time that it was very difficult, if indeed possible, to discover the historical figure Jesus; Jesus was masked by the 'Christ of faith'. Like other theologians he moulded his views of Jesus to his own convictions.

))⟩⟩ *Christianity*

ABOVE: Robert Falcon Scott.
RIGHT: The German theologian and philantropist Albert Schweitzer was awarded both the Nobel Peace Prize and the Order of Merit for his humanitarian efforts in developing countries.

SCOTT, ROBERT FALCON (1868–1912)

British naval officer and Antarctic explorer. Scott commanded the British National Antarctic Expedition of 1901–04 and in 1910 mounted a private expedition to Antarctica aboard the *Terra Nova*. After making preparations and scientific observations for a year, in November 1911 Scott's party of five set out for the Pole. Ponies and motorized vehicles proved useless, so the team hauled their own sledges to reach the Pole on 16 January 1912, only to find that the Norwegian Roald Amundsen had got there a month earlier. The return journey was dogged by appalling weather and resulted in the deaths of the entire party. Scott's diaries preserve the last few days of their expedition, knowing that they were going to die. The last entry reads: 'For God's sake look after our people.'

))⟩⟩ *Roald Amundsen*

SCRAMBLE FOR AFRICA (1880s–90s)

Term used to describe the pursuit of territorial acquisitions in Africa by rival European powers in the 1880s and 1890s. By 1875 European powers already occupied the coastal areas. In 1876 King Leopold II of Belgium convened a conference to discuss Europe's role in Africa. The 'scramble' began in earnest when Britain intervened in Egypt after a nationalist revolt and established authority there. France objected and the race was on to secure territory. The Berlin Conference of 1884–86 laid the foundations for the orderly division of Africa among European powers. By now, however, journeys were already being taken for political rather than geographical reasons and Belgium had appropriated the left bank of the Congo River while France had occupied the right. Treaties divided up Africa between Belgium, Great Britain, France, Germany and Portugal and any areas unaccounted for were claimed by military conquest. By 1900 only Ethiopia and Liberia were still independent.

))))➤ *British Empire*

SELASSIE, HAILE (d. 1975)

Emperor of Ethiopia from 1930. Haile Selassie is regarded as the 225th descendant in a line of succession traced back to King Solomon. He took the titles King of Kings, Lord of Lords, and Conquering Lion of the Tribes of Judah. Although now dead, Rastafarians believe his presence can still be felt as Jah (God).

))))➤ *Rastafari*

SEVASTOPOL, SIEGE OF (1854–55)

Battle during the Crimean War. Central to the English and French strategy in the Crimean War was their laying siege to Sevastopol, the Ukranian fortress on the Black Sea. The siege lasted for a year between September 1854 and September 1855 and was successful for the allies, although military mismanagement had resulted in unacceptably high casualties.

))))➤ *Crimean War*

BELOW: A marble bust of Septimius Severus.

SEVEN YEARS' WAR (1756–63)

International struggle for colonial supremacy. The Seven Years' War arose from conflict between European nations including Austria, Britain, France, Prussia, Spain and Russia. Allegiance between these nations was complex, but Britain fared well, gaining control of India and many French colonies, including Canada. Florida was handed to Britain by Spain, who received Cuba in exchange. Prussia emerged as a great European power through its considerable military success against unlikely odds. The 1763 Treaty of Paris, marking the end of the war, was signed by Britain, France and Spain.

))))➤ *Treaty of Paris*

SEPTIMIUS SEVERUS (c. AD 146–211)

Roman emperor from AD 193. Born in Africa, Severus was a senator with a successful career as a provincial governor when he joined in the civil war following the murder of Commodus in AD 192. Playing off his rivals, he defeated them one by one. Recognizing the importance of military support, he increased soldiers' pay and privileges. In AD 208 he embarked on a war in Britain, designed to toughen his sons and heirs, Caracalla and Geta, and win the dynasty prestige. The campaign proved bloody and inconclusive and he died in York in AD 211.

))))➤ *Ancient Rome*

SHAH JAHAN (1592–1666)

Mogul emperor from 1628–58, and builder of the Taj Mahal. A failed revolt against his father, Jahangir, in 1622 led to reconciliation and his accession at Agra in 1628. The reign saw territorial expansion into Eastern India (the Deccan), and was the highpoint of the Empire, despite the loss of Kandahur to Persia in 1653. However, the vast costs of campaigning meant that the reign saw the Empire pass its peak.

Shah Jahan's enthusiasm for art and architecture included the erection of mosques and the celebrated mausoleum, the Taj Mahal, at Agra. He removed his capital from Agra to Delhi, rebuilt it as Shjahanabad, and erected the fortified palace, called the 'Red Fort', there. Hindusim was tolerated, painting and literature flourished, and the court became renowned for its magnificence.

))))➤ *Taj Mahal*

SHAKESPEARE, WILLIAM (1564–1616)

English poet and playwright. Born in Stratford upon Avon, the son of a glover, Shakespeare attended the local grammar school before marrying Anne Hathaway, a farmer's daughter, who bore him three children. (A certain amount of mystery shrouds Shakespeare's early life: there has, for example, been unproven speculation that his was a family of secret Catholics in an age of potential persecution.) It was only after this that Shakespeare seems to have gone to London to seek the fortune which turned out to await him in theatreland. Though the author of several poems (including what are widely held to be the greatest sonnets in the language), it would be as a dramatist that Shakespeare became the pre-eminent figure of English literature. Comedies like *A Midsummer Night's Dream* and *As You Like It*, and tragedies like *Hamlet* and *King Lear* would be both commercial successes in their day and undisputed classics for all time.

SHANG DYNASTY (c. 1766–1027 BC)

First Chinese dynasty. There are disputes regarding the dates of this dynasty, but what we do know is that Shang China was based in the North China Plain and extended to the modern Shantung Province and Honan Province. The Shang dynasty was an aristocratic society that used priests to keep government records. It was agricultural economy, cultivating millet, wheat, barley and silkworms. They made bronze weapons and tools and worshipped their ancestors and gods, one of whom was Shang Ti. The last Shang ruler was overthrown by the King of Chou – the dynasty that ruled for another 800 years before its demise.

SHANKARA (8TH CENTURY)

Indian scholar. Shankara was a famous scholar of Vedanta (the interpretation of the religious texts *Vedas* and *Upanishads*). He is believed to spent much of his life wandering the country teaching and establishing monasteries. He believed that the purpose of life was to discovered God in oneself. His work *Atma Bodha* ('Knowledge of Spirit') expressed his teaching of non-dualism, in which only God exists – God is in all things and all things are God.

))))➤ *Hinduism*

SHINTOISM

Japanese indigenous religion. There is little agreement about exactly what Shinto means (the term was coined in around the sixth century) but Japan has 100,000 well-supported shrines. Shinto shrines are associated with Kami (spirit entities) for the spirit lives in the Kami. Shinto encourages qualities of purity, honesty and sincerity. Before 1945 Shinto taught that the emperor was divine and the Japanese people were descended from the gods. This encouragement to nationalism was changed after 1945 and Shinto is mixed with popular Buddhist practices. Visits to the shrines require purification from actions and thoughts to restore us to our original state. It is very much a 'this worldly religion'.

))))➤ *Buddhism*

LEFT: William Shakespeare.

BELOW: *A Hindu artesan chisels a statue of Buddha. Buddhism is a faith that has enjoyed an increase in followers in recent years.*
RIGHT: *A Sikh wedding ceremony in London.*

SHIVA

Hindu god. Associated with powers of reproduction and dissolution. Often depicted dancing in a circle of flame – one of the many aspects in which he is worshipped is as lord of the cosmic dance (others are as destroyer and lord of beasts).

)))) *Brahma, Hinduism, Vishnu*

SIDDHARTHA GAUTAMA (THE BUDDHA) (AD 566–486 OR AD 448–368)

Born Siddhartha Gautama into the Sakya clan of a wealthy family, he was married with a son, Rahula. At the age of 29 he saw an old man, a sick man, a corpse and an ascetic. He renounced his life at home and became an ascetic but when meditating under the Bodhi tree he achieved Enlightenment. He was then 35 years old. He spent 45 years in the company of an order of monks and later nuns teaching his philosophy to the people of North India. He taught the 'Middle Way'; between the life of a householder doomed to countless rebirths, and the celibate life of extreme asceticism, which seeks the right goal, but by the wrong means. The goal is nirvana (a place of indescribable peace); one who attains it is enlightened (buddha) and is no longer reborn or subject to karma. At his death he enters into 'nirvana'. Gautama was one in a long line of Buddhas. His teaching has been developed over the centuries and as a missionary religion often takes on something of the culture of that it meets.

)))) *Buddhism*

SIKHISM (16TH CENTURY)

Indian religion, originating in the Punjab, North India. Guru Nanak founded the religion and was followed by nine known gurus. The tenth guru, Gobind Singh, formed the Khalsa (the 'Pure Ones') in 1699. Male members of the Khalsa take the name 'Singh' (lion), females take the name 'Kaur' (princess). Gobind Singh also installed as guru the Sikh holy book, the Guru Granth Sahib or *Adi Granth* ('Original Collection'). This holy book is a collection of hymns and sayings of the first five gurus. It was collected by Guru Arjan (1563–1606) and installed in the newly built Golden Temple at Amritsar. The work 'Sikh' means 'disciple'; Sikhs believe in One God and strive for self-control, forgiveness, humility and social concern. Bad deeds can result in being reborn in an endless cycle. The gurdwara (place of worship) is a central focus for Sikhs who are often identified by the 'Five Ks' – Kesh (uncut hair); Kangha (comb); Kirpan (dagger); Kara (steel bracelet); Kach (shorts) – and by the men wearing a turban.

)))) *Guru Nanak, Guru Gobind Singh*

SILK ROUTE

Ancient trade route connecting China with the West. Using a series of middlemen, the 4,000-mile caravan track originated in Sian and followed the route of the Great Wall of China. It bypassed the Takla Makan Desert, climbing the Pamir Mountains, crossing Afghanistan and ending at the Levant. It was used to transport silk from the East and wool, gold and silver from the West. The goods were transported across the Mediterranean Sea from the Levant.

)))) *Great Wall of China*

SITTING BULL (1831–90)

Sioux Indian chief (Teton Dakota). For his fearlessness during invasions, he was made principal chief of the Sioux nation in 1867. When the Second Treaty of Fort Laramie (1868) was broken, beginning the Battle of Little Bighorn, Sitting Bull and the Sioux tribes wiped out Lieutenant Colonel George Custer and his armies. Forced out of Canada (1877), Sitting Bull joined Buffalo Bill's Wild West Show. He was killed at Grand River during the Ghost Dance uprising.

)))➤ *Battle of the Little Bighorn, George Armstrong Custer*

SIX-DAY WAR (1967)

Third Arab-Israeli war. Ever since the UN voted to partition Palestine and allow the formation of the Independent State of Israel following World War II, there has existed a state of tension between Jewish and Muslim populations in the Middle East. The third Arab-Israeli war or Six-Day War (5–10 June 1967), saw a major offensive by the Israelis. In less than a week they had annexed the Golan Heights in Syria, the West Bank and Gaza Strip in Palestine, and the Sinai as far as the Suez Canal.

)))➤ *Arab-Israeli Wars*

SLAVERY

Involuntary human servitude. Slavery was an essential feature of ancient civilizations, including the Indian, Chinese and Roman ones. During the Middle Ages, despite the spread of Christianity, slavery was not eliminated. Islam recognized slavery from the seventh century and the Prophet Muhammed encouraged his faithful followers to be kind to their slaves.

ABOVE: The great Sioux chief, Sitting Bull.

RIGHT: Joseph Smith, founder of the Church of Jesus Christ of Latter-Day Saints.

During the exploration of Africa and the invasion of the Americas, the modern slave trade gained impetus. Colonists forced the native population to work their land. African slaves were taken to the Americas and the Caribbean to work on the newly formed plantations. Slavery became an essential element of the English colonies in America. Denmark was the first European country to abolish slavery (1792) followed by Great Britain (1807). Despite the United States abolishing slavery in 1808, there were still nearly four million slaves by the year 1860. Slaves did have some legal rights but their masters were not bound to respect them. Mutilation, chaining, branding, rape and murder were widespread despite being prohibited by law. The American Civil War (1861–65) brought about the freedom of four million slaves upon whom the southern economy had depended.

During the late nineteenth century the Arabs were particularly active in the slavery trade in North Africa which was gradually brought to an end as states fell under the power of European countries such as Great Britain and France. In 1926 the International Slavery Convention abolished slavery in all forms. Nevertheless, slavery still continues across the world, notably in West Africa.

)))➤ *American Civil War, Abraham Lincoln*

SLUYS, BATTLE OF (1340)

First major conflict of the Hundred Years' War. The naval Battle of Sluys took place on 24 June 1340. Edward III of England,was planning to invade France through the low countries. He engaged the Franco-Genoese fleet off the Flanders Coast, destroying or capturing most vessels.

)))➤ *Edward III of England, Hundred Years' War*

SMITH, JOSEPH (1805–44)

Founder of the Mormon movement. In 1822 a New York farm boy, Joseph Smith received a vision of the angel Moroni who revealed to him where gold plates were to be found on which were written a

book of God's revelation about North America. In 1830 he founded the Church of Jesus Christ of Latter-Day Saints and published the text of the plates. They told of the lost tribes of Israel coming to America. He believed this to be a restoration of Christianity, building a new kingdom in Utah. Originally condoning polygamy, the practice has been modified, but early followers of Smith were imprisoned in the late nineteenth century. The movement has a strong missionary element.

))))➤ *Mormons*

SMUTS, JAN CHRISTIAN (1870–1950)

South African soldier and prime minister (1919–24 and 1939–48). Smuts was an outstanding military commander and treaty negotiator. He served in both the Boer War and World War I and was a member of the Imperial War Cabinet in 1917. Smuts was a signatory to the peace treaties following both world wars, and was influential in the development of the United Nations.

))))➤ *Boer War*

SOCIALISM

Political movement that believes private property and income distribution should be subject to social control rather than market forces. The term has been used to cover a broad political spectrum from anarchy to social democracy. Similarly, socialist ideas vary from a belief that all or some industries should be state-owned to more decentralized government guided by the free market.

The word first appeared in the early nineteenth century in France, although early philosophers such as Plato wrote about socialist ideas. A successful industrialist, Robert Owen, is generally thought to have started British socialism with his views on a competition-free economy that would benefit all. In 1848 the publication of the *Communist Manifesto* by Karl Marx and Friedrich Engels introduced their vision of 'scientific socialism', in which the working class would take over from the capitalists and the structure of the bourgeois state would crumble. Many socialist parties doubted that capitalism would collapse and advocated a more liberal socialism. The situation

diversified further in the twentieth century. The Soviet Union's centralized socialism was based on strict Communist principles, until its restructuring (*perestroika*) under Gorbachev. Noncommunist socialist governments in Sweden and Britain introduced the welfare state to guarantee basic minimum living standards for all.

))))➤ *Communism, Mikhail Gorbachev, Karl Marx*

SOCRATES (c. 469–399 BC)

Athenian philosopher. Serving at Samos during the Peloponnesian War (440 BC) Socrates rejected scientific knowledge but preferred to 'guide men to clear thought on ethics and politics by pretending ignorance and encouraging others to enter into discussion'. In 399 BC he was accused of impiety, 'corruption of the young', and 'neglect of the gods whom the city worships and the practice of religious novelties', sent to trial and sentenced to death by drinking hemlock.

SOMME, BATTLE OF THE (1916)

Allied offensive during World War I. Half way through World War I, the Allied forces made an offensive move on the Germans at the River Somme in northern France. The Battle of the Somme began on 1 July 1916 and lasted until November. Both sides suffered severe losses, and the Allies advanced a mere 13 km (8 miles). The battle is noted for being the first to involve tanks – originally a code-name – which were invented by the British soldier Ernest Swinton. The first day of the Somme is also remembered as one of the most tragic in history in terms of sheer numbers of dead and wounded.

))))➤ *World War I*

RIGHT: The Battle of the Somme.

SONG DYNASTY (AD 960)

Chinese dynasty. The Song seized control of China in AD 960. They united the many factions into which the country was divided under one central rule. Early emperors established a good bureaucracy, placing a new class of people – the schola-official – in charge. The dynasty also saw the rise of many cities which became important centres for trade. The rise of Confucianism saw a decline in Buddhism during the dynasty and Confucianism became the state religion.

)))➤ *Buddhism, Confucianism*

SOUTH SEA BUBBLE (1720)

First runaway credit boom, centred on the South Sea Company. In 1720 the Company agreed to assume the £80 million national debt in return for guaranteed annual payments, to be obtained from duties on imports, and the monopoly of British trade, mainly in slaves, in the South Seas and South America. Speculation drove the price of shares up dramatically but within months the chairman and some directors sold out and the 'bubble', or market, collapsed. Thousands of investors were ruined. The South Sea Bubble so discredited joint-stock companies that they were widely made illegal for a considerable time.

SPACE RACE (1950s–60s)

Term used to describe the activity of and rivalry between the then USSR and the USA in the exploration of space. From the mid 1950s the two nations successfully launched over 5,000 satellites and space, lunar and planetary probes, as well as manned space flights.

It began with the launch by the Soviet Union of the first artificial satellite, *Sputnik 1*, on 4 October 1957. On 31 January 1958 the United States followed with *Explorer 1*. The manned space programme marked an acceleration of the space race. On 12 April 1961 the Soviet cosmonaut Yuri Gagarin, in *Vostok 1*, made the first successful orbit of the Earth. The Soviets led also in the achievement of true space flight: *Luna 1*, launched in 1959, became the first manmade body to escape the Earth's gravitational field and fly past the Moon. *Luna 2* crashed on the Moon but *Luna 3* (October 1959) photographed the far side of

the Moon. By the time the Soviets landed *Luna 9* on the Moon (1966), the USA had also sent up several craft and received from them countless close-range photographs and information about the Moon's surface. On 20 July 1969 the USA landed two men on the Moon, and a further five landings were made before the programme was curtailed in 1972.

Other ventures in space have looked to the possibilities of planetary exploration, beginning with *Mariner 2* (USA 1962), which passed by Venus, and continuing with *Venera 3* and *Venera 4* (USSR, 1966 and 1967). From 1981 the USA concentrated mainly on the reusable space-shuttle manned research vehicle, but its flights were halted immediately after an explosion that destroyed *Challenger* and its seven crew in 1986. The Russian space station *Mir* finally came to Earth in 2001 after 15 years in space.

)))➤ *Edwin 'Buzz' Aldrin, Neil Armstrong, Yuri Gagarin*

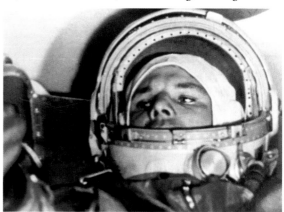

SPANISH ARMADA (1588)

In 1588, a fleet of 130 ships sailed from Lisbon, Portugal, around the north-west corner of Spain, up the west coast of France and into the English Channel. The fleet was the Spanish Armada sent by Philip II of Spain against England. The Spanish Armada had a running engagement with an English fleet of 197 ships, which were under the command of Howard of Effingham and Francis Drake. The Spaniards then weighed anchor off Calais. The English used fire ships to force the Armada to put to sea, and a battle was fought off Gravelines. Half the Armada was lost to gales on its journey home.

)))➤ *Elizabeth I of England, Philip II of Spain*

LEFT: The launch of Russian cosmonaut Yuri Gagarin into orbit in 1961 sparked the space race between the USA and Russia.
RIGHT: The Spanish Civil War began as an anarchic uprising in the streets of Madrid, between the nationalists (fascists) and the republicans.
BELOW: The defeat of the Spanish Armada.

SPANISH CIVIL WAR (1936)

Between 1873 and 1874, Spain became a republic for the first time but ended with the restoration of the Bourbon dynasty. The second republic was proclaimed in 1931, but led to a state of tension, catalyzing the Spanish Civil War.

The republican party, the left-wing Popular Front, won a 1936 election, prompting General Francisco Franco to launch a military rebellion against the government which escalated into civil war. The nationalists under Franco won significant support from the German Nazi Party and Italian fascists, enabling them to defeat the republicans who had limited support from the Soviets. The outcome was that Franco became dictator of a nationalist-fascist regime in Spain. The Spanish Civil War was a particularly barbaric struggle, characterized by 'total war' which saw no distinction between combatants and civilians. Picasso's *Guernica*, 1937, is a poignant comment on the bombing of civilians during the war.

))》 *Francisco Franco*

SPANISH SUCCESSION, WAR OF (1701–14)

Campaign fought over rights to the Spanish throne. Louis XIV of France claimed the Spanish throne on behalf of his grandson Philip V in 1700. This was in defiance of the Partition Treaty which had the Crown of Spain reserved for Charles of Austria (later Holy Roman Emperor, Charles VI). France, Spain and Bavaria fought against an Allied side, comprising Austria, Britain, Denmark, the Netherlands and Portugal. The Duke of Marlborough, John Churchill (1650–1722) played a key military role through the war.

In 1704 came the Battle of Blenheim. The French had marched on Vienna in an attempt to end the war, but the Allies under the Duke of Marlborough and Eugene of Savoy intercepted and defeated them. Marlborough was again successful at Ramillies in 1706, Oudenaarde in 1708 and Malplaquet in 1709. Treaties were signed in 1713 and 1714.

))》 *Louis XIV of France, Charles V*

SPANISH-AMERICAN WAR (1898)

The colonial presence of Spain in the Americas, which had begun at the beginning of the sixteenth century, ended in 1898 with the Spanish-American War. At the time, Spain ruled Cuba and the Philippines plus Guam and Puerto Rico. The brief war saw the USA defeat Spain outright and become a colonial power. The Philippines, Guam and Puerto Rico were ceded to the USA in the Treaty of Paris, and Cuba became independent. As compensation, the USA paid Spain $20 million. The war, which lasted less than four months, saw action in both the Caribbean and the Pacific ocean.

SPARTA (OR LACEDAEMON)

Greek city in the Peloponnesus. Under the constitution attributed to Lycurgus (ninth century BC), all citizens were trained for war from boyhood. The Spartans became proverbial for their austerity, discipline and contempt for luxury and the arts. Sparta distinguished itself in the Persian and Peloponnesian wars but sank into insignificance in the second century BC.

))))◆ *Alexander the Great, Peloponnesian Wars, Persian Wars*

SPHINX

Egyptian monument. At Giza, alongside the pyramids, is to be found the figure of the Sphinx, half-man, half-crouching lion – though this is in fact merely the biggest example of a form often encountered elsewhere in Egypt. The history of the Sphinx at Giza remains obscure, though it is believed to have been built some time before 2500 BC, making it at least as old as – perhaps even older than – the pyramids.

))))◆ *Ancient Egypt, Great Pyramid of Giza*

ST VALENTINE'S DAY MASSACRE (1929)

Chicago gangland murders. During the violence of the Prohibition of Alcohol in America, members of the Al Capone gang disguised themselves as police constables and broke into the premises of the George 'Bugs' Moran gang. They lined the unarmed Moran bootlegging gang members up against the wall and shot all seven men. This mass murder symbolized the rivalry that had been escalating for the control of the illegal liquor traffic during the era of Prohibition.

))))◆ *Al Capone, Prohibition*

STALIN, JOSEPH (1879–1953)

Leader of the USSR (1929–53). In 1929, Stalin introduced the first Five-Year Plan which enforced the government control of agriculture. Farmers resisted by destroying stock and crops: a huge famine resulted and millions of peasants were detained in Siberian labour camps. During the 1930's 'Great Purge', secret police arrested citizens suspected of challenging the government, and millions were killed. In World War II Stalin aligned the USSR  with the Allies, and was one of the three world leaders at the 1945 Yalta Conference. In the post-war period Stalin succeeded in isolating the USSR from the West during a period known as the Cold War.

))))◆ *Cold War, Five-Year Plans, World War II*

STALINGRAD, SIEGE OF (1942–43)

While the Siege of Leningrad cost the lives of a million Russians, the Siege of Stalingrad (Volgograd), August 1942–43, was not quite so devastating. Although 750,000 Soviets died, the Germans lost 4,000 troops in the campaign, and it marked a significant turning point in World War II. The German army besieging the city were forced to surrender on 2 February 1943 having been surrounded by Soviet forces under General Georgy Zhukov.

))))◆ *Siege of Leningrad, World War II*

STONEHENGE

English monument. Though Britain has innumerable stone circles, none matches Stonehenge in sophistication or awesome scale: it is thought to date from 3–5,000 years ago. At that time, the Stone Age would have been giving way to the Bronze Age with the advent of new metalworking technologies and European trade: hence, perhaps, the confidence of a community prepared to tackle so gigantic a construction. Though by far the largest blocks are the lintelled sandstone 'sarsens' grouped around the outer edge, smaller blue stones seem to have been brought from as far afield as Wales, implying a quite astonishing capacity to mobilize and co-ordinate labour. The carving on one stone of the image of a blade of a type associated with Mycenaean, pre-classical Greece, suggests a wealthy culture with commercial contacts the length and breadth of prehistoric Europe.

STRATEGIC ARMS LIMITATIONS TALKS (SALT) (1969–79)

Two long series of arms negotiations between the USA and the Soviet Union. In 1972 the SALT I agreements were signed in Moscow by President Nixon and General Secretary Brezhnev. Two major pacts resulted: the Treaty on Anti-Ballistic Missile Systems and the Interim Agreement on Limitation of Strategic Offensive Weapons. In 1979 SALT II was signed; this agreement set controls on missiles with multiple warheads.
))))► *Richard Nixon*

STUART DYNASTY

Scottish ruling family from 1371, and in England from 1603 until 1714, presiding over religious conflict and England's Civil War and Glorious Revolution.

Originating in the title 'steward', the dynasty began in 1315 when Walter, sixth hereditary High Steward of Scotland, married Robert Bruce's daughter Marjorie. Their son, Robert II, succeeded in 1371. A continuous male line lasted to James V (r. 1513–42).

James V's heir, Mary Queen of Scots, was brought up in France, leading to the French spelling, 'Stuart', becoming used. Mary bore a son, James Stuart, afterwards James VI of Scotland (1566–1625) and I of England (1603–25).

FAR LEFT: *The Sphinx is framed against the backdrop of the pyramids of Giza.*
LEFT: *Soviet leader, Josef Stalin.*
BELOW: *The magical and awe-inspiring stone monument at Stonehenge.*

Charles I, son of James I, nearly destroyed the family's control of the crown when the English Civil War, and afterwards the Commonwealth, ousted the monarchy. The restoration of Charles II in 1660 faltered with his failure to produce a legitimate heir, and fears of Stuart enthusiasm for Catholicism.

In 1685 Charles II's Catholic brother James II succeeded on the understanding his Protestant son-in-law and daughter, William and Mary, would follow. But the birth of a Catholic son, James Stuart (the 'Old Pretender'), by James's second wife, occasioned the Glorious Revolution of 1688, placing William and Mary on the throne. William and Mary (d. 1694) were childless and on William's death in 1702, the crown passed to Mary's sister Anne, during whose reign England and Scotland were joined in the Act of Union.

Anne died with no living heir in 1714, and the crown passed to a distant Protestant descendant of James I, George, elector of Hanover, bypassing the Catholic descendants of James II. James Stuart and his son Charles, the 'Young Pretender', continued to pursue Stuart claims on the throne up to 1745. Charles' son, Henry (d. 1807), was the last of the line.
))))► *Charles I of England, Charles II of England, Restoration*

STURT, SIR CHARLES (1795–1869)

 British explorer, the 'father of Australian discovery'. Sturt discovered and named the River Darling (1828) and followed the Murrumbidgee and Murray rivers to Lake Alexandrina near Adelaide (1829). The expedition of 1844, a year of severe drought, travelled up the Murray and Darling and north-west to the edge of the Simpson Desert. Sturt returned burnt and almost blind. His extensive explorations disproved the existence of an inland sea and showed that the rivers of the south-east drained mostly inland.

SUEZ CANAL (1859–69)

Artificial waterway connecting the Mediterranean Sea with the Gulf of Suez, providing a shortcut for ships operating between Europe or America and the East. The Suez Canal is about 163 km (101 miles) long and can accommodate ships up to 150,000 dwt fully loaded. It was built between 1859 and 1869.

SUEZ CRISIS (1956)

International conflict centred on the Suez Canal in Egypt. The canal, an important passageway for oil tankers, was the centre of an international dispute from July–December 1956. Britain and France, joint controllers of the canal, developed a dispute with Egyptian President Nasser following the US and British withdrawal from a major Egyptian construction project, the Aswan High Dam. Nasser retaliated by nationalizing the canal and taking control of the Suez Canal Company. In October 1956 Israeli troops invaded Egypt and occupied the canal zone, to be joined by French and British military. The United Nations denounced the action, and evacuated the European troops in December.
))))➤ *Abdul Nasser*

SUFFRAGETTES (1792–1928)

 Movement aimed at gaining votes for women. Beginning with Mary Wollstonecraft's book *A Vindication of the Rights of Woman* (1867), John and Harriet Mill presented a petition to parliament from the Woman Suffrage Committee, leading to the formation of many societies. Suffrage bills brought before the parliaments of William Gladstone and Benjamin Disraeli were defeated, Queen Victoria being opposed to the idea.

Women taxpayers were granted the right to vote in municipal elections and sit on county and city councils. In 1897 the National Union of Women's Suffrage Society was formed. Emmeline and Christabel Pankhurst forced the Society into a more militant approach, becoming involved in violent actions resulting in imprisonment, hunger strikes, demonstrations, processions and exhibitions. The Representation of the People Act (1917) allowed women over 30 the right to vote in parliamentary elections. In 1928 the female voting age was reduced to 21, making it equal to that for males.
))))➤ *Emmeline Pankhurst*

SULEIMAN THE MAGNIFICENT (1494–1566)

Turkish sultan from 1520. During Suleiman's reign, the Ottoman Empire reached its climax. At Istanbul (Constantinople) Suleiman (also spelled Sulaiman) built four great mosques, including the Blue Mosque, and he gained a reputation as a poet and law reformer.

In the west advances began well, but met resistance. In 1522 Suleiman took Rhodes, and also advanced into southern and eastern Europe by taking Belgrade in 1521

LEFT: The Suez Canal is an artificially built waterway which connects the Mediterranean Sea with the Gulf of Suez.
ABOVE: Suffragettes are expelled from Westminster after demonstrating for the right to vote.

BELOW: *Surrealist artists like Salvador Dalí borrowed many of their ideas from the dream framework proposed by Sigmund Freud as an expression of the unconscious mind.*

and defeating the Hungarians in 1526 at Mohacz. Although Ferdinand I lost almost all of Hungary he retained Austria when Suleiman failed to take Vienna in 1529. Suleiman's fleet also failed to take Malta in a severe defeat in 1565.

In the east Suleiman was more successful, taking Persia, and much of North Africa, but at his death he was still waging war in Hungary.

SUMERIANS

Civilization of the Ancient Near East. The Sumerians were the first peoples to inhabit Mesopotamia. The civilization grew up around the Tigris and Eurphrates rivers. The Sumerians became an advanced people, building rivers and dykes to control the rivers and harness their properties for their own uses. They built ziggutats, or temple towers, and developed the form of writing that has become known as cuneiform.

))))⯈ *Assyrians, Babylonians*

SURREALISM

Artistic movement. Though associated at first with Dada, surrealism soon abandoned absurdity for absurdity's sake, erecting around itself a theoretical framework based on Freudian psychology. Freud's view that dreams held the key to the unconscious mind inspired Andre Breton in the belief that they could hold the key to art as well, allowing painters and sculptors

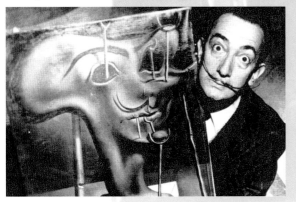

access to a level of creativity richer – and more truly human – than any yet entered. Quite how scientifically seriously this theory was taken seems to have varied considerably from artist to artist: Max Ernst (1891–1976), for instance, strove for ways to bypass his conscious creativity and work straight from his subconscious mind. René Magritte (1898–1967) and Salvador Dalí, on the other hand, worked carefully and – surely consciously – to perfect highly polished pictures of apparently random, dreamlike situations.

))))⯈ *Dadaism, Sigmund Freud*

SWISS LEAGUE (1291)

Union of Swiss cantons formed to defend themselves against their Habsburg landlords. Also known as the Everlasting League, the union was formed in 1291. The Swiss communities of Schwyz, Uri and Lower Unterwalden, populated by many free peasant farmers, had a long history of co-operation with each other. The League was further strengthened when more towns and districts joined them. They eventually won total independence from the Habsburg Empire in the Treaty of Westphalia.

))))⯈ *Habsburg Dynasty, Treaty of Westpahlia*

SYMBOLISM (20TH CENTURY)

Literary and artistic movement. Corresponding with the early years of modernism (from which it cannot straightforwardly be set apart), symbolism was characterized by a rejection of representation as previously understood by artists up to and including the impressionists. Rather than depicting a scene, therefore, a painting had to find a fit symbol for the feeling assumed to be its essence; rather than describe an event or emotion, a poem had to present an image which would of itself inspire the appropriate feelings. The idea that every emotion should have its image, making of art a sort of equation, led to a noticeable bias towards stripped-down spareness and austerity. Though manifest in the flattened forms and bold colours of much modernist art, this taste perhaps found its ultimate expression in the literary vogue for *haiku*, the terse Japanese verse-form popularized in the 1920s by Ezra Pound.

))))⯈ *Impressionism, Modernism*

BELOW: *One of the world's greatest monuments to love: the Taj Mahal in Agra.*
RIGHT: *A Mogul miniature painting showing Emperor Tamerlaine fighting three armed opponents during a battle in the Kar mountains.*

TAIPING REBELLION (1850–64)

Chinese popular revolt. A radical new Chinese movement, the Taiping T'ien-kuoç declared itself a new dynasty in 1851. The group's fanatical religious leader and his followers observed strict moral rules and shared all property. By 1853 they had amassed an army of one million, which attacked and captured the major city of Nanking. In 1864 the city was reclaimed by pro-government troops, and the movement collapsed. But the Ch'ing dynasty was irretrievably damaged by the rebellion, a forerunner of Chinese Communism.

TAJ MAHAL (1632–48)

Indian monument. Built between 1632 and 1648 by the great Mogul emperor, Shah Jahan, the Taj Mahal is one of the most famous buildings in the world. A massive mausoleum of marble, built for the emperor's beloved wife, it stands in Agra, Uttar Pradesh, its distinctive dome dominating the skyline for miles around. A high-point in the history both of Indian and of Islamic architecture, it betrays the influences both of native Hindu and imported Muslim artistic traditions.

))))➤ *Shah jahan*

TAMERLAINE (1336–1405)

Tamerlane ('Timur the Lame') was a descendant of the great Genghis Khan and was himself a Mongol ruler – Samarkand in Uzbekistan – from 1369. In turn, he was the great-grandfather of Babar (Arabic 'lion'), who founded the Mogul Empire of India in 1526. Tamerlane conquered Armenia, Azerbaijan, Georgia and Persia. Between 1395 and 1402 he was busy warring in and around the Middle East. He eventually died on a campaign invading China.

))))➤ *Akhbar, Babar, Genghis Khan, Mogul Empire*

T'ANG DYNASTY (AD 618–907)

Chinese ruling dynasty. Founded by Li Yuan, an official of the Sui dynasty, on whose rule he modelled his own regime. After a power struggle, Li Yuan expanded Chinese control into Asia, Tibet, Korea, creating a vast empire. Avoiding a cumbersome bureaucracy, but improving the Sui policy of recruitment through examination, Li Yuan created an efficient form of government, encouraged small-scale landholdings at the expense of large estates. His descendants continued this trend, controlling aristocrats, improving the bureaucracy and education, and expanding Chinese territory. Although regional and aristocratic ambitions brought the dynasty's downfall, the period saw the invention of printing, and a climax of Chinese culture in music, poetry, painting and Buddhist sculpture.

))))➤ *Buddhism*

TAOISM

The *Tao Te Ching* (the Classic of the Way and its Power) is central to Taoism (pronounced 'Dowism'). The text provides a vision of immortality arising from a life lived in harmony and being non-acquisitive. The notion of ch'i (vital energy) is fundamental. This is characterized by yin and yang, often represented in the yin-yang symbol that, through its curves and light/dark contrasts, suggests movement and constantly changing relationships. If yin and yang can be harmonized internally then the goal of immortality will be achieved – either literally or metaphorically.

TATARS (5TH CENTURY)

Turkic invaders. Originally allied with the Mongols, they originated from the area near Lake Baikal. As part of Genghis Khan's army and later under his grandson, Batu Khan, they ranged into Russia and Hungary. When the Mongol Empire collapsed they settled in Russia. During this period the Tatars were nomads and Ivan IV eventually conquered their lands with the last Tatar state in the Crimea being annexed in 1783. Crimean Tatars collaborated with the Nazis in World War II and Stalin deported many to the east, forbidding their language. Modern-day Tatars live in West Central Russia, Kazakstan and Western Siberia.

))))➤ *Genghis Khan, Tamerlaine*

ABOVE: A Chinese earthenware figurine of a Tang Dynasty tomb guardian.

TENOCHTITLÁN (1325)

Capital city of pre-Columbian Mexico. The capital of the Aztecs, founded around 1325 on a couple of islands in Lake Texcoco, has now been all but erased by the sprawling growth of the modern city. By 1519 itself a considerable size, with no fewer than 400,000 inhabitants, its destruction began with the siege laid by Hernán Cortés and his conquistadors in 1521. Now only a few archaeological sites remain amid the colonial churches and the office blocks of modern Mexico City, but these are sufficient to hint at the wealth and splendour of the one of the great pre-Columbian civilizations of the Americas.

))))➤ *Aztecs, Conquistadors, Montezuma*

TEXAN WAR OF INDEPENDENCE (1836)

Texas is the only one of the 52 US states to have been an independent republic at a point in its history. The region was settled by the Spanish in 1682 and became part of Mexico between 1821 and 1836.

The mission fortress in San Antonio, called the Alamo, was besieged from 23 February to 6 March 1836, by 4,000 Mexicans under the command of Antonio Lopez de Santa Anna, a Mexican revolutionary. His men slaughtered the entire garrison of around 180 men, including Davy Crockett and Jim Bowie.

The garrison was outnumbered 20:1, but managed to hold the enemy off for 13 days. The massacre led to a great deal of anti-Mexican sentiment in Texas and the USA and a quick retaliation was sought. Santa Anna's army was defeated in the same year, on 21 April, at San Jacinto by a US army commanded by General Sam Houston (1793–1863). Following the Texan War of Independence, Texas became an independent republic (1836–45), with Houston as president. Texas finally joined the USA in 1845. Due to its former independence, Texas is nicknamed the Lone Star State.

))))➤ *Alamo*

THATCHER, MARGARET (b. 1925)

British Conservative prime minister, 1979–90. Thatcher was the longest-serving prime minister in twentieth-century Britain and the first woman to ever hold the post. Nicknamed the 'Iron Lady', her policies were characterized by her firm approach to domestic issues and her militaristic stance in foreign affairs. She advocated privatization and the free market, but was sceptical about Britain's participation in the European Economic Community.

Promoting an agenda of 'sound money' policies, she launched her privatization programme (selling off state-owned enterprises to the private sector) at a time when unemployment, inflation and interest rates all rose. These unpopular policies were offset by Thatcher's great triumph during her first term: the British victory in the 1982 Falklands War. Internationally, Thatcher opposed unilateral nuclear disarmament and sanctions against South Africa. She was, however, the first Western leader to meet with the new Soviet leader, Mikhail Gorbachev. Following resistance to her leadership style within her party, Thatcher resigned in 1990.

))))▶ *Falklands War*

THERMOPYLAE, BATTLE OF (480 BC)

Battle in the Persian Wars. The Battle of Thermopylae saw Leonidas, King of Sparta – part of Greece – defend a pass against a greater force of Persians troops.

))))▶ *Persian Wars*

THIRD WORLD

Term that refers to a collection of countries where twentieth century development and progress have been slow. It is also a description of nations that did not support either the West or the Communist bloc during the Cold War. The term is now not used greatly, as politically the world's power structure has changed. But the Third World grouping has been useful as a way of bonding together nations with similar problems in their quest for international aid.

Originally, the Third World definition was part of a broader description, which separated the globe into the 'First World' (the non-Communist bloc, including the USA, Western Europe and Japan), the 'Second World' (Communist countries: the Soviet Union, Eastern European countries and China) and the 'Third World' (underdeveloped countries in Africa, South America and Asia). With the breakdown of many European Communist states and the end of the Cold War, the initial divisions no longer apply. But many of the traits of those nations grouped into the Third World are still relevant – most are still poor, have economies based on agriculture, use traditional methods, and have population problems.

Third World nations have found benefits in uniting together. They are now called the Non-Aligned Movement, representing more than half the world's population. Within the United Nations the group has the biggest share of the total votes in the General Assembly. Non-aligned nations have highlighted contrasts in wealth between the developed and underdeveloped world, but there has not been enough international aid to overcome their huge problems.

ABOVE LEFT: Former British prime minister, Margaret Thatcher.
ABOVE: Third World countries have the majority of their populations living below the poverty line.
RIGHT: The battle of Fleurus in the Thirty Years' War.

THIRTY YEARS' WAR (1618–48)

In the early seventeenth century Germany was divided over religion. Europe was largely Catholic, but there had been a growth in Protestantism or Lutherism, which had started under Martin Luther (1483–1546). Mid-northern Europe became the hotspot for Protestantism and conflict with Catholicism finally began in 1618. The Thirty Years' War lasted until 1648. Another Christian faith akin to Protestantism, Calvinism, had also been founded in Switzerland by John Calvin (1509–64), so the Catholics had their work cut out in the war. The Austrian, Habsburg family were the principal players on the Catholic side, and attempted to control all of Germany. On the Protestant side were the Bohemians, Danes and Swedes. Politics soon took over from religion. After 1634 France's help was enlisted in defeating the Spanish, who were allied with Austria. The Westphalia Treaty saw the German states granted their sovereignty and autonomy.

))))➤ *Jean Calvin, Martin Luther, Treaty of Westphalia*

THOREAU, HENRY DAVID (1817–62)

American writer and thinker. Born in Concord, Massachusetts, it was at nearby Walden Pond that Thoreau would make his name, when he set up as a hermit in a little shack in the woods. His account of his experiences was published as *Walden* (1854): a book which placed him squarely in the solitary tradition of American romanticism. The apparent paradox that Thoreau is remembered not only as complete recluse but also as an influential political thinker is explained by the fact that the philosophy outlined in his great political essay, *Civil Disobedience* (1849), can be seen as simply another form of personal isolationism. Written in response to US policy in the Mexican War of 1846–48, it called for citizens unhappy with their government's behaviour to opt out of what others might see as their collective responsibility.

THREE EMPERORS' LEAGUE (1881)

Secret alliance between the emperors of Germany, Austria-Hungary and Russia, signed 18 June 1881. The league was to last for three years and was called the Three Emperors' League. The three emperors were William I of Germany, Franz Joseph of Austria-Hungary and Alexander III of Russia. The league came about following the assassination of Emperor Alexander II of Russia, by a nihilist terrorist bomb.

TIANANMEN SQUARE MASSACRE (1989)

Chinese people's demonstration that ended in killings by the army. In April 1989 students began a huge pro-democracy demonstration that continued for several months. They were calling for political reform and the resignation of the Communist leadership. The students were joined by workers, intellectuals and civil servants and their numbers swelled to over 1 million in Tiananmen Square which is the largest public square in the world. Premier Deng Xiaping responded by instating martial law on 20 May and then sending in the army on the nights of 3 and 4 June to quell the unrest. At least 2,000 unarmed protesters were killed and many student leaders arrested.

TITANIC (1912)

British luxury liner that suffered one of the worst maritime disasters in history. The *Titanic* (46,000 gross tonnes) was a White Star liner, which, on her maiden voyage from Southampton to New York, struck an iceberg about 153 km (96 miles) south of Newfoundland in April 1912. The *Titanic* had been declared unsinkable, having 16 watertight compartments, but five of these were punctured and the ship sank in under three hours. Of some 2,220 people aboard, more than 1,500 died, partly owing to an inadequacy of lifeboat space. The wreck was found in 1985 and some its contents subsequently salvaged and exhibited.

TITO, MARSHAL (1892–1980)

Yugoslav military commander and premier (1953–1980). Marshal Tito fought in World War I and the Russian Civil War. During World War II as leader of the partisans, he fought valiantly against the Nazis, and in 1941 he headed Yugoslavia's first Communist government. In 1948, following his expulsion by Stalin from the Communist eastern bloc, Tito developed a freer style of Communist rule. His policy of non-alignment built up groups of neutral countries between the Communist East and capitalist West.

TOLTECS (AD 650–12TH CENTURY)

Indigenous Meso-American people. These peoples left the city of Teotihuacn and established their own empire in Mexico. They used their army to conquer neighbouring rivals. The Toltecs built their capital at Tula, which has three pyramidal temples dedicated to Quetzalcoatl. According to Toltec legend the rival god Tezcatlipoca, god of the night sky, drove Quetzalcoatl, the plumed or feathered servant, the god of the morning and evening star, out of Tula in around AD 1000. The Toltecs' art and architecture was a major influence on the Mayans and particularly their city of Chichen Itza. Like the Aztecs the Toltecs believed in human sacrifice.

))))➤ *Aztecs*

TORAH

Holy book of Judaism. The Torah is the revelation of God's will to the Jewish people. The word 'Torah' means 'teaching' and in the Jewish community is referred to as 'Hamash' (meaning 'five' in Hebrew) because it comprises the five books of Moses: Genesis, Exodus, Leviticus, Numbers and Deuteronomy. It includes 613 commandments dealing with issues of ethics, spirituality and diet and encompasses every aspect of life. The books are hand-written on the Torah scroll which is kept in the ark of each synagogue. It is at the heart of worship and processed around the synagogue for all to see. The belief in the divine origin of the Torah (written or oral) is the cornerstone of Orthodox Judaism. The purpose of the Torah is to make 'Israel a kingdom of priests, a holy nation' (*Deuteronomy* 33:4).

))))➤ *Judaism*

TRAFALGAR, BATTLE OF (1805)

Battle during the Napoleonic Wars. The entrance to the Straits of Gibraltar, off the coast of Spain, was the scene for the Battle of Trafalgar, 21 October 1805. It was fought by the British fleet against a combined fleet of French and Spanish ships. Clever tactics by Admiral Horatio Nelson divided the enemy fleet and enabled him to get the upper hand, despite having fewer ships. Nelson died in the battle.

))))➤ *Napoleonic Wars, Horatio Nelson*

TRAIL OF TEARS (1838–39)

Enforced migration of Cherokee Indians. Following the Indian Removal Act of 1830 in the south east of America, 100,000 Indians from the Chickasaw, Choctaw, Seminole, and Creek tribes who had previously refused to trade their cultivated farms for land in the Indian Territory, were forced to leave under military enforcement. The Cherokee Indian trek in 1838–39 became known as the Trail of Tears. The Florida Indians fought resettlement from 1835-42 in the second Seminole War.

))))➤ *Native American Indians*

TRAJAN (c. AD 53–117)

Roman emperor from AD 98. Born in Spain, Trajan was a senator adopted by Nerva (reigned AD 96–8), as heir. Trajan's two campaigns in Dacia (AD 101–2, 105–6), and another in Parthia (AD 113–17), enlarged the Roman Empire to its greatest extent. His forum in Rome included a famous column (which survives) depicting his wars in carved relief, providing invaluable detail about the Roman army. His letters to Pliny the Younger, governor of Bithynia and Pontus, illustrate his firm but considerate method of rule.

))))➤ *Ancient Rome*

TREATY OF PARIS (1763)

Treaty that ended the Seven Years' War. The treaty saw Britain emerge as a burgeoning empire, having gained control of India, Canada, Florida and many French colonies.

))))➤ *Seven Years's War*

TREATY OF ROME (1957)

Foundation document of the EEC (European Economic Community). The economic disarray of post World War II Europe led to calls for a common European Market. Six European countries – France, Germany, Italy, Belgium, the Netherlands and Luxembourg – met in Rome to set out the goals of a free trade system within Europe and establish the European Investment Bank.

TRENT, COUNCIL OF (1545–63)

Collective name for a series of councils of the Catholic Church, held at Trent, Italy. The Council was a response to the Reformation that had broken down the unity of the Church. The Emperor, Charles V, had long advocated such a council but the papacy tended to prevaricate because it might offer a challenge to papal supremacy. The influence of the Society of Jesus helped to secure a powerful re-statement of traditional dogma including a reassertion of papal authority. This indicated

TOP LEFT: Marshal Tito.

LEFT: The Torah is regarded by the Jewish community as the revelation of God's will to them.

BELOW: Richard Trevithick ran the first steam-powered locomotive on the Penydarren railway in Wales in 1804.

the Reformation challenged the Church little in Spain and Italy. Catholicism became more orderly and better disciplined. The supremacy of Catholic Europe would now lie with the pope; Charles V was the last emperor to have a papal coronation. It was, perhaps, the most significant element in the Counter-Reformation.

))))➤ *Counter-Reformation, Reformation, Roman Catholicism*

TREVITHICK, RICHARD (1771–1833)

British engineer, often considered the real inventor of the steam locomotive. His high-pressure steam engines were more efficient than James Watt's low-pressure engines. In 1801 he constructed the first passenger-carrying steam-propelled road locomotive and in 1804 the first steam engine to run on rails. This locomotive carried 10 tons of iron 15 km (9.5 miles) from Merthyr Tydfil to Abercynon, Wales. Trevithick's success encouraged him to build further steam-operated locomotives.

))))➤ *Thomas Newcomen, James Watt*

TRIPLE ENTENTE (1907)

The Triple Entente – Triple 'Intention' – was signed between Britain, France and Russia in 1907. It would last until 1917, with the start of the Russian Bolshevik Revolution. It was a military alliance, especially after 1911 when the threat of the Central Powers, Germany and Austria-Hungary, became more apparent in the build up to World War I. Before Britain joined, France and Russia were the members of the Dual Entente, signed back in 1893.

))))▶ *Bolsheviks, Russian Revolution, World War I*

TRIUMVIRATE (60 BC AND 43 BC)

Board or commission in Ancient Rome consisting of three men. The term applies to the political alliance between Pompey the Great, Julius Caesar and Marcus Crassus, known as the First Triumvirate. The Second Triumvirate followed the murder of Caesar and divided the government of Rome between Octavian (later Emperor Augustus), Mark Antony and Marcus Lepidus. The Second Triumvirate was dissolved in 32 BC after a civil war in Rome.

))))▶ *Ancient Rome, Mark Antony, Julius Caesar*

TROJAN WAR

The Trojan War is an event steeped in myth and legend, because it happened so long ago. So much so in fact that historians disagree on many points. The city of Troy, otherwise known as Ilium, lay on the west coast of Turkey, during the time of Ancient Greece. According to Homer's *Iliad*, legend has it that the Greeks laid siege to Troy to recover Helen, who had eloped with Paris, the prince of Troy. The Greeks finally gained entry by the use of trickery, with a wooden horse, and stole Helen back to Sparta, *c.* 1184 BC.

TROTSKY, LEON (1879–1940)

Adopted name of Lev Davidovich Bronstein, Russian revolutionary and Communist theorist. Trotsky was one of the leaders in Russia's October Revolution (1917) and in the civil war that followed (1918–20). After Lenin's death (1924), Trotsky lost the battle for power to Joseph Stalin and was exiled to Mexico. He continued to oppose Stalin and criticized the Soviet regime in his writing until his assassination by an ice pick, probably carried out at Stalin's instigation.

))))▶ *Vladimir Ilyich Lenin*

TRUMAN DOCTRINE (1947)

US reaction to Communist insurrection. Pronounced by President Harry S. Truman as a means of providing economic and military aid to anti-Communist forces in Greece and Turkey that were believed to be sponsored by the Soviets. Following World War II the USA was determined that the West should not fall under Soviet influence. The doctrine was seen as the means by which the USA could support any nation threatened by Communism during the Cold War.

))))▶ *Cold War, Harry S. Truman*

TRUMAN, HARRY S. (1884–1972)

33rd US president (1945–53). Truman inherited the presidency while vice-president, on the death of Roosevelt in office. He is probably most famous for his decision to drop two atomic bombs on Japan at the end of World War II. Other foreign affairs milestones include his development of the 1947 'Truman Doctrine' (which pledged American support to any 'free nation') fighting Communism) and sending US troops to the Korean War. Truman's sacking in 1950 of Korean War hero General MacArthur sparked a national uproar in the USA. He attempted a wide-ranging reform programme, 'the Fair Deal', but most of the proposals were defeated.

))))▶ *Franklin D. Roosevelt, Truman Doctrine, World War II*

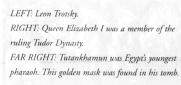

LEFT: Leon Trotsky.
RIGHT: Queen Elizabeth I was a member of the ruling Tudor Dynasty.
FAR RIGHT: Tutankhamun was Egypt's youngest pharaoh. This golden mask was found in his tomb.

TUDOR DYNASTY (1485–1603)

English ruling house. The Tudor period marked the beginning of England's rise to European prominence, as well as the establishment of the Protestant religion.

Descended from a Welshman, Owen Tudor, married to Henry V's widow Catherine, Henry Tudor's claim came from his mother, a descendant of Edward III. Crowned Henry VII in 1485 after defeating Richard III at Bosworth, Henry's marriage to Elizabeth of York, daughter of Edward IV, resolved the dynastic differences of the Wars of the Roses and his restoration of a sound administration ended the political chaos, as well as bequeathing sound finances and a solvent crown.

Henry VIII and Elizabeth I in particular created enduring images of monarchy. However, the dynasty was beset by religious conflict, challenges from the great European powers of France and Spain, as well as problems of succession, and lasted only three generations.

Henry's eldest son, Arthur, died in 1501 and the line of succession passed to the second son, afterwards Henry VIII.

The religious revolution of Henry VIII's reign was founded in the failure of his first marriage to produce a male heir, though the celebrated procession of five further wives, two of whom were executed, yielded two daughters, Mary and Elizabeth, and a son, Edward. Edward succeeded as Edward VI but died young. Both Mary and Elizabeth remained childless, Elizabeth not even marrying. However, James VI of Scotland, succeeded in 1603 as James I of England and was descended from Henry VII's daughter Margaret.

))))➤ *Elizabeth I of England, Henry VIII of England*

TURING, ALAN (1912–54)

During World War II the British made concerted efforts to break the communications codes being used by the German forces. Alan Turing was at the forefront of these developments. He designed a digital tape machine that could decipher code extremely rapidly. He also helped break the Enigma code.

))))➤ *Enigma Machine*

TUTANKHAMUN (c. 1343–1323 BC)

Egyptian pharaoh from *c.* 1333 BC. The son-in-law of the heretic pharaoh Akhenaten, Tutankhamun succeeded as a boy in the aftermath of the regime which sought to establish a new religion based on the sun-god, Aten. Tutankhamun's parentage is uncertain and he may have been a cousin, or even a brother, of his wife. The short reign saw the influence of the priests of Amun revived, a return to the capital at Thebes and the suppression of the Aten. The discovery in 1922 of his tomb caused a sensation and provided vast amounts of evidence for the art and culture of the period.

))))➤ *Ancient Egypt, Lord Carnarvon, Nefertiti*

UNITED NATIONS (1945)

International association of nations. After World War II, the United Nations was created to prevent another international conflict. The organization has representatives from nearly every country in the world and aims to work as an independent body preserving peace. The UN Charter, devised in 1945, was signed by 50 nations – today there are more than 185 member countries. The UN also provides aid and support to developing nations.

The central body of the United Nations is divided into six sections: the General Assembly (international forum); the Security Council (peacekeeping wing); the Secretariat (administrative branch); the Economic and Social Council (contains aid agencies); the International Court of Justice; and the Trusteeship Council. The economic and social council oversees a huge number of agencies such as UNICEF, WHO, the World Bank and UNESCO. These groups provide loans, personnel, food and medical supplies, and much more, to areas in need.

The Security Council has a major function within the United Nations, helping settle major conflicts and making

decisions regarding UN peacekeeping troops. There are 15 member countries, five of which are permanent: France, China, Russia, Britain and the USA. If one of the permanent delegates opposes a decision they use the power of 'veto': this has blocked many UN recommendations.

)))⯈ *World War II*

ABOVE: A propaganda poster issued shortly after the end of World War II, at the formation of the United Nations. It promotes the idea of international co-operation and mutual support.

RIGHT: Tourists view the original Declaration of Independence in the National Archives.

UNITED STATES CONSTITUTION (1787)

Oldest written national constitution. The American Constitution defines government, its jurisdictions and the basic rights of US citizens. It was designed to retain the independence of the states whilst establishing central government. It placed legislative powers in the hands of Congress and executive power in the president's hands. Judicial power was the role of the courts and the privileges of citizens enshrined as Civil Rights which encompassed the Bill of Rights and the First Amendment.

)))⯈ *Bill of Rights, Declaration of Independence, President*

URBAN VI (1318–89)

Italian pope. Born Bartolommeo Prignano he was elected pope in 1378. Noted for his austerity Urban VI proceeded to make a series of imprudent decisions. In August 1378 French members of the Sacred College of Cardinals announced the nullity of Urban's election and elected Clement VII as antipope, beginning the Great Schism in the West, to last for 39 years with two popes claiming to be the head of the Church. Urban had six cardinals tortured and five executed for conspiracy against him. He appointed the Holy Year to be celebrated every 33 years.

)))⯈ *Clement VII, Great Schism*

VALOIS DYNASTY (1328–1589)

French ruling house. The Valois kings of France, a junior line of the Capetian house, ruled from 1328–1589. In 1285, Philip III (r. 1270–85) gave the county of Valois to a younger son, Charles who, on the death of his brother Philip V in 1322, succeeded as Charles IV. In 1328, Charles's son acceded as Philip VI, of Valois. The new dynasty was soon preoccupied with the problems of the Hundred Years' War with England and challenges from French barons. Charles VII (1422–61) brought the war to an end, as well as increasing royal power at the expense of the feudal lords.

The Valois kings strengthened royal power through parliaments, and control of taxation, allowing France to start competing with the Habsburg Holy Roman Empire for territory. These began with inconclusive wars in Italy lasting into sixteenth century. In the late sixteenth century, royal control became weakened as religious factionalism came to dominate French affairs. The reign of Charles IX (1550–74) saw the brutal massacre of thousands of Huguenots in 1572. Although his brother, Henri III (r. 1574–89) attempted to broker a workable relationship between Catholics and Protestants, he assassinated the Catholic leader, the Duke of Guise, fearing that he might be usurped. Henri was murdered himself the following year.

⫸ *Hundred Years' War*

VAUBAN, SEBASTIEN DE (1633–1707)

Marshal and military engineer. During the reign of Louis XIV, France enjoyed the military talents of Sebastien le Prestre de Vauban, a military engineer in the trust of the king, who masterminded many of the campaigns during the unsuccessful 'Expansionist Wars' (1667–68, 1672–78, 1688–97, 1701–13). The final one was the War of Spanish Succession. Vauban conducted many sieges, successful and otherwise, and rebuilt many of the fortresses scattered along the eastern border of France. He is still regarded as one of Europe's finest military commanders.

⫸ *Louis XIV of France, War of Spanish Succession*

RIGHT: The magnificent façade and water feature at the Palace of Versailles.

VERDUN, BATTLE OF (1916)

Campaign during World War I. Verdun, a fortress town in north-east France, was subjected to a fierce onslaught by the Germans in 1916 and it became the symbol of French resistance because it was won by the French without direct assistance from Allied forces. The Battle of Verdun lasted between 21 February and 18 December 1916. There were 400,000 French and German casualties.

⫸ *World War I*

VERSAILLES, PALACE OF (1661)

French monument. Built at the behest of Louis XIV from 1661 onwards, the Palace of Versailles, with its extensive and elaborate ornamental gardens, became the ultimate symbol of the French monarchy in all its splendour – and, ultimately, its decadence. Though his father Louis XIII had had a chateau here, this was not enough for the 'Sun King', who made the construction of a suitably vast and sumptuous palace his life's work. It was here, ironically, that in 1789 a group of deputies excluded from their assembly-chamber took the 'Tennis Court Oath', the opening act of what would become the French Revolution.

⫸ *French Revolution, Louis XIV of France*

VICTOR EMMANUEL II (1820–78)

King of Sardinia from 1849, and king of Italy from 1861. He fought Austria unsuccessfully between 1848–49, in pursuit of Italian unity. After his father's abdication, Victor Emmanuel turned to politics and diplomacy for the cause. Securing French support by handing Napoleon III the province of Savoy, he was provided with enough resources to defeat Austria at Magenta and Solferino in 1859. With the grudging support of the nationalist leader Giuseppe Garibaldi, Victor Emmanuel was declared the first king of a unified Italy and maintained a constitutional monarchy. In 1866 a treaty with Prussia secured Venice. The withdrawal of the French papal garrison in 1871 allowed establishment of a national capital at Rome.

)))➤ *Giuseppe Garibaldi*

VICTORIA, QUEEN OF ENGLAND (1819–1901)

Queen of England from 1837. Victoria's reign saw the climax of Britain's imperial power, and an unprecedented pace of scientific discovery and industrial growth.

Failure of the legitimate direct male line from George III passed the Crown to Victoria, daughter of George's fourth son Edward, duke of Kent, on the death of her uncle William IV. Initial advice and support from the prime minister, Lord Melbourne, was followed by Victoria's marriage to Albert of Saxe-Coburg in 1840. Victoria's lover, confidant and adviser, Albert became the main influence on the middle years of the reign, contributing to friction with her ministers over foreign policy.

Albert's death in 1861 was followed by the Queen's virtual withdrawal from public life until Benjamin Disraeli persuaded her of the value of being proclaimed

LEFT: Victor Emmanuel II.
BELOW: Queen Victoria, in the first few years of her reign.

Empress of India in 1877. Victoria delighted in Disraeli's flattery, but was irritated by the manner of the other great prime minister of the period, William Gladstone. Despite holding strong personal opinions, the reign was strictly constitutional and Victoria acted according to the advice of her ministers.

The Great Exhibition of 1851 marked the aspirations of the time. The Jubilees of 1887 and 1897 were symbolic milestones in Victoria's personal identification with the age, marked by colossal advances in science, industry, communications and learning, as well as styles of art and architecture. The reign elevated royal prestige to its zenith, enhanced by the proliferation of her own descendants amongst the royal houses of Europe.

)))➤ *British Empire, Great Exhibition*

VIETNAM WAR (1963–75)

War between North Vietnam and the south, backed by the United States. Vietnam became a divided country in 1954 in the aftermath of the Vietminh War (1946–54), in which the Vietnamese, under Ho Chi Minh, resisted French attempts to re-assert colonial control. The country was divided into North Vietnam and South Vietnam, at the 17th parallel. North Vietnam was Communist controlled and South Vietnam was US-backed, similar to Korea.

In 1963 a military coup took place in South Vietnam, led by Lieutenant General Nguyen Van Thieu, resulting in the overthrow of the leader Ngo Dinh Diem. By 1964 US combat troops were being mobilized to assist South Vietnam. It was a war fought in the jungle – a factor which proved a serious impediment to the US forces.

By 1975, when the war ended, 56,555 US troops had been killed in action. An appalling fifth of them had been killed by their own side, such was the difficulty with directing gunfire in thick vegetation and bombing – blind – through the canopy of trees. Furthermore, about 200,000 South Vietnamese were killed and an estimated one million North Vietnamese, who were dubbed the 'Vietcong' (a contraction of 'Vietnamese Communists'). A further 500,000 civilians were slaughtered during the campaign.

The US forces were not defeated, but political pressures, especially domestic, resulted in the USA beginning to pull out troops from Vietnam in 1973 following a peace treaty negotiated by Henry Kissinger, for which he won the Nobel Peace Prize, jointly, with Le Duc Tho. Saigon had been captured by North Vietnam by 1975 and in 1976 the Socialist Republic of Vietnam was proclaimed.

))))➤ *Ho Chi Minh, Korean War*

ABOVE: The remains of an American helicopter used during the Vietnam conflict. The war was fought between North (Communist) Vietnam and South Korea (aided by the USA and its allies).

VIKINGS (AD 800–1100)

Nordic raiders and settlers. The Vikings began raiding around AD 800 gradually becoming more determined to settle in the lands. They had conquered much of England by the ninth century and had penetrated as far as Paris in their raids. To begin with, Christian Europe could do little to prevent them apart from paying ransoms, but larger Viking armies appeared in the early eleventh century and the system of paying tribute to the Vikings, or Danegeld, became the strategy. In AD 911 Charles III of France gave the Vikings Normandy and it was these Vikings, now called Normans, that invaded England in 1066. Elsewhere the Vikings had settled in Greenland and North America and had penetrated Russia to reach Constantinople and Baghdad. Swedish Vikings fought for the Byzantines. The Viking impact was not simply destructive and they became a part of the settled European community. Vikings were great storytellers, sailors and warriors.

))))➤ *Danegeld*

VISHNU

Hindu god. Vishnu was a minor god in the Vedic tradition, but has come to be regarded as the supreme being, preserver of the cosmos. Hindus believe that on Earth Vishnu had nine incarnations – or avatars – including Rama and Krishna.

))))➤ *Hinduism, Shiva*

WACO SIEGE (1993)

The Branch Davidian sect, derived from Seventh Day Adventists, led by David Koresh (original name Vernon Howell) was held under siege for several weeks in 1993 before FBI agents stormed the compound on 29 February. The buildings were engulfed by fire and many died. The Branch Dravidians were a millennialist sect recruiting mainly from Seven Day Adventists with Mr Koresh believing he had been singled out by God to usher in a new millennium, operating with God's authority. David Koresh was a charismatic personality who dominated members of the Branch Davidians. The consequences of the fire fight raised issues in the USA of why people, particularly women, join such sects and whether the state has the right to intervene.

WAGNER, RICHARD (1813–83)

German composer. The Leipzig-born conductor and composer enjoyed early success with his opera *Rienzi* (1842), but had much grander, more artistically ambitious ideas, evolving his own revolutionary approach to the composition and performance of opera. What in the Italian tradition had too often been, he felt, little more than a show with songs, should instead be a fully integrated musical drama. In works like *Tannhäuser* (1845) and *Tristan and Isolde* (1865) he achieved operatic music of quite unprecedented emotion and overwhelming sensuality. His deep preoccupation with German myth would lend great beauty to his most ambitious work, the four-opera cycle, the *Ring*, but it went hand in hand with an altogether uglier streak of nationalism and anti-semitism.

WALESA, LECH (b. 1943)

Polish trade unionist and president of Poland (1990–95). Walesa, an electrician at the Lenin shipyard in Gdansk, founded and led Solidarity (1980–90), Poland's first independent trade union. The movement won a number of concessions, both political and economic, from the ruling Communist government until the union was outlawed in 1981 and marshall law declared. Walesa was imprisoned but released a year later. He was awarded the Nobel Peace Prize in 1983. After a series of strikes in 1988 and the country's worsening economic conditions, Walesa negotiated Solidarity's reinstatement and a new 'socialist democracy'. The party won a majority in the elected government and Walesa became president.

WALL STREET CRASH (1929)

Stockmarket crash in the USA in 1929. The growth in the US economy encouraged excessive buying in the domestic market, which pushed prices

up drastically. Some professionals then decided to take profits and sell short. Other investors also switched to selling and prices plummeted. On one day, 'Black Tuesday' – 29 October – 16 million shares were traded and $10 billion wiped off share values. The crash caused innumerable bankruptcies and unemployment rose by two million within six months. Elsewhere in the world banks closed, unable to pay depositors. The crash started the worldwide economic slump called the Great Depression.

))⃤ *Great Depression*

WARLORDS (1916–49)

Independent military commanders in China. Following the death of Yuan Shih-K'ia (1916) many warlords, former officers in the Peiyang army, took power in various provinces. Many served foreign powers, including Japan, Britain and the Soviet Union. None of them was strong enough to destroy the rest and it was not until 1928 when Chiang Kai-Shek reunified China that the warlords were incorporated into his army. Local warlords still existed until the Communist takeover in 1949.

WARSAW PACT (1955)

Military alliance between the Soviet Union and Eastern European Communist countries. The pact was signed by the USSR and Albania, Bulgaria, the former Czechoslovakia, the former East Germany, Hungary, Poland and Romania in response to the rearmament of West Germany and its admission to NATO (the North Atlantic Treaty Organization). The real function of the agreement was to strengthen the Soviet hold over its satellites. Although the Warsaw Pact was renewed in 1985, the political transformation of Eastern Europe in 1989 profoundly weakened the organization and it was dissolved on 1 July 1991.

))⃤ *North Atlantic Treaty Organization, World War II*

WASHINGTON, GEORGE (1732–1799)

1st US president (1789–97). George Washington is known as one of the 'founding fathers' of the United States. He was commander of the colonial army in the American Revolution and a key creator of the US constitution.

Following the Boston Tea Party in 1773, American resentment towards their British rulers intensified. Colonial forces were assembled to fight for independence with Washington as military commander. The troops were badly equipped, but Washington's clever campaigns brought many victories. His 1781 offensive in Yorktown, Virginia, where his forces encircled the British army while the French navy blocked the port, led to the English surrender.

In 1788 the new Constitution of the United States of America was approved, and in 1789 Washington became president. He was celebrated as a national hero, and in office set about laying the foundations of the new structure of government. The US capital city, Washington, was created and named after the first president in 1791.

))⃤ *American Revolution, Boston Tea Party, President, United States Constitution, Battle of Yorktown*

WATERGATE (1972–74)

US political scandal that led to President Nixon's resignation. The story began with the arrest of five men for burglary and wiretapping at the Democrat Party's national headquarters in the Watergate offices in Washington. Nixon's secret attempts to cover up his administration's involvement in the affair, including 'hush money' to the Watergate burglars, were uncovered by news reporters Carl Bernstein and Bob Woodward, who were fed information by a source known only as 'Deep Throat'. Nixon obstructed the FBI's attempts to get hold of his taped conversations, finally releasing some that implicated him in the Watergate affair. He resigned on 8 August 1974 before he was impeached.

))))➤ *Richard Nixon*

WATERLOO, BATTLE OF (1815)

Final battle of the Napoleonic Wars. Napoleon was attempting to stage his comeback, having returned from exile and seized power once again in France. In the opening stages of the battle on 18 June 1815 Napoleon had the advantage: he had caught Wellington's British

RIGHT: After repairing a faulty steam engine, James Watt invented a better model using only a fraction of the coal used by earlier versions.

army isolated from Allied forces and launched a direct offensive. Wellington held Napoleon off long enough however for German, Dutch and Belgian reinforcements to join in the fray. The victory saw the final defeat of Napoleon.

))))➤ *Napoleon, Duke of Wellington*

WATT, JAMES (1736–1819)

Scottish inventor. While repairing a model of a Newcomen steam engine in 1764 Watt devised an exterior condenser, which would allow the working cylinder to remain permanently hot, increasing the efficiency of Newcomen's engine. Watt also invented a pumping engine and a rotative engine and with Matthew Boulton went into production near Birmingham.

))))➤ *Thomas Newcomen, Rail Travel*

WELLINGTON, DUKE OF (1769–1852)

British military leader. Arthur Wellesley became a national hero with his victories in the Peninsula Wars of 1808–14. He became the first Duke of Wellington,

LEFT: The Battle of Waterloo marked Napoleon's biggest defeat, just 100 days after his return from exile.

and was dubbed the 'Iron Duke' by his troops, because he had a fearsome reputation for discipline. His greatest moment came when he defeated Napoleon at the Battle of Waterloo, 18 June 1815.

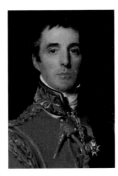

)))➤ *Napoleonic Wars, Battle of Waterloo*

WESTERN WALL

The only remnant of the Second Temple; also known as the Wailing Wall. Jews gather there to pray and the wall has slips of paper with prayers and Bible texts on them inserted between the stones. Many families celebrate Bar-Mitzvah ('son of the commandment') ceremonies there, when a young boy becomes a full member of the Jewish community. The Second Temple was rebuilt in the sixth century BC and destroyed by the Romans in AD 70. It is a very powerful symbol for Jews worldwide. It was at the Western Wall, in the Muslim tradition, that Muhammad tethered his horse when he made his Night Journey.

)))➤ *Judaism, Prophet Muhammad*

WESTPHALIA, TREATY OF (1648)

Treaty that ended the Thirty Years' War. The war had been initiated by religious differences between Catholics and Protestants, but became a political conflict. When peace was negotiated at the Treaty of Westphalia, it marked the end of the Holy Roman Empire's supremacy. France emerged as a new power and Central Europe was reordered.

)))➤ *Holy Roman Empire, Thirty Years' War*

WILLIAM I OF ENGLAND (1027–89)

Conqueror and king of England from 1066. The illegitimate son of Robert, Duke of Normandy, William succeeded Robert in 1035. He claimed the English throne on a verbal promise made by Edward the Confessor, and an oath of feudal allegiance from Harold, then Earl of Wessex. However, Harold succeeded Edward and William invaded to challenge him, winning the Battle of Hastings in 1066. William was crowned on Christmas

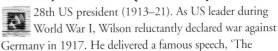

LEFT: The Duke of Wellington, a great warleader and politician.

Day 1066 but four more years of war followed to secure the north, with Scotland capitulating in 1072.

William's wise feudal rule involved suppressing baronial autonomy. Through his archbishop of Canterbury, Lanfranc, the church hierarchy was replaced with Normans. He granted lands and estates to his own men, and in 1086 ordered the compilation of a complete record of land tenure and population in Domesday Book. He died after a fall in France.

)))➤ *Domesday Book*

WILSON, WOODROW (1856–1924)

28th US president (1913–21). As US leader during World War I, Wilson reluctantly declared war against Germany in 1917. He delivered a famous speech, 'The Fourteen Points' (guidelines for a peace settlement), attended the 1919 Paris Peace Conference, and founded the League of Nations, the predecessor of the United Nations.

)))➤ *League of Nations, World War I*

WONDERS OF THE ANCIENT WORLD

List of monuments. Though the Great Pyramid at Giza still stands, that is the only one of the Seven Wonders of the Ancient World to survive (the list seems to have been drawn up by writers in the early centuries of the first millennium). The few stones still to be found can give no real hint of the grandeur of the Mausoleum at Halicarnassus, in what is now Turkey, built by King Mausolus in the fourth century BC to be his own tomb. The gigantic chunks of bronze bought by an Arab merchant in AD 656 and unsentimentally melted down for scrap were, apparently, all that remained of the ancient Colossus of Rhodes. This enormous statue of the sun god Helios, put up in 280 BC, had supposedly straddled the harbour entrance – albeit briefly, since it was destroyed by an earthquake in 224 BC. Other wonders on the list include the temple of Artemis at Ephesus, Asia Minor, the Pharos of Alexandria, a lighthouse some 400 ft high, and the statue of Zeus at Olympia, by Pheidias, the great Greek sculptor of the fifth century BC.

)))➤ *Great Pyramid of Giza, Hanging Gardens of Babylon*

"YOUR COUNTRY NEEDS YOU"

WORLD WAR I (1914–18)

Global conflict. Although action was seen over the Atlantic and Pacific oceans and over much of western Eurasia between 1914 and 1918 the conflict was not particularly ubiquitous and it was formerly known as the Great War. Following the war of 1939–45, confusion over names led to World Wars I and II being used.

World War I was a worldwide campaign in the respect that the Allies enlisted the help of troops from many colonies and dominions globally in fighting the Central Powers: Germany and Austria-Hungary. In fact, the Central Powers had fewer allies of their own

ABOVE: Recruitment posters were introduced during World War I due to a severe shortage of volunteers – there was no obligatory conscription in Britain.
RIGHT: Soldiers lived, fought and died in the trenches during World War I.
FAR RIGHT: World War I involved so many countries that it became known as the Great War. These German troops were on the Western frontline at the Battle of Verdun in 1916.

to turn to because they had not invested so greatly in the colonization of new lands historically.

The war began over tensions between Germany and Serbia. Archduke Franz Ferdinand, heir to the Austrian throne, was assassinated in Sarajevo on 28 June 1914. It was the excuse Austria needed to declare war on Serbia exactly one month later. Russia jumped to the defence of Serbia. Germany then declared war on Russia and France and conquered Belgium. On 4 August Britain entered the war and the scene was set for a war on a scale never seen before.

For the first month of action, fighting was quite fluid. On the Western Front the Germans advanced to a point just short of Paris before being pushed back by British and French forces. On the Eastern Front the Germans, under Paul Hindenburg, managed to encircle and defeat the Russian army at the Battle of Tannenburg. Soon, though, trench warfare would become synonymous with the war as commanders on both sides struggled to understand the dynamics of fighting a war with weapons of mass destruction.

While the First Battle of Ypres raged between the Germans and Allied forces in Belgium, Britain declared war on Turkey (November 1914) who had invaded the Caucuses and Middle East. This led to the disastrous Gallipoli campaign, which saw the Anzacs beleaguered until their evacuation in January 1916. Italy declared

war on Austria in May 1915, and Bulgaria joined the Central Powers against Serbia in the same year.

The Western Front moved little throughout 1915. Both sides became entrenched and tens of thousands of lives were wasted in futile attempts to gain or defend territory. The Second Battle of Ypres witnessed the first use of poison 'mustard' gas by the Germans. The gas, known chemically as dichloroethyl sulphide, caused agonizing blistering to the skin and damage to the mucus membrane in the lungs, resulting in an excruciating death.

In February 1916, the Germans launched their fierce offensive on Verdun at the Western Front. It was to last until June and almost exhaust France of its life's blood of available troops. Somehow the French held on, though and the Verdun became a morale-boosting symbol of French resistance against 'the Hun'. Now it was the turn of the Allies. They launched their own offensive at the Somme in July.

The Battle of the Somme, which ended in November 1916, pushed the German frontline eastward by a mere 12 km (7 miles). The human cost to the Allies was 600,000 troops. Coupled by further French success at Verdun and Russian progress in Galicia, the Allies were, at least, gaining the upper hand. The Somme also introduced the tank to warfare. Although notoriously unreliable in this first incarnation they showed their usefulness at crossing difficult terrain under heavy fire.

Another new feature of warfare was the submarine, or U-boat, as the Germans called them. In the February of 1917, the Germans renewed their campaign of submarine warfare, halted in April 1916. This prompted the USA to join the war in April 1917. On land the Germans withdrew to the Hindenburg line on the Western Front. Meanwhile, in Russia the war was about to lead to the overthrow of the monarchy and the start of the Bolshevik Revolution in November 1917.

In other places the war in 1917 went one way, then the other, seeing victories for both sides, but no decisive

progress. When the war spilled into 1918 though, both sides desperately began to seek an end to the bitter conflict. On the Western Front the Germans launched what was designed to be their final offensive. They forced the Allies back to Marne between March and June. The Allies appointed supreme commander General Ferdinand Foch (1851–1929), to co-ordinate their counter-attack and, at last, the Allies received reinforcements from the USA.

By August the Allied counter-offensive had pushed the Germans back east to the Siegfried line, and in September 1918 Hindenburg requested an armistice, which was offered in October. In November both Germany and Austria-Hungary agreed to the terms of the 'Fourteen Point' armistice and fighting stopped on the Western Front. Fighting had already stopped on the Eastern Front in March with the signing of the Treaty of Brest-Litovsk. In 1919 at a peace conference at Versailles the formalities were sorted out, including demands on Germany that would cause deep resentment and ultimately lead to World War II.

)))➤ *Treaty of Brest-Litovsk, Archduke Franz Ferdinand, General Sir Douglas Haig, Battle of Mons, Russian Revolution, Battle of the Somme, Battle of Verdun, Battles of Ypres*

WORLD WAR II (1939–45)

Global conflict. Following World War I, Germany was plunged into a deep recession when inflation was so exaggerated that millions of Germans became paupers. As a result deep resentment was harboured towards the nations that had formed the Allied forces. Adolf Hitler had served as a volunteer in World War I and felt indignation at the post-war treatment of his peoples: Germans and Austrians.

In 1921 Hitler became leader of the National Socialist German Workers (Nazi) Party. Seeing his opportunity to seduce a disillusioned population he began rallying support by enlisting impressionable youths into his Hitler Youth Movement. The recruits were fed dogma that encouraged thoughts of Arian supremacy and prejudice towards those of other races and creeds, particularly Jews, who had been seen to flourish during the recession, giving the Germanic people an inferiority complex.

By 1934 the Nazis were in full power, with Hitler as Führer. He called his domain the Third Reich (Third Empire) and began plans for its expansion to become the leading power in Europe. Over the following five years Hitler prepared for war and consolidated the epicentre of his German empire by annexing neighbouring territory, including Austria, Sudetenland and

BELOW: An estimated 40 to 60 million lives were lost during World War II. These German troops advance into a burning forest during the Blitzkrieg. BELOW RIGHT: A German warship prepares to attack. FAR RIGHT: Benito Mussolini and Adolf Hitler met several times during the course of World War II claiming they favoured 'frequent personal contact' with each other.

then the rest of Czechoslovakia. Hitler had also formed alliances with Italy, Hungary, Albania and East Prussia, and signed a non-aggression pact with Russia. Now he was poised and ready for World War II.

In the September 1939 Germany invaded its eastern neighbour Poland. This prompted Britain and France to declare war on Germany. The USSR invaded Poland from the east and entered Finland. The Germans launched their Blitzkrieg in early 1940, conquering Denmark, Norway, the Netherlands, Belgium and Luxembourg in only a few weeks, and pushing hard into France. They soon broke the French Maginot line and pushed rapidly westward. From 26 May Britain and France began evacuating troops from the beaches at Dunkirk in northern France, while the Germans' frontline moved ever nearer. They took Paris on 14 June 1940.

July–October 1940 saw the Battle of Britain, intended to weaken British air defence before Hitler's planned

Seelöwe invasion. When Hitler realized defeat he turned his attentions to Russia instead, influenced by the Schlieffen Plan for World War I. In the later months of 1940 Japan invaded French Indonesia and the Italians made an abortive attempt to invade Greece.

Having gone as far as he could westward and northward – Spain and Sweden being neutral – Hitler used 1941 to make headway in the east and south. By April he had taken Greece and Yugoslavia, and June saw him turn traitor on the Soviets, launching a major offensive in the direction of Moscow, taking Romania, Bulgaria, Lithuania, Latvia and Estonia along the way.

By December 1941, the Germans had come within 40 kilometres (25 miles) of Moscow, but they had not been prepared for the bitter Russian climate and it had them frozen to the spot. Moscow unleashed its Mongolian troops on the Germans at the eleventh hour, smashing their hopes of victory. Meanwhile the great Siege of Leningrad (now St Petersburg) had begun. In the Pacific, Japan attacked Pearl Harbor and declared war on the USA and Britain. Germany and Italy declared war on the USA for good measure and a worldwide war was underway.

The year 1942 saw the Axis powers reach their full extent of power and then the tide turned in favour of the

Allies. The Japanese conquered the Philippines in January, but lost the Battle of Midway in June, putting them on the defensive for the remainder of the war in the Pacific. Similarly, the Germans lost the Battle of El Alamein in Egypt, October– November, and were sent on the run westward along the Barbary coast of North Africa.

It was even worse for the Axis powers through 1943. The Russians drove the Germans westward to the Donetz and they were cleared out of North

Africa. The campaign against the Japanese in Burma (now Myanmar) was launched and the Italians surrendered to the Allies. Then, in 1944, came the Allied landings. In January the Allies attacked the beaches of Nazi-occupied Italy. Eventually they won the Battle of Anzio against fierce German resistance. With a foothold in the south, the Allies then launched the D-Day landings on the beaches of northern France. The Germans fought for their lives, but the Allied force was too powerful for them to match, and the counter-invasion of Europe had begun.

By the end of 1944 the Allies and Russians had the Germans surrounded. The Japanese were losing territory as well and the end of the war was in sight. In February 1945 the Russians crossed the German border and headed for Berlin. Hitler took his own life in April and the Germans soon surrendered to the Allies. VE (Victory in Europe) was celebrated on both 8 and 9 May. By July, Japan was surrounded but stubbornly holding on. It took two atom bombs to force a surrender. VJ (Victory over Japan) was celebrated on 2 September.

))))▶ *Blitz, Blitzkrieg, Battle of Britain, Concentration Camps, D-Day, Battle of El Alamein, Adolf Hitler, Nazi Party, Pearl Harbor*

WORLD WIDE WEB

Updated version of the original Internet, allowing for browsing across the realms of the Internet using the generic system, Hypertext or HTML (HyperText Markup Language).

The Internet originated in 1984 as a means of information communications between US universities. Domestic access began in the early 1990s, once demand had made it economically viable. Since then it has expanded to become a global phenomenon, hence the World Wide Web, which connects up realms of Internet worldwide. Information is accessed on web pages (URL addresses) that comprise web sites that, in turn, are stored by web servers.

WOUNDED KNEE, BATTLE OF (1890)

Battle between Native Americans and settlers in North America. Chief Sitting Bull commanded the Sioux at Little Bighorn in 1876 when Custer and his entire regiment were killed. The war was not yet won, though. Fourteen years later Sitting Bull, chief of the Sioux, led his people against the US army on the reservation at Wounded Knee, where the tribe had been confined. Sitting Bull was killed in the fray, along with 146 other members of the tribe.

))))➤ *Battle of Little Bighorn, Sitting Bull*

WRIGHT BROTHERS

American brothers Wilbur (1867–1912) and Orville (1871–1948), pioneers of flying. While running a bicycle repair business they experimented with gliders and the effects of air pressure on wing surfaces. From their own calculations the built propellers, a wind tunnel and finally a machine with a 12-horsepower motor, which they called the *Flyer*. On 17 December 1903 they made the first controlled powered-aeroplane flights. They made hundreds of flights in the succeeding years, the longest lasting some 38 minutes.

YALTA CONFERENCE (1945)

Meeting between British prime minister Winston Churchill, US president Franklin Roosevelt and Soviet premier Joseph Stalin. Critical decisions made during this conference remained secret until the end of

BELOW: Former Russian president Boris Yeltsin.

World War II. The Yalta delegates demanded Germany's unconditional surrender and made plans to divide Germany into four occupied zones under Berlin's control. These and other agreements were widely disputed and led to criticism of Roosevelt in the United States.

))))➤ *Winston Churchill, Franklin D. Roosevelt, Joseph Stalin, World War II*

YELTSIN, BORIS (b. 1931)

President of Russia (1991–2000) An outspoken critic of the traditional Soviet structure, Yeltsin was elected president of Russia in 1991. He was a key figure in the break-up of the Soviet Union and moved Russia towards a market economy. In 1993 he instated both a new parliament and constitution. Despite ill health and growing unpopularity due to the long war in Chechnya, Yeltsin was re-elected in 1996. He resigned in 2000, naming Vladimir Putin as his successor.

YOM KIPPUR WAR (1973)

Name given to the Fourth Arab-Israeli War. The holiest day in the Jewish year is called Yom Kippur. It is the Jewish day of Atonement. Egypt and Syria chose that date to launch a surprise attack on Israel in October 1973 because it marked a national holiday and was likely to catch the Israelis off guard. It was designed to recapture some of the territory taken by the Israelis during the Six-Day War of June 1967.

))))➤ *Arab-Israeli War, Six-Day War*

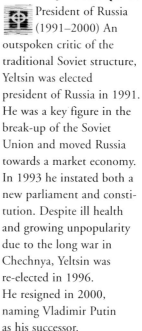

YORKTOWN, BATTLE OF (1781)

Decisive battle during the American Revolution. The Battle of Yorktown raged between September and October 1781. The British army, under General Cornwallis, had been surrounded by French and American troops in Yorktown, Virginia. Reinforcements failed to arrive by sea and the enemy forces accepted surrender on 19 October.

))))➤ *American Revolution, Battle of Bunker Hill, Battle of Lexington and Concord*

YPRES, BATTLES OF (1914–17)

Campaign during World War I. Ypres, a small Belgian town in Western Flanders has become synonymous with the great losses suffered during World War I. There were three battles fought around Ypres between 1914 and 1917; none of which proved progressive for either the Germans or the Allies despite heavy losses.

The Third Battle of Ypres, October–November 1917, was fought on the Passchendaele ridge near Ypres. Passchendaele became the object of an Allied offensive because the Germans had an elevated command of the Allied trenches. The Allies managed to capture the ridge but at the cost of 400,000 British lives.

))))➤ *World War II*

ZOLLVEREIN (19TH CENTURY)

Nineteenth-century German customs union. Friedrich List first popularized the idea to abolish customs barriers that were inhibiting trade among the numerous states of the German Confederations. Prussia led the way in 1818 and by 1845 nearly all the German states were part of the Zollverein. Alsace-Lorraine joined the union in 1872 and the Hanseatic cities followed in 1888. Austria refused to join as it was committed to trade tariffs, so Prussia was able to consolidate its power.

))))➤ *Alsace-Lorraine*

ZOROASTRIANISM (c. 1200 BC)

Monotheistic faith founded in Persia by Zarathustra. Followers worship Ahura Mazda, the god of light in temples where a sacred fire burns continuously. Their central beliefs on heaven and hell, obedience

to God (Ahura Mazda) and the battle between good and evil have a resonance in Christianity and Islam. Zoroastrians in India are often called 'Parsis' (Persians).

))))➤ *Christianity, Islam, Persia*

ZULU WARS (1879)

War between Zululand and Britain. The Zulu kingdom expanded in Natal, South Africa, during the nineteenth century. Cetshwayo, Zulu king by the 1870s, built a highly trained army of approximately 50,000 men and refused Natal's demands to back down. The British army invaded but complacency enabled the Zulus – despite heavy losses – to wipe out a British column at Isandhlwana on 22 January 1879, seizing their rifles and ammunition. The following day a further Zulu army was held back in the celebrated engagement at Rorke's Drift. On 28–29 March 1879, the Zulus were defeated at Kambula. By July the British had captured the Zulu capital at Ulundi. In 1887 Zululand was incorporated into Natal.

ABOVE: Poison gas was first unleashed by the Germans on the enemy during the Battles of Ypres.

CHRONOLOGIES

ART & CULTURE

2600 BC	Great Pyramid of Giza built
449 BC	Programme of works undertaken at the Acropolis
399 BC	Death of Greek philosopher Socrates
AD 80	Inauguration of the Colisseum
1037	Death of the philosopher Avicenna
1122	Death of Omar Khayyam
1198	Death of the philosopher Averroës
1261	Thomas Aquinas begins *Summa contra Gentiles*
1274	Death of Thomas Aquinas
1374	Death of Italian poet Francesco Petrarch
1387	Geoffrey Chaucer begins *The Canterbury Tales*
1501	Michelangelo Buonarroti begins work on his sculpture of David
1504	Leonardo da Vinci paints the *Mona Lisa*
1516	Thomas More publishes *Utopia*
1532	Niccolo Machiavelli writes *The Prince*
1564	Death of Michelangelo Buonarroti
1599	Tommaso Campanella is imprisoned for heresy
1605	Francis Bacon publishes *The Advancement of Learning*
1616	Death of William Shakespeare
1632	Work begins on the Taj Mahal
1637	Réne Déscartes publishes *Discourse on Method*
1661	Work begins on the Palace of Versailles
1742	George Frideric Handel writes *Messiah*
1750	Death of composer Johann Sebastian Bach
1762	Jean-Jacques Rousseau publishes *Émile*
1781	Immanuel Kant publishes *Critique of Pure Reason*
1788	Brandenburg Gate built
1791	Death of composer Wolfgang Amadeus Mozart
1794	Thomas Paine writes *Age of Reason*
1804	Beethoven composes his *Eroica* symphony
1809	Death of Franz Josef Haydn
1827	Death of Ludwig van Beethoven
1837	Charles Dickens begins serializing *Oliver Twist*
1851	Great Exhibition held in London
1854	Henry David Thoreau publishes *Walden*
1883	Death of composer Richard Wagner
1888	Arts and Crafts Exhibition Society established
1889	Construction of the Eiffel Tower

1901	Rise of the Expressionist movement
1907	Rise of the Cubist movement
1910	Rise of the Post-Impressionist movement
1928	Mickey Mouse makes his first appearance in *Steamboat Willie*
1931	Completion of the Empire State Building
1936	Picasso begins work on *Guernica*
1937	*Snow White and the Seven Dwarfs* is first feature-length animation
1950	Bertrand Russell awarded Nobel Prize for Literature
1960	The Beatles form
1962	Marilyn Monroe commits suicide
1970	The Beatles split up
1973	Death of Pablo Picasso
1977	Elvis Presley dies

EXPLORATION & EMPIRE

2686 BC	Old Kingdom established in Ancient Egypt
2500 BC	Rise of the Phoenicians
2000 BC	Rise of the Hittite civilization in Mesopotamia
1991 BC	Middle Kingdom established in Ancient Egypt
1792 BC	Rise of the Babylonian civilization in Mesopotamia
1766 BC	Rise of the Shang dynasty in China
1554 BC	New Kingdom established in Ancient Egypt
1500 BC	Rise of the Mayan civilization in central America
1500 BC	Rise of the Olmec civilization in central America
1050 BC	Rise of the Chou dynasty in China
900 BC	Assyrian civilization of the Ancient Near East
800 BC	Rise of the Etruscan civilization in Italy
206 BC	Collapse of the Ch'in dynasty and establishment of the Han

AD 117	Roman Empire at its height
AD 320	Rise of the Gupta Empire in India
AD 395	Rise of the Byzantine Empire
AD 476	End of the Roman Empire
AD 618	Foundation of the T'ang dynasty in China
AD 637	Fall of the Sassanid dynasty in Persia
AD 768	Beginning of the Carolingian Empire
AD 890	Magyar Arpad dynasty founded
AD 960	Rise of the Song dynasty in China
1100	Rise of the Inca Empire
1196	Rise of the Mongol dynasty
1212	Genghis Khan invades north China
1273	Rise of the Habsburg Empire
1275	Marco Polo begins service at the Mongol court of Kublai Khan
1298	Marco Polo is taken prisoner by the Genoese
1300	Rise of the Ottoman Empire
1325	Azecs found capital city of Tenochtitlán
1368	Rise of the Ming dynasty in China
1405	Cheng Ho sets out on his first voyage of exploration
1487	Bartholomew Diaz sails round the Cape of Good Hope
1492	Columbus sets sail to discover the New World
1497	John Cabot arrives on North American mainland
1498	Vasco da Gama reaches the Malabar coast of India
1503	Albuquerque makes his first trip to the East
1513	Vasco Núñez de Balboa leads expedition to the shores of the Pacific
1518	Hernán Cortés sets out on his trip to South America
1521	Collapse of the Aztec Empire
1521	Explorer Ferdinand Magellan is killed by Philippine islanders
1526	Rise of the Mogul Empire
1526	Babar defeats the Afghan emperor of Delhi
1560	Akhbar begins his campaign for control of India
1577	Sir Francis Drake begins his circumnavigation of the globe
1620	Pilgrim Fathers establish first English colony in the New World
1652	The Dutch settle in South Africa
1724	Vitus Bering explores routes between Siberia and North America

1771	Captain James Cook completes his circumnavigation of the globe
1806	Decline of the Holy Roman Empire
1828	Charles Sturt discovers the River Darling
1855	David Livingstone finds mouth of the Zambesi River at Indian Ocean
1860	Giuseppe Garibaldi conquers Sicily and Naples
1905	Roald Amundsen completes first trip across North-West Passage
1909	Robert Peary reaches the North Pole
1911	Roald Amundsen becomes the first man to reach the South Pole
1912	Robert Scott reaches the South Pole a month after Roald Amundsen
1922	Fall of the Ottoman Empire
1929	Richard Byrd makes the first flight over the South Pole
1947	Kon Tiki expedition
1947	India receives independence
1953	Edmund Hillary and Sherpa Tenzig conquer Mount Everest
1997	Britain returns Hong Kong to China

INDUSTRY

1600	English East India Company established
1602	Dutch East India Company established
1607	Hudson's Bay Company founded
1664	French East India Company established
1720	South Sea Bubble
1773	Boston Tea Party
1801	Richard Trevithick introduces first passenger-carrying steam train
1816	UK adopts the Gold Standard
1848	Beginning of the California Gold Rush
1859	Construction begins on the Suez Canal
1874	Dissolution of the British East India Company

1903	Panama grants the US control of the Canal Zone	**1099**	Crusader knights capture Jerusalem
1906	Launch of *Dreadnought*	**1164**	Lombard League formed
1908	Henry Ford creates the famous Model T car	**1170**	Thomas Becket murdered in Canterbury Cathedral
1928	Joseph Stalin instigates the first Soviet five-year plan	**1198**	Innocent III becomes pope
1929	Wall Street Crash	**1209**	Francis of Assisi founds the Franciscan Order of monks
1929	Great Depression hits the US and spreads worldwide	**1215**	Dominican Order of monks founded
1936	Keynes writes *General Theory of Employment, Interest and Money*	**1232**	Establishment of the Inquisition
		1243	Innocent IV becomes pope
1944	Bretton Woods Conference	**1378**	Great Schism in the papacy
1947	General Agreement on Tariffs and Trades signed	**1378**	Urban VI becomes pope
1947	International Monetary Fund established	**1469**	Birth of Nanak, first Sikh Guru
1950	Schuman Plan lays down foundations for European Economic Community	**1517**	Martin Luther posts '95 Theses' on church door at Wittenberg
1952	Establishment of the European Coal and Steel Community	**1521**	Edict of Worms brands Martin Luther a heretic
		1523	Ignatius Loyola publishes *The Book of Spiritual Exercise*
1976	Concorde goes into passenger service	**1523**	Clement VII becomes pope
1975	Bill Gates founds Microsoft	**1534**	Paul III becomes pope
1987	Black Monday on the US stock market	**1536**	Jean Calvin publishes *Institutes of the Christian Religion*
1988	*Piper Alpha* disaster	**1540**	Ignatius Loyola founds the Society of Jesus, or Jesuits
		1545	Council of Trent

RELIGION

1900 BC	Birth of the prophet Abraham	**1598**	Edict of Nantes ends religious wars in France
479 BC	Death of Confucius	**1652**	George Fox starts the Religious Society of Friends, or Quakers
6 BC	Birth of Jesus Christ	**1699**	Guru Gobind Singh forms the *Khalsa* ('Pure Ones') of Sikhism
AD 31	Crucifixion of Jesus Christ		
AD 62	Death of St Peter	**1708**	Death of Gobind Singh, tenth Sikh Guru
AD 65	Death of St Paul	**1738**	John and Charles Wesley found the Methodist movement
AD 70	Destruction of the Temple in Jerusalem		
AD 325	Council of Nicea called by Emperor Constantine	**1822**	Joseph Smith receives vision leading to foundation of the Mormons
AD 387	Augustine of Hippo converts to Christianity		
AD 520	Bodhidharma carries Buddhism from India to China		
AD 570	Birth of the Prophet Muhammad		
AD 622	Muslim Hijrah		
AD 632	Death of the Prophet Muhammad		
AD 687	Dome of the Rock Built		
AD 804	Death of Alcuin		
1054	The Great Schism		
1095	Pope Urban II makes the call to the Holy Wars		
1096	Launch of the First Crusade		
1098	Cistercian Order of monks founded		
1098	Siege of Antioch		

1830	Joseph Smith founds the Mormons	AD 875	Charles II of France becomes Holy Roman Emperor
1844	Baha'i faith established	AD 893	Charles III ('the Simple') becomes king of France
1886	Death of Hindu saint Ramakrishna	1016	Canute is proclaimed king of England
1917	Balfour Declaration in favour of home for the Jewish people	1189	Richard I becomes king of England
1930	Ras Tafari crowned as Messiah	1193	Death of Saladin, Sultan of Egypt
1933	Beginning of the Holocaust	1259	Kublai Khan becomes First Mongol Emperor
1948	David Ben-Gurion becomes prime minister of the new Jewish state	1272	Edward I becomes king of England
1948	Mahatma Gandhi is assassinated	1327	Edward III becomes king of England
1948	Mother Theresa founds the Order of Missionaries	1328	Establishment of the Valois royal line in France
1964	Ayatollah Khomeni is exiled	1364	Charles V becomes king of France
1978	John Paul II becomes pope	1369	Tamerlaine becomes Mongol ruler

ROYALTY

1379 BC	Akhenaten becomes pharaoh of Egypt	1462	Ivan III ('the Great') becomes Crown Prince of Musovy
1333 BC	Tutankhamen becomes pharaoh of Egypt	1479	Ferdinand becomes king of Aragon
1330 BC	Death of Nefertiti, Akehnaten's queen	1483	Charles VIII becomes king of France
1290 BC	Rameses II becomes pharaoh of Egypt	1483	Richard III becomes king of England
51 BC	Cleopatra becomes queen of Egypt	1493	Maximilian I becomes Holy Roman Emperor
44 BC	Julius Caesar assassinated	1495	Mogul emperor Babar becomes ruler of Turkestan
31 BC	Herod the Great established as king of Judea	1503	Montezuma II becomes last Aztec emperor
30 BC	Death of Cleopatra	1509	Henry VIII becomes king of England
AD 14	Death of Emperor Augustus Caesar	1520	Suleiman the Magnificent becomes sultan of Turkey
AD 37	Caligula becomes Roman Emperor	1530	Death of Babar
AD 41	Roman Emperor Caligula murdered	1542	The infant Mary becomes Queen of Scots
AD 54	Nero becomes Roman Emperor	1546	Death of Barbarossa
AD 98	Trajan becomes Roman Emperor	1547	Henri II becomes king of France
AD 117	Hadrian becomes Roman Emperor	1547	Ivan IV ('the Terrible') becomes Tsar of Russia
AD 193	Septimus Severus becomes Roman Emperor	1553	Mary I becomes queen of England
AD 306	Constantine becomes first Christian Roman Emperor	1556	Philip II becomes king of Spain
AD 434	Attila becomes king of the Huns	1558	Elizabeth I becomes queen of England
AD 527	Justinian becomes Eastern Roman Emperor	1559	Frederick II becomes king of Denmark and Norway
AD 768	Charlemagne becomes king of the Franks	1560	Charles IX becomes king of France
AD 800	Charlemagne becomes Holy Roman Emperor	1582	Japanese warlord Nobunga assassinated
AD 843	Charles II becomes king of France	1611	Gustavus Adolphus becomes king of Sweden
		1613	Establishment of the Romanov royal line in Russia
		1625	Charles II becomes king of England
		1628	Shah Jahan becomes Mogul emperor
		1643	Louis XIV becomes king of France
		1649	Charles I of England is executed
		1658	Aurangzeb become Mogul emperor

1660	Monarchy is re-established in England with Charles II	1770	Boston Massacre
1682	Peter I ('the Great') becomes tsar of Russia	1776	Declaration of Independence in the United States
1697	Charles XII becomes king of Sweden	1783	Treaty of Paris grants American independence
1711	Charles VI becomes Holy Roman Emperor	1787	Establishment of the United States Constitution
1740	Frederick II ('the Great') becomes king of Prussia	1789	Bill of Rights introduced to the United States' Constitution
1760	George III becomes king of England	1789	George Washington becomes first president of the US
1774	Louis XVI becomes king of France		
1793	Louis XVI of France is executed during the French Revolution	1794	Maximilien Robespierre is executed
		1801	Thomas Jefferson becomes president of the United States
1804	Napoleon Bonaparte declares himself Emperor of France	1803	Thomas Jefferson makes the Louisiana Purchase from France
1811	Regency period begins in England	1818	Prussia joins the *Zollverein*
1837	Victoria becomes queen of England	1820	Missouri Compromise
1849	Victor Emmanuel II becomes king of Sardinia	1823	Monroe Doctrine introduced in the US
1851	Napoleon III becomes Emperor of France	1834	Sir Robert Peel becomes prime minister of Britain
1861	Victor Emmanuel II becomes first king of a united Italy	1852	Count Camillo di Camour becomes premier of Sardinia
1877	Queen Victoria is proclaimed Empress of India		
1894	Nicholas II becomes the last tsar of Russia	1857	Indian Mutiny
1908	Carlos I of Portugal is murdered	1861	Abraham Lincoln becomes US president
1912	Last emperor of China is deposed	1862	Otto von Bismarck becomes premier of Prussia
1918	Russian royal family executed	1870	Home Rule movement begins in Ireland
1926	Hirohito becomes emperor of Japan	1871	Bismarck becomes chancellor of Germany
1952	Elizabeth II becomes queen of England	1878	Congress of Berlin
		1878	Treaty of San Stefano

POLITICS

1215	King John of England is forced to sign the Magna Carta	1881	Three Emperor's League signed
		1890	Cecil Rhodes becomes prime minister of Cape Colony
1291	Swiss League formed		
1295	First parliament called in England	1893	France and Russia sign the Dual Entente
1498	Republic of Florence proclaimed	1900	Boxer Rebellion in China
1624	Cardinal Richelieu becomes first minister of France	1901	Theodore Roosevelt becomes US president
		1903	Bolshevik Party formed in Russia
1707	Act of Union between England and Scotland	1904	France and Britain agree the Entente Cordiale
		1907	Triple Entente signed
		1911	Kuomintang established in China
		1913	Woodrow Wilson becomes US president
		1917	First Communist government set up in Russia
		1918	Treaty of Brest-Litovsk signed between Russia, Germany and allies
		1919	Jan Christian Smuts becomes prime minister of South Africa
		1919	League of Nations established

1922	Benito Mussolini becomes Italian dictator
1928	Equal votes for men and women granted in the UK
1929	Joseph Stalin becomes leader of the USSR
1933	Adolf Hitler founds the Nazi Party
1933	Franklin D. Roosevelt introduces his New Deal
1933	Reichstag fire in Berlin
1937	Neville Chamberlain becomes prime minister of Britain
1938	Munich Agreement signed
1939	Franscisco Franco becomes dictator in Spain
1939	Nazi-Soviet Pact
1940	Winston Churchill becomes prime minister of England
1945	Beginning of the Cold War
1945	Churchill, Roosevelt and Stalin meet at the Yalta Conference
1945	Execution of Norwegian fascist Vidkun Quisling
1945	Formation of the Arab League
1945	Formation of the United Nations
1945	Harry S. Truman becomes US president
1945	Potsdam Conference
1947	Jawaharlal Nehru becomes prime minister of India
1947	State of Prussia abolished
1947	Truman Doctrine introduced in the US
1948	Arab league attacks the new Jewish State of Israel
1948	Berlin airlift begins
1948	National Party establishes apartheid in South Africa
1949	Geneva Convention
1949	German Democratic Republic formed
1949	Mao Zedong declares the People's Republic of China
1949	North Atlantic Treaty Organization established
1950	Joseph Stalin signs alliance with new Communist China
1952	Fulgencio Batista begins regime of dictatorship in Cuba
1953	Dwight D. Eisenhower becomes US president
1953	Marshall Tito becomes premier of Yugoslavia
1953	Watson and Crick discover the secret of DNA
1953	Winston Churchill wins the Nobel Prize for Literature

1954	Ho Chi Minh becomes president of North Vietnam
1955	Bandung Conference
1955	Warsaw Pact signed
1956	Abdel Nasser becomes president of Egypt
1956	Suez Crisis
1957	Treaty of Rome
1957	Willy Brandt becomes mayor of West Berlin
1958	Charles de Gaulle becomes president of France
1959	Dalai Lama forced to flee Tibet after Chinese invasion
1959	Fidel Castro becomes Cuban prime minister
1961	Bay of Pigs invasion
1961	Che Guevara becomes Cuban minister for industry
1961	John F. Kennedy becomes US president
1962	Cuban Missile Crisis
1963	President Kennedy is assassinated
1966	Beginning of the Cultural Revolution in China
1966	Indira Gandhi becomes prime minister of India
1967	Che Guevara murdered
1969	De Gaulle resigns as president of France
1969	Richard Nixon becomes US president
1969	Strategic Arms Limitation Talks begin
1970	Anwar Sadat becomes president of Egypt
1972	Bloody Sunday in Northern Ireland
1974	Nicolae Ceaucescu becomes president of Romania
1974	US president Nixon resigns after Watergate scandal
1975	Khmer Rouge regime begins
1976	Pol Pot proclaims himself prime minister of Cambodia
1976	Socialist republic of Vietnam is proclaimed
1979	Idi Amin exiled
1979	Margaret Thatcher becomes prime minister of Britain

1980	Indira Gandhi is re-elected as prime minister of India	**1630**	Death of astronomer Johannes Kepler
1981	Egyptian president Anwar Sadat is assassinated	**1642**	Death of Galileo Galilei
1981	François Mitterand becomes president of France	**1682**	Edmund Halley sights his comet
1981	Ronald Reagan becomes US president	**1705**	Thomas Newcomen invents the steam engine
1983	Lech Walesa awarded Nobel Peace Prize	**1727**	Death of Isaac Newton
1984	Indira Gandhi is assassinated	**1764**	James Watt improves Newcomen's steam engine
1986	President Reagan involved in Irangate scandal in the US	**1790**	Death of US scientist Benjamin Franklin
1988	Mikhail Gorbachev becomes president of the USSR	**1829**	Death of Humphry Davy, inventor of the miners' safety lamp
1989	Fall of the Berlin Wall	**1829**	George Stephenson introduces his *Rocket* steam locomotive
1989	Tiananmen Square massacre	**1838**	Louis Daguerre invents daguerrotype photography
1990	Lech Walesa becomes president of Poland	**1861**	James Clerk Maxwell produces the first colour photograph
1991	Boris Yeltsin becomes president of Russia		
1991	Collapse of the Communist system in Russia	**1865**	Louis Pasteur published his germ theory
1991	Dissolution of the Warsaw Pact	**1869**	Dmitri Mendeleyev publishes his Periodic Table
1991	Maastricht Treaty signed	**1876**	Alexander Graham Bell demonstrates the telephone
1993	Bill Clinton becomes US president		
1993	Waco Siege	**1894**	Death of German physicist Heinrich Hertz
1994	First all-race elections held in South Africa, ending apartheid	**1895**	Wilhelm Röntgen discovers X-rays
1994	Yasser Arafat is awarded Nobel Peace Prize	**1897**	Guglielmo Marconi perfects the wireless
1996	Yasser Arafat elected President of Palestinian-controlled territory	**1901**	Wilhelm Röntgen is awarded Nobel Prize for Medicine
1997	Tony Blair leads Labour Party to victory in British General Election	**1903**	Wright Brothers make the first powered flight
1989	George Bush Snr becomes 41st US president	**1905**	Albert Einstein publishes his theory of general relativity
2001	George Bush Jnr becomes 43rd US president	**1909**	Louis Blériot becomes the first man to fly across the Channel
		1911	Marie Curie wins the Nobel Prize for Chemistry
		1915	Einstein publishes his theory of special relativity
		1919	Arthur Eddington proves Einstein's theory of relativity

SCIENCE & TECHNOLOGY		**1926**	John Logie Baird demonstrates the first television
322 BC	Death of Greek scientist and philosopher Aristotle	**1927**	Charles Lindburgh makes first non-stop solo flight across Atlantic
212 BC	Death of Archimedes	**1927**	Werner Heisenberg develops the Uncertainty Principle
AD 168	Death of Greek astronomer Ptolemy	**1945**	Alexander Fleming receives the Nobel Prize for Medicine
1543	Death of Polish astronomer Nicolaus Copernicus	**1945**	First secret tests of the atomic bomb in New Mexico
		1947	Death of Max Planck, father of Quantum Physics

1961	Yuri Gagarin becomes the first person to travel in space
1967	Christiaan Barnard performs the first human heart transplant
1969	First Moon landing
1975	Niels Bohr shares the Nobel Prize for his work with atoms
1977	Death of Werner von Braun, father of rocket technology
1984	Beginnings of the Internet
1986	Nuclear power station disaster in Chernobyl

SOCIETY

1100 BC	Rise of the Ancient Greek city-states
753 BC	Legendary founding of Rome
658 BC	City of Byzantium founded
510 BC	Roman Republic established
60 BC	Julius Caesar forms the First Triumvirate
AD 43	Julian calendar introduced
AD 79	Mount Vesuvius erupts, burying the town of Pompeii
AD 476	Beginning of the Dark Ages
AD 762	Foundation of the city of Baghdad
AD 991	Danegeld introduced in England to buy off Danish invaders
1066	End of Anglo-Saxon rule in England
1086	William the Conqueror orders *Domesday Book* survey of England
1325	Aztec city of Tenochtitlán founded
1381	Peasant's Revolt in England
1431	Joan of Arc is burned at the stake
1555	Nostradamus publishes his *Centuries*
1582	Gregorian Calendar introduced
1653	Oliver Cromwell becomes Lord Protector of England

1660	Restoration of the monarchy in England
1666	Great Fire of London
1692	Salem Witch hunts
1789	Storming of the Bastille
1799	Discovery of the Egyptian Rosetta Stone
1832	Death of English social reformer and philosopher Jeremy Bentham
1835	Great Trek begins
1838	Trail of Tears begins for the Native American peoples
1854	Florence Nightingale arrives at the military hospital in the Crimea
1859	Charles Darwin publishes *On the Origin of Species*
1866	Ku Klux Klan formed
1867	Sitting Bull made principal chief of the Sioux nation
1872	Friedrich Nietzsche writes *The Birth of Tragedy*
1880	Billy 'the Kid' Garrett is sentenced to death, but escapes
1896	First modern Olympic Games
1900	Houdini begins performing his escapology acts
1901	Nobel Prize first awarded
1907	Florence Nightingale becomes first woman to receive the Order of Merit
1908	Robert Baden-Powell starts the Boy Scouts
1910	Girl Guides founded
1912	*Titanic* sinks on her maiden voyage
1915	Re-emergence of the Ku Klux Klan
1919	Prohibition introduced in the US
1922	Howard Carter discovers the tomb of Tutankhamen
1929	Al Capone masterminds the St Valentine's Day Massacre
1933	Carl Jung writes *Modern Man in Search of a Soul*

1933	Repeal of Prohibition in the US
1937	Airship *Hindenberg* crashes killing 36 of its 92 passengers
1939	Death of Sigmund Freud
1943	Jean-Paul Sartre writes *Being and Nothingness*
1945	Atomic bomb dropped on Japanese city of Hiroshima
1945	Nuremberg trials begin to try those charged with war crimes
1952	Albert Schweitzer wins Nobel Peace Prize
1954	First Commonwealth Games held
1955	Civil Rights Movement begins in the US
1964	Martin Luther King receives the Nobel Peace Prize
1964	Nelson Mandela is sentenced to life imprisonment
1964	US Civil Rights Act bans racial discrimination in many areas
1965	Malcolm X is assassinated
1968	Martin Luther King is assassinated
1971	Greenpeace founded
1977	Steve Biko dies in custody in Pretoria
1979	Mother Theresa awarded the Nobel Peace Prize
1980	Ex-Beatle John Lennon murdered
1981	First outbreak of the AIDS virus in the US
1985	Live Aid rocks the world
1993	Nelson Mandela is awarded the Nobel Peace Prize

WAR

BC 149	Third Punic War begins
BC 218	Outbreak of the Second Punic War
BC 264	Outbreak of the First Punic War
BC 31	Battle of Actium
BC 32	Civil War breaks out between Mark Antony and Octavian
BC 331	Alexander the Great defeats Darius of Persia
BC 431	Outbreak of the Peloponnesian War between Sparta and Athens
BC 480	Battle of Thermopylae
BC 490	Battle of Marathon
BC 499	Persian Wars begin
AD 410	Sack of Rome
AD 61	Boudicca leads a revolt against the Romans in Britain
AD 865	Viking raids on the British Isles
AD 896	Alfred the Great drives the Danes out of England
1066	Battle of Hastings
1337	Hundred Years' War begins
1340	Battle of Sluys
1346	Battle of Crécy
1356	Battle of Poitiers
1415	Battle of Agincourt
1495	Italian Wars between France and Italy
1571	Battle of Lepanto
1588	Spanish Armada
1618	Thirty Years' War breaks out
1642	English Civil War breaks out
1645	Charles I is defeated by Oliver Cromwell at the Battle of Naseby
1648	Treaty of Westphalia ends the Thirty Years' War
1701	War of the Spanish Succession breaks out
1704	Battle of Blenheim
1714	End of the War of the Spanish Succession
1740	War of the Austrian Succession breaks out
1743	Battle of Dettingen
1745	Battle of Fontenoy
1748	Treaty of Aix-la-Chapelle ends War of the Austrian Succession
1756	Seven Years' War begins
1757	Robert Clive defeats the nawab of Bengal at the Battle of Plassey
1763	Treaty of Paris ends the Seven Years' War

1775	American Revolution begins
1775	First Maratha War begins
1775	First shots of the American Revolution are fired at Lexington
1777	Battle of Saratoga
1781	Battle of Yorktown
1789	Revolution breaks out in France
1799	End of the French Revolution
1802	Second Maratha War
1803	Outbreak of the Napoleonic Wars
1805	Battles of Austerlitz and Trafalgar
1805	Russia and Austria declare war on France
1806	Battles of Jena and Auerstadt
1813	Battle of Leipzig
1815	Battle of Waterloo
1835	Texan War of Independence breaks out
1836	Fall of the Alamo
1839	First Afghan War breaks out
1839	First Opium War begins between Britain and China
1842	Treaty of Nanking ends the First Opium War
1845	First Maori War begins
1850	Beginning of the Taiping Rebellion
1853	War breaks out in the Crimea
1854	Battle of Balaclava; Siege of Sevastopol
1856	Second Opium War begins
1860	Second Maori War begins
1861	American Civil War begins
1863	Battle of Gettysburg
1870	Franco-Prussian War begins
1876	Battle of the Little Bighorn
1877	Russo-Turkish War breaks out
1877	Satsuma Rebellion
1878	Second Afghan War breaks out

1879	Beginning of the Zulu Wars
1890	Battle of Wounded Knee
1898	Spanish-American War breaks out
1899	Boer War breaks out in South Africa
1900	Relief of Mafeking
1902	Great Britain finally defeats the Boers, ending the Boer War
1904	Russo-Japanese War breaks out
1914	Battle of the Mons; Ypres campaign begins
1916	Battle of Verdun; Brusilov Offensive
1917	Battle of Arras; Third Battle of Ypres
1917	Revolution breaks out in Russia
1919	Third Afghan War
1936	Spanish Civil War
1938	German–Austrian Anschluss
1939	Battle of the Atlantic begins; it continues throughout the war
1939	Germany invades Poland, triggering World War II
1940	Battle of Britain; the Blitz
1941	Japanese attack on Pearl Harbor instigates US entry in World War II
1941	Siege of Leningrad begins
1942	Battles of Midway and El Alamein; Siege of Stalingrad
1944	Battle of Arnhem; D-Day landings
1950	Korean War breaks out
1956	Arab-Israeli War breaks out
1963	Vietnam War breaks out
1965	Indo-Pakistan War
1967	Six-Day War
1973	Yom Kippur War
1982	Falklands War
1991	Gulf War

GLOSSARY

ABSOLUTE MONARCHY

Rule by a king or queen whereby they are not subject to the laws of government or parliament.

AFRIKAANER

Native of South Africa descended from predominantly Dutch heritage. These people were also referred to as Boers or Voortrekkers.

ALLIES

Term commonly used to describe the countries opposing the Central Powers during World War I: Great Britain, France and Russia. It was also used in World War II.

ANARCHY

Political theory that advocates a society run without the coersive authority from government, religion or education, which imposes limits on the freedom of the individual.

ANTHROPOCENTRISM

Theory which regards human beings as the most important element of existence.

ANTI-SEMITISM

Prejudice against followers of the Jewish faith. Although persecution of Jews is a feature throughout history, anti-Semitism reached its climax just prior to and during World War II, with Hitler's Final Solution: the planned extermination of the race.

ANZAC

Australia and New Zealand Army Corp. Used to denote members of the armed forces of the Commonwealth.

ATOMIC BOMB

Bombs in which atoms of either uranium or plutonium are bombarded with neutrons, causing an explosive release of energy as atoms split apart. The current type of bomb is the much more powerful hydrogen bomb. An atom bomb is used to make hydrogen atoms merge in a fusion reaction.

BRONZE AGE

Period of history characterized by the use of early metals, such as copper and its alloys. The Bronze Age is commonly dated at around 3000–2000 BC, although it began at different times around the world.

CENTRAL POWERS

Term used to describe the nations of central Europe that formed various alliances between 1882 and 1945. Originally they comprised Germany, Austria-Hungary and Italy. During World War I, Italy was absent, but rejoined for World War II. Austria became a member, independent of Hungary, in 1918.

CIVIL WAR

War between the peoples of the same nation, usually proving socially and economically devastating for the country concerned.

COLONIALISM

Political policy by which one country subjugates another to is own rule, with the aim of creating an empire. This can be by economic, religious or military means.

CONSERVATION

Preservation, protection and efficient management of all natural resources, including that of living organisms. The sustainable use by a country of its natural resources has long been recognized as essential for economic growth.

CONSTITUTIONAL MONARCHY

Rule by a king or queen in which their powers are limited by means of a democratic political system.

DEMOCRACY

System of government for the people, by the people, normally through election. The word derives from the Greek words *demos* ('community') and *kratos* ('power').

DESEGREGATION

The reintegration of peoples of different ethnic origins in countries where segregation has been a political force. The best-known examples in modern times are in the United States, where blacks and whites were desegregated in the 1960s after the success of the Civil Rights Movement, or in South Africa with the abolition of the apartheid regime.

DISCIPLES

Anyone who strictly follows the teachings of another person. Usually used to describe the 12 followers of Jesus Christ during his life; these include St Peter, considered to be the founder of the Christian faith, and Judas, who betrayed Jesus.

DIVINE RIGHT OF KINGS

Christian political belief that the monarch is God's representative on Earth and is subject to no man's will or laws. Rebellion against the monarch was therefore rebellion against God and thus considered blasphemous.

ECOLOGY

Study of the relationships between all living things and their environment. Ecology is a broad discipline that encompasses many areas of science, such as biology, chemistry, geology and statistics.

ECONOMICS

The science and study of wealth: its production, distribution and consumption. The first generally recognized work on economics was carried out by Adam Smith, who published *The Wealth of Nations* in 1776.

ECUMENICISM

Religious theory that argues for the mass unity of all denominations of Christianity around the world.

GAUL

Area covering largely what is present-day France during the period of the Roman Empire. It stretched into what is now northern Italy and the Netherlands.

GENETICS

The study of inheritance, genes and their effects. Inherited characteristics are controlled by genes, which are sections of the DNA molecule which make up particular proteins. Genes can have two or more variants, called alleles, which give rise to alternative characteristics, for example eye colour.

GENOCIDE

Deliberate programme of mass murder designed to exterminate a group defined by race, religion or ethnicity. Genocide is most frequently applied to the Final Solution instigated against the Jewish communities, and other groups considered undesirable, such as gypsies, during Germany's Third Reich.

GEOCENTRIC

Scientific theory in which the Sun and other planets all revolve around Earth. The theory was later replaced by Copernicus's heliocentric (Sun-centred) model.

HEBREWS

Hebrews – meaning 'wanderers' – refers to the Semites who lived in Palestine and are the descendants of Abraham. Hebrew is the Jewish liturgical language and the national language of Israel. Hebrew kings and prophets emerged *c.* 1000 BC and so did the concept linking religion with morality.

HELIOCENTRIC

Theory of the Universe first propounded by Nicolaus Copernicus, in which the Sun is the centre with the planets (as they were then known) revolving around it. Although the Sun is now known not to be the centre of the Universe, the theory of orbiting planets was correct.

HUMANITARIANISM

Theory that places importance on the interests of humanity as opposed to personal or national interests. Most recently humanitarianism has manifested itself in environmental policies and aid for the Third World.

ICE AGE

Periods of time, lasting millions of years, when Earth, its oceans and atmosphere experienced a significant drop in temperature causing the formation of large ice masses. The most recent Ice Age began about two million years ago.

IMPERIALISM

Practice of any one state to influence or conquer another in order to expand its its wealth, power and dominions.

IRON AGE

Period of history characterized by the use of iron, a development of the bronze previously used. The Iron Age is usually dated at around 1000–500 BC.

LIBERALISM

Theory that places importance on an individual's civil or political rights, particularly their freedom of speech and expression.

MARSHAL LAW

Policy by which law and order are maintained through military means. Some countries live under martial law, others deploy it as a means of control in times of crisis or rebellion.

MESOLITHIC

Name given to the Middle period of the Stone Age, normally taken to begin when the Ice Age finally receded and Earth's climate took on its present-day status. The Mesolithic era is normally dated from around 10,000 years ago.

NATIONALISM

Pride in, and a sense of belonging to, a nation. In extreme forms, nationalism can lead to hatred of other nations and peoples, such as occurred in Nazi Germany.

NEOLITHIC

Name given to the final part of the Stone Age, after the Mesolithic period, normally dated from around 8000–3000 BC. The Neolithic era is characterized by the development of agriculture.

PACIFISM

Belief in the immorality of war; that it cannot be in any way justified. During World Wars I and II, pacifism became increasingly widespread, with those refusing to fight on grounds of pacifism called conscientious objectors.

PAGANISM

Name given to anyone who followed a religion other than Christianity. First used in the fourteenth century, pagans suffered years of persecution after Christianity was established.

PERIODIC TABLE

Table listing the chemical elements first devised by Dmitri Mendeleyev. The elements are organized in rows by atomic number, with elements having similar atomic structures and chemical properties appearing in vertical columns.

PREHISTORY

Period of history that covers the time from when life first formed on Earth (about 3.5 billion years ago) up until human beings began to keep records.

RACISM

Belief in the superiority of one race over another; often manifesting itself in social discrimination and giving rise to outbursts of violence.

RESERVATIONS

Areas of territory set aside by the United States government on which Native American Indians were forced to live after the expansion of settlers into the West. In theory it was believed that the Natives would continue to live as they had done previously, but in reality they were subject to government laws and continual oppression once inside the reservations.

REUNIFICATION

The reintegration of two or more countries that once shared a common government but have, for political reasons, been separated. After World War II Germany was divided – physically and politically – into East and West. With the end of the Cold War and the fall of the Berlin Wall in 1989, the two countries were finally reunified.

SOCIALISM

Political ideal opposing the theory of class and private ownership. Such ideas can be traced back to Ancient Greece and beyond, but became popular only with the Industrial Revolution and large urban populations.

STONE AGE

The earliest period of human history. As its name suggests, the Stone Age was characterized by the use of stone tools and implements. The Stone Age encompasses those periods of history known as Paleolithic, Mesolithic and Neolithic.

SUFFRAGE

Term used to identify which citizens are eligible to vote in elections. The UK has universal adult suffrage (over 18 years of age) with a few exceptions. Universal suffrage is a key tenet of modern democracy.

BIBLIOGRAPHY

Adams, R. E. W., *Ancient Civilizations of the New World*, Boulder, 1992

Addington, L. H., *The Patterns of War Since the Eighteenth Century*, Indianapolis, 1984

Bakewell, P., *A History of Latin American Empires and Sequels, 1450–1930*, Oxford University Press, Oxford, 1997

Ball, S. J., *The Cold War: An International History, 1947–1991*, London, 1998

Banks, A., *A Military Atlas of the First World War*, London, 1975

Bechert, H. & Gombrich, R. (eds.), *The World of Buddhism*, London, 1984

Black, C. F., Greengrass, M., Howarth, D. et al, *Cultural Atlas of the Renaissance*, Oxford, 1993

Black, Jeremy (ed.), *The Encyclopedia of World History*, Dempsey Parr, Bath, 1999

Blackburn, Simon, *Oxford Concise Dictionary of Philosophy*, Oxford University Press, Oxford, 1996

Blanning, T. C. W. (ed.), *The Oxford Illustrated History of Modern Europe*, Oxford University Press, Oxford, 1996

Bohlander, R. E., *World Explorers and Discoverers*, New York, 1992

Boorstin, D. J., *The Discoverers*, London, 1991

Bowker, John (ed.), *The Oxford Dictionary of World Religions*, Oxford Univeristy Press, Oxford, 1997

Brogan, Hugh, *The Pelican History of the United States of America*, London, 1986

Brogan, Patrick, *World Conflicts*, London, 1985

Bruce, George, *Dictionary of Wars*, HarperCollins, London, 1995

Burkholder, M. A. & Johnson, L. L., *Colonial Latin America* (3rd ed.), New York, 1990

Calvocoressi, Peter, *World Politics Since 1945*, New York, 1991

Cameron, R., *A Concise Economic History of the World: From Paleolithic Times to the Present*, New York, 1997

Carruth, Gorton, *The Encyclopedia of World Facts and Dates*, New York, 1993

Cartledge, P. (ed.), *The Cambridge Illustrated History of Ancient Greece*, Cambridge, 1998

Cavendish, R. et al, *Journeys of the Great Explorers*, Basingstoke, 1992

Chacoliades, Militiades, *International Economics*, New York and London, 1990

Chant, C., & Goodman, D., *Pre-Industrial Cities and Technology*, London, 1999

Clutterbuck, Richard, *International Crisis and Conflict*, London and Basingstoke, 1993

Collier, S., Skidmore, T. E. & Blakemore, H., (eds.), *The Cambridge Encyclopedia of Latin America and the Caribbean*, Cambridge, 1985

Cooper, David E., *World Philosophies: An Historical Introduction*, Oxford, 1996

Cornell, Tim and John Matthews, *Atlas of the Roman World*, Phaidon Press, London, 1982

Cotterell, Arthur (ed.), *Encyclopedia of Ancient Civilizations*, Rainbird Publishing, 1980

Cotterell, Arthur, *The Encyclopedia of World Mythology*, Dempsey Parr, Bath, 1999

Cross, F. L., *The Oxford Dictionary of the Christian Church*, Oxford University Press, Oxford, 1978

Cunliffe, Barry (Foreword), *The Cassell Atlas of World History*, London, 1997

Davidson, Gienapp, Heyrman et al., *Nation Of Nations: A Concise Narrative of the American Republic*, New York, 1996

Dawson, Lorne L. (ed.), *Cults in Context: Readings in the Study of New Religious Movements*, Toronto, 1996

Day, A. E., *Search for the Northwest Passage*, New York and London, 1986

Douglas, J. D. (ed.), *The New International Dictionary of the Christian Church*, Paternoster Press, 1978

Eliade, Mircea, *A History of Religious Idea*s, Chicago, 1984

Evans, Eric (ed.), *The Illustrated Guide to British History*, Dempsey Parr, Bath, 1999

Fagan, B. M., *Peoples of the Earth: An Introduction to World Prehistory*, New York, 1998

Fage, J. D., *A History of Africa*, Century Hutchinson, London, 1988

Featherstone, Donald, *Colonial Small Wars*, David and Charles Publishing, London

Flatlow, Ira, *They All Laughed: From Lightbulbs to Lasers*, New York, 1992

Fraser, Antonia (ed.), *The Lives of the Kings & Queens of England*, Weidenfeld and Nicholson, London, 1993

Friend, W. H. C., *The Rise of Christianity*, London, 1984

Gardiner, Judith, *The History Today Who's Who in British History*, Collins and Brown, London, 2000

Gilbert, Martin, *First World War*, HarperCollins, London, 1994

Gilbert, Martin, *Second World War*, London, 1989

Goodman, M., *The Roman World, 44 BC – AD 180*, London, 1997

Grove, Noel, *National Geographic Society: Atlas of World History*, Washington, 1997

Guirand, Felix (ed.), *Larousse Encyclopedia of Mythology*, Paul Hamlyn, London, 1964

Hall, Michael, *Leaving Home*, London, 1997

Hanbury-Tenison, R. (ed.), *The Oxford Book of Exploration*, Oxford, 1993

Harding, David (ed.), *Weapons: An International Encyclopedia from 5000 BC to 2000 AD*, London, 1980

Hart, L., *The History of the Second World War*, London, 1970

Haswell, Jock, *The Battle for Empire*, Cassell, London, 1976

Heath, Ian, *Armies of the Dark Ages*, War Games Research Group, 1980

Herrin, J., *The Formation of Christendom*, Oxford, 1987

Hillier, Bevis, *The Style of the Century*, London, 1983

Hinnells, John (ed.), *Who's Who of Religions*, Penguin Books, London, 1996

Hobsbawn, E. J., *Industry and Empire*, London, 1990

Hobsbawn, E. J., *The Age of Extremes, 1919–1991*, London, 1994

Holmes, George (ed.), *The Oxford Illustrated History of Medieval Europe*, Oxford University Press, Oxford, 1988

Holmes, Richard, *Battle Plans*, Helicon Press, London

Hopper, R. J., *The Glory that was Greece*, Sidgwick and Jackson, 1980

Hughes, Robert, *The Shock of the New*, London, 1991

Kenyon, N. D. and Nightingale, C., *Audiovisual Telecommunications*, London, 1992

Kinder, Hermann & Hilgemann, Werner, *The Penguin Atlas of World History*, Vols. 1 & 2, London, 1995

La Feber, W., *America, Russia and the Cold War*, 1945-1996, New York, 1997

Langmuir, Erika and Lynton, Norbert *The Yale Dictionary of Art and Artists*, Yale University Press, 2000

Laque, Pierre, *Ancient Greece: Utopia and Reality*, Thames and Hudson, London, 1994

Lenman, B. P. (ed.), *Chambers Dictionary of World History*, Chambers, London, 2000

Ling, Trevor, *A History of Religion East and West*, London, 1977

Litvinoff, M., *Atlas of Earthcare*, London, 1996

Loudon, Irvine, *Western Medicine*, Oxford, 1997

Lundestad, G. *East, West, North, South: Major Developments in International Politics, 1945–1996*, Oslo, 1997

Macfarlane, L. J., *The Theory and Practice of Human Rights*, London, 1985

Maisels, C. K., *The Near East: Archeology in the Cradle of Civilization*, London, 1993

Mallory, J. P., *In Search of the Indo-European: Language, Archeology & Myth*, London, 1989

Manners, John (ed.), *The Oxford Illustrated History of Christianity*, Oxford University Press, Oxford, 1990

McEvedy, C., *The Penguin Atlas of the Pacific*, London, 1998

McHenry, Robert (ed.), *Webster's New Biographical Dictionary*, Miriam Webster, Inc., 1988

Messadie, Gerald, *Great Modern Inventions*, Edinburgh, 1991

Messenger, Charles, *The Century of Warfare: Worldwide Conflict from 1900 to the Present Day*, London, 1995

Moore, R. I. (ed.), *The Hamlyn Historical Atlas*, London, 1981

Morison, Samuel Eliot, Commager, H. S., Leuchtenburg, W. E., *A Concise History of the American Republic* (2nd edition), Oxford, 1983

Myers, Bernard, *Art and Civilization*, Paul Hamlyn, London, 1967

Myers, N. (ed.), *The Gaia Atlas of Planet Management*, London, 1985

Nigosian, S. A., *World Faiths* (2nd edition), New York, 1994

Norwich, John Julius (ed.), *The Oxford Illustrated Encyclopedia of the Arts*, Oxford University Press, Oxford, 1984

Ousby, Ian (ed.), *The Cambridge Guide to Literature in English*, Cambridge University Press, London, 1989

Pakenham, T., *The Scramble for Africa, 1876–1912*, London, 1991

Parker, G. (ed.), *The Times Atlas of World History* (4th edition), London, 1996

Porter, A. N., *Atlas of British Overseas Expansion*, London, 1991

Quirke, S. & Spencer, J., *The British Museum Book of Ancient Egypt*, London, 1992

Roberts, J. M., *The Penguin History of Europe*, Penguin Books, London, 1996

Roberts, J. M., *The Penguin History of the World*, Penguin, London, 1997

Sabrine, George H. and Thorson, Thomas L., *A History of Political Theory*, Orlando, 1973

Sasson, J. M. (ed.) *Civilizations of the Ancient Near East* (Vol. II), New York, 1995

Smallwood, A. D., *The Atlas of African-American History and Politics: From the Slave Trade to Modern Times*, New York, 1998

Solomon, Robert C. and Higgins, Kathleen M., *A Short History of Philosophy*, Oxford, 1996

Spiegel, S. L. & Wehling, F. L., *World Politics in a New Era*, Fort Worth, 1999

Starr, Chester G., *A History of the Ancient World*, Oxford, 1983

Stobart, J. C., *The Grandeur that was Rome*, Sidgwick and Jackson, 1980

Taylor, A. J. P., *From the Boer War to the Cold War*, London, 1995

The DK Science Encyclopedia, London, 1998

The New Grolier Multimedia Encyclopedia, USA, 1991

Thomas, H., *The Slave Trade: The History of the Atlantic Slave Trade,1440-1870*, New York, 1997

Tomlinson, Jim, *Public Policy and the Economy Since 1900*, New York, 1990

Tucker, S. C., *The Great War*, London, 1998

Weller, P. (ed.), *Religions in the UK: A Multi-Faith Directory*, University of Derby, 1997

Williamson, E., *The Penguin History of Latin America*, London, 1992

Wilson, A., *Transport*, London, 1995

Woolf, Stewart (ed.), *Nationalism in Europe*, London, 1996

AUTHOR BIOGRAPHIES

PATRICK O'BRIEN
General Editor

Patrick O'Brien holds the positions of Governor of the Programme in Global History at the Institute of Historical Research, London University, and Centennial Professor of Economic History at the London School of Economics. He has edited and contributed to a wide range of historical journals and encyclopedias.

GUY DE LA BÉDOYÈRE
Royalty

Guy de la Bédoyère is an archeologist and historian with numerous books to his credit on the Roman world, seventeenth-century literature and World War II aviation amongst others. He has also written numerous travel articles on a variety of historical sites for *The Independent* and has made a number of appearances on television and radio history programmes.

ALAN BROWN
Religion

Alan Brown is director of the National Society's Kensington R. E. Centre and R. E. (Schools) Officer of the General Synod Board of Education. He has written a great many books about world religions, as well as numerous articles, reviews and booklets. He is also tutor and examiner for The Open University course, 'The Religious Quest'.

GERARD CHESHIRE
Science & Technology and War

Gerard Cheshire is a specialist science writer. He has written and contributed to many books on the subject, including *Chemical Elements,* as well as magazine articles and part-works. His other areas of research and interest include the history and technology of warfare.

INGRID CRANFIELD
Exploration & Empire and Industry

Ingrid Cranfield is a full-time writer and editor. Her works include *The Challengers*, a survey of modern british exploration and adventure. She contributes to books, magazines and periodicals on a regular basis.

JUDITH HODGE
Politics

Judith Hodge has worked as a freelance writer and editor for 15 years, both in the UK and New Zealand. She writes on a range of subjects for websites and magazines, including history, education, health and business. Judith is the author of a number of non-fiction titles for children.

MICHAEL KERRIGAN
Art & Culture

A contributor to the Time–Life History of the World series, Michael Kerrigan has written extensively on aspects of life and culture from the earliest times to the present day. His books cover everything from world literature to the history of torture; he writes regularly for *The Scotsman* and *The Times Literary Supplement*. He lives in Edinburgh.

JON SUTHERLAND
Society

Jon Sutherland is an experienced writer and lecturer in business studies. He has written and contributed to over 100 books and encyclopedias on a wide range of subjects, including social and military history.

PICTURE CREDITS

The Art Archive: AA/British Library: 9 (b); AA/Archaeological Museum Thasos/Dagli Orti: 11 (r); AA/British Library: 16 (l); AA/Cava dei Tirreni Abbey Salerno/Dagli Orti: 30; The Art Archive: 42 (r); AA/Bibliotheque Universitaire Geneva/Dagli Orti: 43; AA/Bibliotheque Nationale Paris: 45 (l); AA/Imperial War Museum: 63; AA: 66 (b); AA/Musee d'Orsay Paris/Dagli Orti: 77; AA/Dagli Orti: 87 (b); The Art Archive: 93 (b); AA/Galleria degli Uffizi Florence/Dagli Orti: 122 (b); AA/Palazzo Farnese Capranola/Dagli Orti: 124 (b); AA/British Library: 125; AA/Galleria Degli Uffizi Florence/Dagli Orti: 130 (l), AA/Domenica del Corriere/Dagli Orti: 136 (l); AA/Museum der Stadt Wien/Dagli Orti: 137; AA/Egyptian Museum Cairo/Dagli Orti: 139; AA/Museo Tosio Martinengo Brescia/Dagli Orti: 140; AA/RAMC Historical Museum/Harper Collins Publishers: 141 (r); AA/Mireille Vautier: 144 (l); AA/London Museum: 146 (t); AA/Galleria Nazionale Parma/Dagli Orti: 147; AA/ Galleria degli Uffizi Florence/Dagli Orti: 150; AA/Museo del Prado Madrid Album/Joseph Martin: 151; AA/Musée du Chateau de Versailles/Dagli Orti 162 (t); AA/Museo Capitolino Rome/Dagli Orti: 171; AA/Musee de Versailles/ Dagli Orti: 172; AA/Harper Collins Publishers: 177 (b), AA/Dagli Orti: 180 (r); AA/British Library: 182 (r); AA/ Victoria and Albert Museum: 183; AA/Museo del Prado Madrid/Josse: 185; AA/Miramare Palace Trieste/Dagli Orti: 192 (l); AA/Wellington Museum/Eileen Tweedy: 197.

British Film Institute (BFI): 133 (l).

Christie's Images Ltd. 2001: 19, 20, 26 (r), 50, 84, 86, 130 (r), 132, 154 (r), 161, 189 (l), 196 (b).

Foundry Arts: 155.

Graham Stride: 108, 146 (b), 153 (b), 159 (l), 208.

Impact Photos: John Cole/Impact: 10; Mohamed Ansar/Impact: 18 (r); Alan Keohane/Impact: 29 (b); Mark Cator/Impact: 31 (l); Fabrizio Bensch/Impact: 38 (r); Geraint Lewis/Impact: 40 (l); Piers Cavendish/Impact: 45 (r); Stuart Clarke/Impact: 56 (l); Alexis Wallerstein/Impact: 62 (l); Mohamed Ansar/Impact: 62 (r); John Cole/Impact: 67; Alain Evrard/Impact: 71 (r); Simon Shepheard/Impact: 76 (l, r); Julian Calder/Impact: 78 (l); Alain le Garsmeur/ Impact: 90 (l); Ben Edwards/Impact: 91 (l); Caroline Penn/ Impact: 101 (t); Michael Mirecki/Impact: 103 (l); Simon Shepheard/Impact: 106 (t); Javed A Jafferji/Impact: 106 (b); Geraint Lewis/Impact: 109 (b); Mark Henley/ Impact: 111; Robin Laurence/Impact: 112; Jeremy Nichols/Impact: 121; Piers Cavendish/Impact: 124 (l); John Arthur/Impact: 126 (l); Colin Jones/Impact: 160 (l); Philippe Achache/ Impact: 160 (b); Mohamed Ansar/ Impact: 173 (r); Ben Edwards/Impact: 178 (l), Christophe Bluntzer/Impact: 179, Caroline Penn/Impact: 180 (l); John Arthur/Impact: 184 (l); Mark Henley/Impact: 184 (r); Rachel Morton/Impact: 186 (b); Simon Shepheard/Impact: 189 (r); Ray Roberts/ Impact: 191; Colin Jones/Impact: 193; Piers Cavendish/Impact: 202.

Mary Evans: 1, 3, 5, 7, 9 (t), 11 (r), 21 (t), 22, 23 (l), 24 (l, r), 26 (l), 27, 29 (t), 31 (r), 32 (l), 33, 36 (r), 41, 44, 46, 47, 48 (l), 49, 55 (t), 56 (r), 57; Mary Evans/Edwin Wallace 58 (t), 58 (b); Mary Evans/Edwin Wallace 59, 60 (l), 65, 68 (r), 70, 71 (l); Mary Evans/Explorer Archives 72 (l), 74, 78 (r), 79, 80 (b), 81, 82, 83 (t); Mary Evans/ Sigmund Freud Copyrights 83 (b), 85 (l), 87 (t), 91 (r), 92, 94 (l, r); Mary Evans/Douglas Dickins 96, 97 (r), 98; Mary Evans/Harry Price College, University of London 99 (t), 99 (b), 100, 101 (b), 107 (b), 109 (t), 110 (l, r), 113 (t, b), 114 (t, b), 116 (t), 118, 119 (l, r), 120 (l, r), 123, 126 (r), 127; Mary Evans/Explorer Archives 128 (l), 128 (r), 129; Mary Evans/ Edwin Wallace 133 (r), 134, 135 (l, r), 136 (r), 138 (r), 141 (l), 142, 144 (b), 145; Mary Evans/Edwin Wallace 149 (l), 149 (t, b), 156, 157 (l, r), 159 (r), 162 (b); Mary Evans/National Portrait Gallery 166, 167 (b), 168, 169 (l), 174 (t), 187, 188, 194 (b), 195, 200 (l, r), 201, 203, 207, 213 (t).

Topham: 6, 8, 11 (l), 12 (t, b), 13, 14, 15 (t, b), 17, 18 (l), 21 (b), 23 (r), 25, 28, 32 (r), 34 (l, r), 35, 36 (l), 37, 38 (l), 39, 40 (r), 42 (l), 48 (r), 51, 52, 53 (l, r), 54, 55 (b), 60 (r), 61, 64 (l, r). 66 (t), 68 (l), 69, 72 (r), 73, 75 (l, r), 80 (t), 85 (r), 88 (l, r), 89, 90 (r), 93 (t), 95, 97 (l), 102, 103 (r), 104, 105 (l, r), 115, 116 (b), 117, 122 (t), 131, 138 (l), 143 (l, r), 152, 153 (t), 154 (l), 158, 163, 164, 165 (l, r), 167 (t), 169 (r), 170 (t, b), 173 (l), 174 (b), 175, 176, 177 (t), 178 (r), 181, 182 (l), 186 (t), 190 (l, r), 192 (b), 194 (t), 196 (t), 198 (l, r), 199, 206, 211 (b), 214.

INDEX